FIX IT
FAST

FIX IT FAST

AN A-TO-Z GUIDE TO 1,001 HOUSEHOLD REPAIR PROBLEMS

REVISED EDITION

BY STANLEY SCHULER

Illustrated by Marilyn Grastorf

BONANZA BOOKS
New York

This 1990 edition is published by Bonanza Books, distributed by Crown
Publishers, Inc., 225 Park Avenue South, New York, New York 10003, by
arrangement with M. Evans and Company. Originally published as *How
to Fix Almost Everything* by M. Evans and Company in 1975.

Manufactured in the United States of America

Library of Congress Cataloging-in-Publication Data

Schuler, Stanley,
　　[How to fix almost everything]
　　Fix it fast / by Stanley Schuler.
　　　　p.　　cm.
　　Reprint. Originally published: New York : M. Evans, 1975.
　　ISBN 0-517-00169-1
　　1. Dwellings—Maintenance and repair—Amateurs' manuals.
　2. Repairing—Amateurs' manuals.　I. Title.
　TH4817.3.S382　1990
　643'.7—dc20
　　　　　　　　　　　　　　　　　　　　　　　89-18426
　　　　　　　　　　　　　　　　　　　　　　　CIP

ISBN 0-517-00169-1

h　g　f　e　d　c　b　a

CONTENTS

HOW TO USE THIS BOOK

A couple of years ago, I was playing bridge at the home of a close friend. At one point during the evening, when I was dummy, I went to the kitchen for a glass of water. The flow from the faucet was little better than a trickle. Being something of a busybody, I guess, and because I had designed the kitchen, I unscrewed the aerator on the faucet snout, found it clogged, and rinsed it out. It took me about two minutes. Later, it turned out that my host had been wondering for weeks what was wrong with his kitchen plumbing.

Another friend, leaving home with his family for a weekend, found gasoline dribbling from a stone cut in the bottom of his gasoline tank. It was Saturday, and the repair shop couldn't have it welded that morning. They *could* get a new tank—perhaps on Monday. That would be about thirty-five dollars. Or, if he could leave the car on Monday, they could have the tank welded by Tuesday afternoon.

My friend is a choleric man. He fixed the tank himself, at a cost of less than a dollar. His weekend started an hour later than he had planned, of course, but he had the pleasure of driving the car for another year without further trouble, and when he sold it, his gas-tank patch was still intact.

These are random samples. There are dozens of fix-it jobs that need to be done around the house—anybody's house. Half of them are left as lingering nuisances—not because they are difficult, but simply because so many people are afraid that they will botch the job, or don't know what kind of glue to use, or think they have to have special tools, or don't realize that a few minutes' time and a few cents of material may be all that are needed.

We live surrounded by thousands of *things*. And sooner or later, most of them break, rip, rust, chip, tear, stain, leak, or get out of whack in some other way. Something has to be done about them—and to find somebody to do that something often turns out to be either agonizingly slow or astonishingly expensive. Or both.

Not everything in and around the house that breaks down or is broken can be fixed. But hundreds of things *can* be, and fixed well and handily by anybody who can read simple directions and has the normal use of his hands. *Fit It Fast* is intended to tell you what you can use to fix what, and how to use it in the best and easiest way.

What do we mean by fixing? To most people, the word *fixing* implies making a relatively *simple* repair. And that's the way the word is used here. You *replace* a roof, but you may *fix* a leak; you *remodel* a kitchen, but you *fix* a zipper; you *repave* a driveway, but you *fix* a crack in the walk. This, then, is a book about fix-it-sized problems—the hundreds of them that you can handle even though you are not a mechanic. It does *not* include major repairs that are too big or too complicated for the average person. Unless you have special skills, you will find it cheaper and safer and better to let a professional handle these big jobs for you.

Fix It Fast has been arranged to make it as easy as possible to find the specific information you need at the moment.

The first and main section of the book is an alphabetical listing of *things* you may want to fix and also of the materials they are made of. You will find such entries as ELECTRIC

SWITCH, BIRD BATH, BOOT, UMBRELLA, and ZIPPER. You will also find entries such as ALUMINUM, BRASS, CONCRETE, and LEATHER. And sometimes, when there are many related things in one large category, you may find them grouped under such general headings as TOYS or CLOTHING. Where there was more than one likely place to list something, we have used cross-references. If the information you need is in the book, you will be able to find it with very little difficulty.

The second and smaller part of the book will help you if you are a little uncertain about some of the common *techniques* that are used in many repairs. If you are replacing an odd-shaped pane in a window, you will need to know how to cut glass. There are instructions about that in the second part of the book. There, too, you will find sections on soldering, on making basic stitches, on methods of painting, on mixing and handling concrete, on selecting the right glue for a particular job.

Experienced "fixers" will need to refer to this section less frequently than those who are less proficient, but products and practices change over the years, and even the old hands may find some useful hints in these chapters on basic methods.

A word about brand names: You will find several here and there. They are used simply because there seemed to be no other convenient way to specify certain specific types of material in an understandable manner. A long scientific name—if there *were* one—would mean nothing to most readers, and indeed to many experts. The products mentioned are certainly not the *only* ones of their kind on the market. But they *are* widely known, they are available almost anywhere in the country, and when you ask for them by name, the people in the hardware store will know what you are talking about.

No book could conceivably cover all the things that every reader might want to mend. This one is intended to provide usable advice on ways to handle the common fix-it job that the average person can tackle with some assurance of good results. If, in looking through the list, you find some problem that is not covered, it is probably either because the job is too complicated for most householders—or because it is so simple that the procedures are obvious.

So here are some handy directions for ways to handle the thousand-and-one pesky fix-it jobs that all too often remain undone because you don't want to spend a fortune on an "expert" repairman who may not come when you ask and who often doesn't know as much as he professes.

Stanley Schuler

LYME, CONNECTICUT

Section 1/How to Fix Almost Everything

ACOUSTICAL TILE

Loose, bulging. If tile is applied to wood furring strips, nail back to the strips with flathead nails. If applied on plaster, use cement-coated nails. Countersink the nailheads and cover with spackle if necessary to conceal them.

Stained by a leak. First, stop the leak. Then, tile can be painted with any interior paint without damaging its acoustical qualities. But if you prefer to replace the tile, cut it out with a knife. Trim off flanges on new tile as necessary so that it can be fitted into the hole (most acoustical tiles have interlocking edges). Nail tile in place or glue it down with acoustical tile adhesive or linoleum cement.

ACRYLIC, RIGID
(Plexiglas, Lucite, and the like)

Broken, cracked. See PLASTICS—GENERAL. If crack is where a screw has been driven through the acrylic, the trouble probably occurred because the screw and screw hole were the same diameter. In future, always make screw hole only slightly larger than the largest diameter of the screw threads.

Separated from another material. See HOUSEHOLD DECORATIVE ACCESSORIES.

Scratches in surface. You can probably remove tiny scratches by polishing the acrylic with a special acrylic cleaner made for snowmobile and boat windshields. The cleaner, which contains a fine abrasive, will also improve larger scratches, but will not eliminate them.

AIR CONDITIONER, CENTRAL

NOTE. This is too large and complicated a piece of equipment for the average person to fool with. Have it serviced every spring and call a serviceman when you run into trouble. But take the following steps first.

Doesn't run. Is thermostat calling for cooling? Has fuse blown?

Labors. Lubricate blower and motor that circulate air through house, and fan and motor in condensing unit. Clean condensing unit thoroughly.

Not cooling properly. Clean the filters and check them every month hereafter. If blower and duct dampers are adjustable, make sure they are set at high-speed setting.

Ice forms on cooling coil. Turn air conditioner off for several hours until it melts; then turn it on again. If ice forms a second time, call for service.

Noisy. Make sure all bolts, etc., are tight. Check ductwork (see DUCT, HEATING).

AIR CONDITIONER, ROOM

Doesn't work. Is it plugged in? Is outlet operative? Is cord broken? Has the fuse blown?

Labors. Turn it off. Clean filters. If you didn't clean out the entire unit at the start of the cooling season, do so now. Give the condenser special attention.

Your problem may also be a voltage drop. Such drops are sometimes temporary, but sometimes they continue. If conditioner labors only briefly, don't worry. If laboring continues, turn it off and call a serviceman.

Doesn't cool. Make sure thermostat is properly set. Clean filters. Clean entire inside of conditioner, especially condenser.

Freezes. Turn off unit at once. Restart after a few hours.

Turns on and off at short intervals. Try moving up thermostat two points. If this doesn't work, clean condenser and rest of unit well.

Noisy. Check whether grille or window is loose. Shim up conditioner with wedges if it isn't level. Tighten fan belt.

ALABASTER

Broken. Clean and apply epoxy glue to one surface. Press together for several hours.

Stains. See MARBLE.

ALUMINUM

Small holes, tears. Clean metal with steel wool. Apply plastic aluminum.

Large holes, tears. If edges are more than 3/16 inch apart, cut a patch out of sheet aluminum. Clean patch and area around hole with steel wool. Spread plastic aluminum or epoxy glue on patch and press down. Patch can also be soldered (see BASIC METHODS: HOW TO SOLDER METAL).

Seam between two pieces of aluminum open. If previously soldered, heat metal with torch and apply new solder. Otherwise, glue pieces together with plastic aluminum.

NOTE. If there is strain on a patch or seam, riveting is advisable (see BASIC METHODS: HOW TO FASTEN METAL WITH BOLTS, RIVETS, ETC.).

Heavy aluminum broken. Solder or apply epoxy glue to the broken edges and press together.

Aluminum separated from other materials, such as felt, glass, etc. See HOUSEHOLD DECORATIVE ACCESSORIES (*metal*).

Dents. Hold a block of wood over concave side of dent. Hammer out carefully (use light taps, not heavy blows) with a rubber mallet. Hammer from edges of dent toward the center.

Stains. If aluminum is painted, scrub with trisodium phosphate. This may also be effective on unfinished aluminum. If not, brush on an aluminum cleaner containing phosphoric acid; let it stand for 10 minutes, and rinse well. Repeat treatment if necessary.

AQUARIUM

Leaks. Dry and clean the leaking seam on the inside. Remove loose or crumbly caulking. Then squeeze in asphaltic aquarium sealer available from pet stores. Dry for at least 2 hours.

Glass broken. Break it out and pick out all splinters. Scrape cement completely from the slate and frame. Clean thoroughly and let dry. Have piece of glass cut to size. Mix 100 percent Portland cement with linseed oil to a thick consistency; roll into a rope and press firmly into the track at bottom and on sides. Slip glass through top of frame and press securely into the cement. Press cement into track at top.

Let cement dry 1 or 2 days and then trim off excess.

ARMETALE

Broken. Clean and coat edges of this metal alloy with epoxy glue and press together for 6 hours.

Stained. Clean with brass polish.

ARROW

Feathers off or damaged. Remove all feathers, whether damaged or not, and scrape off glue and any thread bindings. Select three feathers from a turkey wing or, if not available, from a large chicken wing. (Arrow feathers are also available from outstanding sporting goods stores.) Be sure feathers come from the same side of the turkey's body or arrows won't fly straight. Split the feathers down the midrib and smooth the ribs on fine sandpaper. Trim feathers roughly to size and allow 1 inch of midrib to extend beyond either end. Arrange feathers at 120-degree angles around the arrow and glue midribs to the wood with cellulose cement. Then wrap fine thread around the exposed midribs and coat with cellulose cement.

Point or metal nock loose. Remove, clean off old cement, and reglue with epoxy.

Nock split. Force epoxy glue into split and clamp.

GLUE MIDRIB TO WOOD AND WIND
EACH END WITH THREAD

1"

ALLOW 1" OF MIDRIB
TO EXTEND AT EACH END

Warped. Heat carefully (don't scorch) over a gas burner or electric plate, bend straight, and hold till set.

Broken. Glue with epoxy or cellulose glue, but odds are the arrow won't be much good.

AUTOMOBILE AIR CONDITIONER

Doesn't work. Check whether fuses for air conditioner have blown, and if they have, replace them. (See your owner's instruction manual.) Check whether a wire has broken or an electrical connection is loose. If air conditioner still fails to work, take it in for servicing.

Doesn't cool adequately. If air flow from ducts is normal and cold, inspect car for air leaks around doors, windows, fire wall, and fresh-air and heater ducts and plug these. If air flow is normal but incoming air is warm, go to a service station.

If air flow is below normal, check fuses, wires, and electrical connections. Check whether there's a leak in the ducts or whether ducts are obstructed. Remove dirt, insects, and papers clogging front of car radiator.

AUTOMOBILE—BATTERY AND ELECTRICAL SYSTEM

Battery weak. Check fluid level and fill to ring in bottom of filler holes. Use ordinary tap water unless you live in an area with hard, acidic, or alkaline water.

Have battery given a light charge to bring it up to snuff.

Battery OK but car doesn't start. The battery cables and terminals are probably badly corroded. Remove cables from terminals by loosening bolts or releasing springs. If they don't come off fairly easily, don't try to force them by hammering or twisting: you're likely to break the connections inside the battery between the terminal posts and plates. Buy a cable puller from an auto supplies store.

When the cables are loose, clean them thoroughly and clean the battery posts. Replace cables if they are frayed. If clamps on cables are floppy or fit too loosely on terminals, either replace the cables entirely or the clamps. When reinstalling cables, make absolutely certain that they fit snugly on the terminals.

Battery dead. You need booster, or jumper, cables. Drive another car alongside or park it front-to-front with dead car. Turn off engine, lights, heater, and other electrical components. Attach clamp at one end of red cable to the positive terminal of the booster battery; then attach other end to the positive terminal of the dead battery. (The positive terminal is identified by a red color, or a + sign or P on the battery post or case.) Then attach the other jumper wire to the negative terminals (black, − sign, or N) on the booster battery and then the dead battery. Be careful not to let cable clamps touch.

Turn ignition key in dead car to *on* and step on starter.

Battery cable insulation worn off. Repair temporarily with friction tape or cellulose electrical tape. For a lasting repair, clean cable and spread plastic rubber on break.

Headlight out. If your car has dual headlights, before replacing a defective lamp, note whether it is marked "1" or "2." You'll find the number pressed into the glass at the top of the lens. Buy a replacement lamp of the same number.

Remove screws holding the chrome trim around the lamp and pull off trim. Then remove the small-headed screws from around the lamp. Do not touch the larger screws, which are used for aiming the lamp. Pull out lamp and withdraw plug. Then replace lamp.

Taillight out. Unscrew trim ring and remove lens and bulb. Clean terminal contacts in socket and on bulb; replace bulb and try once more. If it still doesn't work, buy a new bulb of the same type.

Headlight doors don't open. The doors should open automatically when the light switch is turned on while the engine is running. If they don't, turn lights on, grasp doors at bottom and lift upwards. Have system checked by a serviceman.

Lights, radio, heater, defroster, turn signals, seat belts, clock, power seats, or power windows not working. If specific lights are out, it may be because the bulbs are dead and need replacement. But failure of other individual electrical devices as well as lights is usually attributable to a blown fuse. Consult your owner's manual to find fuse locations, and replace blown fuses with new ones of the same size.

If a new fuse blows almost immediately,

it generally means that there is a short in the circuit. Look for worn or broken insulation on the wires, especially where they are held to the car body by clips and where they pass under the car. If you find the source of trouble, clean wires and overwrap them with electrical tape.

Horn stuck and won't stop blaring. Pull fuse controlling it and go to a service station.

AUTOMOBILE BODY

Paint scratched, chipped. Clean metal with the point of a knife and emery cloth. Be sure to get off any rust. Then paint with touch-up enamel.

Tiny dents. Apply several thin coats of touch-up enamel until dents are filled. The alternative is to fill the dents with body glaze or putty, which comes in a tube. Then paint when dry.

Large creased dents. Remove finish with paint remover and sand metal clean. You can now follow directions below for dents without sharp creases, or you can simply fill the dent with epoxy mender. In the latter case, in very cold weather, heat the metal first with a heat lamp; and to speed curing of the mender, direct a heat lamp on it from about 18 inches away. When mender has set, shape it with a file or SurForm tool and sand smooth. Apply an aerosol paint.

If dent is more than about ¼ inch deep, drill small holes through it in several places and force the epoxy mender through these to improve anchorage.

Large dents without sharp creases. The easiest way to repair these is to buy a dent-puller. Make a very small hole in the center of the dent, screw in end of puller, and pull out dent. Then fill hole with epoxy mender.

A less expensive procedure, which may be slightly more difficult, is to drill one or more ⅛-inch holes through the dent. Drive a sheet-metal screw into each, one after the other; grasp the screw in the jaws of pliers or the claw of a hammer and pull sharply toward you. Then hammer above and below the dent while continuing to pull. When the dent is removed, fill the screw holes with epoxy mender.

Holes. In order to patch a hole, it is obviously necessary to provide some kind of backer to which epoxy mender can be applied. If you can get at the back of the damaged metal, clean the surrounding surface thoroughly, spread on a layer of epoxy mender, and embed in this a patch of galvanized screen wire. Then, when dry, work mender into the front side of the wire and gradually build up to the proper level.

If you cannot get at the back of the metal, it is sometimes possible—as in the case of a rocker panel—to wad galvanized screen wire behind the hole and build up from this with epoxy mender.

Another excellent way to repair holes is to cover them with fiber glass. To do this, remove the paint from around the hole. Then bend in the metal 1 inch back around all edges. Impregnate a piece of fiber glass mat with polyester resin and set in hole. Build up from here with additional patches of fiber glass. See FIBER GLASS, RIGID.

Tears. Clean metal thoroughly on both sides. Bend edges into line. Then apply epoxy mender to both front and back sides. In the case of a very large tear, drill holes through the metal, and bolt or rivet a piece of galvanized steel flashing or even a galvanized steel mending plate to the underside; then apply epoxy mender.

Rust spots. Unfortunately, by the time these start to show up the metal is often so weakened that there's little you can do about the spots. The best you can hope to do is scrape and sand the rust from the front and back sides of the metal; work red metal primer well into the metal, and paint. If the metal is not badly weakened, apply the primer only to the back side and overcoat it, when dry, with fibered asphalt roofing cement. Apply epoxy mender to the front side.

If the rusting occurs in a sealed area—a rocker panel, for example—open up one of the drain holes or drill a ½-inch hole from the back side. Give the metal several days to dry out. Then squirt or spray in red metal primer.

Hub cap dented. Take it off; hold it face down on a block of wood, and tap the dent out.

Use a hard-rubber mallet or hold a block of wood under a steel hammer to remove the worst part of the dent; then tap directly with the hammer to remove small creases.

Chrome strip off. Place the strip over the clips in the body and snap into place. If clips don't hold because strip has been flattened, squeeze the edges of the strip with pliers to return it to its proper shape; then snap onto the clips. It may then be necesary to squeeze the strip tightly onto the clips.

If clips are missing or strip doesn't hold no matter what you do, drill one or more small holes through it and the body and insert self-tapping aluminum screws.

Chromium deeply scratched and rusted. See CHROMIUM PLATE.

Weather stripping off or loose. Clean to remove dirt. Then stick down with adhesive recommended for the purpose by automobile supplies outlet, or use rubber cement.

Leaks around windshield. Clean sealing strip and squeeze in a windshield sealer from auto supplies store.

Door or luggage compartment lock stiff. Squirt into keyhole a little auto-lock lubricant; let it penetrate briefly, then work lock back and forth.

Locks frozen by rain or snow. Warm them up by holding a lighted match against them, squirting with deicer—any way you can think of.

Door doesn't latch properly. Loosen screws holding strike plate in the jamb and readjust position of plate.

Wiper blades worn. Buy replacements.

Radio antenna broken. Buy replacement if antenna is broken through. But if it is simply bent, you can do a reasonably good job of straightening by hand.

AUTOMOBILE BRAKES

Don't hold or too soft. Open master cylinder—a small metal reservoir mounted under the hood either on the fire wall between engine and driver or on the power brake unit. Pour in brake fluid to within ½ inch of top.

NOTE. Fluid in master cylinder should be checked two or three times a year. If level drops frequently, there's a leak somewhere in the system which must be stopped by a mechanic.

AUTOMOBILE COOLING SYSTEM

Radiator overheating. Check water level. Check fan belt to make sure it is not slipping. (See below for how to fix.) Examine front of radiator and clean out dirt, insects, etc., that are clogging it.

Leak in radiator. If a hole is visible and accessible, drain radiator to below that point, clean and dry well and spread on epoxy mender. If hole is invisible or inaccessible, pour radiator sealer, available from service station, into radiator.

Radiator frozen. Fill with water. Replace cap but leave it slightly loose. Cover radiator with a blanket. Start engine and let it idle until steaming stops.

Leaks in hoses. Replace with new hoses. If old clamps are badly corroded, buy replacements for them also.

Fan belt broken. Buy a new one of the same size. To replace, loosen the mounting bolt on the generator or alternator, and move generator toward fan until old belt can be slipped from the pulleys and new one can be installed. Then pull generator tight and fasten mounting bolt. The belt should deflect only ¼ inch when you push down on it with your thumb at midpoint.

AUTOMOBILE ENGINE

NOTE. There isn't much the average person can do about his car's engine. But you can at least manage with the following problems:

Doesn't start. Check gas. If lights and horn don't work, battery may be dead (see AUTOMOBILE—BATTERY AND ELECTRICAL SYSTEM). In wet or humid weather, trouble may be caused by moisture on spark plugs and distributor. Dry plugs, cables, and sockets thoroughly. Dry distributor cap. If you still don't get action, remove distributor cap and dry inside.

Spark plug not firing. Since you can't tell which plug is malfunctioning simply by looking at it, pull off cable and hold the side of a screwdriver blade against the metal cap and the point against the engine block (don't touch the screwdriver blade with your hand). With engine running, observe the sparking. A plug that is bad will not spark or spark weakly. Remove it and replace. In an emergency, it can be partially cleaned (see SPARK PLUG).

Air cleaner dirty. If cleaner is of replaceable paper type, remove paper filter and drop it flat several times on the floor to loosen dirt. Turn over and repeat process. Wipe out interior of air cleaner. Examine the filter paper for holes by holding a light inside it and, if you find any, replace it. Then put filter back in place and turn it half around from its original setting.

If cleaner is of oil-wetted wire-mesh type, slosh it up and down in gasoline; drain thoroughly. Oil well with number 30 oil, drain off excess, and replace.

If cleaner is of oil-wetted urethane type, wash filter in gasoline and squeeze dry. Then soak in number 30 oil.

If cleaner is of oil-bath type, empty oil reservoir and wash the entire cleaner in gas. Refill reservoir to designated mark with number 30 oil.

AUTOMOBILE EXHAUST

NOTE. Fix holes in a muffler or exhaust pipe immediately. The danger of being killed by carbon monoxide is too great to take chances.

Small holes in exhaust pipe. Clean metal with a knife and steel wool. Spread epoxy mender over holes.

Small holes in muffler. Clean metal thoroughly and cover hole with epoxy mender. Pinholes can also be plugged with short self-tapping screws.

Large holes in exhaust pipe. As a temporary repair, cut off the top, bottom, and rims of a tin can. Cut can down the seam, then wrap the metal around the exhaust pipe over the hole. Bind tightly in place with strong flexible wire.

Large holes in muffler. For a temporary repair, cut a steel or aluminum patch large enough to overlap the hole ½ inch on all sides. Clean metal around hole thoroughly and apply a continuous strip of epoxy mender. Set patch in place and bind with string until adhesive sets. You can then, if you wish, drill small holes through the two sheets of metal and secure the patch further with self-tapping screws.

Exhaust pipe loose, dangling. If brackets have rusted out, loop bailing wire twice around the pipe and then secure the ends to the body frame.

AUTOMOBILE GAS TANK

Leaks. For a temporary repair, clean the metal around the hole. If gas is still dribbling out, drain tank down below hole and drive in a self-tapping screw. Then smear on epoxy mender.

AUTOMOBILE INTERIOR

See also AUTOMOBILE SEAT COVER.

Seats torn. Seat fabrics are stretched too tight for you to sew a rip with any assurance that the stitches will not pull out. The only thing you can do is cut a patch out of matching fabric or out of the excess material tucked behind the backseat, coat lightly with appropriate glue, and smooth over the tear. A better solution is to get seat covers.

Fabric on doors, side panels, torn. Spread a light coat of fabric glue under the tear with a spatula; then immediately pull edges of tear together neatly, and smooth down. If the tear is very large, glue one section at a time.

Fabric on armrests worn. Remove screws under armrest. Rip out seams in fabric carefully and use the old covering as a pattern for a new one. Sew new covering out of matching or contrasting material, wrap around armrest, and screw armrest to door again.

Rubber floor mats torn. Clean mat with gasoline or benzine. Roughen surface with sandpaper. Apply plastic rubber to small holes and tears. For large holes, cut a patch from a tire tube or old rubber mat. Clean the back. Apply rubber cement to the patch and to the mat, and smooth patch down.

Stains on carpet. See RUG.

Stains on seats. See CLOTHING—FABRICS.

Stains on plastic surfaces. Wash with detergent. Remove grease and oil with benzine.

Seat belts soiled. Wash with detergent solution. Don't use cleaning fluids, as they may weaken belts.

Retractable seat belt won't pull out. Keep working it in and out and it may eventually come loose. If not, slip a long, slender screwdriver blade into slot and straighten fold in belt. If this fails, you'll have to take up holder from floor.

Screws missing or loose from side panels, etc. You just need some stainless steel or aluminum self-tapping screws. If screws are missing, try an assortment of new screws till you find one of proper length and diameter. If screws are loose—and you can't make them hold—put in new screws that are a little longer and fatter.

Rearview mirror loose, wobbly. Tighten screw in clamp on back side.

Rearview mirror holder falls off windshield. Clean windshield thoroughly. Spread epoxy glue on back of mirror holder and position on windshield. Then clamp it in place for 12 hours with strips of masking tape.

AUTOMOBILE SEAT COVER

Holes in plastic. Cut a patch from matching material. (If you can't buy this, cut a small piece from the seat cover where it is tucked behind the backseat.) Coat with plastic-mending adhesive and glue in place over or under the hole (whichever looks better).

Holes in fabric. Glue a patch of matching material in place with fabric glue.

Holes in fiber. Trim off raw edges. Cut a patch out of matching fiber at least 2 inches wider and longer than the hole. Coat bottom of seat cover with white glue and press down on patch. When dry, spread a little more glue around top edges of hole.

Seams split. Take off cover. Baste edges of material together. Then baste twill tape to both sides of seam and stitch on sewing machine.

AX

Blade badly nicked. Remove nicks with a file. File toward the sharp edge. Then sharpen with a carborundum stone.

Dull. Hone with a small circular carborundum stone. Hold it against the blade at a slight angle and rub with a circular motion.

Handle broken. See HAMMER.

BABY CARRIAGE

Fabric torn. Cut a patch out of matching material and glue over tear with fabric glue.

Seams in fabric split. If the fabric is not too dried out, rip old seams open and cut off edges at thread line. Turn new edges out and baste. Then cover with cloth mending tape or leatherette and restitch.

Mildew stains on fabric. Wash with household detergent.

Wheel off. Pry off hubcap by opening the split metal tabs that clamp around the spokes. Slip wheel on axle and insert new cotter pin in end of axle.

Wheel wobbly. Take off hubcap, pull out cotter pin in axle, and remove wheel. Slip tight-fitting steel washers over the axle, replace wheel, and insert cotter pin.

Brake doesn't hold. Remove rust from brake joint with emery cloth and apply oil. If brake still doesn't hold, bend ends of brake rod slightly toward the wheels so they will grip tighter against the tires.

Joints in frame stiff. Rub off rust with liquid rust remover. Polish metal lightly with very fine steel wool. Apply oil.

BADMINTON RACKET

Handle or frame split. Spread epoxy glue thinly on both split edges and clamp together for 2 hours or longer with C-clamps.

Strings broken. Better have an expert restring the racket. However, you can buy lengths of racket string from sporting goods or mail order stores. Pull broken string ends out through holes in frame and knot them tightly against the frame. Cut replacement string longer than is needed and knot it at one end. Pull unknotted end through hole in top of frame and weave it through the sound strings. At bottom of frame, thread string through hole and knot it against the frame.

Grip on handle loose. Clean off old adhesive. Apply rubber cement to grip and handle and let it set for 5 minutes. Press together and allow to dry for an hour or more.

BALL, INFLATED LEATHER

Leak in bladder. Unlace ball, remove bladder, and patch like a tire. See TIRE.

Leak in laceless leather ball. Send it back to the factory.

Leather dried out. Inflate ball. Rub a damp cloth in saddle soap and rub soap vigorously into leather. Remove excess soap with a cloth dampened in water.

Seams torn. If the ball is laced, you may be able to get inside with your fingers and resew seams with strong cotton thread. A curved needle will help. But don't count on success. If seams in a laceless ball are torn, send the ball back to the manufacturer.

BALL, INFLATED PLASTIC

Holes, tears. Deflate ball. Patch with matching material or patch that comes with plastic-mending adhesive kit. Spread adhesive on back of patch, smooth over hole, and let dry 24 hours before inflating ball.

BALL, INFLATED RUBBER

Holes, tears. Deflate ball. If rubber is heavy and appearance is not important, see TIRE (*tube punctured*). For lightweight, colored rubber, try to secure a scrap of similar material. Clean and roughen surface of ball around tear and back of patch with sandpaper. Apply thin coat of rubber cement to both surfaces and let set for 5 minutes. Press together and allow to dry for several hours.

BAMBOO

Breaks, splits. Apply white glue or epoxy glue and hold in place with clamps, or wrap with thread or light cord until glue sets. For further reinforcement, when glue is dry, wrap neatly with heavy cotton thread (see FISHING ROD) and brush on varnish.

Another way you can sometimes reinforce bamboo is to insert in the hole in the bamboo a wood dowel of approximately the same diameter as the hole. Coat the dowel first with glue.

BAR

Laminated plastic top damaged. See PLASTICS—LAMINATED.

Wood top damaged. See WOOD.

Varnish on top badly scratched. Take it off entirely with paint remover. Sand smooth and then use steel wool. Apply two coats of bar varnish. Use steel wool after first coat to roughen surface slightly before applying second.

BASEBALL

Seams split. With heavy cotton thread, sew leather together in same manner as sound seams: Insert needle under the edge and through leather on one side of seam. Then insert it under the edge and through the leather on the other side of the seam. Continue in this manner to the end of rip, then tack thread securely and draw end of thread back under stitches.

BASEBALL MITT

Seams split. Sew together with strong cotton thread. Match stitches with surrounding seams.

Holes. Out of strong, soft leather cut a patch at least ½ inch wider on all sides than the hole. Feather the edges slightly with a sharp razor blade. Coat back of patch and area around hole with rubber cement. Let dry until tacky, then press patch over hole.

BASEMENT AREAWAY
(window well)

Floods. If water is entering over rim of areaway (the usual cause of flooding), slope or channel the ground away from the areaway. If areaway wall is made of masonry, build up the rim with one or two courses of bricks laid in concrete. If areaway wall is steel, dig out around it, loosen it from the foundation wall (it may not be fastened), and pull it upward a couple of inches. It need not be refastened to the wall since the weight of the soil against it will hold it in place.

If areaway continues to flood, install a 2-inch or 4-inch drainpipe from the bottom of the areaway into the footing drain and cover the top of the pipe with wire mesh. The alternative, if you don't have footing drains, is to lead the drainpipe away from the house to the storm sewer or a low point where the water can be emptied.

BASEMENT BULKHEAD

Badly split, rotten. Replace with a steel bulkhead.

Door hinges loose. See DOOR, GARAGE.

Floods in heavy rains. Fill cracks in the bulkhead and between it and the house wall with silicone or polysulfide rubber caulking. Tack wide strips of thin rubber matting or heavy canvas around edges of doors. To divert water from cracks at the top of the doors, nail 1-inch by 1-inch wood strips to the bulkhead just above the doors. The strips should form a V pointing upward toward wall of house.

If water is coming in under the bottom edges of bulkhead, pull soil away from it so that the top of the masonry walls on which it rests is at least 2 inches above ground level. Caulk open seam between bulkhead and masonry.

BASEMENT FLOOR

Rough, irregular. See FLOOR, CONCRETE.

Leaks around edges. If the leak is active, open the joint between floor and wall with a cold chisel to a width and depth of ½ inch. Clean out crumbs. Cram the joint full of hydraulic cement mixed according to the directions on the package, and hold the patch in place until the cement hardens.

If the leak is not active, open the joint, clean out crumbs, dampen the concrete, and fill the crack with 1 part portland cement, 2 parts sand, and enough water to make a plastic mix. The alternative, which is easier but not quite as good, is to scrape the crack open as much as possible, clean out all dirt, and dampen the concrete. Then trowel latex cement that sets in very thin layers (Top 'n Bond or Watta Bond, for example) into the corner to form a 45-degree angle. Let the cement extend up on the wall and out over the floor about 2 inches.

Other materials that can be used to caulk cracks and joints in concrete are silicone rubber caulking compound and fibered asphalt roofing cement. The concrete must be bone dry when these are applied, however.

Leaks all over floor. Fill individual cracks as above. But if entire floor is cracked and leaking, have a mason cover it from wall to wall with a 2-inch layer of reinforced concrete.

Concrete floor dusty. See FLOOR, CONCRETE.

Floor drain clogged. See DRAINS, PLUMBING.

BASEMENT WALL

Wall weeps or oozes. Remove all dirt, grease, oil, and paint other than cement paint from wall. Mist wall with water. Mix a cementitious coating, such as Thoroseal, with water to pancake-batter thickness, and "lay" it on the wall with a large calcimine brush. Don't try to brush it out too much. Just spread it on the wall at the rate of about 2 pounds of dry powder per 10 square feet. Let dry overnight. Then dampen wall and apply a second coat at half the first rate. If this doesn't stop the weeping, continue applying additional coats in the same way.

Several epoxy materials can also be used for stopping seepage. Their main advantage is that it is not necessary to remove paint on walls as long as it is sound. But they are expensive and quick-drying; and you must work fast to get a batch of the material applied.

Isolated cracks that leak. With a cold chisel, chip out crack to ½-inch width and about the same depth. Cut the sides straight up and down or, better, bevel them backward so crack is wider in back than in front. Blow out crumbs and wet crack with water. Fill with 1 part portland cement and 2 parts sand. An alternate method is to scratch the crack open, remove particles, dampen slightly, and spread a thin-setting latex cement such as Top 'n Bond over it. When dry, paint patch with a cementitious coating or waterproofing epoxy.

If crack is leaking actively, follow first method but use quick-setting hydraulic cement to fill the crack.

Wall drips in many places. Call in a masonry contractor. He will have to excavate down to the footings on the outside of the wall and install a continuous row of perforated drainpipes that empty into a pipe leading to a storm sewer or low spot. He will then cover walls from footings up to grade level with a watertight membrane of concrete plaster and two coats of asphalt. In extreme situations, asphalt building paper is sandwiched between the coats of asphalt.

BASKET

Split-wood basket broken. Weave a strip of thin wood or aluminum flashing into the basket over the break. Coat with cellulose cement and spread cement on broken wood. Clamp broken wood to splint.

Wicker or fiber basket broken. See WICKER.

Handle of wicker or fiber basket loose at one end. The handle is usually woven around a bent wood strip which is inserted in the side of the basket. Pull strip out, coat with epoxy glue, and then replace. Stick together loose bindings on handle with epoxy glue.

Joints in steel wire basket broken. Clean wires with steel wool. Bring them together and, if necessary, clamp with a C-clamp or loop of wire. Heat with a soldering iron or torch and apply solder (see BASIC METHODS: HOW TO SOLDER METAL).

Plastic basket broken. Reglue broken section with plastic-mending adhesive, but if the basket is used to hold any appreciable weight, it will probably come apart again.

BATHROOM ACCESSORIES
(towel rod, soap dish, paper holder, etc.)

Metal accessory mounted on wall surface loose. Reanchor with spring-wing toggle bolts, hollow-wall screw anchors, or ordinary screws driven into lead, fiber, or plastic anchors, depending on wall thickness (see BASIC METHODS: HOW TO SUPPORT things on walls that will not receive or hold nails and screws).

Setscrew in metal accessory lost. Take accessory to hardware store and get new screw that fits.

Setscrew continually loose. Pull off top of accessory and flatten the spindle on the end at the point were the screw touches it. Reset piece and tighten screw.

Flush-type ceramic accessory loose or fallen out. This type of accessory is mounted directly on the subwall so that the base is flush with the surrounding tiles. Remove accessory and scrape off adhesive on back and on wall. Apply new ceramic-tile adhesive or silicone adhesive; press into place, and hold tight to wall with masking tape. After 24 hours, fill joints around accessory with cement grout made for ceramic-tile installations.

Recessed-type ceramic accessory loose or fallen out. Remove accessory and clean out old cement. Apply new adhesive to back and edges, and set in place.

Ceramic accessory broken. Knock off protruding piece and crack the base in two across the center. Then, working from the break toward the edges of the accessory, chip out the base with a cold chisel. Clean out old cement.

Set in new accessory with ceramic-tile adhesive or silicone caulking compound.

Ceramic accessory broken. Clean broken surfaces, apply epoxy glue, and press together. Hold in place for 24 hours with masking tape.

Towel rod set between ceramic end pieces broken. If the rod is made of wood or ceramic (as it usually is), you can glue the ends together with epoxy, but the rod will not have very much strength. It is better to remove it entirely and replace with a steel telescoping rod of appropriate diameter. Cut to proper length, slide into holders, and expand rod. If the telescoping joint is tight, no further work is necessary, but if it is loose, drill a small hole through the overlapping ends and drive in a steel self-tapping screw.

BATHROOM FIXTURES

See also BATHTUB; FAUCET; DRAINS, PLUMBING; SINK, BATHROOM; SHOWER HEAD; SHOWER STALL; TOILET.

Chipped surfaces. Clean and dry the scarred area. With a tiny brush, apply epoxy resin or porcelain glaze made for the purpose.

Stains. Remove rust and green stains with a cleanser containing oxalic acid, such as Zud. Wash other stains with chlorine bleach mixed about 50:50 with water. If this doesn't work, mix cream of tartar and hydrogen peroxide to a paste and scrub the sink. Use a bristle brush and lots of elbow grease.

Paint wearing off painted fixture. Remove paint entirely with paint remover. Scrub with cleansing powder and rinse thoroughly. Roughen surface slightly with emery cloth. Then apply two coats of epoxy enamel made for the purpose. Follow directions on paint can.

BATHTUB

Crack around rim. Clean out old plaster, cement, mastic, grease, dirt, etc. Let wall edge and tub rim dry thoroughly. Then squeeze in silicone caulking compound. Push the caulking ahead of the tube nozzle; that is, as you squeeze in

the caulking, move the tube along the crack nozzle first. Smooth off as necessary with a small artist's pallet knife and remove excess caulking at once. If caulking is misapplied, remove at once with a paper towel.

If crack is very wide, fill it with caulking compound and then cover the joint with quarter-round ceramic tiles made specifically for the purpose. Set them in silicone caulking —not in the adhesive provided by the tile manufacturer.

Drain clogged. See DRAINS, PLUMBING.

Chipped surface. See BATHROOM FIXTURES.

Stains. See BATHROOM FIXTURES.

Rubber nonskid patches peeling from bottom. Scrape and peel off as best you can. Scrub off adhesive remaining with trichloroethylene.

BATTERY-OPERATED APPLIANCES

Don't work. If conventional dry cells are used, they are probably dead and need to be replaced. If rechargeable batteries are used, plug appliance into charger for several hours. No harm is done if you neglect to unplug the appliance after charging is completed. Note that if rechargeable batteries are allowed to become completely discharged, they may not hold a new charge and will have to be replaced. Note also that if relatively new rechargeable batteries cannot be recharged, the charger itself may be defective.

Other problems. Correct like plug-in appliances.

BEADS

String broken. Remove string entirely and arrange beads on a soft cloth surface so they won't roll away from you. Start with largest bead and arrange others on either side in graduated sizes. Knot end of new cord and lace it through the row of beads. After each bead, make a knot in the cord. Before tightening the knot, stick a pin through it and draw it up against the bead; then tighten knot and withdraw pin.

BEAM, EXPOSED INTERIOR

Cracks in wood. Clean out dust and cobwebs with vacuum cleaner. Stain plastic wood to match beam and press into cracks. If beam is painted, fill cracks with spackle and paint.

Shrunken away from ceiling or wall. Clean out crack with vacuum cleaner and fill with spackle. Note, however, that large cracks may open further or contract and crack spackle; in the case of these, it is better to nail small cove moldings over them.

BELT, MACHINE

Slips. Belt is too loose. It should have some play, but not too much. Loosen motor from its base, move further away from machine, and retighten.

Motor not running right. Belt may be too tight. There should be some slack in it but not so much that it slips. Loosen motor from its base, move toward machine, and retighten.

Runs off pulley, frayed. Pulleys on motor and machine are not in line. Check with a straightedge laid across the ends of pulleys. Then loosen pulley on machine (not motor) and move into line.

Squeals. If belt is not frayed, turn off motor and rub belt with a wet cake of soap.

BENCH GRINDER

Doesn't work. Check whether fuse has blown, whether outlet into which grinder is plugged is defective, whether cord is broken.

Grinding wheel cracked. Buy a replacement. When installing wheel, note that the nut for right-hand wheel is tightened clockwise, the one for left-hand wheel is tightened counter-clockwise.

BICYCLE

NOTE. Bicycles used to be easy to repair, but with the advent of the derailleur-type bikes, matters

took a turn for the worse. You can fix these, too, but you need special tools and—most of all—a manual on bicycle maintenance to figure out what should be done to any particular make and model.

Whatever repairs you do undertake, remember that a number of bolts, etc., on bicycles have left-hand threads, so if you come up against one that's difficult to loosen, try screwing it in the opposite direction.

Tire punctured. If location of hole is obvious, wheel does not have to be removed from bicycle. First, take out tire valve. Squeeze tire to unstick it from the rim. Tubular tires are now pushed partway off the rim by hand; but with clincher ties you need a pair of tire irons. When tire is pushed to one side, pull out tube and patch like an automobile tire (see TIRE). Use normal tire-patching kit for clincher tires, a special kit for tubular tires, which are very thin and light.

If location of hole is not evident, remove wheel from bicycle. Take off tire. Use tire irons for clincher tires but never use tools of any kind on tubular tires. Test tube in a tub of water for a leak, and then repair.

Handle grips loose. Remove from handlebar and roughen bar with emery cloth. Coat with rubber cement and apply cement inside grip. Push grip back on.

Handlebar loose—easily twisted downward. If tightening nut at middle of handlebar doesn't correct matters, loosen nut and shift bar to one side. Wrap the middle of the bar with friction tape or two strips of emery cloth glued back to back. Then center bar and tighten nut.

Pedal treads split, worn. Remove nut at back end of tread, knock out bolt, install new tread.

Pedals stiff. If oiling doesn't improve matters, remove both treads as above. Unscrew lock nut on end of center spindle, take out washer, and unscrew nut behind it. Take out ball-bearing sleeve and pull off the entire housing. Clean in kerosene. Fill ball-bearing sleeves with petroleum jelly. Reassemble housing on spindle. Screw on nut that bears against outer ball-bearing sleeve. Screw it tight, then give it a quarter turn in opposite direction to allow for bearing clearance. Then install washer and spindle nut, and reassemble treads.

Pedal crank loose. Take off left pedal and the crank nut (it has a left-hand thread). Then proceed as if you were fixing a stiff pedal, as above.

Coaster brake brakes poorly. The hub needs to be overhauled and lubricated—a pretty big job you may want to leave to an expert.

Expander brake brakes poorly. Adjust brake cable by turning wheel while tightening adjusting sleeve until brake shoes rub on drum. Then release sleeve a fraction and tighten it in place with a lock nut.

Caliper brake brakes poorly. Make sure wheel rim is clean, free of oil or wax. Turn adjusting mechanism at brake handles until brake shoes are about ⅛ inch away from rim.

Front wheel fork loose, moves vertically in head of frame. Loosen nut at top and tighten bearing cone underneath. Then tighten nut.

Slack chain on non-derailleur bicycle. The chain should depress only about ¼ inch at midpoint. To tighten it, loosen nuts holding rear wheel and move wheel backward.

Chain shifts improperly on derailleur-type bicycle. Adjust the limit screws. On a front derailleur, adjust the low-gear limit screw if chain shifts beyond small sprocket or does not go onto sprocket at all; adjust high-gear limit screw if chain shifts beyond or doesn't shift at all onto large sprocket. On a rear derailleur, the high-gear limit screw adjusts for the small sprocket while the low-gear limit screw adjusts for the large sprocket.

Wheel wobbles sideways. At point where rim is bent outward, loosen spokes on bulging side of rim and tighten those on the opposite side. Loosen spokes one turn at a time and tighten one turn at a time. If wheel cannot be straightened this way, you can remove it from bicycle and try bending it over your knee.

Wheel out of round—flat at one point, has a bump at another. Remove wheel from bicycle and take off tire and tube. With a spoke wrench and screwdriver loosen the spokes at the flat point; tighten them at the bump. To check roundness of wheel, tie a string to a nail; hold nail in center of axle hole, and sweep a string around the rim.

BIRDBATH

Concrete basin broken. Clean broken edges with a spray of water and let dry for several days. Apply silicone adhesive to one edge and firmly press broken pieces together. Remove excessive adhesive that oozes out from break. Let dry for 24 hours.

BLANKET

See also QUILT.

Bindings worn, torn. Rip off. Buy new binding material. Turn edges under, fold new binding material around blanket, and stitch down.

Edges frayed. Trim off. Put in two parallel lines of machine stitches close to the edge. Then, if you wish, finish by blanket stitching.

Other problems. See CLOTHING—FABRICS.

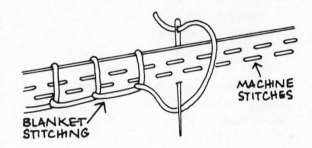

BLANKET STITCHING

MACHINE STITCHES

BLANKET, ELECTRIC

Doesn't heat. Check whether blanket is connected to cord and cord is plugged into house current. Check whether fuse on house circuit has blown and whether outlet used for blanket is operative. Examine cord for breaks and replace if necessary. If these measures fail, you need a new blanket. Repairs are so difficult that professional servicemen can't even make them.

Hot spots or cold spots in blanket. Buy a new one.

Plastic control case broken. If control is operative, disconnect it and coat broken edges of case with plastic-mending adhesive. Press together overnight.

Bindings worn, edges frayed. See BLANKET.

BLENDER, ELECTRIC

Doesn't work. Has fuse on house circuit blown? Is outlet into which blender is plugged defective? Disconnect blender and examine cord for a break. Replace if necessary. If these measures fail, take blender to a service shop.

Hums but doesn't work. *Unplug;* empty container. Reach in and try to turn blades by hand. If this is impossible, unscrew the metal base of the container so you can get at the blades better. If they are still tight, free with penetrating oil; then wash thoroughly in detergent solution and dry well. Apply household oil to base of drive shaft.

Container leaks at base. Unscrew metal base, remove large gasket, clean well, and replace. If leaking doesn't stop, replace gasket.

Blades bent. Try straightening with pliers. If you can't restore blades to the proper pitch and blender runs hard, buy new blades.

Plastic container broken. Clean thoroughly and dry for 24 hours. Coat broken edges with plastic-mending adhesive. Press together and let dry for 24 hours. Just to be on safe side in case glue doesn't hold when container is full and blender is running at high speed, encircle container with one or two strips of cellophane tape.

BOAT, ALUMINUM

Small holes. Clean metal with steel wool and fill hole from both sides with epoxy mender.

Large holes, tears. Use steel wool on metal on the inside and reshape it if it is bent or distorted. Cut a patch out of heavy aluminum flashing, hold over hole, and drill a series of small holes around the edges through both pieces of metal. Then coat underside of patch heavily with epoxy mender and rivet it over hole with aluminum rivets driven from the outside. Make sure that epoxy fills rivet holes. When epoxy has dried, smooth off rough edges and spots with a file.

Dents. See ALUMINUM.

BOAT—FASTENINGS AND FITTINGS

Corroded. Leave corroded screws in the hull. Drill beside them and put in new screws of silicon bronze. Replace bolts with new silicon bronze bolts. Above deck, on fresh water, fastenings can be removed and replaced with brass fastenings, but on salt water use silicon bronze only.

In steel and aluminum boats, use steel and aluminum fastenings respectively.

Fastenings loose. If wood is rotten, treat it with Git-Rot. See BOAT, WOOD (*wood rotting*). If holes are slightly enlarged but wood is sound, fill holes with wood plugs coated with resorcinol glue and drill new holes when glue dries.

BOAT, FIBER-GLASS-COVERED

Scratches, gouges. See BOAT, MOLDED FIBER GLASS.

Holes in fiber glass. Make sure wood is dry. Sand smooth. Sand fiber glass covering around hole to remove paint and marine growth. Brush polyester resin used in fiber glass boat construction on wood and cleaned area of fiber glass. Let it stand for 15 minutes. Then apply a second coat and let stand another 15 minutes. Meanwhile, cut a patch out of fiber glass cloth. Lay this over the tacky resin and smooth down. Brush more resin over patch and let dry. Then sand and apply one or two more coats of resin.

Small leaks. If source of leak is hard to find, pull the boat out of the water and fill it partway with a hose. Watch where the water flows out. Then dry the surface thoroughly and clean. Open the hole slightly with a knife or beer can opener. Fill with a polysulfide rubber caulking compound such as Alroy 707. Work fast, because the stuff hardens rapidly. Then sand smooth.

BOAT—INBOARD ENGINE

NOTE. Never make an electrical repair until you are sure bilges and engine compartment are free of explosive vapors.

Starting motor doesn't operate. Turn off all electrical equipment and wait half an hour for battery to recover. Meanwhile, check battery connections. Make sure they are tight, and clean as necessary. If you still can't get engine going, inspect starter switch for loose connections and broken or bare wires.

Starting motor operates but won't engage. Loosen starting motor from engine. See whether small pinion gear at end is stuck. If so, tap it with a hammer and apply a little oil.

Starting motor operates but engine won't start. Inspect wires from junction box to ignition switch, to coil, and to distributor for damage or loose connections. Dry off spark plugs and cables and inspect cables for damage.

Open distributor, and crank engine to see if distributor points are opening and closing. Stop cranking when you can slip a matchbook cover under the points. Inspect distributor cap to see if contact button is in place and free. Then replace rotor in distributor, close cap, and try to start engine.

If you suspect spark plugs are causing the trouble, hold a spark plug wire ¼ inch from engine while cranking engine with ignition switch on. Don't touch the bare wire with your hands. If spark occurs, clean or replace plug.

If engine still won't start, you may be out of fuel. Make sure shut-off cock on fuel line is open and gasoline tank vent is open. If filter or sediment bowl is not filled with gas, disconnect inlet pipe at fuel pump and blow through line to remove possible clogging.

Remove sediment bowl from fuel pump and clean screen in pump body. Then disconnect outlet line from pump to carburetor to see if fuel flows out when engine is cranked. Ignition must be off when making test.

Remove spark plugs and see if they are moist. If not, carburetor may be out of adjustment. Increase fuel flow by adjusting main jet on carburetor. If spark plugs are wet, engine may be flooded. To dry out cylinders, open throttle wide; put choke in open position and crank the engine several times with ignition on.

NOTE. Always replace flame arrester before cranking engine.

Fan belt broken. If you don't have a replacement, tie a rope around pulleys and tighten movable pulley.

Broken pipe or hose. For an emergency repair, wrap friction tape or even a piece of canvas tightly over the break. Replace pipe or hose when back in harbor.

Propeller nicked. See BOAT—OUTBOARD MOTOR.

BOAT, MOLDED FIBER GLASS

Shallow scratches. Clean with sandpaper. Brush on polyester resin available from boat dealers.

Deep scratches, gouges. Sand thoroughly. Mix ⅛-inch clippings of fiber glass mat with polyester resin to form a putty. Trowel into scratches, allow to dry, and then sand smooth.

Small breaks. Open the hole slightly with a file. Then with a disk sander, grind down the inside surface of the hull around the hole. The sanded area should extend about 3 inches on all sides of the break and should be deeper at the center (i.e., more or less saucer-shaped).

Out of fiber glass mat available from a boat dealer, cut a patch to fill the sanded area. Lay this on a sheet of cellophane and spread polyester resin evenly over the patch. Cover with another piece of cellophane, and with your fingers or a stick of wood squeeze the resin into the fiber glass until it is thoroughly saturated. Paint the sanded area inside the hull with resin. Then remove top sheet of cellophane from the

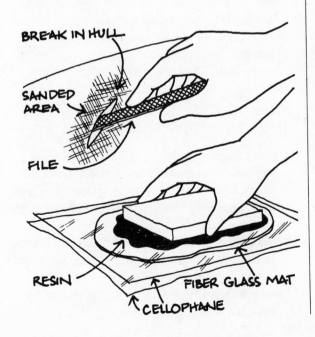

BREAK IN HULL

SANDED AREA

FILE

RESIN

FIBER GLASS MAT

CELLOPHANE

patch, press patch over hole, and smooth it on hull. Let the resin set, then remove cellophane. Sand the patch and then apply additional layers of fiber glass mat in the same way until the patch is the thickness of the hull. Then sand and finish.

If the crack on the outside of the hull is not completely filled, you can then mix ⅛-inch clippings of fiber glass mat with the polyester resin to form a putty. Spread this into the crack.

Large or compound breaks. With a small metal-cutting saw, cut out the damaged area entirely. Then feather back the edges of the hole on the inside of the hull for 3 inches or more. Cover one side of a piece of shirt cardboard with cellophane and lay this over the hole on the outside of the hull (the cellophane should face inward). Tape in place with strong pressure-sensitive tape. Then build up layers of fiber glass mat on the inside of the hull in the manner described above for small breaks. Remove cardboard backing when job is completed, and fill any imperfections in the outside surface of the patch with the fiber glass "putty" used to fill small breaks.

Lightweight aluminum sheet can be used instead of cardboard as a backing material. It is easier to handle if the hole is in an area of complex curves or bends. It does not have to be covered with cellophane.

NOTE. It is preferable to apply patches on the inside of the hull because they are less obvious and need little, if any, finishing. Outside patches are equally serviceable, but require more careful finishing.

BOAT—OUTBOARD MOTOR

Doesn't start. Check: Are you out of gas? Is gas-line valve closed? Is carburetor flooded? Is there water or dirt in fuel system? Is spark plug fouled or cracked? Are electrical connections loose?

Loses power. Check: Is there dirt in fuel system? Is carburetor adjustment too rich or too lean? Have you correct amount of oil in fuel?

Idles roughly. Check spark plugs, carburetor adjustment. Is a gasket blown?

Vibrates. Check spark plug and carburetor adjustment. Is motor properly mounted on boat? Is propeller damaged or fouled?

Motor runs, boat doesn't go. Propeller shear pin is broken. Drive it out and replace with new one.

Motor runs, boat sluggish. Propeller may be fouled or damaged. Motor may not be deep enough in water.

Propeller nicked. If nicks are not serious, smooth them with a fine-toothed file. To maintain propeller balance, try to remove the same amount of metal from each blade. Do this even if only one blade is damaged. If propeller has been dressed in this way several times, have it reconditioned by an expert.

BOAT, PLYWOOD

Seams open. See BOAT, WOOD.

Holes in plywood. Brace on the inside with a piece of exterior-grade plywood that is secured to the hull with resorcinol glue and brass or bronze screws. Then clean paint out of hole on the outside. Prime with new paint. When dry, fill with a plywood patch, or trowel in cement or glazing compound (marine grade). Sand smooth when dry and apply finish paint.

If plywood is also so badly dented that it bulges inward, drill a hole through center of dent and run a bolt through it and through blocks of wood on both sides. Draw up tight for 24 hours or longer. Then patch as above.

Another way to repair a hole is to cut away the splintered edges with a saw. With a disk sander, feather back the edges of the hole on the inside of the hull for about 3 inches. Then fill hole with fiber glass mat (see BOAT, MOLDED FIBER GLASS).

BOAT, SAIL

Spars broken, cracked. If the break is at right angles to the spar, better have a professional repair it. But if the break runs with the grain, coat the broken edges with epoxy glue and clamp together for 24 hours. Then sand the spar in the area of the break to remove the finish. Coat the bare wood with polyester resin used in repairing fiber glass boats. Allow it to stand for 15 minutes, then apply a second coat and allow this to stand for another 15 minutes. Then wrap fiber glass cloth tape spirally around the spar. The tape should extend for about 3 inches on either side of the break. Butt the edges of the tape. When this has soaked up the resin on the wood and cured for a few minutes, wrap another strip of tape over the first, spiraling it in the opposite direction. Brush on more polyester resin and let dry. Then sand lightly and apply a third coat of resin.

If you want the tape to be flush with the surface of the spar, cut a recess about ⅛ inch deep in the wood around the break before applying the tape.

Leaks in centerboard trunk. If these cannot be stopped by caulking with caulking compound available from marine dealers, pull the boat from the water and overturn. Let wood dry thoroughly. Sand off any marine growth in the trunk. Then wrap a piece of wood with felt, dip in Seaprene or Vinylon, and thoroughly coat the trunk on the inside. The coating will dry to form a watertight, flexible seal.

Hull problems. See BOAT, MOLDED FIBER GLASS; BOAT, PLYWOOD; or BOAT, WOOD.

Sails torn. See BOAT—SAILS.

BOAT—SAILS

Holes, tears in canvas. Dry sail. Cut patch of canvas, making cuts parallel with weave of cloth. The patch should overlap the hole in all directions by at least 1 inch. Allow ¼ inch extra to compensate for shrinkage. Place patch in position on sail parallel to sail weave, turn under edges, and draw line on sail around patch. Then baste patch in place, allowing some give in the fabric around the edges. Then stitch around the patch close to the edges. Use linen or cotton thread. Turn sail over and trim out edges of hole, but leave a margin. Turn under the sail edges. Then sew these down with zigzag stitches.

Holes, tears, rips in nylon or Dacron. Dry sail.

Cut a piece out of adhesive-coated nylon or Dacron sold by marine dealers, smooth over hole, and let dry.

Rips in canvas sail. With doubled cotton or linen thread, stitch together with herringbone stitch. Do not knot the thread at start or finish, but cut it off 3 inches or more beyond the ends of the stitching. This will permit sail to shrink without puckering.

Stitching in batten pockets worn. Remove batten. Stitch pocket to sail with doubled cotton, linen, or synthetic thread.

BOAT, STEEL

Small holes. Clean metal thoroughly with steel wool. Smear on epoxy mender and trowel smooth on both sides of hole.

Large holes. Have these welded.

Seams split. Clean thoroughly with steel wool. Press together (if necessary, have someone bear down on the seam with a piece of pipe). Then heat with torch and run in solder (see BASIC METHODS: HOW TO SOLDER METAL). Don't release tension on seam until solder has hardened.

BOAT, WOOD

Topside seams open. Scrape out old caulking and fill with polysulfide rubber caulking.

Bottom seams open. In a carvel plank boat, scrape seams open and refill with polysulfide rubber caulking. Groove caulking inward slightly to allow for swelling of planks. When thoroughly dry, sand and paint.

Seams in a lapstrake boat are not caulked. But clean them well to remove slight or major obstructions that will prevent seams from closing when boat is put in water.

Breaks, splits in wood. Fill with epoxy or resorcinol glue.

Wood rotting. It should be replaced. But for a semipermanent repair, treat it with Git-Rot epoxy sealer. For this to be effective, it must penetrate to the center of the rot, driving out all air. To accomplish this, drill a series of ⅛-inch to ¼-inch holes which will carry the sealer downward into all sections of the rotten area. Space the holes about 2 inches apart in overlapping rows. Pour and brush in the sealer according to the manufacturer's directions. Complete penetration is achieved when the holes remain filled and the surface treated remains shiny. Allow to cure for at least a week before sanding and painting.

Marine borers in wood. Cut open or bore out holes to expose the tunnels. Then treat with Git-Rot.

Canvas deck torn. See CANVAS DECK.

Deck too slippery. Clean, scrape, and paint in usual way. Mix fine clean builder's sand or Perltex into the final coat before applying.

Bright work discolored. Remove varnish. Bleach wood with commercial bleach. Do the entire surface, not just the stained areas. Several applications may be necessary before stains disappear. Then neutralize bleach according to maker's directions (or see FLOOR, WOOD). Sand well, and refinish.

BOLTS

Rusted tight. Squirt on penetrating oil and let it soak into the joint for a while. Tap with a hammer. Then loosen with wrenches. In severe cases, soak the nut in a bath of penetrating oil for a day.

Head of machine bolt battered so that wrench won't hold. Turn with a tooth-jawed Stillson wrench.

Head of stove bolt battered so that screwdriver won't hold. Cut new slot in head with a hacksaw.

Threads stripped, won't hold nut. If bolt cannot be replaced, smear epoxy mender on threads and tighten nut. Put a dab of epoxy mender on the exposed side of the nut.

Threads battered so that you can't screw on nut. Clean out threads with a small triangular metal file.

BONE

Broken. Coat both edges with cellulose cement and clamp together for 6 hours. If the broken object is exposed to weather, use epoxy glue instead.

Separated from metal. Coat with epoxy glue and press together.

BOOK

Page torn. Place a sheet of wax paper under the tear. Put a little white library paste on the torn edges and bring them together. Then rub a strip of white tissue paper into the paste so that it sticks the entire length of the tear. Weight down until paste dries. Then tear off excess tissue, pulling toward the tear from both sides. This repair is easy to make and does not become soiled or discolored like a repair made with cellulose tape.

Page loose. Apply a ⅛-inch strip of white paste to the inside margin of the leaf. Insert in book so that it sticks to adjacent page. To prevent paste from spreading over the two pages, place wax paper between them. Press down loose page until paste dries.

Page corner torn off. Place a piece of matching paper under the torn page and trace missing corner on it with a pencil. Cut the right angle with scissors or a razor blade, and tear along the hypotenuse parallel with the pencil line but ⅛ inch further from the corner. The tear should have a feathered edge. Paste new corner to page with white glue.

Back, or spine, of book torn. If appearance is not important, cover with adhesive-backed cloth tape. Fold tape over top and bottom of back and tuck it in between the cover and the back of the pages. If book is valuable, send to a professional book bindery.

Cover torn from book. Remove cloth and glue from the back of the pages. Cut a piece of muslin 2 inches wider than the back and as long as the book is tall. Center this on the back of the pages and glue with white glue. Rub down smooth and let dry. Then lay the book in its covers and glue the flaps of muslin to the covers. Insert wax paper between the covers and the pages. Close book, lay flat, and weight down. To improve appearance, paste endsheets on inside of covers to hide the cloth ends.

Book warped. Set book on a flat surface in the kitchen, bathroom, or other humid atmosphere. Place a board on top and weight down for several days.

Leather bindings powdery, scuffed. Rub smooth with very fine emery cloth. Heat 2 parts lanolin in a double boiler until it melts; then mix in 3 parts neat's-foot oil. Rub this rapidly and evenly over entire leather surface. Rub in well. Let stand overnight. Then polish with a soft cloth. If you wish, leather can be further protected by brushing on bookbinder's lacquer 48 hours after oil treatment described.

Ink stains on cloth covers. If you can't wipe them off with a damp cloth, leave well enough alone.

Ink stains on pages. Remove with ink eradicator.

Grease stains on cloth covers. Rub lightly with trichloroethylene, but don't count on success.

Grease stains on pages. Place a piece of aluminum foil under the page. Moisten Fuller's Earth with trichloroethylene and spread the paste over the stain. When dry, remove with a cloth. Don't count on success, however.

Mildew stains on cloth covers. Wipe off with a dry cloth. Then wipe with a cloth dampened in soapy water.

BOOKSHELF

Shelf sags. The alternatives are these: (1) Nail a 1-inch by 2-inch wood cleat to the wall under the shelf. The cleat should be at least 16 inches long so that it can be nailed to the studs at the middle of the shelf. It is preferable, however, for the cleat to extend the full length of the shelf. (2) If there are several shelves and the bottom one is well supported, insert a length of 6-inch board vertically between each shelf. Center these supports on the shelves and push them back against the wall where they won't be noticeable. Nail in place. (3) If shelves rest on adjustable metal wall brackets, insert a third bracket midway between the end two. (4) Replace sagging shelf with a new one of thicker wood.

Freestanding bookcase wobbles. Cover the back of the bookcase with ⅛-inch hardboard.

Screw this securely to sides, top, and bottom of frame.

Freestanding bookcase tips forward. Drive shingles under the bottom at the sides. Cut off flush with bookcase when it stands straight. Then if you wish, glue the wedges to bottom with white glue. If bookcase is heavily loaded, an alternative (or additional) method is to drive one or two small screw eyes into wall in back of bookcase. Insert corresponding screw eyes in back of case. Then wire together.

BOOT, OVERSHOE

Holes, tears, in rubber or rubberized areas. See TIRE (*tube punctured*).

Holes, tears in canvas. See CANVAS.

Holes, tears in plastic. Use plastic-mending adhesive kit. Cut plastic patch that comes with kit to proper size, coat with plastic adhesive, and smooth over tear. Patch can also be made out of any transparent or translucent flexible plastic.

BRACE AND BIT

See also ELECTRIC DRILL.

Stiff, hard to turn. Remove rust with steel wool and liquid rust-remover. Oil at all points that move.

Chuck stiff, doesn't hold bits. Unscrew to left until the sleeve comes off. Clean jaws with liquid rust-remover, and oil. Replace as you found them and screw back sleeve.

Bit dull, cutting edges bent. Place in a vise and sharpen with a small file. Be careful not to flatten bit on the outside.

BRASS

Small holes, cracks. Heat metal and run in solder (see BASIC METHODS: HOW TO SOLDER METAL). Fill from reverse side if possible. Touch up visible solder line with metallic paint.

Dents. Hold a block of wood over concave side. Gently tap out dent with a rubber or plastic mallet. Work from sides of dent toward the center.

Brass broken. It is best to have it welded. However, you can do a pretty good job by coating the broken edges with epoxy glue and pressing together.

Brass separated from other materials. See HOUSEHOLD DECORATIVE ACCESSORIES.

Lacquer worn from brass. Rub off remaining lacquer with lacquer thinner. Then clean brass thoroughly with a brass polish, rinse in water, and dry. Apply one or two thin coats of spray lacquer.

Brass plate worn off base metal. Have piece replated by a metalworking shop.

Tarnished. For light tarnish, rub with brass polish until no more dirt comes off on a clean rag. For heavy tarnish, rub with full-strength household ammonia and very fine steel wool. Rinse well when clean. Then apply brass polish.

BRICK

Loose brick broken. If brick is worth saving, clean broken edges and let dry. Then apply silicone rubber adhesive or epoxy glue and let dry for 24 hours.

Brick set in masonry wall, floor, etc., broken. Crack it out with a hammer and cold chisel. Chip off mortar on surrounding bricks. Soak new brick in water for about 30 minutes and thoroughly wet bricks surrounding cavity. Then set in brick with mortar as below.

Mortar joints around brick cracked or eroded. Chip out loose and weak mortar. Blow out dust with vacuum cleaner. Wet cracks with water. Mix 1 part masonry cement with 2 to 3 parts sand, and enough water to make a workable but not soupy mix. Pack into joint and finish to match adjacent joints.

For very small cracks, simply brush in a soupy grout made of equal parts masonry cement and sand. Or scrape cracks open and spread in latex cement.

Efflorescence on brick. Efflorescence is a white, powdery deposit caused by moisture dissolving the salts in masonry. To remove it, scrub with a stiff bristle brush; wash with 1 part muriatic acid in 3 parts water (or use proportions given on container), and rinse thoroughly. If efflorescence returns, check structure for leaks.

Mortar stains. Scrape off chunks of mortar with a chisel. Scrub with 1 part muriatic acid in 3 or more parts water.

Paint stains. Scrape off as much as possible. Then apply paint remover. Scrub off any color that remains with paint thinner.

Oil and grease stains. Blot up large fresh spills with paper towels and cover with cat litter for 24 hours. Pour undiluted household detergent on small spills and let soak in for 10 to 15 minutes. Then scrub with a brush and boiling water. Rinse well.

Old stains are best scrubbed with an emulsifying agent such as Big Red or Clix, available through auto supplies stores. The alternative is to make a thick paste of talc or whiting and benzine or trichloroethylene. Spread this over the stain and let dry. Then brush off and repeat treatment.

To prevent oil penetration into new or cleaned brick masonry, brush on two coats of transparent penetrating masonry sealer.

Rust stains. Scrub with a cleanser containing oxalic acid, such as Zud.

Smoke stains. See FIREPLACE, MASONRY.

Algae or moss on brick. Scrape off thick growth. Scrub what's left with strong solution of chlorine bleach.

Paint flaking off brick. This might have happened because oil-base paint was applied to damp brick. Scrape off loose paint and allow brick to dry thoroughly for about a week before repainting with oil-base paint.

Flaking also occurs in colder climates because moisture penetrates brick, causing it to spall. To prevent this from recurring, remove paint as completely as possible. Prime brick with a transparent masonry sealer, and let dry at least 24 hours before painting with oil-base or latex paint.

BRIEFCASE

Seams split. If possible, restitch with heavy cotton thread and a blunt needle. Run needle in and out of old thread holes. For a quicker but less neat repair, coat facing leather surfaces with rubber cement. Let dry until tacky and then press seams together.

Other problems. See SUITCASE.

BROILER, ELECTRIC

Doesn't heat. Check whether fuse on house circuit has blown. Plug a light into outlet used for broiler to see whether outlet is defective. Examine cord for a break, and replace if necessary. Check whether heating element is broken. If it is, buy a replacement and install the same way as the old one. If these measures fail, take broiler to a service shop.

Food and grease baked on exterior. See CHROMIUM PLATE.

BROILER-OVEN, ELECTRIC

Rotisserie works slowly or doesn't turn at all. Remove gears and clean well. Make sure they are meshing. Then lubricate with light oil. See also BROILER, ELECTRIC.

BRONZE

Small holes, cracks. Heat metal and apply solder (see BASIC METHODS: HOW TO SOLDER METAL). Work on reverse side of metal if possible. If not, visible solder can later be touched up with bronze paint.

Bronze broken. Have it welded for best results. Or apply epoxy glue to the broken edges and press together for 12 hours.

Bronze separated from other materials. See HOUSEHOLD DECORATIVE ACCESSORIES.

Lacquer worn from metal. Remove remaining lacquer with lacquer thinner. Clean metal with brass polish. Wash and dry. Spray on several coats of new lacquer.

Tarnished. Scrub with very fine steel wool and full-strength household ammonia. Rinse well. Then clean with brass polish to remove last vestige of tarnish.

BRUSH, HAIR

Brush head loose from metal handle. Clean back of head and handle cavity. Stick together with four or five dabs of cellulose cement. Then carefully bend or tap the metal edges down around sides of brush head.

BRUSH, SINK

Metal wires holding bristles loose from wood or plastic handle. Dry wires. Let handle dry thoroughly (this may take 2 or 3 days if handle is of wood). Cram epoxy mender into handle and insert wires. Let dry 24 hours.

BUCKET

Holes in metal. Clean metal thoroughly with steel wool. Smooth epoxy mender over hole.

Holes in rubber. Wash surface, dry, and roughen with sandpaper. Spread on rubber cement. If hole is very large, spread rubber cement on bucket and on a patch of rubber, and hold together until adhesive sets.

Holes, cracks in plastic. Wash and apply plastic-mending adhesive. Apply a plastic patch to reinforce.

Holes in porcelain. Chip away a little of the porcelain from around the hole and clean metal with a knife. Spread epoxy mender over hole.

Ear loose on metal bucket. Drill a hole through the ear and the bucket, and rivet together.

Wood handle on bail broken. If it is split, glue it together with resorcinol or epoxy glue. If it is too badly damaged to be saved, slit a short length of rubber hose down one side, wrap around bail, and apply rubber cement to both edges of slit. Let this dry for 5 minutes and press the edges together.

BURLAP

Holes, tears, in loose material. To make a neat repair, unravel strands from a scrap piece of burlap and weave into place with a needle.

If appearance is not important, cut a burlap patch, coat it with fabric glue, and press over hole.

Burlap wall covering loose. Scrape out as much old paste as possible. Spread fresh vinyl wall-covering adhesive or white glue on wall, and press burlap down.

Stains. Have loose material dry cleaned. On burlap wall covering, use spray-on dry cleaning powder or cleaning fluid.

CABINET, FILE

Drawer moves stiffly. Remove drawer. Clean runners and oil lightly. Oil wheels. If drawer is still sluggish, check whether cabinet is resting on a flat surface. Shim up corners with wood shingles if it is not.

Wood front of drawer split. Remove drawer and drawer handle but don't bother to take front off drawer. Coat split edges with epoxy glue. Set drawer front down on wax paper over plywood and force sections together. See FURNITURE—TABLE (*joined boards in top separated*). As further reinforcement, screw small steel mending plates across split on inside of drawer.

Wood drawers broken. See FURNITURE—CHEST OF DRAWERS.

Drawers locked shut after key has been lost. Call a locksmith.

CABINET, KITCHEN

Doors bang when closed. Metal cabinets are equipped with small rubber bumpers. If these are flattened or broken, scrape them off and cut new bumpers out of a tire tube or rubber gasket material. Glue to cabinet frame with rubber cement.

On wood cabinets, glue rubber patches to frame in same way. It may then be necessary to readjust catches so they close and hold properly.

If the banging is made by magnetic catches, stick cellulose tape to the plate screwed to the door. You can apply several thicknesses to cushion the noise, if necessary, without affecting the magnet's action.

Spring catches jammed. Remove from cabinet and soak in paint remover; then clean and reinstall. If old catches are broken, replace with new magnetic catches.

Screws fall out of catches in plastic-covered cabinets. Squeeze a little epoxy glue into the screw holes before resetting screws.

Open space between top of cabinets and ceiling or between sides and walls. If crack remains open at all times, fill with spackle; then sand and paint. If crack contracts and expands, nail strips of ⅝-inch cove molding or ⅝-inch quarter round over it.

Doors bind. See DOOR, CABINET.

Paint on metal cabinets chipped. Touch up with porcelain glaze. If paint is chipped in many places, sand the spots well to remove rust, and feather the edges of the surrounding paint. Wash cabinets with detergent or ammonia solution and rinse. Sand lightly all over to roughen surface slightly. Then apply a good spray enamel. But be sure to cover all surfaces adjacent to cabinets and remove hardware, because the fine spray drifts.

Paint on wood cabinets chipped. Treat as above.

Clear finish on wood cabinets worn. Touching up is almost impossible because you don't know what the original finish was. But if you want to try, apply white shellac or water-white varnish in several thin coats.

A better method is to remove the hardware and then strip off the finish entirely with paint remover (or send the drawers and doors to a furniture stripper). Then apply two or three thin coats of water-white lacquer with an aerosol. Sand lightly between coats. Mask surrounding surfaces.

CABINET, MEDICINE

Enameled surface inside cabinet damaged by medicines. Wash thoroughly and dry. Sand off rust. Apply two coats of gloss enamel. A better solution—if only the bottom of the cabinet is damaged—is to wash the metal well and dry. Then paste on a piece of self-stick vinyl.

Sliding doors stiff. Clean out channels with an old toothbrush and a vacuum cleaner. Make sure all gummy residues are removed. Spray channels with a silicone lubricant.

Light diffusers broken. See ELECTRIC LIGHT.

CAMERA

NOTE. Photographic equipment is very intricate and delicate and should be fixed only by an expert. The only thing you should attempt to do is to clean the camera regularly. Open the back and clean the interior with a clean camel's-hair artist's brush. Remove dust on lens with the brush, but if lens is smeared or spotted, clean with special lens paper, available from photo supplies shop, and—if necessary—lens cleaner fluid.

Flashbulb doesn't flash. Frequently, all you have to do is wet the base well with your tongue before inserting bulb. Check batteries.

Leather camera case ripped at seams. Pull out threads and trim leather edges if frazzly. Coat both edges with rubber cement. Let cement set up for 5 minutes, then press edges firmly together. You can then run a few stitches through the seam, but these shouldn't be necessary.

CAMP COOLER

Plastic liner cracked or punctured. Clean well and smear on silicone glue.

Metal liner punctured. Sand metal until bright and fill hole with epoxy mender.

Lid gasket sticks to chest. Wash and dry well. Dust liberally with talcum powder.

Odors. Wash cooler with a solution of baking soda. Rinse, and dry in the sun for as long as possible. Keep an open box of soda in chest to soak up odors as they occur.

CAMP STOVE

Propane stove won't light or gives a poor flame. Remove cylindrical burner head from torch. Lift or unscrew orifice from end of burner tube; reverse it and hold against the tube end. Then open and close valve quickly, two or three times, to blow gas through orifice. If this doesn't work, you should replace orifice or soak it for several days in lacquer thinner; then blow out again. Don't try to clean orifice with a wire.

Liquid-fuel stove doesn't light. Generator tip is probably clogged with carbon. Remove it with a wrench and replace with a new one.

Pump on liquid-fuel stove not working. Remove pump plunger and apply a few drops of motor oil to it. If the leather is in bad shape, cut a new one from a scrap piece of soft leather, and soak in light oil for a couple of days.

CANDLE

Bent. Place in a barely warm oven until wax softens slightly and candle can be bent straight again.

Colored surface broken off white wax base. Hold chip about an inch over the hole and hold a lighted match underneath so that you soften both the bottom of the chip and the base at the same time. Immediately drop chip into hole. This is a tricky little job, however, because it is difficult to get the chip placed properly in the very short time that the wax surfaces are soft.

If chip is lost, melt paraffin with a crayon in a double boiler and drip into break.

Hollow at center. Melt a matching candle or paraffin in a double boiler and pour into candle. If you need a new wick, dip a cotton string in the melted wax and pull it into a straight piece. Hold this in the center of the hollow while pouring wax around it.

CANDLESTICK

Broken. Apply glue appropriate to the material out of which the candlestick is made and press the pieces together overnight.

Metal candlestick bent. You may be able to bend it straight by hand or in a vise. But if the candlestick is badly bent or very valuable, take it to a qualified metalworker or jeweler. This is particularly important in the case of silver candlesticks.

Removable candleholder stuck in top of metal candlestick. Turn the candlestick upside down in a basin of warm water for about 30 minutes; then try to turn the candleholder loose. If this fails, soak the joint in penetrating oil.

Coated with wax. Scrape off as much as possible with your fingernails or a dull knife. Remove residue with trichloroethylene.

CANE
(walking stick)

Broken. See entry for the material of which cane is made.

Different materials separated. See HOUSE-HOLD DECORATIVE ACCESSORIES.

Tip smooth, skids on floor. Buy a rubber tip from a drugstore handling orthopedic supplies. Take cane with you to get the right size.

CANOE, CANVAS

Canvas ripped. Trim away loose threads. Then carefully pry canvas from wood for about 1 inch on either side of tear and ½ inch at the ends. Cut canvas patch the size of the loosened canvas. Spread resorcinol glue on one side of patch and slip patch through hole and smooth down. Then coat top of patch with more glue and press down loose canvas. This patch is adequate, but is improved by applying a second, slightly larger patch over the tear when the first patch dries.

To make a hurry-up patch, scrape some of the paint from the area around the hole. Cut a canvas or balloon-cloth patch to cover. Spread cellulose cement under torn canvas if it is loose. Then coat patch liberally with cement and spread a thin layer on canvas. Smooth down patch. You'll be ready to go again as soon as cement dries in 30 to 60 minutes.

Ribs, planks, cracked or broken. If breaks are not serious, coat them with resorcinol glue. Ribs can be clamped, in a fashion, with C-clamps. Splits in planks may possibly be brought together somewhat if you turn the canoe over and weight down the broken area with a 50-pound sack of sand. If ribs are separated from planks, cover with wax paper and weight down with sand (or weight from the outside).

If the bottom is buckled or badly broken, get an expert to repair it.

Holes, tears, in caned seats. See FURNITURE —CANED SEAT OR BACK. Use resorcinol glue. You can also cover the seat with canvas, tacking it to the frame underneath.

Paint badly cracked. Remove it before it cracks canvas or lets water rot canvas. Use a paste-type paint remover. Repaint with primer and any good bottom paint. Coats should be thin. Sand each one before applying next.

CANOE PADDLE

Cracked. Dry wood thoroughly. Spread epoxy glue on broken edges. Clamp together for 24 hours.

Blade splintered, cracked slightly at tip. Smooth off splinters with sandpaper. Force glue into splits. To prevent further damage, bend a strip of lightweight copper or aluminum around tip and tack in place with copper or aluminum tacks respectively.

CAN OPENER, ELECTRIC

Doesn't run. Has fuse blown? Is outlet into which opener is plugged defective? Check cord for a break and repair. If you still don't get action, take opener to a service shop.

Doesn't hold cut-off lid. Lift off magnet and wash in detergent solution.

Cutting knife skips, doesn't remove lid completely. Remove cutting assembly if you have a model that has a push-button release. Soak in hot detergent solution and scrub clean. Dry thoroughly. Lubricate back of cutting wheel with a few drops of vegetable oil. Then replace.

If entire assembly doesn't come off, unscrew cutting wheel and spring and wash in detergent solution.

In both cases, clean cogged drive wheel with

a pin and detergent solution. Put a drop of vegetable oil on shaft. However, if cogs are damaged, have a serviceman replace wheel.

Cutting wheel dull. Unscrew it and buy replacement.

CAN OPENER—HAND-OPERATED WALL TYPE

Doesn't work properly. Scrub cutting mechanism under hot water to remove gummy food residue, grease, etc. This usually solves problem. If not, check whether space between cutting wheel and cogged drive wheel is too wide for cans to be held securely. This space can be reduced by tightening nut found either on the front of the cutting wheel or on the shaft behind it.

CANVAS

Holes, tears. With pinking shears, cut a canvas patch that overlaps hole about ½ inch on all sides. Apply fabric glue to reverse side of damaged material. Stick on patch and smooth down. For greater strength, stitch around hole—preferably on a sewing machine—with heavy cotton thread.

Leaks. See TENT.

Canvas frayed at edges. Cut off frayed portion. Then make several rows of stitches just in from the edge—preferably on a sewing machine. To keep edge from frazzling, you can then coat it on both sides with fabric glue.

Soiled. Canvas is extremely hard to get clean, but try washing in a washer in hot water and heavy-duty detergent. Use chlorine bleach on white canvas.

Stains. See CLOTHING—FABRICS.

CANVAS DECK

Hole, tears. Out of new canvas, cut a patch ¾ inch to 1 inch larger on all sides than the hole. Spread white lead—if you can get hold of it—on deck under hole; otherwise brush on a thick coat of oil-base outdoor house paint. Lay patch

under hole and cover with more white lead or paint. Tack down old canvas over patch with copper or aluminum tacks spaced ½ inch to 1¼ inches apart. Apply deck paint when first paint is dry.

CARDBOARD

Torn. On thin cardboard, apply self-stick reinforced wrapping tape. On heavy cardboard, cut a patch out of thin cardboard and apply rubber cement to patch and area around tear. Let set for 5 minutes. Then stick together.

Laminated cardboard separated. Glue together with white glue.

Separated from another material. Reglue with rubber cement.

CARPET, OUTDOOR

Soiled. Vacuum frequently to keep dirt and grit from working into carpet. When carpet is definitely dirty, hose it all over with a hard stream; scrub with a soft bristle brush; and hose again. For an extremely dirty carpet, wet it down with water, then scrub with household detergent and rinse well with hose.

Stains. See RUG.

Edges frayed. Whip with carpet-binding thread or simply cut off the edges with a razor blade.

Surface fuzzy. Clip off the worst of the fuzz with scissors or barber's clippers.

CARPET SWEEPER

Pulley slips, brushes don't revolve. Wrap adhesive tape around the center pulley wheel.

Doesn't pick up dirt. Remove threads and strings around brushes and clean the combs. If brush bristles are worn down, replace with new brushes.

CAST IRON

Cracked, broken. Clean metal thoroughly with steel wool. Coat edges of break liberally with epoxy glue and clamp together. Applying a coat of epoxy mender on the outside of the break will add strength. Nevertheless, don't count on this mend's ability to withstand hard abuse.

Pitted. Clean pits with steel wool and smooth on epoxy mender.

Rusted. Clean metal with a wire brush, steel wool, and liquid rust-remover. Apply a red metal primer and finish paint.

Cast iron separated from other materials. See HOUSEHOLD DECORATIVE ACCESSORIES.

CATCH

See also DOOR LOCK OR LATCH.

Doesn't close or hold properly. Although there are several types of catch, they generally fail for one of three reasons. (1) The two halves of the catch are out of alignment, which means either that the door, window, etc., has sagged or that the catch itself has moved. In the latter case, screw the catch down properly. If the door or window has sagged, it must either be rehung or straightened with a turnbuckle (see DOOR, SCREEN); or the catch must be taken off and repositioned. (2) The moving parts of the catch are frozen by paint, which must be removed with a knife or paint remover. (3) The spring which actuates the catch is broken. Since this is usually troublesome to replace, buy a new catch.

CAULKING

Broken, missing. Scrape it all out of the joint with a screwdriver. Blow out crumbs. Then squeeze in silicone or polysulfide-rubber caulking. Do not use inexpensive oil-base caulking.

CEILING

Cracks, holes. See INTERIOR WALL, GYPSUM BOARD or INTERIOR WALL, PLASTER as case may be.

Slopes badly or very uneven. Repair is a major job. If the ceiling is of normal height or higher, you can build a new ceiling below it. If it's very low, you should probably knock it out so the new ceiling can be constructed close to the joists. The work, in either case, is the same.

First you must cover the existing ceiling or exposed joists with 1-inch by 3-inch furring strips nailed to the joists at right angles. Space the furring strips 16 inches from center to center. Apply the first strips to the lowest point of the ceiling, and work from these to the highest point. To make the strips level, insert shims of wood of the necessary thickness under them. Check the level of the strips frequently with a carpenter's level. You might find that it also helps to stretch a taut string from one end of the ceiling to the other to mark the ceiling level (but you'll also find the string gets in the way when you are nailing up furring strips).

When all the furring strips are installed, cover the ceiling with gypsum-board panels nailed to the strips with annular-ring nails. Use ⅜-inch-thick panels over an existing ceiling, ½-inch if the old ceiling is torn out. The long edges of the panels should be perpendicular to the furring strips. Seal the joints between panels and between the panels and the walls with gypsum board tape and joint compound.

Sound easily penetrates ceiling from floor above. Cover floor above from wall to wall with thick carpet laid on a thick rug cushion. If this doesn't stop sound satisfactorily, cover ceiling with ½-inch or ⅝-inch gypsum board. See INTERIOR WALL, GYPSUM BOARD.

CHAIN

Broken. Repair links of various sizes are available at hardware or mail-order stores. If you can obtain one of the right size, simply insert it in the chain and hammer it closed.

If chain is not subject to great strain (the chain in a toilet tank or a dog leash, for example), you can also cut out the broken link and twist wire of appropriate size through the adjacent links. Twist ends of wire together and tuck into the chain so that they will not snag on anything the chain touches.

Chains subject to strain, such as an anchor

chain, can be mended temporarily with repair links, but should be welded.

Watch chains can be mended satisfactorily by looping tiny copper wire from the ends of an electric cord through the links several times. But for best results, see a jeweler.

Tangles, knots, in watch or similar tiny chain. Don't pull. Drop loosely on a flat surface and pick out the knot with two pins.

Swivel snap on end of chain broken. Buy a replacement at hardware store, slip the bottom loop through the last link of the chain, and hammer it closed.

CHAIN, TIRE

Links broken. Insert a monkey link, available from service station, through adjacent links. It will tighten when you get on the road again.

Entire cross-link broken. You can cut it out with a hammer and chisel and put in a replacement, but it's easier to let a service station do the job.

CHIMNEY

NOTE. If you see smoke curling out of the sides of a chimney or if a chimney feels uncomfortably hot to the touch, damp the fire and call in a masonry contractor at once. You have a real fire hazard. If you suspect that a chimney is leaking, you can test it by building a smoky fire in the fireplace and blocking the top of the chimney with a wet blanket. Smoke escaping through the masonry shows the location of leaks.

Flue encrusted with soot. Cover the fireplace opening to keep dirt out of the house. Climb up on the roof and drop down the chimney a heavy chain attached to a long rope. Scrape the chain up and down the sides of the flue and wave it back and forth.

Leaks water. Check as follows: (1) Is flashing sound and secured to chimney? For repairs, see FLASHING, COPPER. (2) Are mortar joints cracked or eroded? For repairs, see BRICK. (3) Is top of chimney cracked? It's best to have a mason replace the cap. But if cracking is not severe, chip out the cracks, blow out the crumbs, and pack in latex cement. Then cover entire cap with a ¼-inch layer of latex cement. Slope cement away from the flue toward edges of cap.

Throws sparks. Have spark arresters installed.

Crack between chimney and siding. Clean out crack and pack in silicone or polysulfide rubber caulking compound. Smooth it off flush with siding.

Also see FIREPLACE, MASONRY.

CHINA

Broken. Wash broken edges and dry thoroughly. If broken piece is used and/or washed frequently, spread epoxy glue on one edge and press the pieces together for 12 hours. If piece is rarely used or washed, you can use cellulose cement. If piece is used for ornament only, use cyanoacrylate glue, because it is so thin that the mended break is almost invisible. In any case, to hold the pieces together while the glue dries, stick strips of cellophane tape or adhesive tape across the crack.

Separated from another material. See HOUSEHOLD DECORATIVE ACCESSORIES.

Surface chipped; piece missing; glaze gone. These are difficult repairs which in the past could be made only by a professional restorer. But you can now do a professional job yourself by buying a Master Mending Kit for china, porcelain, pottery, and glass from Atlas Minerals and Chemicals Division, ESB, Inc., Mertztown, Pennsylvania 19539. This costs about $17.00 C.O.D., but is worth the price. With it, you can even repaint china.

CHISEL

Top of handle splintered by hammering. Glue down largest splinters with epoxy glue. Sand top smooth and fill cracks with plastic wood. Then tap a round metal furniture glide onto top of handle to protect it in future.

Tang loose in handle. See CUTLERY, KITCHEN.

Dull. Sharpen only on the beveled side. Hold at about a 25-degree angle to a grinding wheel or a flat carborundum stone (in the latter case, hold chisel firmly against a triangular block of wood). Make sure you do not sharpen more at one edge of blade than the other and thus get edge out of square. Sharpen first on rough side of carborundum, then on smooth side. Then turn blade over so that beveled side is up; hold flat against smooth side of stone, and remove any burrs by stroking blade sidewise several times.

CHRISTMAS TREE LIGHTS

NOTE. Repairs to Christmas tree light strings, if not made properly, can start a fire. Be very careful.

Cord broken. Remove ½ inch of insulation from each end of broken wire. Bend wires around each other, twist tight, and always solder them together. Cover with cellophane electrical tape.

Cord pulled out of socket. This happens on series strings, especially those using miniature bulbs. Pull plastic socket cover away from metal socket. You will find that one wire is soldered to the outside of the screw shell, the other into a small hole in the end of the socket. If wire attached to screw shell is loose, simply hold it in place over the solder blob and heat with a soldering iron. If wire in end of socket has broken, as is more often the case, carefully drill out the hole in the socket a little. Cut end of broken wire cleanly and remove ⅛ inch of insulation. Twist strands tight, then melt a tiny bit of solder onto the strands. Insert the wire in the socket hole, and with the point of your soldering iron, heat the edge of the metal around the hole until wire is secure. Make sure bare ends of wires do not touch. Then replace plastic cover. For safety, fill hole in the back of the plastic cover with plastic rubber.

If this repair proves difficult (it is not always possible to separate the plastic cover from the copper socket, for instance), you can simply cut the socket out of the string entirely and splice the two wires.

Wires rarely break at the sockets in parallel strings. But if they do, don't try to repair them. Simply cut the socket out of the string and splice together the wires of the same color (see ELECTRIC CORD, BROKEN).

CHRISTMAS TREE ORNAMENT

Neck broken off glass ornament so wire loop slips out. Close prongs of loop and wrap tightly with paper to size of hole. Apply light coat of white glue or rubber cement to paper and insert roll partway through hole.

Wire pulled out of stuffed or wooden ornament. Squeeze white glue into hole if possible. Apply glue to end of wire and reinsert in ornament.

CHROMIUM PLATE

Scratched, rusted. Clean with a chrome cleaner available from auto supplies stores. If rust remains in deep scratches, carefully scratch it out with the point of a knife. Do not use steel wool or emery cloth. To improve the appearance and protect the chrome against further damage, spray on a chrome protector, also available from auto supplies stores. Fill deep scratches with plastic chrome.

Food and grease baked on. Remove as much as possible with baking soda and a barely damp rag. Dry. Then brush paste-type paint remover on the hard, baked-on brown and black spots of carbon remaining. Let stand for about 10 minutes, until carbon softens. Wipe off. You may also have to scrape some spots a little with a dull knife, but if hard scraping is called for, apply more paint remover. Rinse clear surface with water or mild baking soda solution.

CIRCUIT BREAKER

Circuit breakers are substituted for fuse boxes in most modern homes. They protect the electrical system in the same way. The only difference is that, when there's a short circuit or an overload, the trigger in the circuit breaker automatically flips off. To restore current, simply push it on. If it immediately flips off again, the problem in the circuit has not been corrected. For how to handle short-circuits and overloads, see FUSE BOX.

CLOCK

Glass broken. If glass or plastic is flat, you can easily remove it and replace with a new glass cut to size. But if glass is curved, let an expert replace it.

Plastic case broken. Clean cracked edges and coat with plastic-mending adhesive. Press together and hold in place for 12 hours with strips of masking tape.

Electric clock doesn't run. Examine cord for a break. See ELECTRIC CORD for how to repair. If clock itself is broken, take it to a service shop. Once most electric clocks quit, however, they are worthless and should be replaced.

Electric clock noisy. Try turning it upside down (while continuing to run) for several days.

Pendulum clock running slow. If clock has a small metal spindle projecting through the face (usually above the numeral 12), grasp the spindle with a pair of pliers (or use key if you have it) and turn clockwise about a half turn. If this doesn't correct the situation, give spindle another half turn. Continue thus until clock is keeping time.

If clock doesn't have a projecting spindle, open the back and stop the pendulum. Then lift pendulum out and turn the knob under the weight clockwise one full turn. Replace pendulum and start it again. Continue turning knob clockwise (thus raising the weight) until clock keeps time. As a rule of thumb, one full turn of the knob changes clock speed one minute per day. Even if a clock has a spindle in the face, corrections in speed can be made by raising or lowering the weight on the pendulum.

Pendulum clock running slow. Reverse procedure above; that is, turn spindle or weight counterclockwise.

Pendulum clock operates briefly and stops. Check whether clock is level. It doesn't have to be dead level, but unless it is nearly level, this can make it stop.

If clock is level or nearly so and doesn't run, bend the crutch (the L-shaped piece which projects through the slot in the top of the pendulum) very slightly to right or left until the clock runs and keeps time.

CLOSET, CEDAR

Loses cedar smell. Go over the cedar with fine sandpaper—working with the grain—to open pores.

Open cracks around door. A cedar closet is not effective if moths can enter through cracks. Pry off stops from jambs. Pull door shut. Renail stops closer to door. To seal crack at bottom of door, tack rubber weather stripping to door or install an aluminum threshold with a vinyl strip that bears against bottom edge of door.

CLOSET, CLOTHES

Rod sags. Replace with a new one. Or twist a strong wire around the center of the rod and attach to a screw eye in the ceiling.

Rod loose. Drill a small hole diagonally through the end and nail rod to the wall with a long finishing nail.

Shelf sags. Nail a wood cleat to the wall under the middle of the shelf. The cleat should be long enough to be nailed into at least two studs. If shelf not only sags but is also warped, support it on a large angle iron or on a right-angled metal shelf support screwed into a wall stud.

CLOTHING—BELT

Leather belt delaminated. Spread a thin coat of rubber cement on both surfaces. Let set for 5 minutes and press layers together.

Belt loop worn, broken. Remove from belt and open material to its full size. Use as a pattern for a new loop.

On most men's belts, buckle and belt loop are held in place by metal snaps. Open these. Stitch new loop closed (so it is a complete loop). Slip over end of belt and close snaps.

On women's belts, buckle and belt loop are not usually removable. In this case, before closing the loop, slip one end of the loop material through fold of belt behind buckle and bring it around in front. Dab rubber cement on ends of loop and squeeze ends together. While glue is still wet, stitch ends of loop with thread. When glue is dry, twist stitched ends around under belt.

Tongue of belt buckle on wrong side of buckle. If buckle can be removed from belt, remove it and swing tongue around to top of buckle. Otherwise, with pliers, bend tongue until it can be forced back through buckle; then straighten tongue. To protect finish on tongue, wrap it with adhesive tape.

Snap fasteners behind buckle loose. Open fasteners and with pliers squeeze down on fastener prongs to flatten them slightly. See SNAP FASTENER.

CLOTHING—BUTTONHOLES

Split at end. Stitch back and forth across the end on sewing machine.

Frayed around edges. If buttonhole is not badly frayed, whip the edges with thread. If hole is badly frayed and appearance is not too important, make two closely spaced rows of machine stitches all the way around hole. Then whip the edges by hand, or machine stitch back and forth across the parallel rows of stitches.

CLOTHING—BUTTONS

Button off. Remove old threads. Double new thread and knot it at end. Make a small stitch through material, then bring thread up through one hole and down through another in the button. To make button stand away from the material, slip a pin through the threads on the front of the button; then continue sewing through button, running the thread over the pin. When button is secure, remove pin, pull button out as far as possible, run thread down through hole in button between the button and the fabric, and loop thread several times around the button stitches. Finally, take thread down through fabric and make several overcasting stitches through the threads.

Button torn out. Place a small patch of material under hole and stitch it in place securely. Then sew on button as above.

CLOTHING—COAT

Corners of cuffs frayed. Either leave them alone, because the holes are not likely to enlarge very much, or carefully darn them with threads raveled from an inner seam.

Buttonholes frayed or torn. See CLOTHING—BUTTONHOLES.

Buttons off or torn out. See CLOTHING—BUTTONS.

Holes in pockets. See CLOTHING—POCKETS.

CLOTHING—FABRICS

Specific entries are given for BURLAP, CANVAS, CLOTHING—STRETCH FABRIC, FELT, FIBER GLASS—FABRIC, LACE, LEATHERETTE, OILCLOTH, VINYL.

Light material worn thin. Turn wrong side out. Hold a sheet of white cardboard or paper underneath to determine size of reinforcement needed. Cut a patch out of lightweight material that has some give and that is approximately the same color as material to be mended. Place reinforcement on wrong side of material and pin and baste in place. With thread of proper color, make straight rows of stitches lengthwise on fabric and about ¼ inch apart. Make stitches on right side of material so small as to be invisible; on the wrong side, up to ¼ inch long. Do not draw up each row of stitches; leave them slightly loose.

Heavy material worn thin. Same as above, but use diagonal basting stitch (see BASIC METHODS: HOW TO MAKE BASIC SEWING STITCHES). Rows of stitches can be spaced slightly further apart. The alternative to reinforcing in this way is to darn the weak spot.

Holes. If material can be darned, pull threads from a side seam or ravel those that run lengthwise of a scrap of the same material. Use short threads and a fine needle and imitate as closely as possible the sound fabric. Darn on the right side of the fabric. First make stitches lengthwise across the hole; then weave thread at right angles, going over and under. To help conceal the darn, extend the stitches at different distances into the sound material. Do not pull stitches too tight, especially when you make a turn. Ends of threads should be on the wrong side of the fabric. Do not cut them off too close.

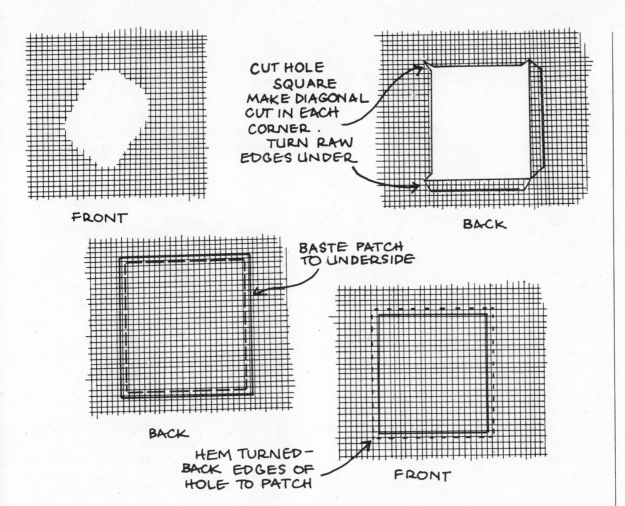

FRONT

CUT HOLE
SQUARE
MAKE DIAGONAL
CUT IN EACH
CORNER.
TURN RAW
EDGES UNDER

BACK

BASTE PATCH
TO UNDERSIDE

BACK

HEM TURNED-
BACK EDGES OF
HOLE TO PATCH

FRONT

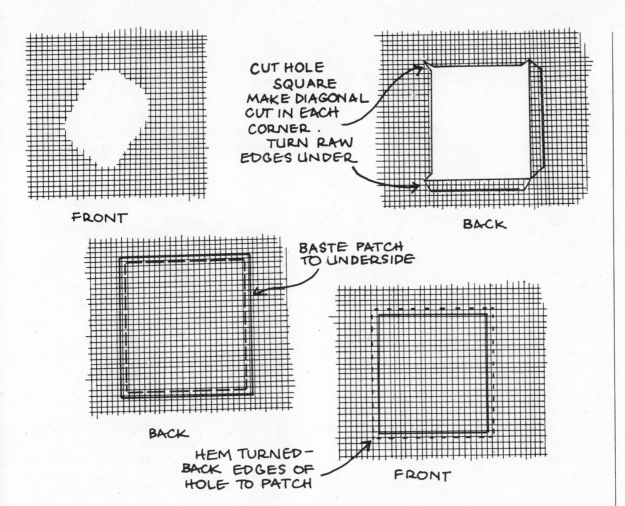

If material cannot be darned, cut a square or rectangular hole around the hole. Make small diagonal cuts in the four corners and turn the raw edges under. Cut a matching patch 1 inch to 1½ inches larger than the new hole, and center it underneath. Baste in place. Then, working on the right side of the fabric, hem the edges of the hole to the patch. Remove bastings. Turn fabric wrong side up and turn under raw edges of patch. Hem them down.

If appearance of patched material is unimportant (as in sheets and men's shorts), cut the hole out cleanly in a square or circle. Place a patch underneath. Pin in place. Then make long, closely spaced zigzag stitches on your sewing machine across the edges of the hole.

Instead of sewed-on patches, you can in some cases mend holes with press-on patches—provided the article is not dried in a dryer. Or you can glue any patch material to the original material with fabric glue.

Tears, slashes. Darn a straight tear like a hole (see above). If it's a right-angle tear, darn each side like a straight tear and overlap the two darns at the corner for extra strength at that point.

Diagonal slashes should be basted first to hold them in place (baste on a reinforcement if necessary). Then darn.

Stains. There are several general points which should be borne in mind when you start working on stains:

1. The sooner you start work the better. The older a stain, the harder it is to eradicate.

2. Remove stains before—not after—laundering.

3. Always test liquid removal agents and bleaches on colored fabrics before tackling the stain.

4. On fabrics that are dry cleaned rather than laundered, use cleaning fluids and absorbent powders only.

5. If a combination greasy and nongreasy

substance causes a stain, treat for the non-greasy substance first. That is, if coffee with cream spills on a dress, treat for the coffee stain before worrying about the grease mark left by the cream.

6. If you're uncertain what caused a stain, let a professional cleaner tackle it.

7. When using cleaning fluids, water, detergent, ammonia, and other liquid agents, work on the fabric right side up, unless the stain was caused by a greasy substance. In that case, try to work on it upside down. In any case, put a pad of clean white absorbent cloth under the fabric to soak up the stain. Use a damp—not soaking wet—cleaning cloth to rub spot, and rub from the edges in. Use straight strokes. Blot frequently with a clean, dry cloth. To stop a ring from forming, lightly apply cleaning agent to area around stain; then blot entire cleaned area as dry as possible.

8. While absorbent powders are just as effective on dark fabrics as on light, they may leave a powder mark which is hard to eradicate. Whatever the fabric, blow off as much of the powder—when it is dry—as you can; then you will not rub so much into the fabric when you brush off the excess.

Follow directions below for removing specific stains:

- *Adhesive tape.* Pick off as much as possible with your fingernails. Then use trichloroethylene cleaning fluid.
- *Alcoholic drinks.* If fabric is white and washable, sponge with cold water, launder in hot. Bleach old brown stains. If fabric is colored and washable, sponge with cold water and then with glycerin mixed with a little water. Let stand for 30 minutes or so. Rinse with 1 part white vinegar and 1 part water. Then rinse with water.
- *Blood.* Soak in cold water for 30 minutes or so, then launder in warm water. If stain is old, soak in 3 tablespoons household ammonia and 1 gallon lukewarm water, then wash in warm water. Soak in an enzyme presoaker and apply bleach if stain persists.
- *Butter, margarine.* Follow directions at *grease, oil,* below.
- *Candle wax.* Scrape off as much as possible with a dull table knife or spoon. Sponge with trichloroethylene. Bleach if color remains.
- *Catsup, chili sauce.* Scrape up, and sponge with cold water. Then work laundry detergent into spot and launder.
- *Cellophane tape.* Pick and scrape off as much as possible, then use trichloroethylene.
- *Chewing gum.* Chill with an ice cube or in refrigerator before scraping off what you can with a dull knife. Sponge with trichloroethylene.
- *Chocolate, cocoa.* Soak for half an hour in cold water, or sponge well. Rub laundry detergent into spot and launder in hottest water that is safe for the fabric. Add a little bleach. Use trichloroethylene to remove any grease that remains. If any color remains, sponge with hydrogen peroxide and launder once more.
- *Cod liver oil.* Sponge with trichloroethylene, then with warm detergent solution. Launder with bleach, if safe for fabric. If stain persists, sponge with bleach and launder again.
- *Coffee.* Soak in cold water. If the fabric can withstand it, pour boiling water through spot, stain side down, from a height of about 2 feet; otherwise, soak in warm enzyme presoaker. Launder. Finally, clean with trichloroethylene if coffee contained cream.
- *Cosmetics.* Rub with laundry detergent and launder. Then sponge with trichloroethylene if cosmetics were greasy. See *lipstick,* below.
- *Crayon.* Wash in detergent solution if crayon was of washable type. Otherwise, sponge with trichloroethylene and launder.
- *Cream, milk, ice cream.* Soak in cold water. Rub laundry detergent into spot and rinse. If grease remains, use trichloroethylene. Bleach if any color remains, or soak in enzyme presoaker.
- *Dye.* If color is light, launder. Then bleach by soaking in 1 gallon warm water and 1 tablespoon bleach.
- *Fruit.* Sponge with cold water and soak in enzyme presoaker. Launder.
- *Grass.* Rub laundry detergent into stain and launder with bleach. Alternative is to rub with denatured alcohol and launder.
- *Gravy.* See *meat juice,* below.
- *Grease, oil.* Rub with laundry detergent and let stand for 30 minutes. Launder in warm water.

If stain remains, sponge with cleaning fluid. Don't count on success with permanent-press or synthetic garments, especially if stain has set.

- *Hair dressings.* See *skin oils,* below.
- *Ink.* If ink is washable, launder. For any other ink, including ballpoint-pen ink, place paper towel under stain. Apply Inknix, available from stationery store, and rub with a clean, hard-bristle brush. Then rinse with warm water. For old ink stains, let Inknix soak in for a while. Repeat application if necessary.
- *Iodine.* Sponge with alcohol and launder. Bleach in sun.
- *Lipstick.* Apply trichloroethylene. Rub with laundry detergent until outline of stain is gone. Then launder in hot water and bleach.
- *Meat juice.* Scrape off excess and sponge with cold water. Soak in enzyme presoaker and launder. Apply trichloroethylene if stain persists.
- *Mercurochrome.* Place in cold water immediately. Then soak in 1 part alcohol and 2 parts water. Then launder with bleach.
- *Mildew.* Rub with detergent, and launder. Mix a little onion juice and noniodized salt; apply to spot, and bleach in sun. If stain is old, use hydrogen peroxide instead of onion juice and salt.
- *Mustard.* Soak in cold water. Rub with laundry detergent and rinse. Soak for several hours in warm detergent solution if spot persists. Then launder with bleach.
- *Nail polish.* Sponge with nail polish remover, and launder. Apply bleach if color remains. But note that nail polish remover should not be used on acetate or rayon—use trichloroethylene instead.
- *Paint.* Blot immediately with clean rag or paper towel. Then sponge with water if paint was latex; use paint thinner, turpentine, or benzine for oil or alkyd paints. Launder. If paint has hardened, try softening with paint remover before cleaning.
- *Pencil.* Clean with a soft eraser as much as possible. Rub with laundry detergent, and launder. For indelible pencil, sponge stain with trichloroethylene or alcohol; then rub with detergent and launder.
- *Perspiration.* Soak in enzyme presoaker, and launder.

- *Rubber cement.* Let dry. Make a wad of dry rubber cement, and rub this over spot to pick up as much as possible. Finally, apply trichloroethylene.
- *Rust.* Sponge with mixture of lemon juice and noniodized salt. Dry in sun. Rinse thoroughly and launder.
- *Salad dressing.* Sponge with cold water. Rub laundry detergent into stain, and rinse. Sponge with trichloroethylene if stain remains. Then launder.
- *Scorch.* Launder with bleach. But if fibers have been damaged, a spot will remain.
- *Shellac.* Sponge with alcohol, and launder.
- *Shoe polish.* Scrape off and work laundry detergent into stain. Launder. If stain remains, apply trichloroethylene or alcohol.
- *Skin oils.* Soak in enzyme presoaker and launder.
- *Tar.* Pick off what you can and apply trichloroethylene. If tar is hard, soften with petroleum jelly before trying to pick off.
- *Tea.* See *coffee,* above.
- *Tomato juice.* See *catsup, chili sauce,* above.
- *Urine.* Launder. If this doesn't work, sponge with 1 part white vinegar and 1 part water. Launder again.
- *Varnish.* See *paint,* above.
- *Wine.* If still damp, cover with salt. In any case, sponge with cold water. Soak in enzyme presoaker. Then launder.

CLOTHING—FOUNDATION GARMENT

Garters or elastic torn. Buy replacements at notion counter and sew into garment.

Girdle seams split. Stitch together on sewing machine with zigzagger. If seam needs reinforcement, sew twill tape over seam on wrong side of garment.

Elastic fabric torn. Reinforce with twill tape and stitch as above.

CLOTHING—GLOVE

Seams split. With a fine needle, restitch to match original stitches.

Hole in fabric glove. See CLOTHING—KNIT-
WEAR.

CLOTHING—HEMS

Plain hem out. Turn in the hem about ⅛ inch,
then turn in again about ¼ inch and hem to
body of fabric. Or you can attach hem by
machine stitching.

Rolled hem out. Roll edge tight and hem down.
Take tiny stitches.

NOTE. These are the two simplest and most common hems. If other types are out, resew like
the sound hem.

CLOTHING—HOOKS AND EYES

Metal hook or eye off. Postion on fabric. Then
attach with overcasting stitches.

Thread eye broken. Snip out old eye. Knot a
doubled thread at the end. Start with one or
two overcasting stitches on wrong side of material. Then bring needle through to right side
of material and form a loop of the proper size.
Secure in material and make a second loop of
the same size. Then whip the four strands of
the loop together with a blanket stitch.

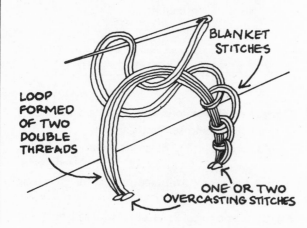

BLANKET
STITCHES

LOOP
FORMED
OF TWO
DOUBLE
THREADS

ONE OR TWO
OVERCASTING STITCHES

CLOTHING—KNITWEAR

Runs. To stop a run, dab clear nail polish at top
and bottom and extend it three or four strands
to either side of run.

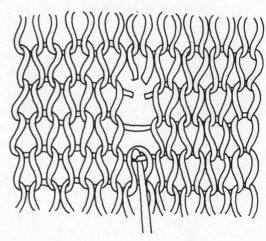

To mend a run, if appearance is not important, simply whip together the threads on each
side of run. If appearance is important, pick up
the free loop at the bottom of the run with a
crochet hook. Then pull through the loop, one
after the other, each of the threads in the run.
Secure the top loop on the wrong side with
needle and thread.

Crosswise splits. Place edges of material together
and whip with matching thread.

Holes. Use a long length of matching yarn. Catch
it in the material at the bottom right corner
of the hole, then weave it through the loops
across the bottom of the hole to the left side
of the hole. Reverse again to left, then to
right until entire hole is covered. Then, starting
at a top corner of the hole, make a series of
chain stitches down across the hole. When
you reach the bottom, thread the yarn straight
back up through the first crosswise stitches
to the top of the hole. Then make the next
series of chain stitches down. Continue in this
way until hole is closed.

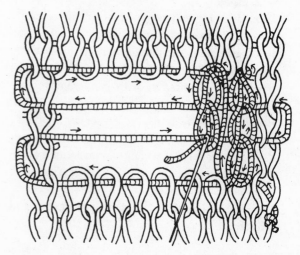

CLOTHING—PAJAMAS

Drawstring in pants pulled out. Pull string all the way out of casing. Put a large safety pin through one end of string. Then work pin through casing. To prevent string from pulling out again, center it at back of pants and stitch in place.

Buttons off or torn out. See CLOTHING-BUT-TONS.

Placket torn. See CLOTHING—PLACKETS.

Holes, tears. See CLOTHING—FABRICS.

CLOTHING—PLACKETS

Torn at end. Baste a piece of twill or bias tape under tear. Lap edges of placket and stitch to tape on sewing machine.

CLOTHING—POCKETS

Holes worn in fabric. Apply a press-on patch on the inside of the pocket. Or machine stitch across the pocket just above the hole.

A better repair is made by ripping out the old pocket and replacing it with a new one purchased at a notions counter.

Garment fabric torn at corner of patch pocket. Rip the pocket to below the tear. Reverse garment and, with running stitches, sew a strip of tape along the length of the tear. Then darn across the tear on the right side of the garment. Stitch the pocket corner down.

CLOTHING—SEAMS

Split. Iron edges of fabric flat together. Pin if split is a long one. Sew with a straight running stitch on a machine or by hand.

Seam edges fray. If material does not fray badly, notch edges with pinking shears. If material is heavy and frays easily, protect edges with deep, closely spaced overcasting stitches. If material is light and frays easily, turn raw edge of each seam under and sew with a straight running stitch.

Hemstitched seam broken. Mending is a painstaking job. It's easier to separate hem edge entirely and rejoin to the body of the fabric with a strip of straight-edged lace. Or, if appearance is not important, simply sew the hem edge over the edge of the fabric on your sewing machine or by whipping.

CLOTHING—SHIRT

Collar frayed. You can turn over the collar if it does not have pockets for stays on the underside. But it is better to buy a new collar at a notions counter. Carefully rip the collar from the neckband (tiny stitches are easily cut with a razor blade). Do not open seam beyond ends of collar. Fold new collar in half and mark center with a pin. Fold neckband in half and mark center with a pin. Insert collar in band, making sure pins are in line. Pin ends of collar to band. Then put in a whole row of pins from one end of collar to the other, and then baste. Make sure that basting stitches go through both sides of neckband as well as collar. Remove pins and carefully stitch collar to band on a sewing machine.

Cuffs frayed. You can turn French cuffs, but it is better to replace all cuffs with new ones from a notions counter. Rip off old cuff. Insert sleeve end into top of cuff. Pin, baste, then stitch on sewing machine like a collar.

Holes. Patch with press-on mending tape.

Buttons off or torn out. See CLOTHING—BUT-TONS.

CLOTHING—STRAPS

Torn loose. Simply stitch in place again. If material is badly frayed or weak, replace strap entirely or cut off damaged end, stitch on new material, and sew in place. Fabric to which strap is sewn may also need to be reinforced.

CLOTHING—STRETCH FABRIC

Holes, tears. Darn with elastic thread. Use regular darning technique (see CLOTHING—FABRICS).

Seams split. Stitch with elastic thread.

CLOTHING—TROUSERS

Bottom edges of cuffs frayed. Easiest solution is to cut stitches at side seams and rip stitches that tack down end of fabric inside of trouser leg. Cut about ¼ inch from end of fabric. Now make a new cuff that is about ¼ inch narrower than the original one by pulling down the outside layer of fabric ¼ inch, pressing top of cuff flat, then pulling fabric up on inside of trouser leg and stitching in place. Frayed edge is now inside trouser leg. Cover the tear with press-on mending tape.

If you have the scrap material cut from the trouser legs when trousers were purchased, a better solution is to cut stitches holding frayed cuff at seams and to rip out stitches inside of trouser leg. Open material, flatten it, and cut it off somewhere between the bottom of the trouser leg and the top of the cuff (in other words, on the inside layer of the cuff). Stitch the new fabric to old on a sewing machine. Then form new cuff. Press. Stitch end of material inside of trouser leg and stitch cuff to outside seams.

Belt loops off. Restitch at top or bottom as necessary. If ends of loops are badly frayed, remove loop. Make new one from scrap material or from excess material in cuffs or seams.

Buttonholes frayed or split. See CLOTHING—BUTTONHOLES.

Buttons off or torn out. See CLOTHING—BUTTONS.

Holes in pockets. See CLOTHING—POCKETS.

COAT HANGER

Hook loose. Push hook down through hole and coat the end with epoxy glue. Dribble a little glue into the hole. Then pull hook up and let glue set for 6 hours.

Wood hanger snags clothes. Sand or scrape smooth. For good measure, coat the wood with shellac or varnish.

COFFEE MAKER, ELECTRIC

Doesn't work. Try another cord: the original may be broken. Check whether fuse has blown, whether outlet into which pot is plugged is operative. If these measures don't work, take coffee maker to a service shop.

Stains on inside. Wash and wash again with detergent solution. If necessary, partially fill pot with solution and turn on heat. Rinse and rinse again.

White spots in pot are caused by hard water. To remove them, scrub with vinegar.

COLUMN, WOOD

Solid column rotting. If rot has not progressed too far, dig it out with a chisel and saturate wood with pentachlorophenol wood preservative. Let dry 48 hours. Then fill hole with water putty. However, if column is badly rotted out, replace it.

Base rotting. Cut base out entirely and make a new one to fit. Cut a cross-shaped groove in bottom ½ inch deep by half the width of the base so air can circulate under it. Soak for 24 hours in pentachlorophenol and set in position. Anchor with finishing nails or silicone adhesive.

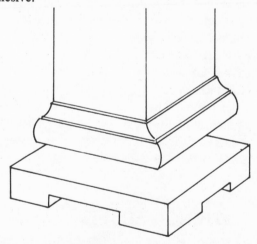

Hollow column rotting. If the rotten area is fairly small, cut it out in a rectangle with a saber saw. Bevel the edges of the hole so it is narrower in back than in front. Shape a patch to fit out of a board and glue in the opening with resorcinol glue. When glue has set for 24 hours, plane down patch to match the surrounding wood.

Seams open in round hollow column. If the cracks are narrow, fill them with wood putty.

If wide, shape strips of white pine to fit; glue them into seams with resorcinol glue, then shape them with a plane to blend into column.

Ornamental capital chipped. Fill holes with water putty and shape it to conform with surrounding area.

Ornamental capital broken. If capital is wood, glue back broken piece with resorcinol glue. If capital is plaster, glue with silicone adhesive.

COMB

Comb loose from metal back. Clean top edge of comb and inside metal channel. Apply a light coat of cellulose cement to both surfaces and reset comb in channel. Crimp metal edges along sides of comb if they are loose.

COMBINATION STORM AND SCREEN SASH

Water leaks inside. Remove glass insets (and screen if you like). Unscrew frame from window and scrape off whatever caulking is underneath. Apply a thick ribbon of polysulfide rubber caulking around four sides of window frame; press storm sash frame into these, and screw it up tight.

Water accumulates on windowsill behind storm sash. Weep holes should have been provided in the storm sash frame at sill level. Clean these out. If they were not provided, drill two or three ⅛-inch holes through frame at sill level with an electric drill. If kept clean, these should carry off any water that accumulates. If they don't, make them a little bigger.

Sash slides hard. It's possible that when the sash was installed, the sides of the frame were pinched in a little at the sides. Check with a straightedge whether this is so. If sash is distorted, remove and install again (see above). It's more likely, however, that tracks need to be cleaned thoroughly to remove grease and dirt. Clean edges of sash. If frames are made of unfinished aluminum, sand edges and sashes thoroughly to remove corrosion.

Catches don't hold. Squirt oil in them and work them back and forth repeatedly until they're free.

Glass broken. Have dealer reglaze it.

Screen mesh torn. On new sash, screen mesh is pressed into channels around edges of sash and held in place by plastic splines. Carefully pry out splines and remove mesh. Cut new piece of mesh to same size. Press it into top channel and set in spline. Stretch mesh and press into bottom channel and set in spline. Then finish the sides.

Unfinished aluminum badly corroded. See ALUMINUM.

CONCRETE

For how to use concrete, see BASIC METHODS: HOW TO MIX AND HANDLE CONCRETE.

Cracks. Chip open as deeply as possible with a cold chisel. Blow out crumbs. Let concrete dry thoroughly. Fill with latex cement and trowel smooth.

If a very wide crack has opened up in a slab of concrete resting on uneven ground, break out a wide strip between the two pieces with a sledge. Cram sand or gravel under the pieces to raise and level them. Wet broken edges and brush on a creamy mixture of cement and water. Immediately pour into crack a mixture of 1 part portland cement, 1¾ parts sand, and 2 parts gravel of not more than ¾ inch diameter. Pack this down well and force it against broken edges. Then strike off level with the broken pieces with a board and trowel smooth. Cover with damp burlap for 48 hours.

Holes. Handle like cracks.

Surface pitted, rough, uneven. Clean thoroughly and wash. Let dry. Spread on latex cement and trowel smooth.

Thin sections of ornamental concrete broken (as in a birdbath or jardiniere). Clean broken edges thoroughly and allow to dry completely. Apply silicone adhesive or epoxy glue and press pieces together. Clamp if necessary. Let dry for 24 hours.

Surface dusty. See FLOOR, CONCRETE.

Efflorescence. See BRICK.

Stains. See BRICK. If stains are old or don't come up, mix muriatic acid with an equal amount of water and scrub on stains with a fiber brush. Rinse. Repeat as necessary.

CONCRETE PATIO BLOCK

Broken. Clean edges thoroughly; coat with epoxy glue, and press together for 6 hours. Be sure block is placed on a level base, otherwise it may break again along the same line.

Stains. See BRICK.

COPPER

NOTE. The best way to mend copper is by soldering. Use an acid flux except for electrical work, which requires a rosin flux (see BASIC METHODS: HOW TO SOLDER METAL). It is perfectly feasible, however, to make many repairs with epoxy mender. See GALVANIZED STEEL.

Small holes, tears. Clean metal thoroughly, apply flux, and heat with a torch. Then run in solder.

Large holes, tears. If edges are more than $\frac{3}{16}$ inch apart, cut a patch out of copper flashing. Use steel wool, patch an area around hole thoroughly. Apply flux. Then heat patch and apply a thin layer of solder on one side. Do same thing to metal around hole. Lay patch over hole, tinned surface to tinned surface. Heat until solder flows together.

Seam between two pieces open. Clean with steel wool. Heat and press together. If old solder is not sufficient, apply a little more.

Scratches. Rub with very fine steel wool.

Dents. Hold a block of wood over concave side. Hammer reverse side lightly with a rubber mallet. Work from edges of dent toward the center.

Green or dark brown stains. Scrub with full-strength household ammonia and fine steel wool. Rinse well. Then, for a soft, lustrous finish, apply brass polish. For a shiny finish that will also prevent further staining, spray on one or two coats of clear lacquer.

Tarnished. Follow directions for stains.

CORK

Holes, dents. Cut a piece of waste cork or even a bottle cork into tiny slivers (use a kitchen grater if you wish). Mix with white shellac or clear lacquer and immediately spread into hole. Sand smooth when dry.

Burns. If stain cannot be removed by sanding, cut it out and fill hole as above.

Loose from base. Scrape out old adhesive and stick down with linoleum cement.

Pieces of cork separated. Coat both surfaces with rubber cement and let dry until tacky, then press together.

Cork separated from other materials. See HOUSEHOLD DECORATIVE ACCESSORIES.

Stains. Wash with mild detergent and lukewarm water. If stains persist, sand lightly with fine sandpaper.

CRIB, BABY

Plastic teething surface broken. You can try gluing it to the wood rail with plastic-mending adhesive. Coat broken edges with adhesive, too. But if the surface isn't perfectly smooth, you'd better remove the entire strip.

Lifting mechanism on side broken. Examine the central latch to make sure rods are connected to it. Fasten down guide straps that hold rods in the groove in the bottom of the side. If the rods are bent, remove the entire mechanism and straighten them carefully.

Crib wobbly. Tighten all bolts. If this doesn't work, cut a long strip of wood about ½ inch by 1 inch into two equal lengths to use as braces. On the back side of the crib, screw the end of one strip to the edge of the footboard, level with the top of the side. Screw the other end to the bottom of the side midway between the headboard and footboard. Then screw the other strip to the headboard at the top of the side and to the bottom of the side between the headboard and footboard. This forms a V.

Casters fall out of legs. Wrap the shanks of the casters with adhesive tape and force them into the holes in the legs.

CROQUET MALLET

Head loose from handle. Remove handle and clean dirt from end and from the hole in the head. Let wood dry completely if damp. Spread resorcinal or epoxy glue in the hole and on end of handle. Tap together and let dry for 24 hours.

Handle broken. If the break parallels the grain, coat both surfaces with epoxy glue and clamp together with C-clamps or by overwrapping with waxpaper and string. If break is across grain, make a new handle out of a broomstick.

CURB

Concrete curb broken. Break out loose concrete and brush surfaces clean. Coat two boards lightly with automobile oil and stake on either side of curb so top edges are even with curb top. Greased surfaces should face inward. Wet concrete between boards with water and let it stand for several hours. Before this dries, trowel in a stiff mix of 1 part portland cement, 2 parts sand, and 2 parts small gravel (or 1 part cement and 3 parts sand, if hole is small). Compact thoroughly and strike off level with tops of boards.

Brick curb broken. Crack out broken brick and surrounding mortar. Set in new brick. See BRICK.

Blacktop curb broken. Chip out crumbly and broken blacktop. Stake ungreased boards on either side of curb with top edges level with curb top. Pack in blacktop, compacting frequently as you add more. Smooth off top level with boards. Then remove boards and compact sides of curb.

CURTAIN ROD

Cord on traverse rod loose, dangling. If cord is looped through a spring pulley on the wall or floor, close curtains, pull out knot in one end of the center carrier until cord is taut. Then reknot. If cord is in two pieces (not looped through a pulley), attach weights to the pulling ends.

Curtains on traverse rods do not close at center of window. Open curtains wide. On the back of one of the center carriers, you will find a hook around which the cord is looped. Loosen cord. Push carrier as far to the side of the window as possible. Tighten cord by pulling on the end, then loop it around the hook again.

Sags in middle. For lightweight hollow or brass rods, screw a screw hook into the casing or wall, at the center of the rod. For a large wood or metal rod, attach to the casing a bracket with a U-shaped cutout in the end (similar to the brackets supporting the ends of the rod). For a traverse rod, install a center support bracket designed for the particular make of rod.

CUSHION, BENCH

Holes, burns. Cut small round patch of matching material. Glue down with fabric glue if cover is a fabric, plastic-mending adhesive if it is plastic, vinyl cement if it is leather or vinyl.

Buttons off. See MATTRESS.

Needs stuffing. See FURNITURE—UPHOLSTERED.

CUTLERY, KITCHEN

Tang loose in handle. Remove handle and clean tang with steel wool. Make sure hole in handle is dry. Coat tang and hole with epoxy glue and reset tang in handle. Allow glue to dry 24 hours

Handle split. If it is wood, dry thoroughly and force epoxy glue in the split. If plastic, use plastic-mending adhesive. Clamp the handle in either case until glue dries.

Wood handle roughened, bleached by hot water. Smooth with fine sandpaper and steel wool. Then saturate wood with linseed oil and rub it in well.

Metal rusted. This happens only to very old cutlery, not to stainless steel. Rub liquid rust-remover on the metal. Then go over it with fine steel wool or emery cloth.

Knife dull. Use a flat carborundum stone (the bigger, the better). Hold blade almost flat on this and sharpen with a circular motion.

CUTLERY, TABLE

Knife blade loose in handle. Remove blade and clean tang with fine emery cloth. Apply epoxy glue and reset in handle.

If hole in handle is much larger than the tang of the blade, take knife to a jeweler for repair. Hollow-handled knives are filled with a white cement which occasionally erodes and needs to be replaced entirely if blade is to hold tight.

Fork tines bent. Wrap with paper or cloth and bend them straight with pliers.

Tips of silver spoons bent. You can usually straighten these with your fingers, but don't try anything more violent.

Ceramic or bone handle broken. Apply cellulose cement to both edges and clamp together for 6 hours.

Silver tarnished. See SILVER.

Carving knife dull. See CUTLERY, KITCHEN.

CUTTING BOARD

Soiled. The real danger of a soiled cutting board is that the bacteria that cause food poisoning hide in scratches and wait to come in contact with a new serving of food. Boards should, therefore, be washed thoroughly after every use with hot water, detergent, and a scrubbing brush. In addition, they should be scrubbed weekly with a strong chlorine solution (at least 1 ounce chlorine bleach in 1 gallon water).

Stains. Scrub with detergent. When thoroughly dry, rub with medium-fine steel wool or sandpaper. Remove particles of steel wool with a damp cloth. Wash and dry. Rub in mineral oil (not cooking oil) about once a month.

For difficult stains, scrub with chlorine bleach mixed 50:50 with water, and let bleach stand for a while. Wash thoroughly to remove flavor of chlorine.

Rough, scratched. Sand with the grain, preferably with an oscillating-reciprocating sander. Start with medium paper and work down to very fine. When wood is smooth, rub with mineral oil to seal pores.

DECK, WOOD

See also CANVAS DECK or PORCH, WOOD.

Heaved by frost. The footings are inadequate. You must dig out below each post that supports the deck—one at a time—and build a poured concrete pier that extends to below the average frost line. The pier itself should measure 8 inches by 8 inches in cross section, and it should rest on a footing measuring 16 inches by 16 inches across by 8 inches deep. Extend the pier at least 6 inches above ground level. Set a steel post anchor in the top, and bolt the post to this. For concrete, use a mixture of 1 part portland cement, 2¾ parts sand, and 4 parts pebbles of not more than 1½ inches diameter.

Wobbly, weak. The posts may not be large enough (they should never measure less than 4 inches by 4 inches) or they may not be spaced close enough. The only way to answer these questions for sure is to have an experienced carpenter examine the deck. Before doing this, however, you might nail diagonal braces between the posts. Arrange these in a W pattern; don't run them all in the same direction. Use 2-by-4s for braces under 8 feet long; 2-by-6s otherwise. Secure them with 4-inch to 5-inch nails, and if they stop the deck from wobbling, add lag screws or bolts.

Floor vibrates. Install bridging between the joists at 10-foot intervals. Make the bridging of 1-inch by 4-inch boards and nail it in an X between each pair of joists.

Tree growing up through hole in deck battering deck when wind blows. Either cut down the tree or enlarge the hole in the deck.

DEHUMIDIFIER

Doesn't work. Is fuse on circuit blown? Is outlet into which dehumidifier is plugged inoperative? Has cord broken? Is collection bucket full, shutting off unit automatically?

Collects widely varying amounts of moisture from day to day. Don't worry. This is very probably attributable to normal changes in the atmosphere of the house.

Operating sluggishly. Check whether fan is running at full speed. It may need cleaning or oiling. Humidistat may be malfunctioning. Call a serviceman.

Rusting. Sand metal clean. Brush on red metal primer and one or two coats of alkyd gloss enamel.

DISHWASHER

Doesnt work. Check: Has fuse blown? Is dishwasher turned on? Is cycle selection button pushed in all the way? Is door or lid closed tight?

Hums but doesn't work. Check: Is anything jamming impeller? Is strainer in outlet clogged?

Doesn't fill with water. Your water pressure may have dropped too low. If this condition doesn't quickly correct itself, call a serviceman.

Doesn't empty. Inspect drain hose to make sure it isn't kinked or clogged. Clean strainer and outlet in tub.

Dishes don't wash clean. Is water in dishwasher 140 degrees or higher? It should be. Have you scraped dishes adequately? (They still need it despite manufacturer's claims that they don't.) Is dishwasher loaded properly? Try changing detergent.

Dishes water-spotted or not dried thoroughly. Try adding a wetting agent to each wash cycle.

Soap dispenser doesn't open. Clean thoroughly. Make sure catch that holds dispenser closed has not been bent.

Water on floor. Check if door gasket is torn or flattened. Inspect hose connections under dishwasher and sink.

White film on sides of tub. Scrub with white vinegar. Or fill two small bowls with a cup of vinegar, put them on the bottom rack, and run the dishwasher through a complete cycle.

Wood top scratched, stained. See CUTTING BOARD.

DISPOSAL, GARBAGE

Doesn't work. Check whether fuse has blown and disposal is turned on. Then call a serviceman.

Stops suddenly. If you filled it unusually full, it is probably simply overloaded. Let it cool for several minutes; then press the red overload reset button near the bottom of the disposal. If this doesn't work, disposal may be jammed. If yours isn't a new model with antijamming features, consult manufacturer's instruction manual. Depending on the model, you may need only to click a switch to reverse the cutting wheel. Or you may have to reverse the cutting wheel by inserting a special wrench, which came with the disposer, in the bottom of the unit. Or you may have to turn off the electricity and turn the cutting wheel with a broomstick.

Other problems. Let a serviceman cope with them.

DOG COLLAR

Studs loose. Turn collar upside down on a board and hit it with a hammer to bend down the flanges on the studs. If this doesn't work, put a blob of epoxy glue under the loose studs and press them into place.

Other problems. See CLOTHING—BELT.

DOG LEASH

Swivel snap broken. With a hacksaw, cut the loop that fastens the snap to the leash. Buy a replacement snap at hardware store. Slip the loop through the end of the leash, and hammer it closed.

Leather handle broken. Cut the broken ends off cleanly. Apply rubber cement to one side of one end and the other side of the other end. Let dry until tacky. Then overlap the ends about 1 inch and press together. When glue has dried, punch a hole through the overlap and insert a steel rivet.

Leather leash damaged. If badly weakened, cut out the bad leather, overlap the cut ends, and glue and rivet together as above. If leash is simply delaminated, spread rubber cement on the laminations and press together.

Chain broken. *See* CHAIN.

DOLL

See also STUFFED ANIMAL.

NOTE. Some doll repairs are very easy, others quite difficult. Before attempting to fix a broken head or a torn body it is well to find out— if you can—what material you are dealing with. This can save you time in selecting the right glue and/or patching material. But don't worry too much if the answer escapes you. If the first things you try don't work, you can always try something else.

If the doll has pulled apart, the first thing to determine is how it was put together. Then, can you get inside the body to fix it? Also do you have the materials you need?

Finally, before mending a doll, decide how much you value it. If it is just an ordinary doll and repairs seem relatively easy, go ahead and make them. But if repairs look difficult for one reason or another or if doll is an antique with real or sentimental value, then it is better to take it to a doll hospital.

Head, limbs, body, made of solid material broken. Coat broken edges lightly with cellulose cement and let dry. Then apply a second coat and press pieces together. If the broken part is known to be made of a modern plastic (other than polyethylene), use plastic-mending adhesive instead of cellulose cement.

Holes, cracks, in soft rubber body. Cut a patch out of thin flesh-colored rubber or any thin, flesh-colored fabric. Coat patch and area around hole with rubber cement. Let dry. Apply a second coat of cement to both surfaces and smooth patch down. Be sure not to stretch or bend the body from its normal position when applying patch, because if you do, patch will be permanently wrinkled.

Holes, cracks, in soft plastic. Use plastic-mending adhesive kit. Apply patch from kit or cut a patch out of any thin, flesh-colored vinyl. Spread over hole when body is in normal position (not bent or stretched).

Holes, tears, in cloth. Cut a patch out of matching material and glue over hole with fabric glue.

Limb off jointed doll. Jointed dolls made during the past several generations are held together with wire hooks connected to one or more thick rubber bands. A single limb may come off when the hook to which it is attached becomes disengaged either from the rubber band or from the mount inside the limb. In either case, bend a stiff wire into a hook, reach through limb socket, slip hook around rubber band, pull band out, and hook the doll wire around the rubber band or the limb mount as the case may be. Pinch the hooks in the doll wire closed, then let limb snap back into socket.

Four limbs and head off jointed doll. The rubber band connecting the head and limbs has probably broken. If you can buy a replacement from the doll manufacturer or a doll hospital, do so. Otherwise use the 1/8-inch-wide elastic used in dressmaking. Cut this into a length slightly longer than the broken rubber band, or if the band has disappeared, cut a length about double the length of the doll's body. Tie a square knot in the ends. Insert the elastic loop into the body through the neck; stick a long nail through it at the neck end (where the knot should be), and lay the nail across the neck opening so that the loop won't get away from you. Then hook the legs, arms, and finally the head onto the elastic. Remove the nail from across the neck opening and let the head snap into place. If the limbs and head are held tight to the body, fine. If not, pull out head and retie the knot to shorten the loop. When you are satisfied with the adjustment, sew down the ends of the knot in the elastic to prevent it from loosening.

Limbs off jointed wood dolls. The limbs on many wood dolls are constructed with a tongue that fits into a slot in the piece above it. The two pieces are held together by wire or pegs. The easiest way to repair these is to insert a piece of small wire through the holes in the slot and tongue and bend or twist the ends so the wire can't come out.

Limbs off a soft body which does not have rubber bands inside. These are attached in various ways and you will just have to investigate the proper repair. Limbs that are ordinarily sewn on should be resewn. Molded-on rubber or plastic limbs are most easily attached with material wrapped around and glued to them and then to the body (see HOLES, CRACKS, above). In some cases, excess material at the top of a limb is simply wedged under a cardboard disk which is held tight to the body by a spring inside.

Limbs off floppy rag doll. Add stuffing to limb if needed. Stitch opening closed. Then sew limb on body.

Stuffing out of body. Fill with cotton, soft rags, whatever seems appropriate. If the doll head is easily removed, it is best first to close the hole in the body by sewing or gluing on a patch, and then to stuff the body through the neck opening.

Rag doll too floppy. Additional stuffing will correct matters. Or, open body and insert a stick of wood or, for greater flexibility, a strip of aluminum sheet. In arms and legs use semi-flexible wire. Be sure to bend ends of wire into closed hooks so that they can't poke through the "skin" of the doll.

Eyes out of sockets. The eyes and balancing weight are mounted in a metal bracket that is clamped on a projection inside the head. You can pull back head and try to squeeze the bracket on the projection from which it sometimes comes loose, but the odds are against you. Better let someone who specializes in repairing dolls take over.

Eyes bang when they open. Pull off head and glue a patch of red flannel, about ¾ inch square, behind the mouth. Use white glue.

Shoes keep coming off. If your child doesn't object, spread rubber cement on sole of foot and in the bottom of the shoe. Let dry. Apply a second coat of cement and put on shoe. If doll has socks, first glue these to foot, then glue on shoe.

Hair off. Reglue with cellulose cement.

DOOR, ACCORDION

Works stiffly. Clean the overhead track and coat it very lightly with petroleum jelly.

Touches latch jamb at top but not at bottom. Unscrew door from opposite jamb. Loosen all the screws in the overhead track except the last one before the latch jamb. Starting at the opposite jamb, insert wood shims under the track until door hangs parallel with the latch jamb. Then screw track tight. For appearance's sake, the long wedge-shaped crack between the track and the top jamb should be covered with a ¼-inch quarter round.

Touches latch jamb at bottom but not at top. Loosen all the screws in the overhead track except the last one before the opposite jamb. Shim the track down, as above, until door hangs parallel with latch jamb.

Holes in vinyl covering. Cut a patch out of matching vinyl and glue over hole with plastic-mending adhesive. Let dry about 6 hours before moving door.

DOORBELL

Won't ring. Tighten nuts that hold small bell wires to low-voltage side of transformer. Have someone push the door button. If you hear a hum, the wiring is OK. If you don't, attach short wires to another bell and hold these to the low-voltage terminals of the transformer. Bell should ring if transformer is all right. If it doesn't ring, shut off house current and tighten connections on high-voltage side.

If bell still doesn't ring when power is restored, check whether bell clapper strikes bell. Bend it if it doesn't. Clean contact points inside bell box with emery cloth or fine sandpaper. Bend contact tab on one side of bell to correct vibration speed of clapper rod (some bells have a screw to make this adjustment). If bell still doesn't ring, remove door button and check wire connections. If they appear to be OK, lay a knife blade across the two terminals. If this makes bell ring, clean contact points in button with emery cloth. If bell doesn't ring, however, buy a new button.

If bell still doesn't ring, examine exposed wires running through the house for a break. If you can't see any, attach short wires to a test bell. Then, starting at the transformer, scrape a bit of insulation from the wires at 3-foot intervals, and touch exposed wires with test bell wires. When test bell stops ringing, you are near break and can easily find it by feel. Then splice broken wires together.

DOOR, BIFOLD

Out of plumb. Adjust pivot at bottom of door.

Doesn't close flat. Take down the door and plane the free edge, but be careful not to take off too much wood, because when the door contracts in the winter there will be too much of a gap between it and the latch jamb.

Opens and closes jerkily. Clean track attached to top jamb and spray with silicone lubricant. Inspect guide on top of door to make sure it is not worn.

Wood damaged. See PAINTED SURFACE or VARNISHED SURFACE.

DOOR, CABINET

Door sticks. Rub paraffin on all edges. If this doesn't work, and if door sticks at top or bottom, remove it and scrape and sand the edge. If door sticks at the sides and fits tight in the door opening, remove it and plane down the hinge edge. Then deepen the hinge mortises and rehang the door.

If door binds at the latch edge or hinge edge and there is a gap at the opposite edge, insert shims under the hinges in the jambs. See DOOR, HINGED.

Panel in door split. See FURNITURE—CHEST OF DRAWERS.

Other problems. See DOOR, HINGED.

DOOR CHIME

Won't ring. Follow procedure for mending doorbell. When checking whether chime is clean, remove it and slide out rod and spring you will find inside. Clean these in gasoline before replacing.

DOOR CLOSER

Door bangs shut or closes too slowly. Most door closers have some sort of adjusting screw that controls the speed with which they close doors. Turn this until door operates properly.

Closer without adjusting screw sluggish. Open door as far as possible and clean piston rod with light household oil.

Closer comes loose from jamb. Remove screws in jamb. Shape wood pegs to fit the screw holes, coat with resorcinol glue, hammer them in, and let glue dry for 24 hours. Then trim off pegs flush with jamb, drill screw holes, and install closer.

DOOR, FLUSH

Hole kicked through front or back surface. Better replace the door—and don't buy a cheap one made of matchstick-thick wood next time. A satisfactory repair is impossible if door has a natural finish. If it's painted, however, it may get by.

Trim off splintered edges with a sharp knife and fine-toothed hacksaw blade. Cut blocks of wood to the exact thickness of the hollow space in the door and glue them to the back of the unbroken side. Fill the hole as much as possible with the blocks, but take particular pains to place them under the edges of the hole. Then cut a piece of plywood or hardboard the same thickness as the door panel to fit the hole, and glue it in over the blocks. Finally, fill the crack around the hole with plastic wood or spackle; sand smooth, and paint.

DOOR, FOLDING

Sagging or hanging on slant. Tighten screws that hold track to the top jamb. If screws don't hold, drive glued wood pegs into screw holes and reset screws.

Vinyl covering torn. Reglue to base with vinyl cement. If necessary, cut a patch out of matching vinyl and glue over tear with vinyl cement.

Wood damaged. See VARNISHED SURFACE or WOOD.

DOOR, GARAGE

Overhead door operates stiffly. Lubricate moving parts of hardware with oil or powdered graphite. Spread a little heavy grease in tracks.

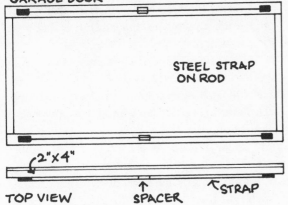

INNER SIDE OF OVERHEAD GARAGE DOOR

STEEL STRAP ON ROD

2"x4"

TOP VIEW   SPACER   STRAP

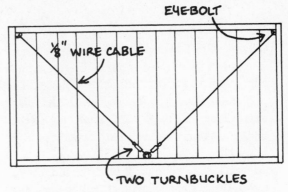

EYEBOLT

⅛" WIRE CABLE

TWO TURNBUCKLES

Tighten screws holding tracks to framing of garage.

Overhead door sags when open. If door has horizontal steel rods or straps on the top and bottom rails, tighten nuts on the ends. If there are no rods, buy a pair from the garage door dealer and attach them to the door on the inside. Insert a 4-inch block of wood under each rod at the middle so the rods bow outward. Then tighten the nuts at the ends of the rods.

A somewhat less effective solution is to insert eyebolts in the two upper corners of the door and a third eyebolt in the bottom rail at the center of the door. Stretch ⅛-inch steel cables with turnbuckles from the corner bolts to the bottom bolt, and tighten the turnbuckles until the sag disappears.

Lower panels of overhead door rotten. This may happen to doors with inset panels. First, carefully cut out panels with a saber saw or jigsaw. Cut new panels from ¼-inch exterior-grade plywood or hardboard. Hold in place in frame with ¼-inch quarter-round strips nailed around opening on front and back of panels.

Hinges on out-swinging door loose. If screws cannot be tightened because wood has rotted or hinges have rusted, remove them entirely. Drill through hinge holes to other side of door. Secure hinge with nuts and bolts.

Out-swinging door sags, but hinges tight. Drive wedges under dropped corner of door until it hangs straight. Strengthen corners with right-angle steel mending plates. Then install metal door brace with turnbuckle (see DOOR, SCREEN).

Top edge of out-swinging door rotting. If rot has not progressed too far, cut out soft wood and fill with plastic wood. Saturate with pentachlorophenol wood preservative. Out of aluminum flashing, cut a narrow strip 2 inches wider than thickness of door. Fold this over top edge of door and nail along both sides with aluminum nails.

DOOR, HINGED

Warped door won't latch. If warped along the hinge edge, install a third hinge midway between those at top and bottom. If warped along the latch edge, pry up the stop on the latch side of the frame. Close door and draw a pencil line on the frame along the inside edge of the door. Nail the stop along this line.

Door closes with a bang. Chances are the top slants in toward the jamb. Check with a spirit level. Then remove top hinge from jamb and reset it further away from the stop bead, or move bottom hinge further in toward the stop.

Door won't close because it strikes jamb on latch side. Check if there is a wide crack on

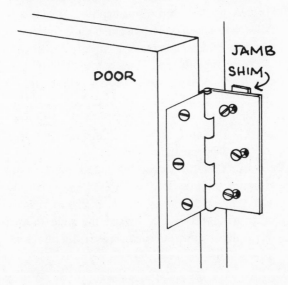

DOOR

JAMB

SHIM

hinge side. If there is, screw hinges down tighter. If this doesn't produce results, loosen hinges from jamb and insert under their inner edges thin strips of cardboard (shims). This pulls door away from latch jamb. If there isn't a crack on the hinge side, door has swelled and to make it close you must shave down the hinge edge.

Door won't close because it binds against hinge jamb. If there is a wide crack on the latch side, loosen hinges from jamb and insert shims under their outer edges. This pushes door toward latch jamb.

Door won't close because it strikes jamb at top. If there is a wide crack at the bottom, unscrew

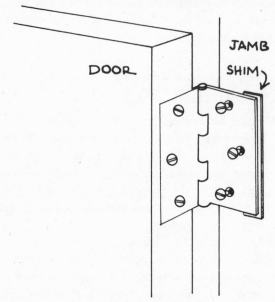

DOOR

JAMB

SHIM

hinges from jamb and, with a sharp chisel, extend the mortises downward. Plug old screw holes with glued plugs of wood. Rehang door in new position and fill in exposed hinge mortises with plastic wood or glued chips of wood.

Door won't close because it strikes threshold. Reverse above procedure.

Door latch doesn't reach strike plate. Insert shims under outer edges of both hinges. If this doesn't work, remove hinges entirely and insert thick cardboard or wood shims the full size of the hinges in the mortises.

Door won't latch because latch and strike plate are not in line. If difference in alignment is not great, unscrew strike plate, clamp it in a vise, and, with a file, extend the hole in the plate up or down as necessary. If difference in

alignment is considerable, unscrew strike plate and, with a chisel, extend mortise in jamb up or down.

Door hangs on a slant. Insert shims under top or bottom hinge as necessary.

Door rattles. Move strike plate toward the stop. The mortise in the jamb must be enlarged so you can do this.

Draft under interior door. Tack felt or rubber weather stripping along bottom edge.

Air leaks around exterior door. Tack flexible metal weather stripping to sides and top of jamb. The tacked edge should face the door when it is open. Tack rubber weather stripping to bottom of door or install a new metal threshold with a plastic insert that rubs against bottom of door.

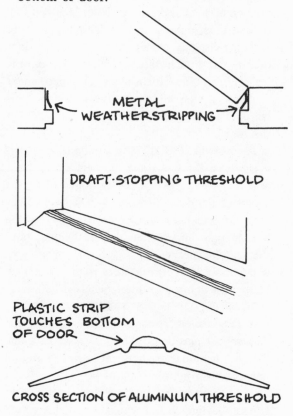

METAL WEATHERSTRIPPING

DRAFT-STOPPING THRESHOLD

PLASTIC STRIP TOUCHES BOTTOM OF DOOR

CROSS SECTION OF ALUMINUM THRESHOLD

DOORKNOB

Loose. Loosen setscrew in shank of knob. Turn knob to right until it is firm, and reset screw (make sure it seats against flat side of spindle). If knob is still loose, loosen setscrew again and turn knob to left until it pulls free of spindle. Pull out other knob with the spindle. Replace spindle.

Glass or porcelain knob loose from metal shank. Better get a new one. But if you must save the old one, try drilling a hole through the metal behind the knob and squeeze in cyanoacrylate glue. If you're lucky, it may hold for a while.

DOOR LOCK OR LATCH

Latch or lock tongue stiff. Scrape off any paint that may be binding it. Squirt powdered graphite on the tongue and into keyhole. Work door knob back and forth. If this doesn't do the trick, remove lock by unscrewing setscrew in one of the doorknobs and pulling out both knobs. Then remove screws holding lock in edge of door and pull out lock assembly. Take to a locksmith for repair.

Latch or lock broken. If it is a modern lock or latch set, remove as above and take to a locksmith. Note, however, that so much inferior hardware is being used in postwar houses that it may be better in the long run to replace the unit entirely. If you suspect this to be the case, take the lock or latch set to a builder's hardware dealer and ask for his advice.

If lock or latch set is of old-fashioned tumbler type, remove it from door as above. Unscrew cover plate and examine mechanism. If parts have slipped out of place, reassemble them properly; squirt in powdered graphite, and replace lock in door. If parts are broken, take set to a locksmith. Repair of this type of lock is easy, but parts are not generally available in hardware stores.

Latch tongue doesn't seat in strike plate. See DOOR, HINGED.

DOOR, PANELED

Paint around edges of panels ridged; unpainted wood exposed. Make this repair at start of heating season, after panels have contracted. Scrape and sand off bad paint thoroughly. Prime bare wood with an alkyd primer. When dry, brush on alkyd semigloss or glass enamel.

Panels cracked through. If you can loosen broken pieces from the surrounding wood into which panels are set, spread white glue into the crack and force the pieces together. If you can't loosen broken pieces, pack crack full of plastic wood; let dry 24 hours. Then sand smooth and repaint.

DOOR, SCREEN

Screening corroded, torn, etc. See SCREEN, WINDOW.

Door sags. Buy a long metal door brace with screw eyes in each end and a turnbuckle in the middle. Extend the brace to its greatest length. Screw one end of brace to the rail at the center of the sagging corner. Screw the other end as far up on the hinge-side stile as possible. Then tighten turnbuckle until corner of door is raised.

Bangs shut. Replace door spring with a pneumatic closer.

Joints loose. Pull open slightly and run in resorcinol glue. Then hammer joints closed and reinforce them with steel mending plates.

DOOR, SLIDING

Warped. There is no positive cure, but you may be able to prevent door from binding against frame or other doors by screwing door guides to floor.

Door jumps track. If this happens repeatedly and door appears to be straight and hanging properly, the cause may be the size of the wheels in the track. If these are less than 1 inch in diameter, install new track with larger wheels.

Hangs on a slant. Loosen hangers on back of door. Line up door with door frame. Then tighten hangers in the proper position.

DOOR, SLIDING GLASS

Moves stiffly. Clean out tracks with a vacuum cleaner, then scrape out hardened paint, wax, etc. Polish lightly with steel wool. Then rub a light film of oil on the track.

Leaks at the bottom. If water enters under the track, force caulking compound under it. Otherwise, call in dealer.

DOOR, SWINGING

Works stiffly. Remove cover plates from both sides of hinge at bottom of door. Clean dust, lint, etc., from mechanism. Squirt powdered graphite into pivot and spring. Work door back and forth.

Strikes jamb. Check whether hinge and pivot at top of door can be moved closer to the hinge jamb. If they can't be, the swinging edge of door will have to be planed down slightly.

DOOR—THRESHOLD

Interior threshold worn, splintered, scuffed. Saw it in two, pry out pieces, take to lumber dealer, and buy a matching threshold. Use old threshold as pattern for the cuts to be made in new one. Use fine-toothed saw for cutting. Pry off stops on door jambs. Place threshold in place in doorway and nail down with 3-inch finishing nails (drill holes for the nails first). Countersink nailheads and cover with plastic wood.

Exterior threshold worn, cracked, rotten, etc. Take down door and pull off the side casings. Slip a hacksaw blade under each side jamb and cut through nails holding the threshold. You may then be able to pull out the threshold, or you may have to saw it in two to pull it out. Buy a new oak threshold and cut to the same size. Slip in under the jambs and nail in place. Renail side casings and hang door.

DRAINS, PLUMBING

Bathroom sink drain clogged. Proceed in this order: (1) Remove pop-up stopper and clean. On some modern stoppers, a thin rubber flange stops water from flowing out when stopper is closed. But in time the rubber becomes flabby and distorted and may also stop outflow even when open. Replace with a new flange.

(2) Remove rod that controls pop-up stopper by unscrewing large nut on back of drainpipe just under lavatory. Bend a small hook in the end of a stiff wire about 15 inches long. Poke this down drain and fish out glup in bottom.

(3) Unscrew clean-out plug at base of U-trap (if there is a plug). Put a bucket underneath, and fish out stoppage on either side of U with a hooked wire. If you have a small spring auger of type usually used to clean toilet drains, crank it down drain.

(4) Replace rod that controls pop-up stopper, but not the stopper. Plug overflow opening with a wet rag. Fill lavatory with about 3 inches of hot water. Place cup of a plumber's friend over drain and pump handle up and down rhythmically about six times. On last stroke, pull cup sharply loose from drain. Repeat process three or four times. (New product called Drain Power can be substituted for plumber's friend. It works the same way.)

(5) Use a commercial drain cleaner according to directions on package.

(6) Remove U-trap by unscrewing large nuts at either end. Push a 25-foot spring-type auger down drain.

Kitchen sink drain clogged. Use chemical drain cleaner—*but only if you do not have a garbage disposal.* If this doesn't work, pour boiling water mixed with household ammonia into drain. Let stand for a few minutes. Then fill sink with about 3 inches of hot water and use plumber's friend as above. If this still doesn't work, remove U-trap and clean drain with a 25-foot spring-type auger.

Tub drain clogged. If tub doesn't have a pop-up stopper, follow directions for kitchen sink. On a tub with a pop-up stopper, unscrew from the end wall of the tub the escutcheon holding the drain control. Lift up out of the hole the arm that connects the control handle to the stopper. Remove stoppage from coil at bottom end of arm.

Shower stall drain clogged. Remove cover and clean out drain with hooked wire. If this doesn't work, use boiling water, ammonia, and plumber's friend as above.

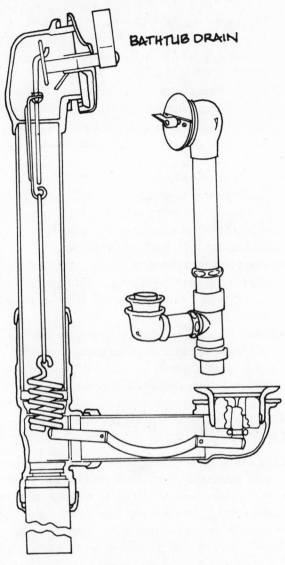

BATHTUB DRAIN

Toilet drain clogged. For this you need a plumber's friend with a flexible fold-down rim. Open out rim and fit it into toilet outlet. Pump handle up and down rhythmically. On last stroke, pull cup sharply loose from drain. Repeat several times.

If drain is still clogged, push hooked end of a short spring-type toilet auger into drain opening and crank it down into drain as far as possible. Pull out stoppage.

Floor drain clogged. Take off strainer and clean drain with a hooked wire and spoon. Pour in several gallons of boiling water and ammonia.

House drain clogged. Call a plumber. Special tools are required.

Leaks in joints of kitchen or bathroom sink drain. Unscrew large nut at joint where leaking occurs and pull it away from joint. Remove

string that you will find wrapped around pipe. Wrap new soft cotton string around pipe three or four times to form a washer. Wrap clockwise. Push nut over string and into place, and screw it tight.

Leaks in joints of drains in basement. If drains are copper, heat joints with a torch until solder melts and flows into joints. Feed in a little additional solder. On steel and iron drains, clean joints thoroughly and smear on epoxy mender. Don't run water through drains for at least 6 hours.

Drains frozen. Heat with a heat lamp or rags soaked in boiling water. Work from point where drain leaves house back toward fixtures.

DRAINS, UNDERGROUND

Cracked. Dig out soil around all sides of pipe and brush and hose dirt from pipe. Mix 1 part portland cement and 2 to 3 parts sand, and put around pipe in a 1-inch- or 2-inch-thick layer. Extend concrete well beyond crack on both sides. Form concrete around pipe. Do not backfill trench until concrete has hardened.

Cast-iron or clay pipe broken. This is a difficult repair to make properly—which is by installing a new length of pipe. Better call in a plumber contractor. But you can do a pretty good job on a pipe that carries water only—not household wastes—by removing broken pieces. Then wrap a sheet of copper or galvanized-steel—not aluminum—flashing metal around the pipe, over the break, and tighten it with twisted wires. Pour concrete, as above, all around the flashing. Extend it well beyond the edges of the flashing.

DRAPERIES

Small holes, tears. Darn or patch. See CLOTHING—FABRICS.

Large tears. Anything you do for a large horizontal tear will be makeshift. If fabric is heavy, the least obvious repair will be made by bringing torn edges together carefully and covering with press-on mending tape. If fabric is sheer, machine stitching is best.

For large vertical tears, rip the material all the way to the bottom, turn edges under, and sew on a machine. An even better job is done by putting a seam in all the way from the bottom to the top of the drapery.

See also CLOTHING—FABRICS; CLOTH-ING—HEMS; CLOTHING—SEAMS.

DRIVEWAY, BLACKTOP

Holes, cracks. Cut out loose material down to solid base. Make sides of hole straight up and down. Pour in packaged blacktop, rake it well to fill voids, and tamp hard.

Edges broken. Cut out loose material, wash with water, and let dry. Lay a board along the edge and stake in place. Pack in packaged blacktop between driveway and board, and tamp well.

Heaved by frost. Cut out heaved area, level base, and fill as above.

Dry, crumbling, sheds gravel when cars pass over. Patch holes first and let new blacktop cure for 2 months. Then seal entire driveway with a bituminous sealer. Use only a quality product such as Jennite; discount-house stuff isn't very good. Air temperature must be above 50 degrees; humidity, low.

Sweep driveway thoroughly to remove every particle of dirt, sand, etc. Using a leaf blower helps. Pour on sealer and spread it with the squeegee end of special applicator; work it into cracks and other voids with the brush on the applicator. Smooth out evenly; don't leave puddles. Let dry for 48 hours or longer. Don't walk or drive on pavement during that time.

DRYER, CLOTHES

NOTE. Call a serviceman if machine doesn't work properly, but before doing so check and correct the following points.

Doesn't work. Check whether fuse in machine has blown (if there is one). Check whether fuse or fuses in fuse box have blown. Is dryer door closed tight?

Runs but doesn't heat. An electric dryer has two 30-amp fuses. Make sure one of them has not blown. On gas dryer, see if gas is on. If not,

turn dryer control off, turn on gas, wait 10 minutes, and start dryer. Also make sure pilot light is not out. If it is, follow directions in your instruction manual.

Takes too long to dry. Clean lint screen. Remove back of dryer, shut off current at fuse box, and carefully vacuum out lint accumulated inside. Open vent pipe to outdoors and vacuum out lint.

Drum rotates slowly. Shut off current at fuse box. Remove back of dryer and check drive belts. If loose, loosen sheave on motor pulley, push it in or turn clockwise to tighten belt. If belt is broken, buy replacement from dealer.

Shorts out. Check whether a bobby pin, nail, or other metal object has worked through a hole in the clothes drum so that it rubs on parts behind it.

Enamel chipped or scratched. Scratch out rust and touch up with porcelain glaze.

Light in control panel burned out. Replace according to manufacturer's directions.

DRY WELL

Clogged. Before opening the well, run a spring-steel plumber's snake down through the drain pipe leading into well. This may eliminate the clog. If not, remove soil over well; take off top and remove stones from inside the well (but don't disturb the well lining unless it has collapsed). Clean out thoroughly and toss stones back in. Don't pack them tightly. Then cover the well with coarse aluminum mesh or flashing. Over this lay 1-inch-thick boards. Replace soil and sod.

Collapsed. Take out all the old stones and rebuild sides. Use rectangular stones; but if they're not available or too difficult to handle, use curved, perforated concrete cesspool blocks. When lining is finished, fill well with loosely packed stones and cover as above. The top of the dry well should be at least 1 foot below ground level.

DUCT, HEATING

Leaks at joints. Make sure duct is straight. If sagging, loop wire or, better, metal straps around it and attach to joists overhead. Wrap joints with self-stick polyethylene duct tape or seal with silicone caulking or epoxy mender.

Vibrates and is noisy. Secure to joists in basement with additional wires or metal straps. Check whether there is a canvas connector between the main duct and the furnace or air conditioner; if not, have a heating contractor or sheet-metal contractor install one.

EARTHENWARE

Follow directions for fixing china. See CHINA.

Pieces used for ashtrays and ornamental purposes rough on bottom, scratch tabletops. Cut a piece of felt to cover bottom and coat one side with rubber cement. Let dry. Then apply cement to earthenware and again to felt. Let set for a few minutes until tacky, and smooth felt down.

ELECTRIC CORD

NOTE. Always disconnect cord before making repairs.

Outer insulation frayed, cut, or broken but wires intact. Wrap securely with cellophane electrical tape.

Lamp cord, extension cord, or cord to motor broken. If break occurs in a small lamp cord or extension cord, cut cord in two and snip off broken ends of wires. Insert the two pieces in a clamp-on splicer available from hardware or electrical store. Follow directions of splicer maker.

If a large cord is broken, cut it in two. Remove 4 inches of the outer insulation from the two cords and 2 inches of the insulation from the ends of all the wires. Bend opposing wires around each other and twist together. If you have a soldering iron, apply solder. Then wrap each of the mended wires with cellophane electrical tape. Be sure no metal is exposed. Then bundle the wires together and overwrap with additional tape.

Heater cord (for irons, toasters, other heating appliances) broken. In an emergency, fix as

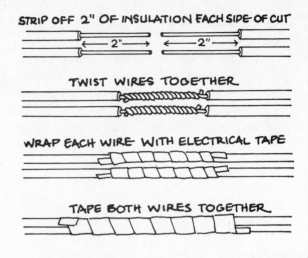

STRIP OFF 2" OF INSULATION EACH SIDE OF CUT
2" 2"

TWIST WIRES TOGETHER

WRAP EACH WIRE WITH ELECTRICAL TAPE

TAPE BOTH WIRES TOGETHER

above. But replace cord with a new one as soon as possible.

Lamp cord broken at socket. Cut off below socket and pull socket apart. Loosen the two screws that hold broken wires. Remove ¾ inch of insulation from end of each of the wires in the cord and twist strands tightly together. Insert both wires through socket cap, tie Underwriter's knot as illustrated, and wrap each wire clockwise around one of the screws. Tighten screws and reassemble socket.

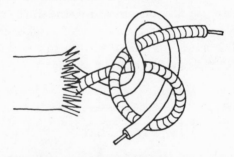

UNDERWRITER'S KNOT

Cord broken at plug. Cut off cord. If cord is used for lamps or extension cords, replace old plug with clamp-on type. Don't remove insulation from wires. Just insert end of cord in plug and clamp in place.

If cord contains two wires and is too large for clamp-on plugs, separate the wires for about 2 inches. Strip off ¾ inch of insulation from end of each wire and twist strands together. Push them through hole in back of plug and tie Underwriter's knot. Then loop one wire around one prong, wrap copper strands clockwise around adjacent screw, and tighten screw. Loop other wire around other prong and screw and tighten.

If a cord has three wires, follow same procedure. Attach black wire to gold screw, white wire to silver screw, colored ground wire to third screw.

Cord broken at outlet plug. Use clamp-on plug on thin cord, old-style screw-on plug on thick cord. Proceed as above.

ELECTRIC DRILL

Doesn't work. Check whether fuse has blown, whether outlet into which drill is plugged is defective, whether cord is broken. If operating drill on an extension cord, make sure that isn't broken either.

Runs slowly or noisily. Lubricate according to maker's directions.

Sparks excessively. Check if carbon brushes are worn down to about 1 inch or less. If so, replace with new brushes of same size.

Chuck loose. Unplug drill and remove and replace chuck according to maker's directions.

Sandpaper flies off sanding disk during operation. Try using two pieces of sandpaper on disk instead of one. If this doesn't work, rub disk adhesive on back of sandpaper.

ELECTRIC HEATER

Doesn't heat. Proceed as follows until you find problem: (1) Check whether fuse on house circuit has blown. (2) Check whether outlet is defective by plugging in a light. (3) Disconnect and check whether heater cord is broken and, if so, replace it. (4) Disassemble heater (each one is put together differently, but the manner in which they come apart is usually obvious). Tighten wires at terminals. (5) If heater still doesn't work, heating element has probably burned through. Some of these unscrew like a light bulb and are easily replaced. If break occurs very close to one of the terminals, pull wire straight and connect it to terminal. Otherwise, take heater to service shop for expert attention.

ELECTRIC JUNCTION BOX

Wires in box loose. Most junction boxes are octagonal or square, flat boxes usually found in the attic or basement. They are used when several cables are connected together. Sometimes when an outlet or switch doesn't work, the fault can be traced to loose connections in a junction box.

Shut off current at fuse box. Remove cover from junction box. Check whether connections of wires are tight. If not, scrape dirt off ends of wires and twist them together tightly. To cover the joint, slip on a cone-shaped plastic cap, called a wire nut, of appropriate size and screw it on tight. The cap should completely cover the bare wires; if not, remove it, snip the ends off the wires, and replace the cap.

If a wire nut is not available, wrap the bare wires completely with friction tape or cellophane electrical tape. In this case, however, it is best first to solder the wires.

ELECTRIC LIGHT

Socket of incandescent ceiling or wall fixture defective. While light is turned off, remove bulb and bend metal contact in base of socket upward slightly. If this doesn't work, shut off current at fuse box. Take down fixture and disassemble it as necessary to expose socket. If the small wires connected to socket are molded into the socket body, remove the coverings on the wire splices and untwist wires (if they are soldered together, melt solder with a soldering iron or simply cut off soldered portion). Pull socket from fixture and replace with new one. Connect black wire on socket to black cable in ceiling or wall and white wire to white cable by stripping about ¾ inch of insulation from ends of wires and twisting ends together. Cover the joined ends with wire nuts, and screw nuts tight. The bare wires should be completely covered so they cannot touch any bare metal in the fixture. If they are not covered, remove wire nuts, shorten wires slightly, and replace nuts. Reassemble fixture.

If the small wires to the socket are connected to screws on the sides of the socket body, simply loosen screws and remove wires. Install new socket and attach wires to it.

Pull-chain broken below incandescent light. Buy a new chain with a split clamp. Open one end of clamp, slip bottom bead of old chain into it, and squeeze clamp together.

Pull-chain broken within light. Turn off current. Pull socket apart and note how chain is threaded into it. Open or pry out the clamp holding the last bead of the chain, thread new chain into socket, and place in clamp. Re-assemble socket.

Fluorescent light doesn't light. If the tube is an instant-start or rapid-start type, replace it. If the tube is a preheat type, remove it; then remove the starter (small metal canister) that is revealed. To do this, press down and twist until the starter is loose. Replace it with a new starter of the same number. Then replace tube, which should now light. If it doesn't, install a new tube.

Fluorescent light blinks repeatedly. In preheat fluorescents, it is common for the light to blink once or twice before it comes on, but if blinking continues, the starter usually needs to be replaced. Put in a new tube only if the new starter fails to stop the blinking.

Fluorescent tube lights at ends but not in middle. Replace starter.

Fluorescent light makes humming sound. Remove tube and cover of fixture. Tighten bolts holding ballast in fixture. If this doesn't work, insert fiber or rubber washers around bolts between ballast and fixture. If this still doesn't work, replace ballast with new one of the same size.

Light diffuser broken. If made of glass, apply cellulose or cyanoacrylate glue to edges and press together. If made of plastic, use plastic-mending adhesive.

Incandescent fixture broken, worn, outdated. Shut off current at fuse box. Remove nut or screws holding fixture. Then pull apart wires; if soldered together, cut the small wires just below the soldered splice and remove ¾ inch of insulation from the ends of the wires. Attach new wires in fixture to large wires leading into the steel outlet box. Black wire goes to black

wire, white wire to white wire. If both of the small fixture wires are the same color, the solid-colored one corresponds to the black wire; the other has a colored thread running through it and corresponds to the white wire. If the large outlet wires seem to be the same color because they're dirty, examine them closely and you will find one is really black, the other white. To attach the wires, use wire nuts. First wrap the bare ends of the two black wires around and around each other clockwise; then screw the wire nut over them clockwise. The bare wires must be completely covered by the wire nut; if not, remove the nut, snip a little off the ends of the wires and replace the nut. Handle the white wire in the same way.

In some cases, a ceiling fixture is attached to the outlet box with two screws driven into the holes in the flanges of the box. If the holes in the fixture and box do not align, screw a mounting strap to the box and then screw the fixture to the mounting strap. If there is a large boltlike stud protruding from the center of the box, the mounting strap is slipped over this and held with a nut. If the fixture is heavy, it is screwed directly to the stud; no mounting strap is required.

Wall fixtures are usually fastened to the box by a headless bolt called a nipple. The nipple is screwed into the center hole of a mounting strap screwed to the outlet box. The fixture is

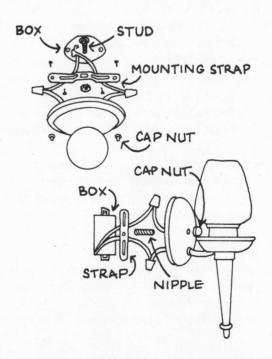

then slipped over the bolt and held by an ornamental nut.

Note that many wall fixtures have built-in switches. If a fixture is controlled by a wall switch somewhere else in the room, ignore the built-in switch. Just push the wires connected to the switch out of the way, or cut them off.

If the fixture is controlled only by its built-in switch, on the other hand, note first that both of the switch wires are black and both of the light wires are white. Attach one of the black switch wires to the large black outlet wire. Attach the other black switch wire to one of the light wires. Then attach the other white wire to the large white outlet wire.

ELECTRIC MOTOR

NOTE. Oil motors only in accordance with manufacturer's instructions. If you don't have these, but if motor has obvious oiling points, put in a few drops of SAE number 10 oil every 2 or 3 months. If motor has no oiling points, leave it alone.

Doesn't run. Check whether fuse has blown on house circuit. Plug a light into outlet into which motor is plugged to see if outlet is defective. Disconnect motor and examine cord and plug for breaks. Make necessary repairs (see ELECTRIC CORD). If these measures don't produce results, call in an expert.

Hums but doesn't start. Disconnect and examine mechanism driven by motor to make sure it turns freely. If it is stiff or frozen, grasp shaft with pliers and turn until it moves easily. Apply oil at oiling points in mechanism. Check whether belt driven by motor (if any) is too tight (see BELT, MACHINE). If trouble continues, call a serviceman.

Turns too slowly. Disconnect and check mechanism driven by motor as above. Make sure that motor is securely bolted or screwed into motor housing.

Overheats. Turn off at once and get a serviceman.

Sparks excessively, runs unevenly. If you have oiled an AC-DC motor frequently, it may be that commutator and brush ends are covered with oil. Shut off current. Remove housing and clean commutator with a toothbrush dipped in trichloroethylene. Do not use gasoline or benzine. Unscrew metal or plastic caps on brush holders and slide out little springs and brushes. Clean these, as well as holders, with trichloroethylene. Then replace in exactly the same position that you found them.

If carbon tips (called brushes) on ends of springs are worn down to about ¼-inch length and if motor continues to spark a great deal after cleaning as above, stretch springs slightly to increase tension of brushes on the commutator. But buy replacement brushes of same size as soon as possible. Replace both brushes even though only one is worn badly.

Blows fuse when starting. Circuit is overloaded. Turn off other things on circuit before starting motor. Or replace present fuse with a time-delay fuse of same size. Best answer, however, is to connect motor to a new circuit of its own.

Motor flooded. If it was installed within the last 10 years and was new at the time, the chances are good that it will start up safely without major overhauling. Pump down water and let motor drain for a couple of hours before turning on. If it doesn't start immediately, turn off switch, pull out motor, and take to a repair shop or have repairman come to you.

Older motors almost always must be baked out thoroughly before they are restarted. You can do this by focusing a couple of heat lamps on it for a day or so, but it's simpler and safer in the long run to have a motor repair shop take care of the job.

ELECTRIC OUTLET

Defective. Shut off current at fuse box. Unscrew outlet plate, then take out screws holding outlet and pull it out of box. Loosen wires and install a new outlet. Scrape corrosion off bare wires before connecting; wrap the wires around the terminal screws counterclockwise and crimp them; then tighten screws. Always attach black wire to gold screw, white wire to silver screw, colored wire (if there is one) to colored screw. Push outlet into box carefully and make sure bare wires do not touch sides of box. Screw outlet to box, and plate to outlet.

Note that most new outlets have small holes in the back into which wires can be inserted to make a connection. You can use either these or the screws. If using holes, straighten ends of wires and snip off all but ⅜ inch.

ELECTRIC PAINT REMOVER

Doesn't work. Has fuse blown? Is outlet into which remover is plugged defective? Is cord broken? Is extension cord (if in use) broken?

Heats inadequately. This happens when remover is attached to an extension cord. Use an extension cord with number 14 wires if no more than 25 feet long. Use cord with number 12 wires if over 25 feet long.

ELECTRIC PLUG

See ELECTRIC CORD.

Body of plug cracked. In an emergency, tape it up with friction tape or electrical tape. But replace as soon as possible.

ELECTRIC SWITCH

Single-pole switch defective. A single-pole switch has two terminals; the word *off* is stamped into the top of the handle, *on* is stamped into the bottom of the handle. To replace a defective switch, shut off the current at the fuse box. Unscrew the cover plate, take out the two screws holding the switch in the outlet box, and remove the switch from the box. Unscrew wires from switch, and scrape the ends bright. Attach new switch in the same way the old one was attached. That is, if only one cable enters the box, attach the black wire to the gold screw, the white wire to the silver screw; on the other hand, if two cables enter the box, attach the two black wires to the screws (it makes no difference which wire goes to which screw). Then splice the ends of the two white wires and cover them with a wire nut.

For exactly how to connect the wires to the switch, see ELECTRIC OUTLET. Be sure to install the switch so that the *off* side of the handle is at the top.

Three-way switch defective. A three-way switch has three terminals. The switches are made in different ways, but in all cases one of the terminals is slightly darker than the others and is marked *common* (you'll find the word on the back of the plastic or porcelain enclosure). This common terminal is usually located by itself.

To replace a switch, shut off the current at the fuse box, unscrew the cover plate, and pull the switch carefully from the outlet box. Before unscrewing the wires, note which one is attached to which screw. It's a good idea to tag the wire attached to the common screw.

When attaching new switch, connect the common wire to the common screw, the other two wires to the remaining screws. Push the switch back into the box and make sure the bare ends of the wires do not touch the box. It makes no difference which end of the switch is up. Fasten switch to box and replace cover plate. Test the switch. If it doesn't control the light properly, reverse the positions of the two last wires but leave the common wire alone.

Four-way switch defective. A four-way switch has four terminals and is used when a light is controlled from three or more points. To replace a switch, tag which wire is connected to which screw, and attach the new switch in the same way.

ENGINE, SMALL GASOLINE

NOTE. Let an expert make repairs on gasoline engines. But first check points noted below for small engines such as those on lawn mowers. Remember, however, that engines differ, and you may not have to take the same steps for one that are required for another. Keep your instruction leaflet and don't lose it.

Doesn't start. Are you out of gas?

Is valve on fuel line open?

Is spark plug wire attached?

Is metal tab pushed away from spark plug?

Is starter and running control properly adjusted to "choke" or "start"?

Is spark plug dirty or cracked? Perhaps you need a new one.

If engine has been run dry of gas or if it has not been used for a long time, push primer button several times to force fuel into carburetor.

Runs unevenly. Is gasoline old and gummy?

Is air filter clean?

Is oil in crankcase at proper level and is it clean?

Is oil filter clogged?

Is spark plug dirty or cracked?

Are cooling fins clogged with grass and dust?

Does carburetor need adjustment? Follow manufacturer's directions.

EXPRESS WAGON, CHILDREN'S

Nut on steering yoke pulls out from bottom of wagon. Take off nut and pull out bolt. Slip a wide steel washer under head of bolt and insert bolt shank through hole in wagon bottom and yoke. Then screw on nut.

Handle loop bashed. If this can't be straightened, replace it with metal handle from a child's aluminum snow shovel. Bolt to handle post.

Axle broken. Cut a new axle out of a round steel rod. Drill holes in ends for cotter pins. Slip into frame. Put large, tight-fitting washers over the ends. Then put on wheels and more washers. Set cotter pins in holes.

Holes in steel wagon bottom. Scrape off paint around holes and clean metal with steel wool. Spread on epoxy mender, and smooth.

EXTERIOR WALL—ALL TYPES

See also the following entries.

Open cracks between siding and window or door frame, chimney, etc. Scrape out loose caulking, if any. Fill with new silicone or polysulfide rubber caulking. Squeeze into large cracks with a caulking gun; squeeze from tube or use a putty knife for small cracks.

Paint blistered and peeling. Scrape down to the base with a putty knife or scraper, steel brush, and coarse sandpaper. If a lot of paint must be removed, use a paste-type paint remover or electric paint remover. If you scorch surface, sand well to remove carbon.

Before repainting, remember that blistering is an indication of some deep-seated problem. If blisters are concentrated around windows and doors, water may be entering around the frames, so renew the caulking. If blisters are under eaves, make sure gutters are in good shape. Install metal drip edges along roof edges to force water to fall straight into gutters or to the ground. If blisters are widespread, you probably have a condensation problem in the house. See BASIC METHODS: HOW TO STOP CONDENSATION.

Covered with tendrils of vines. Scrape these off as well as you can: it's harder than it looks. Then scrub with a fairly strong solution of trisodium phosphate to loosen the roots and remove the stains.

EXTERIOR WALL, ALUMINUM

Leaks. Look for trouble (though it's rare) in vertical joints. Caulk joints with polysulfide rubber or silicone.

Dents. If large and objectionable, sand off finish and smear in epoxy mender. File smooth and level when dry. Then repaint.

Dirt and stains. Wash with trisodium phosphate. Use chlorine bleach to remove mildew.

Rattles in wind. It should have been installed with backer strips of insulation, but there isn't much you can do about that now. Locate the sections that make the most noise and squirt caulking compound under the butt edges.

EXTERIOR WALL, ASBESTOS-CEMENT SHINGLE

Broken shingles. See ROOF, ASBESTOS-CEMENT SHINGLE.

Copper and rust stains. Scrub with household cleaner. If this is not completely effective, use a cleanser, such as Zud, containing oxalic acid.

Moss growth. See ROOF—ALL TYPES.

EXTERIOR WALL—ASPHALT ROLL SIDING

Bulges. Carefully pry up bottom edge of the siding strip above the one affected and then slightly loosen the nails along the top edge of the bulging strip. If bulge does not disappear after a few days of warm weather, loosen the bottom edge of the strip and with a stick reach up under the strip and smear asphalt roofing cement under the bulge. Press down. If this does not eliminate bulge (don't count on it) the only thing left to do is carefully cut through the bulge along the "mortar" lines in the siding, spread asphalt roofing cement under the cut edges, overlap the edges, and wedge a board flat against them for several days.

EXTERIOR WALL, BRICK

Brick broken, loose. See BRICK.
Mortar joints cracked. See BRICK.
Efflorescence on brick. See BRICK.
Water leaks through wall. If walls become slightly damp on the inside during prolonged wet weather and the problem is not attributable to cracks, the entire wall needs to be damp-proofed. Use either a transparent, colorless silicone waterproofing compound, or portland cement paint. To apply former: clean walls, remove old oil paint and whitewash but not cement paint. Let walls dry. Then brush or spray on two coats of silicone. This should be renewed in 5 years.

To apply portland cement paint, remove old oil paint and clean wall thoroughly. With a scrubbing brush apply first coat of paint mixed according to manufacturer's directions. Work it well into pores. Let dry for several hours, then fog wall with clear water several times during next 24 hours. Apply a second coat of paint on damp surface. After it has set, keep damp for 48 hours.
Stains. See BRICK.

EXTERIOR WALL, CONCRETE BLOCK

Water leaks through wall. See BASEMENT WALL or EXTERIOR WALL, BRICK.

Mortar joints cracked or eroded. Chip out loose and weak mortar and blow crumbs from joints. Wet with water. Mix 1 part masonry cement and 3 parts sand, and pack into joints. Finish to match surrounding joints.

For very small cracks, brush in a soupy grout made of equal parts of masonry cement and fine sand.
Efflorescence. See BRICK.
Stains. See BRICK.

EXTERIOR WALL, HARDBOARD

Holes. Fill with water putty and repaint. If hole is large, cut it out in a rectangle with a sharp chisel. Nail in a patch of hardboard. And fill joints with water putty.
Stains. See PAINTED SURFACE.

EXTERIOR WALL, PLYWOOD

Holes. Fill small holes with water putty or plastic wood. Cut out large holes in a rectangle with a sharp chisel or circular saw. Nail in a patch of same thickness. Fill joints around edges with water putty.
Rotten. If only a small area is affected, scrape out rotten wood. Saturate the area with pentachlorophenol and let dry for 48 hours. Then fill with water putty. If rot is extensive, cut out the area and set in a patch.
Delaminated. Make a slit through the veneer with a sharp knife. Spread resorcinol glue underneath. Nail down veneer with small galvanized nails or put a brace against it until glue dries. Then spread plastic wood or water putty into cut.
Stains. See PAINTED SURFACE.

EXTERIOR WALL, STEEL

Leaks. Look for leaks in vertical joints and caulk with polysulfide rubber or silicone.
Scratches, scars. Sand immediately to eliminate rust; apply metal primer, and repaint.
Rattles in wind. Siding should have been installed with insulation backing. You can't correct this now, and there's not much you can

do to stop rattling entirely. Locate sections that make the most noise and run a bead of caulking compound in under the edges.

Dirt and stains. Wash with trisodium phosphate. Use chlorine bleach to remove mildew.

EXTERIOR WALL, STONE

Mortar joints cracked, crumbling. Chip out broken mortar. Blow out crumbs with vacuum cleaner. Then pack in 1 part cement and 3 parts sand mixed to a thick plastic consistency. Finish to match old joints.

Water leaks through walls that are not cracked. See EXTERIOR WALL, BRICK.

Stains. See BRICK.

EXTERIOR WALL, STUCCO

Cracks. Cut open with a chisel or old screwdriver. Blow out crumbs with vacuum cleaner and wet with water. Fill with prepared stucco mixture from a masonry supplies outlet.

Loose, broken, bulging. Remove all defective stucco. If wire lath is broken or rusted, cut it out and nail in a new piece after covering the sheathing with waterproof building paper. Wet edges of surrounding stucco with water before applying each of three new coats of stucco.

For the first coat, mix 1 part portland cement, 3 parts sand and hydrated lime equal to no more than one-tenth of the weight of the cement. Trowel firmly onto lath and cover the surface with crisscross scratches so the next coat will adhere. After stucco has set up, keep it damp for 48 hours. Then sprinkle with water, and trowel on second coat mixed in same way. It should come to within ¼ inch of the wall surface. Scratch surface and keep damp for 48 hours. Then let dry for 5 days.

Use the same mortar for the third coat or buy prepared stucco mixture. Apply to a damp surface. Finish to match surrounding stucco. Keep damp for 48 hours. Cover with damp burlap if exposed to sun.

EXTERIOR WALL, VINYL

Leaks. Look for leaks in vertical joints and caulk with silicone caulking.

Dirt and stains. Wash with trisodium phosphate.

EXTERIOR WALL, WOOD

Holes. If holes are small, fill with spackle made for exterior use. For large holes, use water putty after priming the holes with oil-base paint. For very large holes, cut a piece of wood to fit and nail or glue in place; then fill nail holes and cracks around edges of plug with spackle.

Siding warped slightly. Try to straighten gradually by driving screws through the siding and tightening them bit by bit until board is more or less flat again. Fill wide cracks left around board with silicone or polysulfide rubber caulking.

Badly warped, cracked, or rotten siding. Cut out defective section with a saw and chisel. Replace with new length of wood and secure in place with galvanized nails.

Stains. See WOOD.

EXTERIOR WALL, WOOD SHINGLE

Holes. Fill with water putty and groove lightly with a comb or nail to match the shingle grain. If shingles are stained or natural, use plastic wood instead of water putty and mix it with a little stain before applying.

Shingle cracked. Loosen overlapping shingles slightly, reach up under them with a hacksaw blade, and cut nails holding defective shingle. Trim new shingle to fill space and hold it in place by driving two or three galvanized finishing nails through it just below the butts of the overhanging shingles.

Shingle warped. Replace it if the warp is very bad; otherwise simply drive a galvanized nail through it and push it back slightly into place. Drive nail in a bit further about a week later, a week after that, and so forth until shingle lies flat.

EYEGLASSES

Plastic frame broken. Apply plastic-mending adhesive to break. Allow a little excess glue to remain on surface of frame; it will add strength, but being transparent it will not show. Press pieces together until glue sets.

Steel frame bent. Bend back into shape by hand or with smooth-jawed pliers.

Plastic on nosepiece cracked. Coat with a thin layer of plastic-mending adhesive.

Pin missing. Use wire or paper clip until it can be replaced with new screw.

FAIENCE

Broken. Clean and coat broken surface with a thin layer of cellulose cement. Press together for 6 hours. See also EARTHENWARE.

FAN, ATTIC

Doesn't run. Check whether switch is on. Check if fuse has blown. Then call a serviceman.

Runs slowly. Apply oil at oiling points. Examine drive belt and adjust tension. Check motor (see ELECTRIC MOTOR). Then call a serviceman.

Vibrates noisily. Make sure fan is securely mounted. Examine and, if necessary, replace vibration dampeners under it. If noise continues, call serviceman.

Fan blades loose. Make sure fan is positioned properly then tighten. You may need an allen wrench of the proper size to do this.

FAN, ELECTRIC

Doesn't run. Disconnect and examine cord and plug. If broken, repair (see ELECTRIC CORD). If the switch doesn't seem to work properly (the push-button type often fails to catch when it is old) and if it's possible to open fan housing easily, replace the switch. Should these measures fail, take fan to a service shop.

Runs slowly. Disconnect and turn blades by hand. If they feel stiff, apply a couple of drops of light oil either at oiling point (if there is one) or on shaft where it enters motor housing. Turn blades to loosen them. Then, if shaft was oiled, remove excess oil with a rag.

Doesn't oscillate. Clean grease, oil, and dirt from oscillating mechanism under fan and apply a couple of drops of SAE number 10 oil to moving parts.

Fan blade bent. Try straightening by hand. If this is impossible, take blades off shaft, lay bent blade on a flat surface, and tap out the bend with a block of wood or a wood or hard-rubber mallet.

FAN, VENTILATING

Doesn't run. Is switch on? Has fuse blown? Remove grille and check whether lead wires are connected tightly. If fan still doesn't work, call an electrician.

Noisy, slow. Remove grille. Clean out grease and dust by scraping and with sponge soaked in detergent solution. Lubricate motor at oiling points with light oil.

Wind cover doesn't close when fan is off. Remove hood and clean out grease and dirt by scraping and with detergent solution. Oil moving parts.

FAUCET

Compression faucet drips. Shut off water to faucet. Pull off handle and escutcheon cap, if any. Unscrew large packing nut at top of faucet assembly and screw out stem assembly. (Wrap nut with adhesive tape so you don't scratch it.) Unscrew old screw holding washer with a screwdriver, or if the screw head is damaged, with pliers. If screw breaks off in stem, place stem in vise and carefully bore it out with a small metal drill. Replace old washer—and old screw if damaged—with a new one of the same size. Use either a washer that is flat on both sides or one that is conical on one side. In the latter case, install the washer with the conical side pointing down. Reassemble the faucet.

Note that the washer is surrounded at the base by a tiny collar of brass. If the collar breaks off at one point, file the entire thing off. Then slip on a "no-rotate" washer, which is held in place by prongs rather than a screw.

If the faucet continues to drip, the valve seat below the washer is probably rough and uneven. If the faucet was made before World War II, the seat can be smoothed with a special tool, called a valve seat grinder, available from a hardware or plumbing supplies store. To use this, turn off the water and remove the stem assembly of the faucet. Screw the cone-shaped part of the grinder into the top of the faucet, and then carefully revolve the spindle until the seat is smooth.

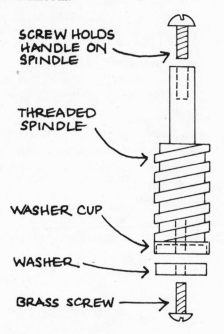

SCREW HOLDS HANDLE ON SPINDLE

THREADED SPINDLE

WASHER CUP

WASHER

BRASS SCREW

In more modern faucets, the valve seat is designed to be screwed out of the faucet with a large allen wrench or, in a pinch, a screwdriver. Replace it with a new seat.

Compression faucet leaks around faucet stem. Remove faucet handle and escutcheon, if any, and tighten the packing nut slightly until the drip stops. If this doesn't work, turn off water, unscrew packing nut and stem assembly. If there are small rubber rings, called O rings, on stem, replace them with new rings of the same size, and close faucet up again. If the stem is devoid of rings, wrap graphite wicking around the stem once or twice and force it into the packing nut. Then reassemble the faucet. If graphite wicking is unavailable, cotton string

can be used instead, but don't count on its lasting.

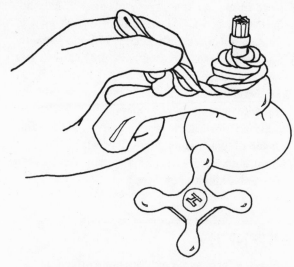

Faucet chatters when water is turned off. On a compression faucet, the trouble may be caused by a worn or loose washer or because the packing nut is loose. Repair as above. On other faucets, tighten the stem assembly slightly.

American-Standard Aquaseal faucet drips. In this faucet, a rubber diaphragm takes the place of the washer and valve seat found in a compression faucet. Shut off water. Lift off faucet handle and tighten big cap nut slightly. If drip doesn't stop, unscrew cap nut and lift out valve stem. Pry out rubber diaphragm in the valve body below the stem (but it may come out with the stem). Replace with a new diaphragm.

American-Standard single-lever faucet drips. In this faucet, hot and cold water are controlled by one handle, which tips back to turn on water and swings to right or left to control the temperature. Shut off both hot and cold water supply. Remove the escutcheon and unscrew two large cap nuts on either side of faucet assembly. Lift out wire mesh screens and wash them. Take out stainless steel valves and polish the faces with a pencil eraser. Clean valve seats with eraser. Then replace parts.

American-Standard push-pull faucet drips. In this faucet, water flow is controlled by pulling handle out or pushing it in; temperature is controlled by turning handle. Directions for fixing faucet are printed on a paper hidden behind a removable plate in the back of the faucet. To stop dripping, turn off hot and cold water. Disconnect pop-up rod under bowl and lift it out through top of faucet. With a ³⁄₁₆-inch allen wrench, remove the bushing through which pop-up rod ran. Grasp the front of the spout and lift it off with a slight rocking motion. Remove the little screen, valve stems, and spring assemblies. Clean rubber surface of the valve seats with a pencil eraser. Replace stem assemblies and screens. Slightly deform screens to an oval shape so they will fit tight.

On some models of this faucet, the screens are omitted. In that case, simply pull out the springs and valve stems and clean the valve seats.

In either case, if the valve seats are damaged, remove them with a ⁵⁄₁₆-inch allen wrench and replace with new seats.

Crane Dial-ese faucet drips. Turn off water. Remove handle screw and lift off handle with a wrench, remove locknut by turning it counterclockwise, but leave gasket alone. Remove Dialese control unit with a wrench. Unscrew the large piece at the top of the control and pull the rest apart. Replace the small seat ring near the bottom of the control unit with a new ring. Apply a little heavy grease to the threads of the long, narrow stempiece, then reassemble the entire control unit. The large top piece should be screwed hand-tight, no more. Replace the control unit in the faucet and screw on locknut.

Moen single-handle faucet leaks. Turn off hot and cold water. Remove handle cover, handle, and stop valve. Lift out retainer clip and pull valve cartridge out of the body. Push new cartridge all the way into the body until the front of the ears on the valve cartridge are flush with it. Replace the retainer clip so the legs straddle the cartridge ears, and slide it down in the bottom slot in the valve body. Replace stop tube, handle, and handle cover. When mounting handle, be sure the red flat surface on the stem of the valve cartridge points up.

Delta single-handle faucet leaks. Turn off hot and cold water. Loosen small setscrew in handle and pull off handle. Unscrew round cap under handle. Pull up stem to remove cam and ball to which it's attached. From the body of the faucet lift and replace the two rubber seat-and-spring assemblies. If the ball on the stem is rough

around either of the two small holes, it should also be replaced. Then reassemble, making sure that the slide in the side of the ball is inserted over the pin in the body above the seat assemblies, and that the lug on the side of the cam is inserted in the slot on the side of the body. Make sure round cap is tight before replacing handle. Also tighten the adjusting ring at the top of the cap.

Delta two-handle faucet leaks. Turn off water. Take out cap in top of handle, remove screw, and lift off handle. Unscrew the topmost nut that is exposed. Note how the stem assembly is installed, and pull it out. Remove the seat and spring assembly in the body of the faucet and replace it. Then replace the stem in the position you found it, and tighten nut securely around it.

Delta faucet with single knurled handle leaks. Turn off hot and cold water. Pull out plastic cap in top of handle, remove screw, and lift off handle. Then follow directions above for single-handle faucet.

Bradley single-handle faucet leaks. Turn off water. Pull out cap in top of handle, remove screw beneath, and lift knob and lever handle from the serrated end of the cam. Press the cam down. Swing knob and lever back roughly 90 degrees, slide them to the right, and remove the lever. Then remove the three screws at the base of the cam bearing and lift off bearing. Remove cam, sleeve, and cartridge from faucet body. Install a replacement sleeve. Be sure to line up the flat on the serrated end of the cam with the flat in the serrated hole in the knob. Reassemble handle.

Bradley faucet with single knurled handle leaks. Turn off hot and cold water. Pull out cap in top of handle, remove screw underneath, and lift off stem. Remove the three screws at the base of the cam bearing, lift off bearing, and proceed as above.

Faucet aerator clogged. Unscrew by hand or wrap it with adhesive tape and use pliers. Remove strainers, noting exactly how they were installed. Wash under running water. Then replace strainers in the same sequence and positions you found them.

Faucet escutcheons loose, water and dirt seep out from underneath. Remove faucet handles. To tighten or loosen an escutcheon that is not held in place by any visible means, simply turn it with your hand. Other escutcheons are held by small nuts (which may resemble washers) at the top. If these cannot be turned by hand, use a wrench and take pains not to damage the metal, by covering it, if you can, with adhesive tape.

FEATHER

Ornamental feather bent, broken. Poke a stiff wire of appropriate diameter up through the quill and well past the break. If you can work some cellulose glue into the break, so much the better.

Edge of ornamental feather torn from quill. Usually there is a sliver of quill still attached to the feathers. Glue this to the body of the quill with cellulose glue.

FELT

Holes, slashes, in loose felt. Cut a patch about ¾ inch larger in all dimensions than the hole. Feather edges with a razor blade. Apply fabric glue and smooth down.

Holes, slashes, in pasted-down felt. Hold a scrap over the damaged area and cut a square through both layers at once with a razor blade. Remove damaged felt and set in patch with appropriate glue.

Felt loose from wood. Clean off old glue. Apply a thin layer of white glue to felt and smooth down.

Felt loose from glass, ceramics, metal, plastics, etc. Clean off old glue. Apply a thin layer of rubber cement to both surfaces. Let set for 5 minutes and press together.

Felt loose from wall. Clean off old glue. Reglue with wheat paste.

FENCE, SOLID STEEL

Posts set in concrete wobble. Chip out concrete about 1 inch around posts and blow out crumbs. Fill with quick-setting cement and round it off at the top so water drains away from the posts.

Rusted. Chip off loose paint with a cold chisel, old screwdriver, or stiff putty knife. Remove rest of paint with a rasp. Sand well to remove particles of rust. Prime with red metal primer and follow with one or two coats of exterior alkyd trim paint.

Pickets or other parts broken. If break is clean, remove rust, apply epoxy glue to both surfaces, press together, and clamp with splints on either side of break. Separate steel from splints with wax paper. This repair will not take much abuse, however.

Pickets eaten away by rust, pieces missing. Have new pickets made by a blacksmith. To remove old pickets, cut through them on top and bottom of the rails and drill out what's left with an electric drill. When setting in new pickets, use epoxy glue and epoxy mender to hold them in rails; however, they should really be welded.

FENCE, STEEL MESH

Posts set in concrete wobble. Chip out concrete around base of posts and blow out crumbs. Pack in quick-setting cement and round it off at the top so water will drain away from posts.

Rusted. Wire-brush to expose clean metal as much as possible. Apply a red metal primer, then one or two coats of exterior trim enamel. To save work, apply paint with a roller with a very long nap.

FENCE, WOOD

Posts wobble. If posts are sound, clean thoroughly and saturate them with creosote or other oil-base wood preservative such as pentachlorophenol. Dig holes 16 inches deep and 12 inches wide around them. Pour in concrete made of 1 part portland cement, 2¼ parts sand, and 3 parts gravel of not more than 1½-inch diameter. Tamp well. Slope top of concrete away from posts.

Posts rotten. Replace with redwood or cypress posts or with posts made of other wood that has been soaked for 24 hours in creosote or oil-base pentachlorophenol.

Posts rotting at top. If you don't have to replace

them, dig out soft wood completely and soak with pentachlorophenol. Fill with plastic wood or water putty. Then cover top with a slanting board or with aluminum flashing.

Rails, pickets, boards rotting. If rot has not progressed too far, dig out soft wood, saturate holes with pentachlorophenol, and fill holes with water putty or plastic wood.

Wide top rails hold water and are split. The best solution is to replace rails entirely. Install new ones on a slight slant so water will run off. If you must salvage old rails, cut down the top and edges with a drawknife so water will run off. Saturate splits with pentachlorophenol and then fill with plastic wood or water putty.

Rail in post-and-rail fence broken. If the break runs with the grain, coat the edges with resorcinol glue and clamp together. Then to reinforce the mend, drive long screws or bolts through the broken pieces.

If the rail should be replaced, you must dig out around one of the posts on either side of the break so it is very loose. This will allow you to move the post back and forth so you can set in the new rail. The job is almost impossible otherwise.

FIBER GLASS—FABRIC

Holes in fiber glass fabrics. Darn with fiber glass yarn or sew on a patch of matching fabric with cotton thread. See CLOTHING—FABRICS. Patches can also be glued to the fabric, but you must use methyl methacrylate "invisible" glue.

Grease stains on fiber glass fabrics. Place a blotter or absorbent rag under stain and drip trichloroethylene on stain. Don't rub. This method works pretty well on solid-colored fabrics but will probably fade prints (and unfortunately there is no other way to clean the latter).

Rust stains on fiber glass fabrics. These are impossible to remove. Make sure that drapery hooks and hardware you use are rustproof.

Other stains on fiber glass fabrics. Sponge on lukewarm, soapy water. Do not rub.

Paint on fiber glass fabrics. Pick paint off with your fingernails when it dries.

FIBER GLASS, RIGID

Shallow scratches. Sand clean and brush on polyester resin available from boat dealers.

Deep scratches, gouges. Sand. Mix 1/8-inch cuttings of fiber glass mat or cloth with polyester resin to form a putty. Trowel into scratch. Sand smooth when dry.

Breaks in opaque fiber glass. Open small breaks with a file. Then, with a disk sander, feather back the edges around the hole for about 3 inches. Out of fiber glass cloth or mat, cut a patch to cover sanded area. Lay it on a sheet of cellophane, spread polyester resin uniformly over it, cover with another sheet of cellophane, and, with your hands or a wood paddle, work the resin thoroughly into the fabric. Then brush polyester resin on area to be patched. Remove top sheet of cellophane from patch, lay patch over hole, and smooth down. When resin has set, remove cellophane. Sand patch and apply additional patches in the same way until the desired thickness is reached. Then sand, and brush on one or two most coats of resin to obliterate the weave of the cloth. See illustration under BOAT, MOLDED FIBER GLASS.

If break is large and compound, cut the damaged area with a metal-cutting saw and feather back the edges of the hole. Mold a thin sheet of aluminum or a piece of shirt cardboard covered with cellophane over the hole on one side and hold in place with masking tape. Then patch hole with fiber glass cloth or mat as above.

Polyester resin cures best at a temperature of about 70 degrees. Below 55 degrees it will not cure satisfactorily. However, you can use the resin at this temperature if an infrared bulb is directed on the patch from a distance of no less than 14 inches.

If the repair must match a colored surface, you can add a color pigment to the resin. But an exact match is difficult to achieve. It is easier to apply paint. If doing this, sand the fiber glass well to roughen it. Then apply an epoxy primer followed by epoxy enamel or alkyd enamel.

Breaks in translucent fiber glass. If this type of material is not used for decorative purposes repair it like opaque fiber glass. Otherwise, clean the broken edges, dry thoroughly, and glue together with polyester resin. But note that the joint is very weak and will last only if the fiber glass is not subjected to strain; therefore, it may be advisable to reinforce it by bolting small pieces of fiber glass across the back of the break.

FIGURINE

Wood figurine broken. If the break is large, apply white glue to one edge and press together. But if the break is too small to offer an adequate gluing surface (for example, if an upraised hand breaks off at the wrist), a strong repair is difficult to make with glue alone. In this case, push a straight pin about ¼ inch into one broken edge. Cut off all but ¼ inch of the exposed pin. With a tiny drill or awl make a corresponding hole in the other broken edge. It can be larger than the pin in order to permit perfect alignment of the broken pieces. Apply a thin coat of cellulose cement to both broken edges and let dry. Then apply a second coat to the edge with the hole and fill hole, too. Bring pieces together, align, and hold in place until glue sets.

Instead of a pin, a round toothpick can be used if the broken edges are large enough to permit drilling for the toothpick. Use white glue to stick pieces together.

Ceramic figurine broken. If the break is large, coat both edges with cellulose cement and press together. If break is small and figurine is hollow, try cyanoacrylate glue. If this doesn't work, shape a short length of balsa wood to fill the hollow. (Lacking balsa wood, use a small roll of paper.) Insert it halfway in one broken piece. Then coat broken edges with cellulose cement. Slip other end of the "splint" into other broken piece and press the pieces together until glue sets.

Wax figurine broken. If broken surface is large, hold the two pieces close together and melt both surfaces at the same time with a match. Immediately press together. If break is small, stick a needle halfway into one broken piece.

Align edges as best you can. Then stick bottom end of needle into other broken piece. If figurine is not handled too much, this repair will be adequate, but there is a good chance that the top piece will swivel on the needle. If this happens, replace needle with a flat-sided toothpick or a small flat strip of metal.

FILE, CARPENTER'S

Teeth clogged, file smooth. Brush with a wire brush. If soft metal such as solder has clogged teeth, scrape clean with a knife.

Tang loose in wood handle. See CUTLERY, KITCHEN.

FIREPLACE, MASONRY

Smokes. Take the following steps in the order given:

(1) See that damper is working properly. Scrub off caked-on carbon with a wire brush and putty knife. Oil the pivots. If broken, have it replaced.

Reach up into firebox and clean off smoke shelf behind damper.

(2) Clean chimney. See CHIMNEY.

(3) Check whether chimney is high enough. It should rise at least 2 feet above the peak of a pitched roof, 3 feet above a nearly flat roof. If it doesn't meet these specifications, cap the chimney as follows.

First, lay up four columns of bricks on top of the chimney at the corners. Lay the bricks flat. Cement them together and to the chimney top with a mixture of 1 part masonry cement and 3 parts sand. Then cement a thin flagstone cut the size of the chimney to the tops of the columns. The four openings under the flagstone must have a combined area at least equal to the area of the chimney flue. If there are two or more flues in the chimney, build withes—solid walls of brick—between them. These should extend from the chimney top to the flagstone and across the width of the chimney. The area of the three openings surrounding each flue should equal the area of the flue.

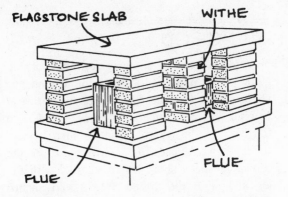

FLAGSTONE SLAB WITHE FLUE FLUE

(4) Decrease the size of the fireplace opening. First build a fire in the firebox. Hold a long wide board against the chimney breast and lower it gradually over the fireplace opening. When smoke stops billowing into the room, measure the distance from the bottom of the board to the top of the opening. You can now have a metal hood made to cover the top of the opening to the same point.

The alternative is to build up the bottom of the firebox to a height equal to the board. Try this first with bricks laid without mortar, and build another fire. If fireplace draws correctly, as it should, set new firebricks permanently in the firebox with fire clay, a type of mortar available from masonry supplies outlets.

Multiopening fireplace smokes. Follow steps 1 through 3 above. If these don't correct problem, call in a mason who is an expert in building fireplaces. He may have to install heat-resistant glass doors in one or more of the openings or install a small exhaust fan in the flue.

Wind or rain blows down chimney. Cap it.

Mortar joints in firebox and hearth cracked. Chip out bad mortar and blow out crumbs. Wet edges of bricks. Pack in fire clay.

Hearth settling. Call in mason.

Large cracks between hearth and floor. Shape strips of wood matching floor to fill cracks and glue in place with white glue.

Smoke stains on fireplace breast. Scrub with cleansing powder.

FIREPLACE, PREFAB METAL

Smokes. Clean flue. Increase height of flue or cap chimney.

Joints open in fireplace or flue pipe. Brush off soot and wash with detergent. Dry and clean metal with steel wool. Then spread on epoxy mender.

Dents in fireplace. Hold a block of wood against concave side and hammer out dents. Use light blows, especially if exterior is porcelain-enameled.

FIREPLACE SCREEN

Hole in mesh. Weave in steel wire and paint black or gold.

Flexible screen slides stiffly. Clean out track with a toothbrush and cleaning fluid. Squirt in powdered graphite.

Traverse-type flexible screens don't meet at center of fireplace. See CURTAIN ROD.

Rusted. Brush hard with a steel brush. Apply red metal primer followed by an oil-base enamel.

FIREPLACE TOOLS

Tip of poker loose. Remove tip by unscrewing. Clean threads and hole. Coat threads with epoxy mender and screw tip back in place.

Hole in bellows. Cut a patch out of any impermeable, flexible matching material such as light leather or vinyl, and glue over hole with rubber.

Tool broken. Have it welded.

FISHING LURES

Hooks rusted. Rub them over fine emery cloth.

Hooks missing from lures. Buy new hook and open screw eye from tackle store. Screw screw eye part way into lure; slip hook into eye. Close eye with small pliers, and screw screw eye in tight.

If screw eye doesn't hold tightly in lure, dip end in epoxy glue before screwing into lure.

Paint on lure damaged. Scrape or sand paint off carefully or dip the lure in paint remover to soften paint. Smooth lure as necessary with steel wool, but don't change the shape. Prime with an exterior alkyd primer and overcoat with exterior alkyd gloss trim paint. To improve life of paint, put on a final coat of clear epoxy or spar varnish.

The easiest way to paint most lures is by dipping into paint. Be careful, however, to remove blob that hangs on the bottom before it dries. The alternative is to spray the lures. Brushing is the least desirable because it's difficult to get an even coat; but some brushing is usually necessary to paint on eyes or gills or, of course, when the body is several colors.

FISHING REEL

NOTE. If you keep a reel clean and lubricated, it presents few problems. Make a habit of taking it apart at least once—and preferably two or three times—a year. A reel that is exposed to salt spray should be cleaned monthly, and if it is ever wet with salt water, it should be cleaned at once.

When cleaning, take the reel apart as much as you can and spray the entire thing thoroughly with gun solvent. Then go over it with a paper towel and soft cloth. Finally, lubricate thoroughly but sparingly. An aerosol is good for this. In the gear boxes of spinning reels, use a very lightweight grease recommended for the purpose (but it's generally best to leave the gears alone unless it has been a long time since you looked at them or unless you know that water has gotten into them).

Parts worn or broken. Save yourself trouble and buy replacement parts.

Level-wind doesn't work properly in bait-casting reel. Take out screw holding the level-wind bar and remove the bar. Then shake the level-wind until the small brass pawl comes out. Replace with a new pawl that is lightly oiled.

Line jammed behind spin-cast reel spool. Remove hood of reel and line spool. Pull out line and place it behind the pin that picks it up when in use. Then reassemble the spool, pull line through hole in hood, and screw on hood.

FISHING ROD

Line guide off or loose. Clean rod and position guide on it. Wrap cellophane tape around one leg to hold it in place. Use silk or nylon thread to bind legs permanently in place. Wind from the base of the leg to about ⅛ inch beyond the end. To anchor the starting end of the thread, drape a short length parallel with the leg and wind the thread over it. To anchor the other end, as you approach it, loop a piece of monofilament line from the eye of the guide out beyond the end of the leg and back to the eye. Wrap the thread tightly over this for about eight turns; stick the end through the loop, and pull it back under the wrapping by pulling on the loop. Then cut off the loose ends of line and thread.

The thread must, of course, be wrapped tightly so the turns touch. When completed, brush on a fixative such as that used on toy models. Overcoat with rod varnish.

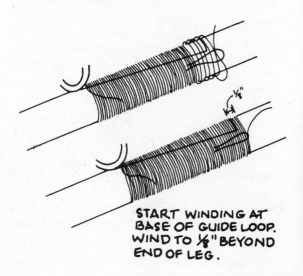

START WINDING AT BASE OF GUIDE LOOP. WIND TO ⅛" BEYOND END OF LEG.

Ferrule loose. Remove it and clean off rod. Melt and smear ferrule cement on end of rod and replace ferrule. Make sure it's straight. If ferrule seems to be a little too big for rod, wrap the rod tightly with nylon or silk thread and cover this with the cement before replacing ferrule.

Tip broken. Heat the tip guide just enough to

soften ferrule cement so guide can be pulled loose. If guide is not held with cement, bore out the broken rod. Cut off the rod end cleanly. Test whether guide will fit over it; if not, you must thin the rod down very slightly with a knife. Then coat with ferrule cement, quickly push on tip guide, and let dry.

Cord handle deteriorating. Cut it off down to the base and clean the base well. If you can buy a preshaped replacement handle of the proper design, do so. Glue it on with resorcinol or epoxy glue. The alternative is to buy cork rings made for the purpose. These are about the size and shape of circular napkin rings. Dry-fit them on the handle base. If the holes need to be enlarged, soak the corks in boiling water so you can drill or shape them without damaging them. Glue the fitted rings to the handle and to one another with resorcinol glue. Let dry for at least 24 hours. Then shape the cork to the proper size and contour with a rasp, file, and sandpaper.

FLAGSTONE

Mortar joints between stones cracked or eroded. Chip out loose and weak mortar. Blow out dust with vacuum cleaner. Mix 1 part portland cement and 2 to 3 parts sand with just enough water to make a plastic, but not runny, mixture. Pack this into joints and smooth to match nearby joints. Wipe off mortar stains on stones with a wet rag.

Broken. Clean edges well; coat with epoxy glue, and press together for 6 hours. Make sure base on which stone is set is level; otherwise, stone may break again along the same line.

Stone set in mortar loose. See WALK, STONE.

Stone set in sand heaved or sunken. See WALK, BRICK.

Stains. See BRICK.

FLASHING, ALUMINUM

Leaks around edges. Pry up the metal slightly and smear fibered asphalt roofing cement underneath. Then nail down tight. Remember that flashing around chimneys and plumbing vents should overlap the roofing. If for some reason it doesn't (usually because the roof was reroofed incorrectly), take up shingles and put the flashing over them.

Small holes. Use steel wool on surface and smear on epoxy mender or asphalt roofing cement.

Large holes, tears. Cut a patch out of aluminum flashing. Use steel wool on area around hole and underside of patch. Spread epoxy mender on flashing and embed patch in this. Fibered asphalt roofing cement can be used instead of epoxy but is not as permanent.

Chimney flashing buckled or loose. Force together seams that have come apart, crimp edges, and seal with epoxy mender. If metal has pulled loose from mortar joints or mortar is crumbling, clean out joints. Force aluminum back in place. Fill joints with silicone or polysulfide rubber caulking.

FLASHING, ASPHALT ROLL ROOFING

Holes, tears. Nail down as necessary with asphalt roofing nails. Smear fibered asphalt roofing cement over break.

Leaks. The flashing should be replaced, but if you want a shortcut, simply brush on several coats of unfibered asphalt roofing cement.

FLASHING, COPPER

Leaks. See FLASHING, ALUMINUM.

Small holes. Clean with steel wool until bright. Smear on epoxy mender.

Large holes, tears. Solder on a patch of copper. See COPPER. For safety, use a soldering iron rather than a torch.

Chimney flashing buckled or loose. Force together seams that have come apart, and solder. If metal has pulled loose from mortar joints or if mortar has crumbled, rake out joints and pack in latex cement. Or wet joints with water and pack in mortar made of 1 part portland cement and 2 parts sand.

FLASHING, GALVANIZED STEEL

Leaks. See FLASHING, ALUMINUM.

Small holes. Clean thoroughly with steel wool. Remove all rust. Cover with epoxy mender. Prime with red metal primer and apply finish paint or unfibered asphalt roofing cement.

Large holes, tears. Cut a patch out of galvanized steel. Use steel wool on one side of patch and metal around hole. Spread on epoxy mender and embed patch in it.

Chimney flashing buckled or loose. See FLASHING, COPPER.

FLASHING, RUBBER

Leaks. Rubber flashing is used only around vent stacks. Raise edges, clean them, and spread fibered asphalt roofing cement underneath.

Holes. Roughen rubber with sandpaper. Squeeze plastic rubber into holes.

FLASHLIGHT

NOTE. For a flashlight to work, electric current must flow from the positive terminal (the small brass button) of the battery to the filament and back to the negative terminal (the zinc bottom) of the battery. In a tubular flashlight the current flows from the brass button of the top battery to the bottom of the bulb, through the filament, then out through the screw base of the bulb to the reflector, then to a metal strip attached to the bottom of the turn-on switch, then to the coiled spring in the base of the flashlight, and finally to the zinc base of the bottom battery. For the circuit to be complete, the batteries must be arranged so that the brass button of the bottom battery touches the zinc base of the one next nearest the light; the brass button of the top battery must touch the base of the lamp; the metal strip on the bottom of the switch must touch the reflector; and the spring in the base of the flashlight must touch the zinc base of the bottom battery.

In an electric lantern, the circuit is completed in the same way, but in this case the positive and negative terminals of the large square battery are close together on top of the battery. They make contact with the bulb and switch by an arrangement of metal strips which are readily located when the lantern case is opened.

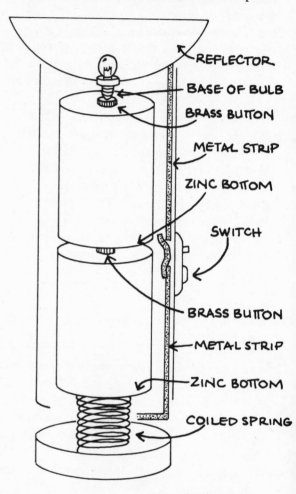

Light dim. If the batteries are not weak (have them checked), clean positive and negative terminals with fine sandpaper or emery cloth, or by scraping with a knife. Clean contact point at base of lamp socket. Remove spring from base of flashlight case, clean thoroughly, and stretch it slightly. With a screwdriver, scrape out rust in case below spring.

Light blinks. Clean and stretch spring in base of case. Seat reflector securely and make sure metal strip on switch touches it. Clean all other contact points.

Light doesn't work at all. Be certain that batteries are not reversed. Have them tested. Have bulb tested. Clean all contact points with sandpaper or a knife. If switch is difficult to operate, clean under the metal strip inside the case with sandpaper. Bend metal strip so it touches reflector.

FLOOR, ASPHALT TILE

Tile broken. Crack tile with a hammer into small pieces and dig them out. Work from the center of the tile toward the edges so you don't damage the edges. Scrape adhesive from subfloor. Spread in new asphalt-tile adhesive and set in tile. If subfloor is uneven, heat tile briefly in a low oven until it is slightly pliable, and set in place at once.

If new tile is a trifle larger than the hole, place it upright on a large piece of coarse sandpaper and scrape it back and forth to sand the edge down slightly.

Holes. Replace tile as above.

Tile loose. This usually occurs when tiles are laid over a concrete floor containing too much moisture. There's nothing to do but take the tile up and scrape adhesive off the back. Remove adhesive from subfloor. Let concrete dry out thoroughly. Then reset tile in fresh adhesive.

Stains. See FLOOR, VINYL.

FLOOR, CERAMIC TILE

Cracks between tiles. Clean out old mortar completely. Soak tile edges with water. Then smear on a prepared tile grout; shape to match other joints, and remove excess with a damp rag.

Other problems. See TILE, CERAMIC.

FLOOR, CONCRETE

Cracks. See CONCRETE.

Badly broken. Break out bad area with a sledgehammer. Wet edges with water. Fill with 1 part portland cement, 2¼ parts sand, and 3 parts pebbles of no more than 1½ inches diameter. Compact mortar thoroughly to eliminate voids. Level it by drawing a board across the surface. Let it set until moisture on the surface starts to disappear. Then smooth it with a wood float or steel trowel. Keep covered for several days with damp burlap.

Surface pitted, uneven. See CONCRETE.

Concrete dusting. Clean floor thoroughly. Then mix 1 part zinc fluosilicate with 4 parts magnesium fluosilicate. Mix ½ pound of this mixture in 1 gallon water and mop evenly over floor. While this dries, mix 2 pounds of fluosilicate mixture in 1 gallon water. Mop on floor when it is dry. After second application dries, mop floor with clear water to remove encrusted salts.

Stains. See CONCRETE.

Paint coming off. If it's flaking off, that's because the concrete is damp, and unless you can eliminate all dampness now and in the future, you might as well leave floor unpainted. If paint is wearing off under traffic, the only solution is to clean the floor thoroughly and repaint with the best oil-base deck paint available. But that will wear out also.

FLOOR, CORK

Holes, burns. See CORK.

Tile damaged. See FLOOR, VINYL. Stick tile down with linoleum cement.

Cracks between tiles. See FLOOR, VINYL.

Stains. See CORK.

FLOOR, LINOLEUM

Small holes. Grate a waste scrap of linoleum and mix with clear lacquer to form a thick paste. Spread in hole immediately. Sand smooth when dry.

Large holes. Lay a scrap piece of matching linoleum over the hole, hold tight, and with a very sharp knife cut through both layers at once. Then dig out old linoleum, scrape out adhesive, and apply new linoleum paste. Set in patch and weight down.

Cuts, tears. Lift edges and spread linoleum paste underneath. Use a spatula or thin knife, or squirt paste from a clean oil can. Weight down.

Bulges. Make small cut through bulge, spread

linoleum paste underneath, and weight down.

Stains, rubber heel marks. Never use chemical cleaners. Scrub with a damp cloth and mild cleansing powder or white appliance wax. Use fine steel wool if necessary.

Nail polish, tar, lacquer, varnish, other deposits on flooring. Scrape off with a dull knife and rub with fine steel wool.

Dirty wax buildup on floor. See FLOOR, VINYL.

FLOOR POLISHER

Doesn't work. Check whether fuse has blown, whether outlet is defective. Examine cord for a break—especially near the plug and the connection to the polisher. If you still don't get any response, take polisher to service shop.

Sparks excessively. Replace the carbon brushes (see ELECTRIC MOTOR).

Liquid dispenser clogged. Remove and fill with warm water for about half an hour, then rinse.

Internal dispensing system clogged. Fill dispenser with hot water and run machine until clog is broken. If you don't get action quickly, add household ammonia to the water.

FLOOR, QUARRY TILE

Tile broken. With a cold chisel and hammer, chip tile out. Work from the break toward the edges. Chip out concrete around edges of hole, and chip down the concrete in the bottom a fraction of an inch. Spread ceramic-tile adhesive or silicone rubber caulking on back of tile and center it in hole. Let adhesive dry for 24 hours. Then fill joints around tile with 1 part portland cement and 2 to 3 parts sand.

Stains. See TILE, CERAMIC.

FLOOR, RUBBER

Tile damaged in any way. Replace it. Cut across the middle, insert chisel or putty knife underneath, and pull up. Scrape out old ad-hesive and spread in new rubber flooring adhesive. Set new tile and weight down.

Stains. See FLOOR, VINYL.

FLOOR, SEAMLESS

NOTE. Unless you know for sure what the floor is made of, you should let a seamless-flooring dealer make repairs.

Floor dull and cloudy. It needs to be reglazed. Acrylic floors require this treatment every 6 months; urethane floors usually need it only every 3 to 5 years. If floor is acrylic, simply clean it thoroughly. Remove all wax. If floor is urethane, clean thoroughly and then sand well. Apply new glaze (clear plastic liquid) with a paint roller. Take pains not to leave any ridges. Let dry for 12 hours before walking on floor.

Stains. Most come up by scrubbing with detergent. Treat others as on a vinyl floor.

FLOOR, VINYL

Small holes. Shred a scrap of the vinyl flooring into tiny shavings and mix with a small amount of methyl ethyl ketone or acetone until a putty is formed. Surround hole with masking tape to keep mixture from spreading. Apply putty with a spatula or knife to the level of the tape. After it has set for a few minutes, remove tape. Added thickness created by tape will allow for shrinkage of the mixture as it dries. Smooth with fine steel wool when completely dry.

Large holes. Hold a piece of vinyl flooring tightly over the hole and cut through both layers at once with a sharp knife. Dig out old flooring and adhesive. Spread in new vinyl flooring cement. Set in patch and weight down.

Cuts, tears. Lay a 1-inch strip of smooth, heavy-duty aluminum foil over the cut and fasten one end with friction tape. Smooth the foil down with your finger. Heat a hand iron to highest temperature. Then pull the point of the iron over the foil toward you several times. Do not bear down or hold iron in one spot. Edges of cuts should now be sealed together.

Wipe foil with a damp rag and remove it. Clean vinyl with water and an abrasive household cleanser to remove dull streak left by foil.

Bulges. Make small cut through bulge, spread vinyl flooring adhesive underneath, and weight down.

Burns. Scrape with a dull knife until only a small residue remains. Then rub with a damp cloth and abrasive cleanser.

Tile damaged. Cut tile across the middle, insert chisel under cut, and pry up two pieces. (Do not pry up a tile from the sides: you might damage adjacent tiles.) Scrape out old adhesive and spread in new vinyl flooring cement. Set new tile and weight down.

Cracks between tiles. These result from laying the tiles on a single-thickness wood subfloor. The inevitable expansion and contraction of the wood causes cracks to open between the tiles (as well as between sheets of resilient flooring). There is no way to fix these short of relaying the floor on a double-thick wood subfloor.

Stains, heel marks, grease, tar, crayon. Rub with white appliance wax. If this doesn't work, rub with powdered cleanser and very fine steel wool dipped in water.

Chewing gum, paint, on floor. Scrape off with a dull knife. Rub with a little cleaning fluid.

Nail polish on floor. Scrape off with dull knife. Rub with fine steel wool and household cleanser.

Dirty wax buildup on floor. Remove with a one-step, packaged wax remover. Mix in water and apply liberally to a 10-square-foot area. Let stand 3 minutes, then scrub with stiff fiber brush or electric floor scrubber (fine steel wool can also be used, but not on shiny vinyls). Sponge up moisture when wax is off and do another area.

Hard lacquer finish worn off in traffic lanes. All hard finishes wear off unevenly and should therefore never be applied. You can't remove them with solvents without ruining the flooring. Your only hope is to rub them off laboriously with fine steel wool.

Finish worn on shiny floor. Recoat with special finish made for this purpose, available from flooring dealer.

FLOOR, VINYL-ASBESTOS TILE

See FLOOR, ASPHALT TILE. Unlike asphalt tile, however, vinyl-asbestos is flexible enough to be laid over an uneven surface without heating.

FLOOR, WOOD

Isolated scratches. If scratch is in the finish only and if the floor was finished with a penetrating or gym seal, remove the wax with fine steel wool or benzine and brush on new penetrating seal. If floor was shellacked, remove wax and rub shellac with alcohol, which will soften the shellac and hide the scratch. If floor was finished with any other material, the only thing you can do is rub on some more paste wax.

If scratch goes through to the wood, brush oil stain into it to match rest of floor. Then follow directions above.

Deep scratches, gouges. Fill with plastic wood. This must be stained to the color of the floor before you apply it. Better make several test batches first. After plastic hardens, sand smooth and refinish.

Burns. Scrape out charred wood with a sharp knife or razor blade. Work with the grain. Sand smooth. If hole isn't deep, apply new stain and finish. If hole turns out to be too deep for this, fill it with plastic wood as above.

Entire floor badly scratched, stained, dirty, etc. Rent a large drum sander and an edger, or disk sander, and redo the entire floor. You will need to buy three types of sandpaper for both machines—coarse, medium, and fine.

Remove everything from the room. Nail down loose boards. Drive down high or protruding nails with a hammer and nail set. Remove shoe moldings around baseboards. Close all doors and open windows.

Sand the center of the floor first with the drum sander. Start with coarse sandpaper; then use medium paper, and always finish with the fine paper. If the boards are badly cupped, sand diagonally across them with the coarse sandpaper. Otherwise, always sand with the grain.

When using the sanders, keep them moving. If they are held in one spot for any time, they will dig a hole in the floor. Starting at one end of the room with the drum sander, make a pass straight across the floor to the other end of the room; then back up over the same area. Then move over and do the next boards in the same way.

When using the edger, hold it level and go back and forth from one end of the room to the other. It makes no difference whether you sand with or across the grain.

Sweep the floor frequently during sanding operations. Use the stuff you take up as a garden soil conditioner.

To remove the old finish in corners, around radiator pipes, and in other spots the sanders can't reach, use a sharp hand scraper and work with the grain.

Stains that cannot be sanded off should be bleached with a commercial bleach or ½ cup of oxalic acid crystals mixed in 1 quart of water. Swab on the stains and let dry; keep applying more until the natural color returns. Then neutralize with 1 cup of borax in 1 quart of hot water. Let dry, and sand by hand to smooth the surface.

Before finishing the floor, vacuum it again thoroughly. If you want to change the color of the wood, brush on oil stain evenly. Let it soak in for a few minutes, and wipe off the excess with clean rags. Then rub hard with another clean rag to even out the finish. Let dry for at least 24 hours. Finally, brush on two coats of floor finish—preferably a penetrating seal. Finish with a coat of paste wax.

Parquet floor in bad condition. Since the blocks are laid at right angles to one another, this kind of floor is very difficult to refinish without showing scratches. Have the job done by a professional.

Boards split. If board is loose, drill through it at an angle in several places along the break. Drive in 3-inch or 4-inch cement-coated or galvanized finishing nails, and countersink the heads. Fill split and nail holes with plastic wood stained to color of floor. To replace a badly damaged section, cut across the board

with a sharp chisel or circular saw. Then cut off the tongue of the board with the chisel or saw. Pry board out. Cut new board to fit and plane off tongue. Set in the hole and nail it down with finishing nails.

Boards loose or raised. Drill small holes at an angle through the boards, and nail down with 3-inch or 4-inch cement-coated or galvanized finishing nails. Countersink heads and fill holes with plastic wood.

Adjacent boards warped upward at the edges. Run a circular saw along the joint to sever the tongue on one of the boards. (You can also use a sharp chisel.) Then drive long flat-head screws through the curled edges into the subfloor and tighten them gradually over a period of several weeks. Countersink the screw-heads and cover with plastic wood.

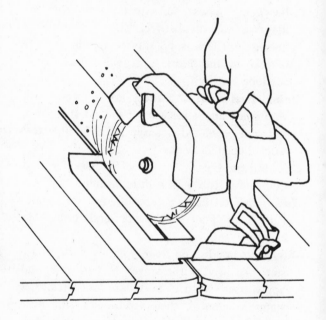

If the warp is very bad and hidden by a rug, either cut out the boards entirely and replace them, or simply saw out the warped area with a circular saw, shape a piece of wood to fit the hole, and nail it in.

Parquet block loose or warped. If it is laid over a wood subfloor, nail it down like strip flooring (see above). If it is laid on concrete, better leave well enough alone. The only thing you can do is to insert a very thin chisel or putty knife into the cracks around the block and cut through the tongues connecting it with the adjacent blocks. Then lift out, clean out old mastic, and glue down with silicone adhesive.

Wood plugs in pegged floor missing. You can buy plugs at some lumberyards; otherwise you must cut your own from hardwood dowels. Clean out openings for holes and put a little white glue in the bottom. Press in plugs. If they are very loose in holes, work glue in around the edges. When glue is dry, carefully trim off the tops of the plugs flush with the floor with a sharp plane. Then stain and finish.

Floor squeaks. If you can get at the underside of the floor, drive wood wedges between the floor and the joists. If there's a ceiling below the floor, drill small holes at an angle through the boards. Nail down boards with long cement-coated or galvanized finishing nails. Countersink the heads and fill holes with plastic wood or simply floor wax.

Graphite squirted into cracks between squeaky boards often silences them, but the graphite is very messy. If you can find it in a hardware store, use Dry-Lube instead.

Floor sags. Raise it on one or more jack posts. Set a pair of 2-inch by 4-inch timbers, one on top of the other, flat on the floor under the sagging joists or girder. Place the jack post

on this base and screw it up until it touches the girder. If there isn't a girder, place two more 2-inch by 4-inch timbers on top of the jack post at right angles to the joist, and raise the floor on these.

When you first install the jack post, screw it up tight and then raise it about ½ inch. From then on, raise it another ¼ inch to ½ inch every 6 or 7 days until the floor is level. Then replace the jack post with a steel Lally column or 6-inch by 6-inch timber.

Floor vibrates. You can repair the floor only if the underside is exposed. If the joists do not appear large enough (they are usually at least 8 inches high), install new timbers next to them and nail them together. If the joists seem adequate, you probably need more bridging. Cut 1-inch by 3-inch boards to match the bridging already installed, and nail in one or two rows midway between the existing rows. (You can also buy prefabricated steel bridging.)

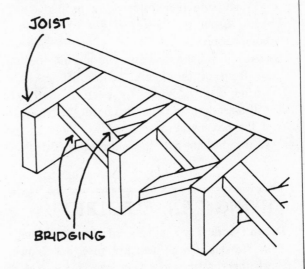

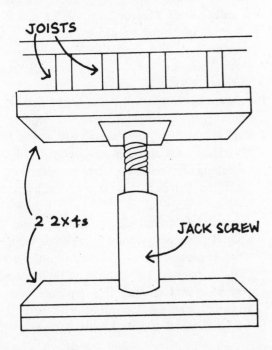

Stains. The stains are probably in the wax or finish, not in the wood. First try to eliminate them by rubbing with liquid floor wax or white appliance wax. Then rub with very fine steel wool or benzine.

If a shellacked floor is spotted by alcohol, rub lightly with steel wool and apply new shellac which is thinned with denatured alcohol.

Remove water spots by rubbing with cigarette ashes and oil.

Scrape off paint with a sharp knife and remove the excess that remains with benzine.

If stains go through into the wood, see WOOD.

FREEZER, FOOD

NOTE. Call a serviceman if freezer doesn't work properly, but first check the following points.

Doesn't work. Is it plugged in? Has fuse blown? Is cord broken?

Runs too warm, foods starting to melt. The freezer probably needs defrosting. Do this first, even though the buildup of ice on the shelves and walls may not seem excessive.

Remove dust and lint from around compressor with a vacuum cleaner.

Check door seal by inserting a dollar bill. If it pulls out easily when door is closed, clean gasket and door jamb. If gasket is worn or flabby, have it replaced.

Make sure thermostat is set properly.

Labors. Clean out dust and lint from around compressor.

Sweats. If sweating occurs only around the top or front of the freezer, check if gasket is sealing tightly. Wash. If sweating continues, call a serviceman. You also need a serviceman if the box sweats in one or two spots on the surface but not over the entire surface.

FRYING PAN, ELECTRIC

Dosen't work. Try another cord; the original may be broken. Check whether fuse has blown, whether outlet into which pan is plugged is operative. If you still get no action, take frying pan to a service shop.

Teflon finish damaged. See TEFLON.

Grease and carbon baked on exterior. See CHROMIUM PLATE.

FUR

Seams in furs ripped. Loosen and turn back lining. With a very sharp needle, sew heavy cotton twill tape to both leather edges. Use a back stitch. Fold tapes under and stitch together.

If the skins are very dry, the tapes must be sewn as far back from the edges as possible.

Coat cuffs worn. Loosen sleeve lining, pull worn fur up into sleeve, and sew down. Then resew lining.

Other problems. Take the fur to a furrier.

FURNACE FLUE

Small holes. Clean metal with steel wool and fill holes at once with epoxy mender.

Large holes. Replace flue section immediately.

Joints between pipe sections loose. Straighten pipes and support them on wires from joists. Remove dirt and rust with steel wool. Then cover joints with thin layer of epoxy mender or asbestos cement.

Joint between flue pipe and chimney open. Plug with asbestos cement.

FURNITURE—BED

Slats fall out. Check whether slats are too short and cut new ones. Also check whether the small wood rails on which slats rest are secure. If not, screw them to the side rails with additional screws, and add white glue for good measure.

Box spring sags. One or more of the bed irons (heavy angle irons on which the spring rests) may be loose. If it cannot be tightened because screw holes are worn, remove it and install it in sound wood.

Bed squeaks. Inspect all joints in the bed frame and reglue any that are loose or wobbly. If slats fit too tightly between rails, cut a little bit off the ends and rub them with paraffin. If squeaking continues, the slats are probably to blame, so replace them with steel bed irons that hook over wood rails.

Bedpost finial broken off. Sometimes finials are integral parts of bedposts; sometimes they are separate pieces that are doweled into the posts. If the former type is broken, turn the repair over to a professional. If a separate finial is broken, saw off the dowel flush with the base of the finial. Drill a hole in the bottom of the finial. Cut a new hardwood dowel and glue it into the hole with white glue.

Headboard or footboard split. See FURNITURE —TABLE (*joined boards in top separated*).

Stains. See WOOD or VARNISHED SURFACE.

FURNITURE—CANED SEAT OR BACK

Holes. Buy cane from crafts supplies or chair-seating outlets. Soak in a solution of 3 tablespoons glycerine to 1 pint warm water until pliable. Trim off old broken ends under seat or behind back. Weave in new canes and conceal ends under old. When cane is dry, glue ends to old cane with epoxy glue, cover with wax paper, and clamp between boards.

FURNITURE—CANVAS SEAT OR BACK

Holes, tears. See CANVAS.

Canvas done for. Rip it off. Pull tacks (if any) out of frame. Using old canvas as a pattern, cut new canvas to size. Sew edges if necessary for strength or to prevent raveling. If canvas is tacked to wood, double the material at the tacked ends. Use 5/16-inch copper or aluminum tacks and space them about 1½ inches apart.

Stains. See CLOTHING—FABRICS.

FURNITURE—CARD TABLE

Legs wobble. Tighten all screws. If screw holes are worn, fill them with plastic wood before setting screws. If top of wood leg is attached to a wood axle and the joint is loose, remove leg entirely. Separate leg slightly from axle and fill joint with glue. Then screw tight.

Top on wood table torn. This can be patched with adhesive-backed mending tape. But it will look better if it's replaced. Rip off fabric and carefully dig out the fabric in the slots around the edges of the opening. Clean glue from slots. Cut new fabric top just large enough to cover the opening and fit into slots. Cover hardboard top with thin cotton batting or felt. This should

come just to the slots. Lay the fabric and notch the four corners slightly. Run a little white glue into the slots. Then carefully push edges of fabric into slots.

Top on metal table torn. The fabric top is wrapped around a hardboard base. Loosen cleats holding the base, lift out, and tear off fabric. Use old fabric as a pattern, but add an inch to all sides of the new fabric. Wrap this over the hardboard base and down around and under the edges. Set top back in table and anchor one side with the cleats. Then pulling on the extra fabric under the table, tighten the fabric top on the other sides and anchor with cleats. Cut off excess material.

FURNITURE—CASTERS

Loose. If caster fits into a metal socket in the furniture leg, remove it from socket and wrap the shank with friction tape. If shank of caster is set directly in wood, hold in place with epoxy glue. If caster is secured to furniture with screws, fill screw holes with plastic wood and reset screws.

Frozen, won't swivel. Check whether sticking is caused by thread or string wrapped around the caster. Clean thoroughly. Apply a drop of oil and work caster back and forth. Remove excess oil.

FURNITURE—CHEST OF DRAWERS

Drawer sticks in summer. Rub edges with paraffin. If this doesn't help, burn a light bulb inside the drawer to shrink the wood. (Don't let bulb rest on wood, and keep drawer open slightly for ventilation.) Then coat all surfaces inside and out with shellac or varnish to prevent wood from soaking up moisture from the summer air.

Drawer sticks in winter. Try rubbing edges with paraffin. If this does no good, plane or scrape down the bottom edges of the sides a fraction of an inch and sand smooth.

Drawer too loose. In some old chests, the drawers slide only on rails fastened to sides of chest. To keep drawer from wobbling when you open or close it, glue small strips of wood to the tops of the rails close to the drawer sides. In other chests, drawers are held straight by a wood strip, called a center guide, under the middle of the drawer. If this is loose, just screw or nail it tight. If broken, replace with a new wood strip—preferably of a hardwood.

Drawer joints loose. Pull sides apart and scrape off old glue. Apply white glue and refit sides. Tighten with a tourniquet as shown in drawing.

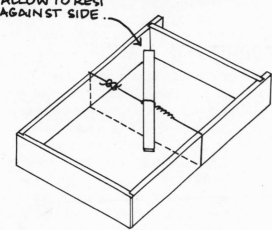

TIE HEAVY CORD LOOSELY AROUND DRAWER, PASS STICK OR OTHER RIGID OBJECT UNDER, THEN OVER CORD TO FORM LOOP, TWIST UNTIL TIGHT, ALLOW TO REST AGAINST SIDE.

Bottom of drawer loose. Remove bottom and scrape glue from edges. Also clean glue out of grooves in the sides and front of the drawer. Spread white glue in grooves and set in bottom. Nail a small brad through the bottom edge of the back of the drawer into the drawer bottom. If bottom panel is loose in the grooves, force glue-coated toothpicks into the cracks.

Bottom of drawer broken. Cut a piece of ⅛-inch hardboard to the size of the drawer and lay it over the old bottom. For a better job, replace the bottom entirely with hardboard or plywood of the proper thickness. Glue this in place as above.

Wood damaged. See WOOD. Also see VENEER.

Side panel split. Remove the drawers. Working on the inside, pry one piece of the panel loose from the frame with a knife or chisel. Coat broken edge with white glue. Then join with

other piece and glue a very thin strip of wood, as from a bushel basket, lengthwise to the back of the split.

Top split. Remove top by loosening screws underneath or by knocking off the triangular pieces used to glue it to the base. Apply glue to broken edge and press pieces together. See FURNITURE—TABLE (*joined boards in top separated*).

Top warped. Remove as above. See FURNITURE—TABLE (*top or leaf warped*).

Pulls loose. See FURNITURE—KNOBS AND PULLS.

Drawers and interior of chest smell. Spray with a disinfectant such as Lysol. Take outdoors and expose to the sun for 3 or 4 days. If odor persists, apply two coats of white shellac to the interior of the chest and inside and outside the drawers (but not, of course, to the fronts). Take pains to brush the shellac into the corners.

FURNITURE—DESK

Wood top damaged. See FURNITURE—TABLE.

Veneered top damaged. See VENEER.

Felt top torn. Remove felt and scrape and sand wood base clean. Cut new felt top to fit. Apply white glue to wood and smooth felt into this. Trim edges as necessary with a razor blade.

Linoleum top damaged. See FLOOR, LINOLEUM.

Leather top torn. If tear is not obvious when leather is pressed down, simply spread white glue under torn edges and weight down. If damage is severe, replace top as you would a felt top.

Acrylic top cracked. See PLASTICS—GENERAL.

Burn in leather top. Carefully scrape out charred particles. If the scar is not too deep, you can pretty well conceal it with leather polish. If burn goes through leather, however, lay a scrap of matching leather over the hole; hold tight, and cut through both layers at once with a razor blade. Make a round or oval hole if possible. Apply rubber cement to back of patch and to base. Let dry until tacky and then stick down patch. Polish well and often.

Stains. See WOOD or entry for appropriate material.

FURNITURE—FOLDING CHAIR

Slat seat in wood chair broken. It's difficult for anyone except an expert to set in a new slat. But you can make a sound seat simply by cutting a piece of ⅛-inch hardboard to the size of the seat opening and gluing it to the slats with epoxy glue.

Holes in upholstered seat of folding wood bridge chair. Replace with new covering. See FURNITURE—UPHOLSTERED (*seat of side chair torn, shabby*).

Holes, tears, in upholstered seat of metal chair. Unscrew the seat from the frame (if the chair is assembled in this way). Remove old fabric and use it as a pattern for the new cover. Cut, fold around seat, and tack in place. Then reset seat in frame.

In an older type of chair, the seat is slipped into a frame made of U-shaped metal. The part that forms the back of the seat frame is held to the rest of the frame by strong steel clips. Pry one of the clips loose with the claw of a hammer. Remove seat, take off cover, and cut a new cover out of vinyl fabric. Tack to the base of the seat. Then slide seat into frame and hammer on the back channel.

Rubber tips on metal legs broken. Replace round, cup-shaped tips (like those on crutches and many ironing boards) with new tips available from most hardware stores. The rubber "tips" used on chairs with more or less flat, rectangular legs are another matter. These consist of a straight piece of hard rubber stuck to the bottom of a more or less T-shaped metal piece. To replace them, knock rubber and metal T off the bottom of the leg with a hammer. Then insert an entirely new tip, available from the chair supplier, in the hole in the end of the leg.

Chair wobbly, squeaky. Tighten up all bolts and screws, and oil the joints lightly. That's about as much as you can do.

FURNITURE—KNOBS AND PULLS

Wood knob or pull loose. Remove bolt driven into back of knob. Put a dab of silicone adhesive on back of knob near the center, set knob in place, and drive in screw until knob is tight.

If threads of bolt are worn and don't hold in knob, coat them with silicone adhesive before tightening.

If bolt is attached to knob and threads are worn, remove nut, coat threads of bolt with silicone adhesive, and reset nut. Then put a dab of silicone adhesive behind it as an extra safeguard. Epoxy glue or mender can be used instead of silicone adhesive but will make it almost impossible to remove the knob at a later date, should you desire to.

FURNITURE—ROCKING CHAIR

Rocker split. Spread epoxy glue on split surfaces and clamp wood together with C-clamps. If additional reinforcement is needed, drill ¼-inch holes up through the rocker after glue has hardened. Coat ¼-inch dowels with glue and tap into holes. Cut dowels off flush with surface when glue sets.

Other problems. See FURNITURE—WOOD CHAIR.

Stains. See WOOD.

FURNITURE—ROPE SEAT OR BACK

Sags. Find starting point of the rope. Working from there, pull each succeeding loop of rope taut. Put a new knot in the end and cut off the excess.

Broken. Don't remove rope. Make a rough measurement of the amount of new rope required and purchase this at hardware store. Then, when you're ready to install this in the chair, study how old rope is laced into frame and make a rough diagram on paper. Then cut out old rope and lace in new. Pull it up as tightly as possible to accommodate somewhat for eventual sagging.

FURNITURE—RUSH SEAT

Rushes broken, frayed. Buy chairmaker's rush to match. Cut old broken rushes off cleanly—preferably under the chair. Cut new rush strips long enough to fill in the breaks and add about 4 inches. Flatten the ends of the old and new rushes. Glue new strips to old with white glue.

FURNITURE—TABLE

Legs wobbly. Try to break joints and reglue, or try to force new glue into joints. If this is impossible, cut a triangle out of a piece of 1-inch-thick wood. Notch 90-degree corner to fit around the leg. Place block tight against inside surfaces of leg and screw it to the frame.

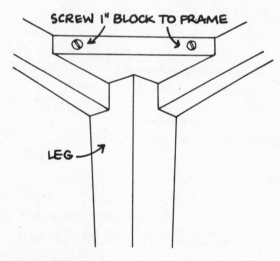

SCREW 1" BLOCK TO FRAME

LEG

Wood damaged. See WOOD. Also see VENEER.

Top or leaf warped. Remove top from frame and lay it concave side down on several layers of damp rags. Over the top, hang one or two heat lamps. Keep lamps lighted and rags wet until wood straightens. If warp returns, repeat process. Once you're sure wood is stable, varnish the unfinished underside.

If warp is irregular, so that top is actually twisted, follow above procedure and weight down the highest parts with heavy weights.

NOTE. This repair is likely to damage the finish on the wood, but you have no choice.

Joined boards in top separated. Remove top from base. Scrape the old glue from edges of boards. Apply white glue and press boards together. To assure that joints are tight, nail a straight board to the floor or to a sheet of plywood. Cover with wax paper. Push one end of tabletop against the board and, when joints are tight, nail a board along the opposite end of table.

Top or leaf split. Same as above.

Pedestal tabletop wobbly. Turn table upside down and tighten screws attaching top to frame. If screws don't grip, fill holes with plastic wood or glued wood plugs, let dry, and then drive in screws.

Leg on pedestal table loose. If possible, pull it completely loose. Scrape glue from dowels and mortises and apply new white glue. Then reset leg. If leg refuses to come off, spread epoxy glue in joint between it and the pedestal, and clamp leg in place. But don't be surpised if nothing you try works. You may need help from a cabinetmaker.

Stains. See WOOD.

Top marked up with lines made by people writing. The tiny dents made by ballpoint pens and hard pencils cannot be eradicated except by sanding down the entire top until smooth. This is a major and difficult job, and if the table is valuable, you should let a professional refinisher do it. On an inexpensive table, use a reciprocating sander. Start with medium-coarse sandpaper and progress to very fine. Always sand with the grain. Take care not to sand the edges more than the center. Finish with steel wool.

FURNITURE, UPHOLSTERED

Seat of side chair torn, shabby. Turn chair upside down and remove the four screws that hold seat in place. Remove old cover and use it as a pattern for new cover. (If using a strongly patterned print, be sure that feature of design is centered.) Wrap new cover tightly around seat and secure four sides with tacks or staples. Miter corners. Then tack all the way around the seat with 5/16-inch tacks or staples spaced about 1½ inches apart.

Seat of overstuffed chair or sofa sagging. Turn chair upside down, remove dust cover and webbing. Tie bottom coils of springs together and to the frame. Be sure springs are evenly spaced in straight lines. Replace old webbing with new. The strips should be spaced so that each spring rests squarely on a crossing of the strips. Double the ends of the webbing to increase holding strength and fasten to bottom of chair frame with ¾-inch tacks. Webbing should be interwoven and pulled flat and tight across bottom of frame. To pull it tight, use a webbing stretcher, or fold end of webbing around a board, brace board against chair frame, and bend it down. Tack webbing strip once to hold. Then cut it off about 2 inches beyond the chair frame, double back the end, and put in three or four more tacks. To assure against movement of springs, sew them to webbing with coarse thread or light string. Replace dust cover.

REPLACE WEBBING SO THAT EACH SPRING RESTS ON AN INTERSECTION

TIE AT ALL FOUR POINTS

USE A WEBBING STRETCHER

Seat of overstuffed chair or sofa lumpy. Remove upholstery fabric and muslin underneath. If the lumpiness is in the padding, simply smooth it out. If necessary to add new padding, use cotton and lay it in thin sheets with tapered edges. (It is available in long, wide rolls for upholstering.) Then replace the muslin and upholstery fabric or buy new material.

If the lumpiness is caused by the springs, which have come loose, remove all the padding and burlap over them. Tie down the springs as described above. The outer coils must be pulled down toward the edges of the chair to give the seat a rounded contour. Then replace the burlap, adjust the padding, and replace the muslin and finish fabric.

Loose seat or back cushion flabby. To make it thicker, cut stitches at the cord line along a rear edge. Add padding like that already in cushion, or replace padding entirely with urethane or latex foam. Cut foam about ¾ inches larger in both directions than the cover measurements from cord to cord. Double it over, slip into cover, open it flat, adjust in position so cover is snug. Sew up opening.

Arm or leg loose. Peel off upholstery and stuffing. Reglue broken joint and/or fasten it to the frame with angle irons.

Wood damaged. See FURNITURE, WOOD.

Stains. See WOOD or CLOTHING—FABRICS.

FURNITURE, WICKER, RATTAN, REED, OR BAMBOO

Bindings loose, broken. If full length of binding remains and is not too brittle, apply epoxy glue to joint, rewrap binding over it, and nail end in place with small brad. If binding needs to be replaced, soak new strip in water until pliable. Dry with a rag. Then apply resorcinol glue to joint, wrap binding around it, and secure with a brad.

Wicker, rattan, reed, or bamboo strips broken, split. If possible (the angle of the break and size of the material may cause trouble), coat the broken edges with epoxy and press together. To hold the ends while glue is drying and to strengthen the joint, it may be necessary also to wrap thread tightly around the break or to insert a pin (sharpened at both ends) or a wood dowel into the opposing ends.

If the broken strip is part of a rather dense weave (as is often the case with wicker), an easier solution may be simply to coat it with glue and clamp it to the other strips in the weave. The break can be further reinforced by tiny wires wound through the weave and around the broken strip.

FURNITURE, WOOD

Minor scratches. Rub with paste floor wax, the meat of a nut, or a mixture of equal parts boiled linseed oil, turpentine, and water. Hide with shoe polish if necessary.

Severe scratches. Rub with a wax stick of the proper color.

Burns. With a sharp knife, carefully scratch out all charred wood. Work with the grain. Clean with benzine. Smooth with fine steel wool or sandpaper. Apply oil stain to match surrounding finish.

If stain doesn't eliminate black look, brush white shellac on scar. Then blend enamel to match surrounding finish and rub on a light coat with your finger. Let dry. Add more paint if necessary. Then apply a very thin coat of white shellac. Sand off gloss when dry, and apply furniture polish or wax.

If scar is deep, fill it with stick shellac matching the finish. Heat a small spatula over an alcohol flame or on an electric burner, press it against shellac stick, and let the melting shellac drip into hole. Smooth with heated spatula. Sand with fine sandpaper when dry and rub down with rottenstone and a rag dipped in sewing machine oil.

Dents. Cover with a damp cloth. Place a bottle cap upside down directly over dent and rest a warm flatiron on top. If dent doesn't rise after several applications of heat, remove finish with steel wool and try again.

Stains. See WOOD. Also see LACQUERED SURFACE, SHELLACKED SURFACE, or VARNISHED SURFACE, as case may be.

FURNITURE—WOOD CHAIR

Joints loose. Pull joint apart. If this proves impossible, try to loosen it by rapping it sharply with a hammer that is thickly padded with rags. When joint is separated, sand off old

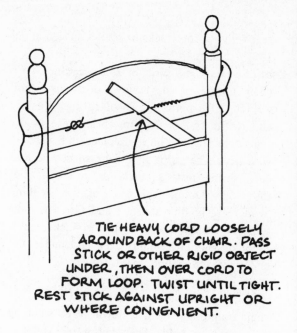

TIE HEAVY CORD LOOSELY AROUND BACK OF CHAIR. PASS STICK OR OTHER RIGID OBJECT UNDER, THEN OVER CORD TO FORM LOOP. TWIST UNTIL TIGHT. REST STICK AGAINST UPRIGHT OR WHERE CONVENIENT.

glue on the tenon and in the mortise. Apply white glue and reset the joint. Keep joint under pressure for 24 hours. This is most easily done by looping a strong cord around legs, arms, or back of chair and tightening like a tourniquet. Pad the cord where it bears on the wood.

If joint keeps coming loose no matter how much or what glue is applied, try one of the following tricks: (1) After joint is glued and set, tap glue-coated wooden toothpicks into mortise around the tenon. Cut them off flush with joint when glue dries. (2) Apply glue to tenon, wrap with thread, apply more glue, and force into mortise. (3) This is frowned on by cabinetmakers but it works. After joint is glued and set, drive a small screw at right angles into the tenon from the outside of the mortise. Countersink head and cover with a glue plug of wood which is cut off flush and stained to match chair.

Arm loose. Repair as above. In some cases, however, arms are held to the back legs and seats by screws that are concealed under little wooden buttons or plugs set flush with the surface. Pry out buttons and save them. Drill out flush plugs. Remove screws. Then pull out arm and reglue. Replace screws and tap buttons into holes or set in new plugs of wood.

Broken rung, slat, leg. If the break runs with the grain, apply epoxy glue to the split and clamp together for 24 hours. If clamps are difficult to adjust because of contours of wood, bind wood with wax paper and string.

If break is across the grain, the piece must be doweled together. Let an expert do this. Lining up the holes in the two pieces is difficult.

If a rung is beyond repair and is difficult to pull out of its hole, cut it off close to the mortise and then drill out mortise. Have new rung made to match the old one.

Legs different length. Set chair on a level surface. Put a thick dab of plastic wood on a piece of wax paper and embed short leg into it. File to shape when dry. If you're lucky, this repair will last a long while. But a better procedure is to stand chair on a flat piece of plywood. Lay saw flat on the plywood and saw off end of longest leg. Repeat process as necessary, sawing off only the thickness of the saw blade each time.

Legs wobble. Try to break joints and reglue, or force glue into cracks of joints. If this doesn't work, either turn chair over to an expert, or brace legs with angle irons.

If chair wobbles even though all joints seem tight, you can brace it with a metal stretcher. Insert metal hooks in four legs and connect them to turnbuckle. Tighten turnbuckle until wobbling stops. This is not an attractive repair.

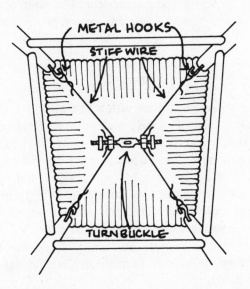

METAL HOOKS
STIFF WIRE
TURNBUCKLE

Wood seat split. Apply white glue to crack. Lay boards across top and bottom of seat and hold together, but not tightly, with C-clamps. Then loop strong cord around the seat and tighten like a tourniquet. If clamping boards are not too tight, tourniquet will draw broken seat pieces together; the clamping boards will keep it from buckling.

For additional reinforcement of a split seat, screw iron mending plates across the bottom. If seat is cracked in several places, cut a piece of 1/8-inch hardboard slightly smaller than the seat and screw it to bottom instead of mending plates.

Wood damaged. See WOOD.
Stains. See WOOD.

FUSE BOX

NOTE. Fuse boxes are generally located at the point where the electrical service enters the house, but in many houses—especially large ones—additional fuse boxes may be located elsewhere. Three kinds of fuses are commonly used. Plug fuses have screw-in bases like those on light bulbs. Fustats are made in two pieces. The body resembles a plug fuse but the screw-in base is of smaller diameter. It screws into a threaded shell, which, in turn, screws into the fuse box. Fustats and plug fuses can be used interchangeably. Cartridge fuses resemble firecrackers with brass caps on both ends. They are pushed into clips in the fuse box or on the back of a rectangular plastic unit with a handle. The entire unit pushes into the fuse box.

Plug fuse or Fustat blown. When this type of fuse blows, the window in the back usually becomes cloudy, and the strip or coil of metal inside is burned through. Before replacing it, turn off the house current at the meter, then try to determine the cause of the failure. Usually this is an overload—meaning that you have been using more electrical devices on the affected circuit than the circuit can carry. Turn off the last device you turned on, and replace the fuse. If this doesn't blow, you have nothing more to worry about.

If a short circuit caused the fuse to blow, you may have seen a momentary flash of light in one of the electric cords or appliances you were using. Or you may notice a burn mark on a cord, socket, etc. In either case, before replacing the fuse, disconnect the device or wire that has been affected and don't use it until it has been fixed.

If a replacement fuse blows when you install it, the circuit is either still overloaded (although that is pretty unlikely if you have already turned off the last device turned on) or it is still shorted. Disconnect all lamps, extension cords, and appliances on the circuit and install a third fuse. If this doesn't blow, look for the short in one of the disconnected devices; but if it does blow, it means there is trouble somewhere in the wiring system and you should call in an electrician. Don't use the circuit until he has checked it out.

Cartridge fuse blows. A blown cartridge fuse looks just like a good one, so in case a circuit protected by two fuses fails, you can't tell which fuse is good and which fuse is bad, and you may have to replace them both. The cause of failure is usually a short circuit, in which case you should call an electrician. However, if the circuit serves a water pump or other appliance or lights installed at a distance from the house, and if you have recently had a thunderstorm, it may have been knocked out by lightning, in which case you can replace the fuse (or fuses).

CAUTION. Whatever type of fuse blows, always replace it with a new fuse of the same size. Never replace a plug fuse or Fustat with a penny.

GALVANIZED STEEL

Small holes. Remove rust and dirt with steel wool. Cover holes with epoxy mender, or, if steel is used for roof flashing, you can coat it with fibered asphalt roofing cement.

Large holes. Use steel wool thoroughly on surfaces. Cut a patch out of galvanized steel sheet. Spread epoxy mender around hole and weight patch down in it.

Paint on new galvanized steel flaking. The metal should not have been painted until it had weathered at least 6 months. It should then have been primed with a zinc-dust primer before finish paint was applied. Remove paint

entirely, or let it flake off the rest of the way; then apply zinc-dust primer and finish coat.

Rusted. Sand off rust thoroughly. Apply a red metal primer and follow with one or two coats of oil-base trim paint.

GARBAGE CAN

Hole in metal. Scrub with detergent and water and clean with steel wool. Cover with epoxy mender.

Metal bottom rusting. Scrub clean, sand as smooth as possible, and paint with asphalt roofing cement. Let dry thoroughly before using. This is a good precaution to take with any new metal garbage can.

Split in plastic. If plastic is of relatively thin type used in kitchen garbage cans, oxidize the surface with a torch (see BASIC METHODS: HOW TO GLUE THINGS TOGETHER). Cut a strip of polyethylene to cover break and oxidize that. Then apply plastic-mending adhesive.

If plastic is of thick type used in outdoor cans, cut strips of aluminum flashing to fit across break and rivet them to the can.

Metal handle on metal top torn off. Bore holes through the flanges of the handle and the top, and rivet the pieces together. Use steel rivets on steel cans, aluminum on aluminum cans.

GARDEN DUSTER

Nozzle clogged. Clean with a fine wire. If necessary, take off nozzle and wash it. Dry thoroughly.

Flit-gun type doesn't pump air. Remove cap at end of air cylinder, pull out plunger, and coat edges of leather with car grease. If end cap is not easily removable, pull plunger out as far as possible and apply heavy oil through holes in end of cylinder on leather. If duster still doesn't throw dust properly, replace the leather entirely.

Crank on crank-type duster works hard. Apply a few drops of oil to handle. On some dusters, there is a grease cap under the handle. Remove this, clean out old grease, and apply new.

This kind of duster also works hard when the gears become clogged with dust. Remove end housings and clean dust compartment and gears thoroughly. Do not apply oil to moving parts except as noted above.

GARDEN HOSE

Rubber hose broken. Cut in two and join pieces with a hose mender made for a rubber hose.

Rubber on hose cracked. As long as it's not leaking, there's no need to do anything about it, but you can rejuvenate it to some extent by painting it with neoprene rubber, plastic rubber, or even rubber cement.

Vinyl hose broken. Cut in two and join pieces with a hose mender made for a plastic hose.

Hose leaks at couplings. If a new washer doesn't help, pry or cut off coupling and replace with a new one.

GARDEN SHEARS

Blades do not come together properly. Tighten nut holding the two blades together. If this does not correct problem, check whether one blade (or handle) is bent; then disassemble shears, place defective blade in vise, and bend slightly. Do not exert too much pressure, especially on cheap shears.

Dull. If cutting edges are scissorslike, clamp shears in a vise and run a fine-toothed metal file up and down them several times. Be careful not to change the angle of the cutting edges.

If shears have only one cutting blade, take them apart and sharpen on a carborundum stone.

GARDEN SPRAYER

Sprayer does not hold pressure. Check gasket under top of air cylinder. If worn or distorted, replace it. If this is not the cause of trouble, examine tank for pinholes, especially in or near the bottom. Solder these if tank is copper. Seal with epoxy mender otherwise.

Pump action does not produce air. Make sure that rubber diaphragm at bottom of air cylinder is not stuck to metal and that air holes are clear. For a temporary repair, pry cylinder from plunger handle and coat leather on bottom of handle with heavy grease. For a permanent repair, install new leather.

On sprayers of the flit-gun type, pump action can be improved somewhat by pulling the plunger all the way back and squirting heavy oil through the hole near the end of the cylinder on the leather.

Spray nozzle clogs continually. Trouble may be caused by nothing more than undissolved chemicals and bits of garden debris. But it may also be caused by corrosion products in bottom of tank. In this case, partially fill with kerosene and let it soak for several days. Empty and scrape sides and bottom as well as you can with a long stiff brush or stick of wood. Soak with kerosene again. Then empty and rinse with soap and water.

Hose cracked. Smear rubber cement on the holes. If hose is badly cracked at end near tank, cut it off and clamp the new end over the pipe stub on the tank. Install new hose if tank is cracked in several places.

GARDEN SPREADER

Fertilizer, etc., comes out in uneven stream. Empty spreader and examine the toothed axle and shutoff plate. They may be badly clogged with rust. The teeth of the axle may be bent or even missing. Clean entire mechanism thoroughly (expose the bare metal) and prime with a red metal primer. Straighten teeth.

Hereafter, make a habit of hosing down your spreader well every time you have used it for applying chemicals.

Fertilizer, etc., comes out in too heavy stream or too light stream. Be sure the control is set properly. If it is and the flow of fertilizer is still wrong, you must recalibrate the spreader. For the test, use a balanced fertilizer and note on the package how much coverage it should give (for example, 25 pounds covers 2,000 square feet). Then calculate how many pounds and ounces are needed to cover 100 square feet.

Determine the distance that the spreader must travel to cover 100 square feet by measuring the width of the spreader opening and dividing this figure into 100. (For example, if spreader width is 18 inches (1½ feet), travel distance is 66 feet; if spreader width is 21 inches (1¾ feet), travel distance is 57 feet.)

Establish a place where fertilizer dropped from the spreader can be retrieved for weighing purposes. If the basement or garage floor (the most suitable locations as a rule) is not long enough for the distance to travel, cut the measurement in half and go over the area twice.

Set the spreader opening to give you what you think is the correct distribution rate, pour some fertilizer into the hopper, and roll the spreader across the test area. Then sweep up the fertilizer and weigh it.

Continue testing in this way until you find the correct spreader opening.

Spreader doesn't shut off instantly and completely. Go over the entire control mechanism and shutoff plate to remove corrosion. Then lubricate at all moving points.

Wheels frozen. Apply penetrating oil to the axle.

GARDEN SPRINKLER

Clogged. Clean spray holes with a fine wire. If trouble persists, soak sprinkler in vinegar for several days and then clean with wire.

GARDEN TILLER

NOTE. Tillers are much more subject to wear than other power equipment used in gardening, so it's essential that you follow the maintenance directions in the instruction manual to the letter. Regular lubrication is of top importance. Let an expert make repairs. But check following points first.

Doesn't start? Are you out of gas? Is valve on fuel line open? Is oil level low? Is choke adjusted? Is spark plug dirty or cracked?

Runs unevenly. Is gasoline stale, gummy? Is air

cleaner clean? Is oil level adequate? Is spark plug clean? Is it cracked?

Vibrates excessively. Tighten all bolts.

Engine erratic. Clean air cleaner and hereafter check it frequently.

Drive belts or chains loose. Adjust tension according to instruction manual.

Cutting blades bent. Grasp them between the jaws of a large adjustable wrench and bend straight. If you can't get enough leverage, slip a long steel pipe over wrench handle.

GARDEN TOOLS

See also AX; GARDEN SHEARS; GARDEN DUSTER; GARDEN SPRINKLER; GARDEN SPRAYER; LAWN MOWER, HAND; LAWN MOWER, POWER; RAKE, LEAF; WATERING CAN.

Handle broken. File off heads of rivets, if any, and drive them out. Dig or drill wood out of ferrule. If this proves difficult, put tool head in a fire and burn handle out. Insert new handle in ferrule and rivet in place with steel rivets. If there are no holes for rivets, bore them with an electric drill, or simply coat handle with epoxy glue before inserting in head.

Tool head bent. Place in vise and bend slowly. Hammering does little good.

Hoe, spade, trowel, mattock, dull. Clamp tool head in a vise and sharpen with a medium-coarse metal file. Hold the file at both ends and stroke it toward the cutting edge of the tool. Do not file on the back stroke. And do not feather the cutting edge too much—it should resemble a chisel edge, flat on the back and beveled in the front.

Sickle, scythe, grass whip, dull. Stroke a scythestone along the beveled edge of the blade. The stroke should not be completely parallel with the blade edge but at a slight angle toward it (in other words, at the start of the stroke, the top edge of the stone is touching the blade; at the completion of the stroke, the stone is touching the blade near its bottom edge). Stroke from the point of the blade toward the handle.

Tools rusted. Rub with coarse steel wool, then

smear on liquid rust-remover and rub with steel wool. Henceforth, clean and dry tools thoroughly after you use them, and store them in a dry place.

GARDEN TRACTOR

NOTE. Without the manufacturer's instruction manual, you can't expect to operate a garden tractor very long or satisfactorily. Even with it, you can't do much about fixing it when it acts up. Most repairs call for an expert. But before calling him, check the following.

Won't start. Is battery dead? Are battery cables broken? Are you out of gas? Is fuel shutoff valve open? Is spark plug dry, clean, and sound?

Moving poorly. Check whether belts are slipping, and adjust according to your instruction manual.

Vibrates. Tighten nuts, bolts, and fittings.

Noisy. Check oil. Lubricate entire tractor.

GARMENT BAG

Tears. Cover tear on the inside with adhesive-backed mending tape.

Zipper broken. See ZIPPER.

GATE

Post loose in ground or concrete. See entries for FENCE.

Post loose from a masonry wall. The post is probably held to the masonry by screws driven into lead anchors that are set in holes in the masonry. If anchors do not hold when driven back into the masonry, pull them out and force a little fast-setting cement or epoxy mender into holes and then immediately reset the anchors. If this doesn't work, replace lead anchors with machine-screw anchors or drive anchors (see BASIC METHODS: HOW TO SUPPORT THINGS on walls that will not receive or hold nails and screws).

Sagging. Make sure hinge screws are tight. If they are, take gate down and force it back into

square. Then nail a diagonal brace across the back from the top corner on the hinge side to the bottom corner on the latch side. The alternative is to install a metal door brace with a turnbuckle (see DOOR, SCREEN).

If the gate is very wide, a diagonal brace will probably not be enough to correct the problem over the long run. The best solution is to replace the post to which the gate is hinged with a 4-inch by 4-inch or 6-inch by 6-inch post (depending on the weight of the gate) about twice as high as the gate. Install an eyebolt in the post just below the top and another in the top of the gate on the latch side. Install a stainless steel cable between the bolts; jack the gate up until it is level, and secure the cable.

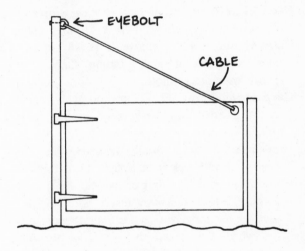

GLASS

Broken. Apply a thin layer of cellulose cement to both broken edges and press together for 6 hours. Use epoxy glue if the glass is subject to much wind pressure or is frequently wet.

Edges rough. Polish with silicon carbide cloth available from hardware store. Keep edges wet while working.

Scratched. The glass can't be repaired. Replace it.

Separated from other material to which it is joined. See HOUSEHOLD DECORATIVE ACCESSORIES.

Insulating glass broken. Replace it: It has lost

some of its insulating value because it's no longer hermetically sealed.

For how to cut glass, see BASIC METHODS section.

GLASS BLOCK

Mortar joints cracked, broken. Scrape clean. Blow out crumbs with a vacuum cleaner. Pack in mortar of 1 part masonry cement and 2 parts sand. Smooth to match surrounding joints.

Joints stained. See BRICK.

GOLF CLUB

Head of iron scratched. Rub scratch with medium, then fine emery cloth. A file may help.

Head of iron nicked. Remove or at least reduce nick with a file or on a grinding wheel; then polish with emery cloth.

Head of wood cracked. Clean thoroughly; work epoxy mender into crack; sand smooth, and dry.

Face insert in wood badly scarred. Pad the head well and lock it in a vise. Then remove insert screws. Make four or five closely spaced vertical cuts across the insert with a fine-toothed hacksaw. Be careful not to cut into the wood. Chisel out the pieces of the old insert and smooth the wood in the mortise. Make a paper template of the mortise to show exact location of screw holes. Then, using template, drill screw holes in new insert; fit insert into head, and screw it in place.

Grip deteriorated. If grip is rubber, slit it from end to end with a razor blade, peel it off and scrub off the adhesive on the shaft. Wrap double-faced tape made for purpose (such as that available from Golf Day Products, Lake Forest, Ill., 60045) around shaft, working from bottom of grip up. Leave ⅛ inch between the spiral turns, and fold about ¼ inch of tape over end of shaft. Then wet tape and inside of new rubber grip with paint thinner and slide grip on shaft. Tap it down firmly against butt end of shaft. Let dry for 12 hours. Remove an old leather grip in the same way,

and after cleaning shaft, slip a plastic starter (which comes with new grip) into end of shaft. Press grip collar over starter on to shaft and slide it down the shaft. Wrap double-faced tape spirally around shaft from bottom up. Apply paint thinner to tape and inside of grip, and slide grip on shaft. After glue dries for 12 hours, remove plastic starter from shaft and replace it with a screw-on cap or insert. At base of grip, trim off excess leather; slip collar up over end, and cement in place.

Shaft bent or broken. Don't try to replace a shaft on a wood. The job is occasionally easy; but it may also turn out to be extremely difficult. Fixing an iron, however, is relatively simple.

Since iron heads are generally cemented to the shafts with epoxy glue, heat the old shaft and head with a torch until the glue is soft; then immediately twist off head. If head is pinned to shaft, find the small pin in the neck and drive it out with a punch. Buy a new shaft with the proper tip diameter. Slip colored rings and ferrule up on to lower end of shaft. Roughen shaft tip with sandpaper and coat evenly with epoxy glue. Insert in head. Then, holding the head in your hand, bring the butt end of the shaft down hard on a concrete floor to set the shaft. Let the glue dry for 12 hours. Finally, slip the ferrule and rings down against the head.

GRASS CLIPPERS, MANUAL

Blades open too wide or not wide enough. Tighten or loosen nuts on eyebolt connecting handle to the rocker arm that controls the moving blade.

Blades separated vertically so they fold grass between them. Tighten nut on axle on which moving blade pivots. This tightens springs that hold moving blade tightly to fixed blade.

Blades dull. You can do a pretty good job of sharpening them with a fine-toothed file, but it is better to take the clippers apart and sharpen the blades on a stone. Follow directions at SCISSORS.

Rubber handles badly worn. Replace with short

lengths of small rubber tubing or wrap with friction tape.

GRASS CLIPPERS, CORDLESS ELECTRIC

Don't work. Have they been fully charged? Is there anything wrong with the outlet into which they were plugged? Are they locked? Are the blades clogged?

Sluggish. Remove bottom screws and lift off blades. Clean out housing that's exposed.

Dull. Sharpen with a small medium file held at the same angle as the original setting. You will do a better job of sharpening if you unscrew the blades and clamp them in a vise.

Blades jammed by metal burr. Remove blades from housing and file off burr.

Plastic case cracked. Clean the broken edges and smear on plastic-mending adhesive. Press together and hold in place with masking tape until glue is dry.

GRASS CLOTH

Dirt, stains. First try sponging with water. Use a sponge that is well wrung out. Then try a mild detergent solution. Then try dry-cleaning fluid or spray-on cleaning powder.

Other problems. See VINYL WALL COVERING.

GRILL, CHARCOAL

Hole in firebox. Scrub metal with detergent; rinse and dry. Then clean with steel wool and coat hole heavily with epoxy mender. Henceforth, don't build fire directly on the metal. Put in a layer of gravel or sand.

Grid post stuck in slot. Soak in detergent solution to remove grease. Dry. Then saturate crack between post and slot with penetrating oil and try to tap post out with a hammer and blunt chisel. Don't pound too hard. If post doesn't loosen, apply more penetrating oil and let it soak in for several hours. Then use your hammer again. When post finally comes out,

clean it and the slot with steel wool. In the future, remove and clean the post periodically. Sprinkling with powdered graphite will help.

GRILL, ELECTRIC

Doesn't heat. Check whether fuse has blown, whether outlet into which grill is plugged is operative. Check cord for a break, and replace if necessary. Remove grids from grill. If coiled heating element is broken, you can make a temporary repair by twisting the ends of the wire together several times. Make sure they do not make contact with the shell of the grill. Then, as soon as you're through using the grill, remove the heating element entirely and replace it with a new one available from a wiring supplies outlet or appliance service shop.

If none of these repairs works, take grill to service shop.

Grids dirty, stuck up. Soak in detergent solution. Uncoated metal grids can also be scrubbed with powdered cleanser and fine steel wool.

Food and grease encrusted on body of grill. See CHROMIUM PLATE.

GUTTER, ALUMINUM

Small holes. Clean metal with steel wool and cover holes with epoxy mender. Or coat the entire trough with asphalt roofing cement.

Large holes. Clean out dirt; spread a liberal coat of fibered asphalt roofing cement over hole. In this, lay a strip of freezer-grade aluminum foil. Smooth down and cover with more roofing cement.

Gutter sags. Adjust hangers or install new ones. If gutter is bent, try straightening it by hand while it is still in place; but if this doesn't work, take it down.

Straps on hangers broken. Most gutter hangers consist of a loop of metal strapped around the gutter. From the top of this strap, another strap makes a forward loop back up on the roof, where it is nailed. The straps are riveted together, but frequently the rivet breaks. When this happens, join the two straps with a small nut and bolt.

If the strap bent up on the roof breaks (usually just above the rivet), loosen it from the roof. Make another hole in the lower end, bolt it to the strap around the gutter, and reattach to the roof.

Gutter clogged. Clean out leader (see LEADER). Clean gutter thoroughly, then cover it from end to end with a mesh gutter guard made of aluminum or vinyl in a long roll 6 inches wide. Slip upper edge of mesh under roofing, bend front edge down below rim of gutter, and tie it to the gutter hangers.

Leaks at joints. Squeeze silicone caulking compound into the joints.

Ice builds up in gutter, backs up melt water, which leaks through roof. This can be prevented by looping electric heating cable in a zigzag along the edge of the roof and over the front edge of the gutter. When the cable is warm, it cuts channels through the ice and permits water to run off over the gutter to the ground. (In an alternate arrangement, the cable is installed in a zigzag on the roof and run through the gutter and down through the leader, so water will run off by its normal route.)

The only permanent cure for this problem, however, is to remove the roofing from the

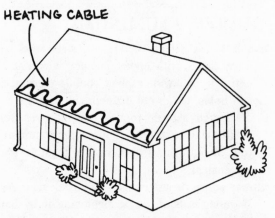

lowest part of the roof and install an eaves flashing strip of asphalt roofing. The strip should extend up the roof to a point 1 foot inside the inside wall line.

Corroded. Clean with heavy-duty aluminum cleaner and steel wool. Prime with zinc chromate primer and overpaint with one or two coats of alkyd trim enamel.

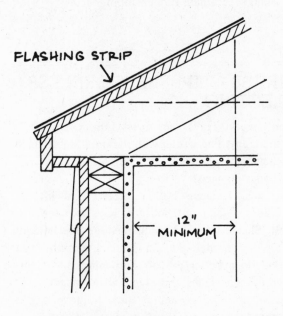

GUTTER, COPPER

Fix like an aluminum gutter with these exceptions: Soldering joints that leak is preferable to caulking. Don't worry about corrosion; it does no harm. If you dislike the appearance of the gutters, however, scrub them with detergent solution and apply an alkyd primer and alkyd trim enamel. Use only vinyl gutter guards to prevent clogging with leaves.

GUTTER, GALVANIZED STEEL

Fix like an aluminum gutter with these exceptions: Use only vinyl gutter guards. To prevent corrosion, paint the inside of gutter anually with unfibered asphalt roofing cement. If gutter rusts on the outside, use steel wool thoroughly to remove all traces of rust. Then prime with a red metal primer followed by a couple of coats of alkyd trim enamel.

GUTTER, VINYL

Small holes. Clean and daub with silicone caulking compound.

Large holes. Clean. Cut a patch out of heavy vinyl and glue it over hole with plastic-mending adhesive.

Gutter sags. Check if gutter has pulled loose from metal hangers into which it snaps. Are hangers loose from house? If the sag occurs between hangers, take gutter down (with the aid of an assistant) and install additional hangers.

Gutter clogged. Install vinyl gutter guard. See GUTTER, ALUMINUM.

Leaks at joints. Squeeze in silicone caulking compound.

Ice builds up in gutter. See GUTTER, ALUMINUM.

GUTTER, WOOD

Split. Clean out dirt and let dry thoroughly. Coat trough with asphalt roofing cement. Smooth freezer-grade aluminum foil into this. Cover with more roofing cement.

If splits are bad, try to nail wood together. Tack a sheet of aluminum flashing to trough. Spread asphalt roofing cement over this. Finally, when splits dry out, fill them with water putty or plastic wood.

Rotten. Dig out soft wood completely. Saturate with pentachlorophenol wood preservative and let dry. Then fill hole with water putty or plastic wood. Coat trough with asphalt roofing cement and renew coating every year thereafter.

Leaks at joints. Open joints and squeeze in silicone caulking compond or polysulfide rubber caulking.

Ice builds up in gutters. See GUTTER, ALUMINUM.

GYM, CHILDREN'S OUTDOOR

Rocks when children are playing on it. Attach legs to T-shaped steel anchors which are buried in the ground (gym-set dealers have these). Or make your own anchors out of "brass" curtain rods.

A better alternative is to dig holes about 12 inches wide and 15 inches deep under the legs. Pour in concrete made of 1 part portland cement, 2¼ parts sand, and 3 parts coarse aggregate. The concrete should come to within about 2 inches of the ground level. Firm it well around the legs.

Swing chains broken. Buy replacements from dealers.

Supports rusted. Remove rust with a scraper and wire brush. Apply red metal primer, then exterior trim paint.

HAIR DRYER, ELECTRIC

Doesn't work. Check whether fuse on house circuit has blown. Disconnect dryer and examine cord and plug for breaks and make necessary repairs (see ELECTRIC CORD). Make sure outlet into which dryer is plugged is operative. If dryer still doesn't work, take it to a service shop.

Tear in hat. Lap edges of tear and glue together with plastic-mending adhesive. Or apply a patch cut out of matching material with plastic-mending adhesive.

Hole in hose. Use plastic-mending adhesive kit. Coat patch in kit with adhesive and smooth over hole.

Hose loose from end connectors. Coat end of hose with plastic-mending adhesive and screw into connector. Let dry overnight.

Plastic case broken. Clean broken edges, apply plastic-mending adhesive, and press together for 12 hours.

HAMMER

Head loose. Hold hammer, head up, on a firm base. Drive small metal wedges, available from hardware store, into top of handle. You can also use hardwood wedges, but in this case it is necessary first to make a small split in the top of handle.

Handle broken. Saw off handle just below head. Then drive rest of handle out through bottom of head. Shape new handle to fit with a rasp, drive into head, and secure with a metal wedge.

Face or claw nicked or burred. Smooth with a file.

HAMMOCK

Fabric hammock ripped. Out of lightweight canvas or sailcloth cut a patch to extend at least 2 inches to either side and either end of the rip. Coat it with fabric glue and smooth under the hammock. Let dry overnight.

Net hammock cut. Tie cut cords at nearest joints so they cannot come loose. Then weave in new cords of same kind and tie to net. For extra security, dab fabric glue on the knots.

Hook pulls out of tree, wall, etc., to which hammock is attached. Screw it in at another point. If it still doesn't hold, drill a hole all the way through wood; insert a galvanized steel eyebolt; slip a large washer over the threaded end; and screw on nut.

HANDBAG

Frame sprung. Bend straight by hand. If this proves difficult, wrap the sprung edge with paper and squeeze it straight in a vise.

Twist-type catch hard to open or close. Wrap the two prongs, or knobs, with adhesive tape and carefully bend them slightly apart. If this proves difficult, overlapping edges can be filed down with a metal file; but of course this ruins the finish at that point.

Twist-type catch doesn't stay closed. Wrap the prongs with adhesive tape and bend them toward each other.

Spring-type catch doesn't catch. Check whether frame is bent, and if so, correct this. Otherwise, with a small metal file, open the catch as far as possible and deepen the groove that fits over the small prong on the other half of the frame.

Handle off. Sew back on. Or use appropriate glue or metal rivet.

Lining at top of handbag loose. The lining should be wedged into the channel in the frame. With a screwdriver, pry up edge of channel just enough to stick the lining back underneath. Squeeze frame back together with pliers (wrap the jaws with adhesive tape).

Handbag material damaged. See appropriate material entry.

HARDBOARD

Cracked. Coat both edges with white glue or resorcinol glue. Bring together carefully, trying not to break the flakelike layers, and let dry overnight. If the board is subject to any strain, you should then reinforce the break with a strip of hardboard or wood glued over the back.

Gouged. Prime with paint and let dry. Then fill hole with spackle or water putty.

Scratches. Rub a hammerhead over the scratch. Press down hard. Then rub with a wax stick of appropriate color.

Pieces of hardboard separated. Coat with white or resorcinol glue and clamp pieces together overnight. If the joint is subject to strain, bolt or rivet the pieces.

Hardboard separated from another material. If the other material holds nails and screws, cardboard can be rejoined to it with either of these. Otherwise, use bolts or rivets or appropriate glue (see HOUSEHOLD DECORATIVE ACCESSORIES and use same glue as specified for wood).

Paint finish marred. See PAINTED SURFACE.

Stains. See PAINTED SURFACE or WOOD.

HEATING PAD, ELECTRIC

Doesn't heat. You can repair a broken cord plug (see ELECTRIC CORD), but don't fool with the pad otherwise. Buy a new one.

HEATING SYSTEM—ALL TYPES

Also see DUCT, HEATING; PIPE, HEATING; RADIATOR, HOT WATER; RADIATOR, STEAM; REGISTER, WARM AIR.

System not working. Is the thermostat calling for heat? Is the switch on? Has the fuse blown?

Open thermostat cover and examine contact points. Run a dollar bill between them to remove dirt. If thermostat has a small vial of mercury instead of contact points, leave it alone.

Heating inefficiently. Turn off system and vacuum soot from walls of combustion chambers made of steel or brick (but leave those with a fabriclike fiber lining alone). Take down smoke pipe and clean out soot with a brush and/or vacuum cleaner. Have chimney flue cleaned.

Check radiators. See directions in following entries for your particular kind of heating system.

Make sure furnace room is ventilated so burner receives sufficient oxygen.

Thermostat may be in wrong location. See HEATING SYSTEM—THERMOSTAT.

HEATING SYSTEM—COAL STOKER

Doesn't start. Check for blown fuse. Turn off stoker and check for obstruction. Follow manufacturer's directions for removing any obstruction. If you still have trouble, call heating contractor.

Jams. Turn off stoker and remove obstruction according to manufacturer's directions.

NOTE. Don't lose manufacturer's instructions for operating stoker. Keep them available near stoker. Follow directions for oiling.

HEATING SYSTEM, ELECTRIC

Room heaters blow fuses. Somebody didn't install wiring of adequate size, so the heaters are overloading the circuits. Don't use the heaters until heavier wiring has been run in.

Room cold. Thermostat may not be properly calibrated. You can correct this provided you have the manufacturer's directions; otherwise, call a serviceman.

Room insulation may be inadequate. Perhaps all you need is to install storm windows and doors.

Baseboard heaters click and pop. Tighten all screws holding units in place, but don't count on dramatic results. There's really no cure.

Fans in recessed wall and ceiling heaters noisy, laboring. Remove grilles and give fans a couple of drops of light oil.

Excessive condensation on bathroom walls.

This happens because the extrathick insulation, storm windows, and tight vapor barriers required in electrically heated homes do not permit moisture vapor to escape from the houses as rapidly as it does ordinarily. To correct problem, install small ventilating fans in all bathrooms. Don't take such hot, long baths or showers.

Cracks in plaster ceiling with embedded heating cables. Knock out plaster covering cables and replace with gypsum board.

HEATING SYSTEM—GAS BURNER

Doesn't come on. Check whether thermostat is calling for heat. Is the electric switch on? Has the fuse blown?

Check whether pilot light is out. If it is, turn off electric switch and main furnace gas valve. Relight pilot according to instruction plate on the furnace.

Smells. Shut off main gas control valve at once and call a serviceman. Don't under any circumstances go hunting for the leak with a lighted match. Don't even turn on the electric light in the furnace room.

HEATING SYSTEM, HOT WATER

Water level in gauge glass too low. Open valve on water inlet pipe and let in water until it reaches point marked on boiler.

Water rusty, filled with sediment. Open drain valve near bottom of boiler and draw off water until it runs clear. Also draw water to fill a pail from expansion tank. Then introduce fresh water.

Circulating pump stops or labors. Lubricate with SAE number 30 oil. If it still doesn't work, press reset switch on circulator, or, if there isn't a reset switch, rap the circulator sharply with your hand.

Radiator problems. See RADIATOR, HOT WATER.

HEATING SYSTEM—OIL BURNER

Doesn't start. Check whether thermostat is calling for heat. Is burner switch on? Has fuse blown? Is there oil in the oil tank? Don't trust the gauge: jar it by hitting the tank close to it. Drop a dipstick into the tank.

Press the red reset button on the control box mounted on burner, furnace, or the smoke pipe running to the chimney. If burner goes on and continues running, fine. If burner doesn't make a sound, or goes on and then turns off within a short time, call a serviceman.

Operates but house doesn't get warm enough. Open fire door. If flame seems small, call a serviceman.

Smells of oil. Call a serviceman.

HEATING SYSTEM, STEAM

Water level in gauge glass too low. Open valve on water inlet pipe and let in water until it reaches middle of gauge or point marked on boiler.

Boiler goes on and off at brief intervals. This usually happens in the morning when the heat is turned up from the low nighttime setting. Steam leaves boiler faster than condensate can return from radiators, causing water level in boiler to drop and low-water cutoff to shut off boiler. Don't worry.

Water rusty, filled with sediment. Open drain valve and draw off water until it runs clear. Add fresh water if necessary.

Pipes bang. See PIPE, HEATING.

Radiator problems. See RADIATOR, STEAM.

HEATING SYSTEM— THERMOSTAT

Heating plant doesn't turn on. The thermostat is rarely to blame, but it just might be if it is old. In that case, it very probably has open contacts which have become covered with dust. Remove cover of unit and run a piece of paper carefully between the contacts to clean them. If the heat still doesn't come on, trouble is somewhere else.

House not heating properly. If this has been a problem for some time, there's a good chance the thermostat is not in the right location. The rules for locating the right spot are long but simple:

Install the thermostat 4 feet off floor in a central location that is frequently occupied or used—for example, the living room, dining room, family room, or center hall, but not a bedroom, bathroom, or kitchen.

Avoid interior halls, locations directly over the furnace, and rooms with fireplaces you use often.

Don't install thermostat on an outside wall, and be sure the inside wall doesn't contain heating pipes, ducts, or a chimney.

Keep thermostat away from sunny windows, radiators, registers, television sets, often-used heating appliances, and large incandescent lamps, because the heat they give off will make thermostat slow to call for heat from furnace. Also keep it away from outside doors, large windows and glass walls because the cold they bring in will turn thermostat on before heat is needed.

Install thermostat in an open location where it's exposed to circulating air—not behind a door or drapery, for instance.

Before moving your thermostat, hang a thermometer in the location you're thinking about for several days. If it shows the heat in that location runs fairly even, it's a simple job to disconnect the thermostat, move it, and reconnect it in exactly the same way.

Mercury thermostat not working properly. In this type of thermostat, a little spring is attached to a glass vial containing mercury. To work properly, the thermostat must be dead level. Lay a carpenter's level across the top or up and down the side to make sure it is.

HEATING SYSTEM, WARM AIR

Operating inefficiently. Clean filters. Do this monthly during heating season. Vacuum blower compartment in furnace and wipe blower blades clean.

Not delivering heat. Turn off furnace and oil blower motor and fan with number 30 oil. Replace fan belt if broken, badly worn, or cracked. If belt is slipping because it's loose, tighten it by loosening allen screw on sheave at end of pulley and turning sheave clockwise, or by turning cradle bolt beneath blower motor.

Stains on wall above registers. See REGISTER, WARM AIR.

HEAT PUMP

NOTE. Heat pumps are far too complicated for the layman. Have them checked every spring and fall, and let a serviceman make all repairs. In summer, however, there are several minor measures you can take to meet common problems. See AIR CONDITIONER, CENTRAL or AIR CONDITIONER, ROOM, depending on whether you have a central or room heat pump.

HEDGE CLIPPER

Doesn't cut—simply folds twigs between blades. Tighten nut joining blades. If trouble continues, one or both of the blades may be slightly bent; in which case, take them apart and straighten carefully.

Dull. Sharpen blades with a medium-fine file; or separate the blades and sharpen them on a bench grinder. Be sure to maintain the original bevel of the cutting edges.

HEDGE TRIMMER, ELECTRIC

Doesn't work. Is trimmer plugged into extension cord and is cord plugged into outlet? Has fuse blown? Is outlet defective? Is there a break in the extension cord?

Make sure that pigtail on trimmer has not broken or become disconnected inside the handle, by turning on clipper and wiggling cord back and forth. Open handle and check connections.

Works slowly. Extension cord is probably undersized. Up to 75 feet, use cord with number 18 or, better, number 16 wires. Up to 125 feet, use cord with number 16 or number 14 wires. Over 125 feet, use cord with number 14 or number 12 wires.

Sparks noticeably. Replace carbon brushes.

Works stiffly. Unplug trimmer and examine blades to make sure nothing is jammed between teeth. Clean off resin and dirt on blades. Lubricate according to manufacturer's directions.

Blade nicked. Remove nick with fine-toothed file or sharpening stone.

Blade dull. Remove reciprocating cutting blade and file each tooth with a small, fine-toothed file. Maintain original bevel of the cutting edges.

HINGES

Stiff. If pin is removable, tap it out with a nail and scrape off paint. Scrape paint from hinge leaves, too. Coat pin with light oil and replace. If pin is not removable, scrape off paint around it and the joints, and squeeze powdered graphite into the joints.

Leaves bent. Place on a hard surface and hammer straight.

Shift position. Screw down tight. If screws don't hold, take them out and fill holes with plastic wood. Then reset screws. Note that some hinges have elongated screw holes to permit the position of a cabinet door to be changed. With these, if door is accidentally knocked out of place, simply position door properly and tighten hinges.

Screws tear through hole in hinge. This happens sometimes in cigar-box hinges, piano hinges, and others made of light metal. If the leaves do not come together when the hinge is shut, you can make a washer out of thin aluminum sheet or a tin can, place over screw hole, and drive in a roundheaded screw. Then file top of screw flat. If the hinge leaves do come together when shut, drive screw almost all the way through the enlarged hole in the hinge, then coat edges of hole with epoxy glue and turn screw tight.

HOCKEY STICK

Broken. Coat the broken edges with epoxy glue and clamp together for 24 hours. Sand finish off the stick in the area of the break and coat the wood with polyester resin used in fiber glass boat construction. Then wrap fiber glass tape diagonally over the break. Butt the edges of the tape and smooth it into the resin. Let dry. Then sand and brush on two more coats of resin.

HOT PLATE, ELECTRIC

Doesn't heat. Examine element to see if it is broken. If so, disconnect appliance, take out element, and replace it. Check also whether fuse on house circuit has blown, whether outlet into which hot plate is plugged is defective, whether cord is broken. If hot plate still won't work, take it to a service shop.

HOT WATER BOTTLE

Holes, tears. See TIRE (*tube punctured*).

HOUSEHOLD DECORATIVE ACCESSORIES
(such as bookends, ashtrays, sconces, candle holders, ornaments).
See also FIGURINE and VASE.

Material of which object is made broken. See appropriate material entry.

Different materials separated. In almost all cases the materials can be rejoined with the appropriate glue as shown in chart that follows. (For how to glue, see BASIC METHODS: HOW TO GLUE THINGS TOGETHER.) The addition of screws or rivets may be advisable if the joint needs to be extrastrong.

To use chart, find one of the materials in the vertical list, find the other in the horizontal list. Use the glue called for at the intersecting lines.

Key to chart:

C—Cellulose cement.   F—Fabric glue   R—Rubber cement   W—White glue
E—Epoxy glue   P—Plastic-mending adhesive   Re—Resorcinol glue

	Ceramics (china, earthenware, etc.)	Cork	Felt	Glass	Leather	Metal	Plastics	Rubber	Stone	Wood
Ceramics (china, earthenware, etc.)	C or E									
Cork	R	R								
Felt	R	R	F							
Glass	C or E	R	R	C or E						
Leather	R	R	R	R	R					
Metal	C or E	R	R	C or E	R	E				
Plastics	P	R	R	C	R	P	P			
Rubber	R	R	R	R	R	R	R	R		
Stone	E	R	R	E	R	E	C	R	E	
Wood	C or E	R	W	C	R	C or E	E or P	R	E	W or Re

HUMIDIFIER

Doesn't work. Has fuse blown? Is outlet into which humidifier is plugged operative? Is cord broken?

Is humidifier properly filled with water? If unit has an automatic feed, valve controlling flow may be defective and need replacing.

Is humidifier clogged with mineral deposits? Clean thoroughly. If unit has a spray nozzle, clean carefully and thoroughly. Wash evaporative belt or pad. Vinegar dissolves hard-water deposits.

Not delivering enough moisture. It's probably clogging up. Clean thoroughly.

Rusting. Scrape metal bare. Prime with red metal primer and follow with one or two coats of alkyd gloss enamel.

ICE BUCKET

Glass liner broken. If you can figure out who the maker was, see if he can't replace the liner. Otherwise, you must cut through the seal around the top with a sharp knife and carefully lift out the broken pieces. Glue together with epoxy glue and hope for the best. After replacing liner in the outer shell, seal the edges around the top with silicone caulking.

Plastic liner broken. Drain out any water that has dripped through the bucket and give the cavity as much time to dry as possible. Press the broken edges together into line. Squirt silicone caulking into the break and smooth it over the break.

INSULATION

Soggy with water. Stop the leak that caused the trouble and let the insulation dry out; it's still good. If insulation inside a wall becomes soggy, however, it may settle and leave an uninsulated area at the top of the wall. But, unfortunately, there is no way of telling whether this has happened short of opening the wall.

Vapor barrier on the back of insulation torn. Cover the tear completely with packaging tape made of plastic reinforced with cord.

Blanket or batt insulation in roof or under a floor drooping. Wedge it back between the rafters or joists and tack chicken wire underneath.

Rigid perimeter insulation loose from foundation wall. Remove it and clean off the back and the wall. Stick it back in place with silicone-rubber adhesive.

INTERIOR WALL—ALL TYPES

Admits too much sound from adjoining rooms. This is primarily a problem with gypsum-board walls but can affect other types as well. See INTERIOR WALL, GYPSUM BOARD.

Damaged by chairs pushed back against it. Glue a small strip of felt of the appropriate color across the back of a flat-backed chair just below the top. If chair back is curved, glue a short strip to the outermost edge.

A better solution is to nail a molding, called a chair rail, across the entire wall. Install the rail at the height of the chairs giving the most trouble. Drive finishing nails through the rail into the studs.

INTERIOR WALL, CERAMIC TILE

Crack between tiles and bathtub. See BATHTUB.

Crack between tiles and wood or metal. Clean out old filler, if any. Since there is a difference in the rate of expansion and contraction between the materials, fill crack with silicone caulking compound.

Other problems. See TILE, CERAMIC.

INTERIOR WALL—CORK

Also see CORK.

Wallpaperlike covering made with thin layer of cork loose. Pry up edges very carefully and spread vinyl wall-covering adhesive underneath. Smooth down.

INTERIOR WALL, FIBER BOARD
(Celotex and the like)

Tears, cracks. If board is textured, there is no way of fixing it so it will look right. Replace. If board is smooth and sufficiently rigid, spread gypsum-board joint compound over hole and embed in it a strip of gypsum-board tape. Smooth and cover with a thin layer of compound. Let dry. Then sand smooth and spread on more compound in a wider strip. Let dry and sand again. A third application of compound may be necessary if ridge made by compound is too apparent.

Joints between boards expand and contract. This happens with changes in weather. There is no cure. Cover joints with wood moldings.

Holes. Replace panels.

INTERIOR WALL—GLUE-ON BRICKS

If bricks are made of clay, clean them and repair mortar joints between them like conventional bricks. See BRICK.

Plastic bricks damaged. Cut them out and scrape off adhesive on subwall. Buy new plastic bricks to match along with adhesive and joint compound recommended by the manufacturer. Cut bricks to fill hole exactly. Apply adhesive to back and stick to wall. After 24 hours, fill joints.

INTERIOR WALL, GYPSUM BOARD

Nail holes, gouges. Fill with spackle or gypsum-board joint compound and sand smooth.

Holes up to about 4 inches wide. Cut a piece of cardboard slightly larger than hole. Insert a string through the center and knot at the back. Push cardboard through hole, center it, and hold onto string. Fill hole to about half its depth with patching plaster and hang onto string until plaster sets. Then cut off string at the plaster and fill hole the rest of the way with patching plaster or gypsum-board joint compound. Strike off smooth and flush with wall surface. Sand when dry.

Large holes. Cut out hole with a saw to make a rectangular opening. Out of a scrap of gypsum board, cut a patch or plug 2 inches greater than the hole in both directions. Turn upside down, measure in 1 inch from all edges, and draw lines parallel to the edges. Cut along these lines with a knife, and bend edges backward to break the plaster. Then carefully cut out the cut strips of plaster down to the back of the paper on the front of the gypsum board.

Trowel a thin layer of gypsum-board joint compound around the edges of the hole. Insert the plug in the hole and smooth the paper flanges into the compound. Then apply another thin layer of compound over the exposed edges of the flanges. Let dry, and sand. Apply additional compound, feathering out the edges beyond the flanges. Sand when dry and apply a third layer of compound, feathering out edges even further from the flanges. Sand smooth when dry, and paint.

Boards bulging along edges. Nail down with annular-ring nails spaced 6 inches apart. If the crack between board shows, trowel a strip of gypsum-board joint compound over it and smooth a piece of gypsum-board tape into it directly over the joint. Over this apply another thin layer of joint compound. Let dry, and sand. Then apply two more layers of joint compound, feathering out edges beyond the joint until the strip of compound is about 8 to 12 inches wide. Finish by sanding smooth and painting.

Nails holding board have popped through the paper surface. Drive them into the board about 1/16 inch with a hammer. Then drive another new annular-ring through the board about 2 inches away from each popped nail. Cover heads with several layers of gypsum-board joint compound.

Cracks, bulges, depressions, show through paint where gypsum boards come together. Scrape open cracks slightly. If bulges are bad, chip off joint compound covering them and tear off paper tape underneath. Then smooth new tape into a thin strip of compound. From this point, all problems are handled in the same way. Apply several layers of joint compound, feath-

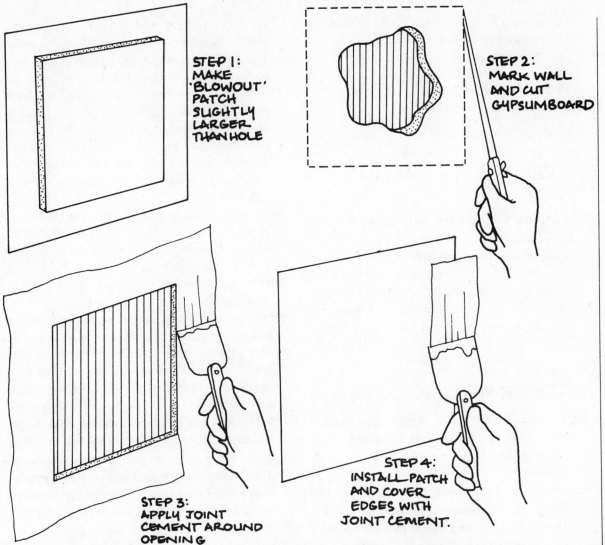

STEP 1: MAKE 'BLOWOUT' PATCH SLIGHTLY LARGER THAN HOLE

STEP 2: MARK WALL AND CUT GYPSUMBOARD

STEP 3: APPLY JOINT CEMENT AROUND OPENING

STEP 4: INSTALL PATCH AND COVER EDGES WITH JOINT CEMENT.

ering the edges further and further away from the joint, until the joint is completely concealed. Then sand smooth and paint.

Nails, screws, don't hold in wall. See BASIC METHODS: HOW TO SUPPORT THINGS ON WALLS THAT WILL NOT RECEIVE OR HOLD NAILS AND SCREWS.

Sounds easily penetrate wall. Remove baseboards and other moldings and trim around doors and windows. Apply a new layer of ½-inch, or better, ⅝-inch gypsum board directly over the existing wall. The boards must be installed so the joints do not fall over those in the existing wall. Offset them one stud spacing. Install the new panels either with annular-ring nails that are long enough to penetrate well into the studs, or with the adhesive recommended by the gypsum board manufacturer.

Fur out trim around doors and windows with boards the same thickness as the gypsum board. Outlet and switch boxes must be brought forward flush with the new board.

For even better results, build a new framework of studs and plates in front of the existing wall. Use 2-inch by 2-inch lumber. Install the studs midway between the existing studs. Then cover the new framework with ½-inch or ⅝-inch gypsum board.

INTERIOR WALL, HARDBOARD

Panels buckling, loose. Renail with annular-ring nails driven into the studs or furring strips. Before driving nails, drill ¹⁄₁₆-inch-deep holes to receive the nailheads. Set the heads into the holes with a nail set—don't try to drive them all the way in with your hammer, because the face will damage the hardboard surface. Then cover with spackle or colored filler sticks sold by hardboard manufacturer.

Other problems. See HARDBOARD.

INTERIOR WALL—MIRROR TILE

Tile broken. Chip out tile and remove adhesive tape that secured it to wall. Buy new tile and attach double-faced adhesive tape to the back. You can use either two strips of tape, the length of the tile, under the vertical edges, or four small squares of tape under the four corners. Stick tile to wall and press down firmly.

INTERIOR WALL, PLASTER

Hair cracks, small holes. Scrape open slightly with a beer can opener and fill with spackle or gypsum-board joint compound. Sand smooth when dry.

Large cracks, large holes. Scrape open to ¼-inch width. If possible, make the opening wider at the back than on the surface. Dampen crack with water. Fill immediately with patching plaster. If the job is not too extensive, the plaster can be mixed with water only. The mixture hardens quickly. To slow hardening, if you are doing a big job, mix plaster with ⅔ water and ⅓ vinegar.

If the lath is missing behind a hole (as where a light was installed), cut a piece of cardboard a bit larger than the hole. Insert a string through the center and knot in back. Push cardboard through hole. Center it. Hold on to string. Fill hole part way with patching plaster and when it has set, cut string. Then fill hole rest of the way with plaster. For a smooth, hard finish, wet trowel with water frequently. For a sand finish, mix plaster 50:50 with clean fine sand or Perltex.

Very large holes. Chip out loose plaster and sprinkle exposed surfaces with water. Fill to within ⅛ inch of wall surface with prepared plaster mix from a masonry supplies house. Fill rest of the way with gypsum-board joint compound or patching plaster.

If lath is broken or rusted out, cut back plaster to studs on either side of hole. Nail in new lath and build up from this with prepared plaster mix and gypsum-board joint compound. To make patch flush with wall, draw a steel straightedge across it while joint compound is soft.

Holes and cracks in wall above bathtub. Repair as above but for plaster use Keene's cement and dry hydrated lime mixed in the proportion of 4 pounds to 1 pound.

Bulges. Break out bulging plaster completely and repair as above.

Plaster cracked into large pieces which are loose from plaster but otherwise strong. The only proper solution is to knock out the plaster completely and replaster or replace with gypsum board. If plaster is applied to wood lath, however, there is a simpler answer: Drill small holes here and there through the loose pieces and fasten them to the lath with 1¼-inch flathead screws driven through small washers. Then cover washers and screws with gypsum-board joint compound. (Special perforated, slightly concave washers called plaster buttons are available in some hardware stores.)

Plaster soft, crumbly, powdery. Check for water leak and stop this first. Then scrape out all loose material and let dry for several days. Fill hole, if not deep, with gypsum-board joint compound; otherwise, fill partway with patching plaster and finish with joint compound.

Picture hooks chip plaster, don't hold. Fill holes with spackle or gypsum-board joint compound. Stick scraps of masking tape over spackle when dry and drive picture hook nails through this.

Screws don't hold in plaster. Fill holes with steel wool and drive in screws. Or insert fiber plugs and drive screws into these. If screws still don't hold, replace them with toggle bolts or hollow-wall screw anchors (see BASIC METHODS: HOW TO SUPPORT THINGS on walls that will not receive or hold nails and screws).

New paint peeling off old paint. Old paint may

have been calcimine. You should never paint over this. About the only thing you can do now is take off the new paint—and old paint, if it comes off, too—with paint remover and a scraper. Then scrub off whatever calcimine remains with warm water. When dry, repaint with latex.

INTERIOR WALL—PLASTIC TILE

Tiles broken. See below.

Tiles loose. With a thin putty knife, carefully pry off tile (don't use too much pressure or tile will break). Scrape out as much of the adhesive as possible. Make sure wall is sound and dry underneath. Spread back of tile with plastic-tile adhesive and press tile firmly in place. Smooth out joints.

If wall behind tile is unsound, it must be repaired before tile is reset.

Cracks betwen tiles. Scrape out old cement and fill joints with new plastic-tile adhesive. Smooth off with a small knife, nailhead, or blunt pencil point. Remove excess from surface with plastic-tile adhesive cleaner. Let joints dry 24 hours before exposing to moisture.

Joints stained. See TILE, CERAMIC.

INTERIOR WALL, PLYWOOD

See also INTERIOR WALL, WOOD.

Hole kicked in thin plywood. This cannot be repaired attractively. You should really replace the entire panel. But if you insist on trying, cut plywood back on the sides until at least ¾ inch of the front surface of the studs is exposed. Cut the plywood straight across the top and bottom of the hole. Cut a 2-by-4 into two pieces to fit snugly between the studs. Nail them into place between the studs along the top and bottom edges of the opening so that the old wall surface and new patch will bear on them. Cut a new piece of plywood to fit exactly in the hole. Nail to studs and cross blocks with brads, and nail down the surrounding panel.

INTERIOR WALL—RIGID PLASTIC PANELS

These panels are similar to those used to surface kitchen counter tops. In the home they are used primarily in bathrooms—usually in bathtub recesses and shower stalls. They are glued to a subwall of moisture-resistant gypsum board or exterior-grade plywood.

Bulging and loose around rim of tub or shower stall receptor. This happens if the subwall was not properly constructed and water seeps into the joint, weakening the glue and subwall. The only satisfactory cure is to rip out the entire panel and have it replaced or reinstalled by a carpenter over a new subwall. You can, however, improve the appearance of the wall to some extent and prevent further trouble if you don't use the shower for a couple of months so that the subwall can dry out completely. The plastic will then return to a more or less level contour. To hold it in place, scrape out the old caulking around the tub (or shower receptor) rim and fill with new silicone caulking compound. Then install curved strips of ceramic tile over the joint. See BATHTUB.

INTERIOR WALL, WOOD

Joints open. If joints open and close as weather changes, you can tack batten strips over them. The strips should be attached only on one side of the joints. If the joints are permanently open, you can apply batten strips or fill the joints with narrow wood strips set flush with the surface. Note, however, that any such treatment may end up in a wall that is worse-looking than the one you have now.

Gouges, dents, etc. See WOOD.

Finish marred. *S*ee LACQUERED SURFACE, PAINTED SURFACE, SHELLACKED SURFACE, or VARNISHED SURFACE as case may be.

IRON, ELECTRIC

Doesn't heat. Check whether fuse has blown. Make sure outlet into which iron is plugged is operating. Disconnect iron and examine it for a break or loose connection at terminals. Tighten connections. Replace cord if broken. If these measures don't work, take iron to service shop.

Soleplate scratched. Smooth with ultrafine emery cloth. Then heat iron slightly and run it over a piece of wax paper.

Starch burned on soleplate. Rub a steel plate with very fine steel wool. On Teflon, use a heavy-duty detergent.

Steam iron clogged, not steaming. Clean with special chemical made for dissolving mineral scale. This is available from hardware store.

IVORY

Broken. Coat broken edges with cellulose cement and press together for 6 hours.

Separated from another material. See HOUSEHOLD DECORATIVE ACCESSORIES. Use glue recommended for ceramics.

Stained yellow. Rub with alcohol and expose to sunlight. But note that ivory yellows naturally with age and you may not be able to change its appearance very much.

JEWELRY

NOTE. Better let a jeweler fix your valuable pieces, but you can do a pretty good job on the others. You will find, however, that, because many clips and clasps are made of spring steel, you can't replace them with ordinary metal if they break. You must, instead, either let a jeweler take over, or replace the entire clip.

Stone loose. Try bending little prongs or claws that hold stone secure. If these are worn or broken off and if jewelry is not valuable, glue stone in place with cellulose cement.

Pin or brooch latch broken. In the usual latch, the pin slips into an incomplete ring and a small trigger slides across the opening in the ring to lock the pin in place. If the trigger doesn't stay closed, pinch the sides of the ring in which it slides. If it doesn't close, insert a knife point in the slotted edge of the ring and force the slot open slightly.

Ring-type latch on necklace broken. This is similar to the preceding latch except that it contains a spring which automatically closes the trigger—provided the slotted sides of the ring are not pinched together. If spring fails, replace the latch. Simply pry open the ring at the end of the necklace so the latch ring can be removed. After replacing latch, to assure that the ring at the end of necklace won't reopen, solder the joint or put a dab of epoxy glue on it.

Earring clip loses spring, won't grip earlobe. The spring is a tiny straight strip of metal built into the clip. If this is bent outward, pinch it closed with small-nosed pliers. If strip is flabby, open the bent prongs holding it and pull it out of clip; turn it over, and reclamp it in the prongs.

Tonguelike necklace clasp doesn't hold. Simply bend the two leaves of the tongue further apart

Necklace or bracelet hasp doesn't stay shut. Open the moving arm of the hasp and bend the end inward slightly so it grips the body of the hasp when shut.

Chain snarled. See CHAIN.

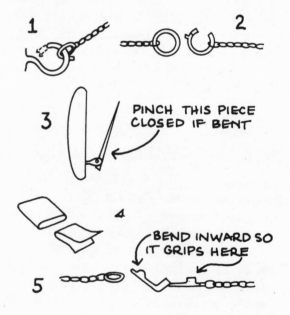

KITE

Tears in paper. Out of tissue paper, cut a patch ½ inch larger than the tear in all directions. Paste down with white glue.

Wood-framing pieces broken. If break parallels

the grain of the wood, coat the broken edges with resorcinol glue and clamp together. If break is across the grain, use epoxy glue and reinforce with a short strip of very thin wood, such as a veneer, glued to one side of the broken piece. Matchsticks laid edge to edge, parallel with the grain, may be used instead of the veneer.

For a neater joint, cut a shallow recess in the framing member wood, on one side, and lay the reinforcement in this.

KITCHEN UTENSILS

Holes in metal. Scour surface thoroughly, rinse, and dry. Spread plastic steel into and over hole. This withstands up to 600 degrees F., and will therefore not be affected by oven heat, but it will break down under high direct heat. However, even under these circumstances the patch will hold as long as the utensil has liquid in it.

Holes in porcelain enamel. Scour surface and dry. Chip off a bit of the porcelain from around the hole. Then cover bare metal with plastic steel.

Glass utensil broken. Wash broken edges and dry thoroughly. Coat both surfaces with epoxy glue and press together for 24 hours. Utensil can be used again for oven cooking.

Earthenware utensil broken. See EARTHENWARE.

Aluminum, copper, steel, dented. Hold a block of wood over concave side of dent and tap out dent with light hammer blows.

Bottom warped. You probably can't flatten it completely, and don't try to because you may fracture the metal. However, you can flatten it enough to sit steadily on a burner by turning the utensil upside down and pressing down on the bottom with the palm of your hand. Do not use a hammer.

Handles broken. If made of plastic, coat the broken edges with plastic-mending adhesive and press together overnight. If handle is wood, use waterproof glue.

Handle broken from utensil. You can drill holes (if none exist) through the handle and the utensil and rivet the pieces together with steel or aluminum rivets. But it is preferable to take utensil to a metalworking shop and have handle spot-welded on.

Cap on whistling teakettle spout doesn't spring closed. Unscrew the bolts holding the handle to the kettle. Lift up trigger that controls the cap. Remove the coiled spring and replace with a new one purchased at hardware store.

Cast iron rusted, pitted. Remove rust with liquid rust-remover and fine steel wool. Smooth plastic steel into pits. Henceforth, do not wash cast-iron utensil with scouring powders or steel wool; a slight coating of grease on the surface prevents rusting.

Copper discolored. Sprinkle with salt and then rub with vinegar.

Copper bottom on Revereware utensil burned and flaking. This happens when an empty utensil is left on a hot burner. Simply scrub and wash off the flaking metal. No serious harm is done.

Aluminum darkened. Scour with fine steel wool. If necessary, wash the stain with vinegar or mix 2 teaspoons cream of tartar in 1 quart water and bring to a boil in the utensil.

Enamelware stained. Scrub with a household cleanser. If stains remain, fill with a solution of laundry bleach and let stand overnight.

Brown stains on stainless steel. Scour with a household cleanser.

Tinware rusted. Remove rust with liquid rust-remover. (Do not use steel wool because it will remove the tin coating as well as the rust, and rust will then spread.) If tinware is painted (a bread box or canister, for example), prime cleaned metal with a rust-inhibiting paint. Then apply gloss enamel.

Food burned on utensil. Soak overnight in a strong solution of household ammonia. Then scrub off.

KNIFE, ELECTRIC

Doesn't run. Has fuse blown? Is outlet into which knife is plugged operating? Check cord for a break and replace it. Otherwise let a service shop handle repairs.

Sparks, runs unevenly, smells of ozone. Open handle of knife. Screw out carbon brushes on each side of the motor and replace with new ones of the same size. At the same time, make sure springs holding brushes have enough tension. Clean the commutator against which brushes bear with fine sandpaper while turning the commutator by hand.

KNIFE, POCKET

Handle sides (bone, plastic, etc.) loose. Spread epoxy glue between body of knife and handle and clamp.

Blade broken. If knife is worth saving, reshape blade on a grinding wheel.

Dull. Lay blade almost flat on a carborundum stone and sharpen with a circular motion.

Blades rusted shut. Soak in liquid rust-remover. Then clean with emery cloth. Oil.

LACE

Holes. Cut a patch of matching lace, place under hole and whip it down. Then carefully snip out old material.

LACQUERED SURFACE

Minor scratches. Dip a tiny artist's brush in lacquer thinner and lightly run it along the scratch. Thinner will soften lacquer, obliterate scar.

Larger scratches. Fill by rubbing with a colored wax stick made for use on furniture. Or touch up with matching lacquer.

Water spots. Rub with cigarette ashes and a cloth dipped in salad oil or sewing machine oil. If this doesn't work, rub with rottenstone and cloth dipped in salad oil. Clean off residue with paint thinner.

Heat marks. Rub with rottenstone and oil as above.

Paint spots. Scrape off the paint with the point of a sharp knife. If surface is damaged slightly in the process, rub down with rottenstone and oil.

Nail polish. Handle like paint spots.

Candle wax on lacquer. Remove as much as possible with your fingers, then scrape off residue with a dull table knife and wipe entire surface quickly and lightly with paint thinner.

Crayon or lipstick. Rub with white appliance wax.

LADDER

Also see STEPLADDER.

NOTE. Don't let a hasty, patchwork job kill you. A new ladder is cheaper than a broken neck.

Rung of wood ladder broken. If the rung passes all the way through the side rails (so you can see the ends), saw it off close to the inside of the rails. Then drill out wood remaining in rails with a brace and bit and cut out the nails that held the ends of the rung with a triangular metal file. Secure a piece of hickory the same size as the holes. Apply resorcinol glue in the holes and insert the rung by driving it carefully through from one side of the ladder to the other. Anchor the ends of the rung with galvanized finishing nails.

If the broken rung is set into mortises in the rails (the ends are not visible), cut it off about 3 inches from each rail. Then, with a hammer and chisel, split the remaining pieces and pull them out (but don't bend them back and forth so violently that the rails are split). Cut nails that held rung with a file. With a brace and bit, bore one of the holes all the way through the rail. Apply glue in holes. Then insert a new hickory rung by driving it through the open rail hole, across the ladder, and into the mortise in the other rail. Secure ends with finishing nails.

Rail cracked. This can be braced with a long 2-by-4 bolted to the rail, but that will make the ladder even more awkward to handle, and anyway, why take chances? Get a new ladder.

Rung in metal ladder broken. If the rung is bolted to the rails, as is the case in cheap ladders, you can easily install a new one. But if the ladder is welded, let a metalworker make the repair.

LAMP

NOTE. Always disconnect lamp before making repairs.

Cord broken. If socket is mounted on top of a straight stem, unscrew socket from stem, pull it apart, loosen screws holding wires, and pull cord out through bottom. Run new cord up through base and stem and attach to socket. See ELECTRIC CORD (*lamp cord broken at socket*).

If socket is mounted on an arm attached to the stem, unscrew wires from socket as above. Then unscrew nut in base of lamp and pull out cord. The various pieces of which the lamp is made will now either fall apart or you can unscrew them. This will make it possible for you to thread new cord into arm on which socket is mounted. After cord is in, reassemble pieces and tighten them together. Then install socket.

Socket broken. Simply unscrew it from lamp and install new one. See LAMP SOCKET. Also see ELECTRIC CORD (*lamp cord broken at socket*).

Table lamp loose at joints. Remove felt (if any) from base. Tighten nut on the spindle that holds parts of lamp together.

If metal base that holds socket wobbles on top of a glass or ceramic pedestal, loosen nut in base of lamp until socket base can be pulled free of pedestal. The socket base, in many instances, is a cup that fits over the top of the pedestal. Clean this out, fill with wet plaster of Paris, and place over pedestal immediately.

Light diffuser broken. If made of glass, coat broken edges with cellulose cement and press together. If made of plastic, use plastic-mending adhesive. To hold pieces together while glue is drying, put strips of adhesive tape across the break.

LAMPSHADE

Shade loose from wire frame. Remove binding at top or bottom as case may be and replace with adhesive-backed mending tape. Stick tape to outside of shade first and smooth it carefully. Then wrap over frame wire and stick down.

Thick plastic shade cracked. Apply plastic-mending adhesive to break and press pieces together. Hold them in place with masking tape until dry.

Glass shade broken in many pieces. See VASE.

LAMP SOCKET

Lamp won't light. Disconnect. Pull halves of socket apart. Tighten screws around wires and make sure cord is not broken at any place. If lamp still doesn't light, remove bulb again and, with a screwdriver, bend metal contact in bottom of socket upward. If lamp still doesn't light, difficulty is in the switch. Replace socket with a new one. See ELECTRIC CORD (*lamp cord broken at socket*).

Bulb broken, base stuck in socket. Disconnect lamp. With small-nose pliers, grasp edge of bulb base (it won't hurt to bend it a little) and turn counterclockwise. If base is rusted in socket and doesn't come out, replace socket.

LATTICE

Strips bent away from one another. The usual practice is simply to nail them together with tiny box nails and clinch the points, but the result is unattractive from the back side. Use slender flathead screws instead. They should be just a fraction shorter than the thickness of the two lattice strips.

Strip broken. If break runs with the grain, apply resorcinol glue to one of the edges, and clamp the pieces together for 24 hours. If break is across the lattice strip, saw the strip back to the cross strips on either side of the break. Make the cuts at a 45-degree angle across the strip. The triangular pieces should overlap the cross strips, and should be fastened to the cross strips with small screws. Then out of a new piece of lattice cut a piece to fill in the gap, and screw it into place. This, admittedly, is a rather fussy way to make a simple repair, but it looks better and is stronger than any other approach.

LAUNDRY TUB

Porcelain chipped. See BATHROOM FIXTURES.

Stains. See BATHROOM FIXTURES.

Drain clogged. See DRAINS, PLUMBING.

Faucet problems. See FAUCET.

Basket-type strainer-stopper leaks. Buy a new one.

LAWN MOWER, HAND

Rattles, stiff. Tighten all bolts. Lubricate at oiling points regularly.

Blades stick. Lower the front edge of the under-knife by loosening bottom screws at the side of the knife and tightening top screws. Turn reel by hand to make sure contact is even along the entire blade. Some mower under-knives are adjusted by thumbscrews.

Doesn't cut. Reverse above procedure; raise the underknife.

Dull. You can touch up edges of blades with a fine-metal file, but it's better to take mower to a shop where blades can be sharpened properly.

Wheels spin, reel doesn't. If you loosen the bolts that hold the wheels and remove the wheels, you will find inside a cogged gear. Pull this off its shaft and you will then find a short piece of steel inserted through the shaft. This is beveled on the ends and positioned so that when you push the mower forward it catches in slots inside the gear and turns the reel, but when you pull the mower backward, the gear does not catch. When this metal piece, called a pawl, becomes worn, it no longer catches properly in the gear when you move forward. Then it needs to be replaced. Take it to a lawn mower dealer and buy a new piece, or have a metalworking shop make one.

Wood roller falls off. Stuff the holes in the end tightly with steel wool and reset the screws that hold it on the mower.

LAWN MOWER, POWER

Doesn't start. On gasoline mower, check: Is valve on fuel tank open? Is stop switch pushed away from spark plug? Is spark plug clean and sound? Is choke adjusted? Are you out of gas? Is oil level low? On electric mower, check if there is a break in the cord and whether fuse on house circuit is blown.

Runs unevenly. On gasoline mower, check: Is gasoline stale, gummy? Is filter clean? Is oil at proper level and is it clean? Are cooling fins clogged with grass and dust? Is spark plug clean? Is it cracked? For an electric mower, see ELECTRIC MOTOR. Be sure to examine carbon brushes.

Stalls. If you're not mowing grass that's too high for the mower to handle, stop machine and check it for accumulations of grass. Clean underside of blade housing.

Vibrates excessively. Stop mower and look for loose parts or damage. Correct problems. If vibration persists, have mower checked by a serviceman.

Engine erratic. If you've been using the mower for a long time without trouble, chances are that the air cleaner is clogged with dust and dirt. Remove it and clean it as best you can by jarring it. Order a replacement.

Rotary mower blade dull, nicked. Disconnect spark plug and remove blade from housing. Set in a vise and file the beveled edges (on top side of blade only) with a medium- and then a fine-toothed file, or sharpen on a grinding wheel. The two ends of the blade should be exactly the same size and shape.

Balance the blade after sharpening by inserting a bottle cork in the center pivot hole. Drive a small hole through the center of the cork and insert through this a knotted string. Suspend the blade by the string. If blade dips at one end, file more metal from that end. Continue thus until blade balances perfectly. (If it doesn't, you may wreck the engine or bearings.)

When replacing blade in mower, make certain it is top side up.

Reel blades dull. These require special sharpening equipment; so let an expert work on them. You can improve matters to some extent, however, by filing the stationary cutter bar under the reel. File the bottom beveled edge only, and make sure the edge is straight.

Grass catcher torn. Patch with matching fabric and fabric glue.

Grass catcher zipper broken. See ZIPPER. If you can't get it fixed immediately, pin grass catcher shut with safety pins. A few leaks between pins won't stop catcher from working.

LAWN SWEEPER

Basket torn. Cut a patch out of matching fabric and paste over tear with fabric glue. If plastic bottom of basket is broken, rivet a piece of aluminum flashing to the underside.

Doesn't sweep clean. Brush may be set too low or too high. If set too low, sweeper is hard to push; if set too high, sweeper passes over many leaves without picking them up. Raise or lower the height adjustment lever. If this doesn't correct the problem, the brush may be worn down and require replacement.

Hard to push. Brush may be set too low. Axle of brush may be snarled with vines. Lubricate wheels.

Brush doesn't turn although sweeper moves easily. Remove wheels and gears and check whether pawls (short, flat, steel strips) are worn or improperly installed. Replace if worn. Make sure they engage flat surface inside small cogged gears.

LEAD

Small holes. Clean metal thoroughly with steel wool and cover hole with epoxy mender.

Large holes. Clean area around hole until metal shines. Cut a patch out of sheet lead and clean one side. Sprinkle shavings of tallow on both surfaces and melt it with a warm iron (this serves as the flux). Then tin both surfaces with a special tin-lead-bismuth solder. Hold patch over hole and heat it with a not-too-hot iron until the solder melts. Do not let iron rest long in one place, because lead has a low melting point.

LEADER
(downspout)

Clogged. Remove straps fastening leader to house wall. Take leader down and clean out stoppage with a plumber's snake or stick of wood, or by forcing it out with a hose.

Seam split. Remove clog that caused split. If leader is copper or galvanized steel, bend metal back in shape, heat with a torch, and solder.

If leader is aluminum, fill seam with epoxy mender after cleaning metal and bending into shape. If leader is vinyl, clean broken edges and glue together with plastic-mending adhesive. Wrap several lengths of small aluminum wire around the leader and twist them tight to reinforce the mend.

Joints in copper or galvanized steel leader broken. Take down leader, clean joints with sandpaper, and resolder.

LEAF BLOWER

Doesn't start. Are you out of gas? Is valve on fuel line open? Is starting-running control properly adjusted? Is spark plug clean?

Runs unevenly. This may be attributable to a dirty or cracked spark plug, gummy gasoline, clogged air cleaner, dirt on cooling fins, low oil level or dirty oil, carburetor out of adjustment.

Blowing power reduced. Clean leaves off air intake.

Vibrates. Tighten all screws and bolts. Trouble may also be in engine, which is running unevenly.

LEATHER

Tears, slashes. If leather has a solid backing, apply white glue under torn edges, butt edges carefully, and press down. Several applications of polish will help to conceal the scar. If leather is not backed, apply adhesive-backed mending tape to one side of tear. Or cut a patch out of leather, coat with rubber cement, and coat torn area with cement. Let dry until tacky and then press together. Very soft leather can also be patched with needle and thread (see CLOTHING—FABRICS).

Holes. Cut a patch out of matching leather and feather the edges with a razor blade. Lay over hole and draw a pencil line around it. Coat back of patch with rubber cement. Apply cement around the hole within the pencil line. Let glue dry until tacky. Then smooth down patch.

Stitches in leather articles ripped out. If leather

itself is sound, resew with thread of appropriate strength and color. Very soft leather, like that in gloves, can be sewn on a machine. Thick leather must be sewn by hand with a very sharp needle. Don't try to resew leather that is old, worn, and weak. Use glue.

Layers of leather delaminated. Coat facing surfaces with rubber cement. When this becomes tacky, press together. If stitches along edges are ripped, resew them.

Leather separated from wood, glass, ceramics, metal, rubber, paper, plastics. Clean surfaces. Apply light coat of rubber cement to both surfaces. Let dry until tacky and then clamp together.

Leather stiff, brittle. Wet a rag, rub it in saddle soap, and rub on leather. Work soap in well. Rinse with a damp sponge and then polish with a dry cloth.

Grease stains. As soon as possible, brush rubber cement over the stain and peel off when dry. Repeat operation several times, if necessary. Don't count on success, however.

General discoloration. Rub a damp cloth in saddle soap and then rub evenly over leather. Work soap in well. Then rinse with a damp sponge and dry.

LEATHERETTE

Holes, tears. Cut a patch out of matching material. Apply a thin coat of fabric glue to the back and smooth over the hole. Let dry several hours.

LIGHTNING ROD

You can reset a loose rod, splice and solder a broken cable, or clamp or solder a loose joint between cable and ground rod. But beyond that, leave repairs to a professional installer.

LOUVERED OPENING

Louver broken. Cut it out carefully with a small saw or hacksaw blade flush with the sides. Make a new louver of the same size. It should be long enough so you can just wedge it into place. Coat the ends with white or resorcinol glue and set in position.

MAILBOX, OFFICIAL U.S.

Loose or broken from post. Remove board screwed under bottom of box. Replace with a new board of same size. Check whether post wood is sound. Center board on post and nail down securely with 4-inch nails. Then set box over board and drive screws through sides of box into board.

To secure box further, you can screw angle irons to the board and post at the front and back of the box. But these shouldn't be necessary if post is sound and at least 4 inches across.

Post wobbles. See FENCE, WOOD.

MARBLE

Small scratches. Rub with ultrafine sandpaper. Then wet surface with water, sprinkle on a pinch of tin oxide, dampen a cloth, and rub briskly until shine reappears.

Large scratches, pits, general roughness. Repair is a tedious, hard job best left to a professional. But if you insist on doing it yourself, take marble to a place where you can make a mess without doing any damage. Buy necessary supplies from a marble dealer, or Vermarco Supply Company, division of Vermont Marble Company, Proctor, Vermont 05765. Directions from the Marble Institute of America follow:

"The secret of polishing marble is to buff or rub the surface persistently and evenly with abrasive materials of successively finer grit sizes. The coarse abrasive materials are usually purchased in the form of small hand-size bricks, each brick being composed of abrasive grit of a specific size. Those used in marble finishing range from the coarsest, No. 45, through 120, 220, and 280 to the finest grit size brick, which is called hone. Finally, polishing powder composed of tin oxide to which has been added a few grains of oxalic acid is used during the final polishing stage to give the marble its glossy, high-polished finish. No oxalic acid should ever be used with the tin oxide for polishing green marble or any marble which is to be outdoors.

"1. Examine the surface carefully to determine how much buffing or polishing will be required. Rough surfaces, containing swirl marks, deep scratches, and pits, will require extensive effort and a great deal of time to bring them to a final smooth, high polish. Polished surfaces with only faint ring marks, or with small spots only slightly rough to the touch, can often be buffed to a shine with polishing powder alone.

"2. The condition of the surface will determine which abrasive material to start with. On a very rough surface the No. 45 or 120 grit size brick should be used first to rub the surface evenly and persistently so that all scratches, marks, and blemishes, except of course those left by the brick itself, are rubbed away. The remaining abrasive bricks in the series should then be employed successively. These remove the marks left by the previous abrasive until a smooth but nonglossy surface, known as a hone finish, is achieved. Remember that the lower-numbered, coarser abrasive bricks should be used first; the higher-numbered finer abrasive bricks last. A back-and-forth rubbing motion rather than a circular motion is recommended. Water should be applied frequently to the face of the stone during the rubbing process. Abrasive residue should be sponged away to prevent clogging of the surface of the brick in contact with the marble. Work on only about 4 square inches of surface area at any one time; then move on to the adjacent area.

"3. Once a honed surface has been produced, the surface of the marble should again be sponged thoroughly to remove all grit. The surface should be carefully reexamined to make sure that all spots, pits, and scratches have been removed; otherwise they will show through the final polish. Expert hand polishers agree that the smoother the hone finish, the better the final high polish. The final hone should have a satin finish which, though not glossy, does have a slight luster.

"4. The final polish is achieved by steady and persistent buffing or rubbing with polish-

ing powder. After sprinkling the powder lightly on the surface, use a pad of medium-hard felt, hard wool carpeting, or chamois which has been dampened with water to do the actual buffing. The best buffing pad is one which has been saturated and compacted with polishing powder and water. Add a few drops of water whenever additional lubricant seems necessary. More powder may also be added so that a thin, dry slurry appears over the surface of the marble. After a lengthy period of vigorous rubbing, the surface will start to take on the characteristic shine of polished marble. Continue rubbing until the shine is uniform, then rinse the surface and dry it with a soft cloth."

Broken. Wash edges if dirty and let dry. Apply epoxy glue to one edge and press together for 12 hours.

Loose from wall, floor, etc. Lift out and scrape loose cement from back of marble and the base. Apply several large dabs of silicone adhesive to back of marble and press firmly into place.

Separated from another material. See HOUSE-HOLD DECORATIVE ACCESSORIES (*stone*).

Oil stains. Scrub with Vermont 50-50 Liquid Cleaner (Vermarco Supply Company); let stand for a few minutes, then rinse. Repeat several times as necessary. If stains persist, mix the cleaner with whiting to form a thick paste. Trowel on stains and keep paste covered with a damp cloth and piece of glass for 24 hours; then scrape off and rinse.

Coffee, tea, wine, fruit, and other organic stains. Pour hydrogen peroxide mixed with a few drops of household ammonia on stains. Let stand until stains disappear. If stains persist, mix peroxide with whiting to form a thick paste. Trowel on stains and sprinkle with a few drops of ammonia. When bubbling action stops, scrape off and rinse. Throw old poultice outdoors to let it cool off. If the peroxide etches the surface slightly (as it may), polish with tin oxide powder.

Rust stains. Sprinkle Vermont Crystal Cleaner on stains. Let stand for a very short time. Follow manufacturer's directions. For persistent stains, mix cleaner with whiting and water to form a paste. Spread on stains and cover with glass for 24 hours. Then scrape off and rinse.

Paint. Scrape off with a razor blade. Clean with Vermont Liquid Cleaner.

Smoke. Clean with liquid cleaner and, if necessary, apply a poultice of the cleaner.

Dirty. Wash with a mild dishwashing detergent. When completely clean, apply a marble sealer available from Vermarco Supply Company. Renew this every 6 months or whenever marble is washed thoroughly. On doors, reapply sealer every 4 months. Do not apply any other type of finish or polish.

NOTE. Never clean marble with lemon juice, vinegar, or other acid, because it etches the surface.

MATTRESS

Buttons off. With a needle long enough to go all the way through the mattress, thread a strong cord (upholsterer's twine preferably, or the equivalent of fishing line) from the bottom of the mattress to the top. Run cord through button and then thread it back through to other side of mattress. Loop through the bottom button. Have someone compress the mattress as much as possible at that point. Draw ends of string tight and knot them securely.

If you don't have a long needle, you can try doubling a small, stiff wire in two lengths greater than the thickness of the mattress. Make the bend as sharp and pointed as possible. Push the wire through from the top of the mattress to the bottom. Thread cord through the bend and pull the cord back to the top of the mattress. After looping cord through button, insert bent wire from bottom of mattress, secure end of cord, and draw it back to the underside.

Holes in fabric. Patch with press-on mending tape.

Mattress lumpy, sagging. It's impossible to fix it short of having it completely rebuilt. But you can improve it some by covering with a 1-, 2-, or 3-inch topper of urethane foam.

MATTRESS, AIR

Holes in rubberized mattress. To find hole, inflate mattress and immerse in water. Bubbles will rise from hole. Then let all air out of mattress and dry fabric completely. Use patching kit provided by mattress maker or cut a patch out of rubber or rubberized fabric. Apply rubber cement to patch and mattress and let dry. Apply a second coat to patch and smooth over hole.

Holes in plastic mattress. Find hole and release air as above. Use patching kit provided by manufacturer or use plastic-mending adhesive kit. Spread adhesive around hole and immediately smooth on plastic patch in kit. Let dry overnight before inflating mattress.

MELAMINE DINNERWARE

Broken. Clean edges well; apply plastic-mending adhesive, and clamp together firmly overnight.

Broken, scratched. See PLASTICS—GENERAL.

MICROWAVE OVEN

NOTE. Don't fool with this. Call a serviceman if it is not operating or if it is operating improperly.

Surface nicked. Touch up with porcelain glaze or epoxy touch-up enamel.

MIRROR

Broken. See GLASS.

Edges rough. See GLASS.

Silver gone, scratched, or discolored. Have mirror replated.

Loose from wall to which it has been cemented. Cement alone will not hold a mirror permanently. Don't try to scrape off old adhesive. Screw plastic or metal mirror hangers to wall around edges of mirror. Place the hangers, if possible, so that screws can be driven through the wall surface into the studs. This is especially important in the case of the bottom hangers.

Special metal strips are also available for hanging mirrors. They are more difficult to install but are almost invisible.

Acrylic mirror loose from wall to which it has been cemented. Do not remove old adhesive or tapes from back. Drill a hole through each upper corner of the mirror. The holes should be $\frac{1}{16}$ inch larger than the shanks of the screws you will use. Then screw mirror to wall. If mirror is very large, additional screws at bottom should also be installed.

MIXER, ELECTRIC

Doesn't work. Check whether fuse on house circuit has blown, whether outlet into which mixer is plugged is defective. Then disconnect mixer and examine cord for a break. Repair or replace if necessary (see ELECTRIC CORD). If mixer still doesn't work, take it to a repair shop.

Mixer sparks and sputters intermittently, may smell of ozone. The carbon brushes are probably worn or loose. Unscrew large plastic screw caps on side of mixer and pull out springs and brushes. The latter (actually sticks of hard carbon) should be about $\frac{1}{4}$ inch long. Replace if they are not. Check tension on springs; if loose, replace them, too. Both brushes and springs are available from hardware store or appliance serviceman handling your kind of mixer. Make sure you get new brushes and springs of the correct type.

Bowl doesn't turn. Lift turntable and scrub off gummy residue underneath. Put a drop of light oil on spindle.

Beater shafts bent. Clamp in a vise and carefully bend them straight. But it's difficult to do a perfect job.

Beater blades bent, broken. Bends can be removed with pliers. If joint where blades cross at the bottom is broken, it can be resoldered. See STAINLESS STEEL. But a good repair is hard to make. You may be better off buying new blades if these don't work smoothly.

MOLDING

Pulled away from wall or ceiling, floor, or baseboard. Drive 3-inch or 4-inch finishing nails (depending on thickness of molding) diagonally through molding into the studs or joists. If crack remains along either edge of ceiling molding or at top edge of base molding, fill with spackle and sand smooth. If base molding can-

not be nailed down tight to floor, check whether there are bobby pins, grit, or dirt underneath.

Joints open in corners or between lengths of molding. Nail down ends of strips and fill joints with spackle or water putty.

Elaborate molding badly damaged. If lumberyard doesn't have matching molding, you can probably get it from Driwood Molding Company, Post Office Box 1369, Florence, South Carolina 29501. To insert new piece, carefully pull molding from wall and saw out damaged area. Make cuts at 45-degree angles in a miter box. Cut ends of replacement piece also at 45-degree angles. When renailing molding to wall, either glue new piece to ends of old or drive a small finishing nail through each diagonal overlap.

If it's impossible to replace a damaged molding, your only hope is to fill in the area with water putty. Shape the putty to match molding while it is still soft. Use a knife, pencil point, fingers, whatever seems to work. When putty is dry, sand or file smooth.

MOTHER-OF-PEARL

Broken. Clean edges, coat with thin layers of cellulose cement and press together for several hours.

NOTE. Don't let a baby have a glued mother-of-pearl teething ring.

MOTORCYCLE

Doesn't start. Is it out of gas? Check if strainer is clogged and clean if it is. Check if gas-tank air vent is clogged. Make sure gas is getting through to carburetor by removing the gas line at the carburetor and turning on the tap. Check if orifice in idle jet is plugged.

Is battery dead? Are any wires disconnected? Is insulation sound?

Dry off spark plug and cables if they are damp. If spark plug is damaged, replace it, if it is fouled, clean it as best you can or replace it. See SPARK PLUG. (To test plug, remove it and place on cylinder head. Turn on ignition, and watch whether the plug sparks when engine is cranked.)

Inspect breaker points in magneto to make sure contacts are clean. Clean with ultrafine emery cloth or, better, flexstone. If contacts are badly pitted, replace points and also the condenser.

Runs but stops in short time. The gas-tank air vent may be plugged or there may be dirt in gas line. Clean both.

Engine doesn't run smoothly. Spark plug may be cracked, fouled, improperly gapped. Clean and adjust contact points. Check and clean idle jet in carburetor.

Idles unevenly. Adjust idle air screw according to your operator's manual.

MOVIE CAMERA

Pictures soiled. Clean lens with a camel's-hair artist's brush or with lens paper from a photo supplies store. If lens is very smeary, you will also need a fluid lens cleaner.

While you're at it, clean entire interior of camera with artist's brush to remove dust, lint, etc.

Camera operating too slowly. Replace batteries. Clean camera carefully with artist's brush.

Pictures exposed improperly. Replace tiny battery controlling photoelectric cell.

MOVIE PROJECTOR

Pictures dirty, spotted. Clean projector lens with a camel's-hair brush or with lens paper. Use fluid lens cleaner to get fingerprints and other smears off glass.

Operates slowly. Clean entire machine thoroughly with a camel's-hair brush. Pay special attention to sprockets and spindles. Lubricate projector only as specified by manufacturer. Use light sewing machine or typewriter oil.

Belt broken. If you can get at it, this is easy to fix temporarily. Use plastic-mending adhesive to put together a plastic belt. If belt is a coiled steel spring, straighten the wire just enough to hook the two ends together.

MOVIE SCREEN

Torn. Bring edges of tear close together. Coat a patch of lightweight canvas with fabric glue and smooth it over back of tear. When glue dries, touch up line of tear with paint.

MUSICAL INSTRUMENTS

NOTE. If a good instrument is damaged, let an expert repair it. Anything you do may alter the tone. On inexpensive instruments, proceed as follows.

Dents in metal parts. Where possible to do so, place a wood block on the concave side of the dent and tap the reverse side lightly with a block of wood or, preferably, a rubber mallet. In cases where it is impossible to do this, solder a short length of stout copper wire to the center of the dent. Grasp the end of the wire with pliers and pull out the dent. Then melt off the solder on the instrument.

Wood parts cracked. Coat edges of crack with white glue and press them firmly together for 6 hours.

Plastic parts cracked. Coat edges with plastic-mending adhesive and press together firmly overnight.

Hole in accordion bellows. Cut small patch out of matching material or vinyl sheet. Coat back of patch and area around hole with rubber cement. Let dry, then apply a second coat of cement to patch and immediately press into place.

NAMBE

Broken. Coat edges of this metal alloy with epoxy glue and press together for 6 hours.

Stained. Clean with brass polish.

Water-spotted. Don't wash in dishwasher. Use hand-dishwashing detergent and dry immediately. Rubbing with a little cooking oil helps to preserve the luster of the metal.

NETS—BADMINTON, BASKETBALL, FISHING, ETC.

Holes. Repair with cotton twine. In a square-meshed net, first tie new lengths of twine to the broken cords (or knots) along the top of the hole. Call these strings 1, 2, 3, 4, etc. Then tie a length of twine to the topmost broken string at the left side of the hole. Call this string A. Now draw string A to the right to meet string 1; form desired mesh opening, and tie strings together with a square knot. Then draw string A to string 2 and knot, and so on across the hole. Repeat process with horizontal strings B, C, D, etc. until hole is filled.

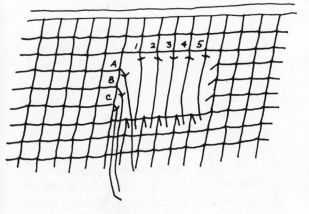

The procedure is the same in a net with a diamond-shaped mesh except that all strings run diagonally downward.

Professionals use a special net knot instead of a square knot, but this is more difficult for the amateur to make.

OILCLOTH

Holes. Trim out hole neatly. Place a scrap of matching oilcloth, shiny side up, underneath and draw an outline of the hole on it. Take out patch and scrape off the shiny surface around the outline. Then spread a thin layer of fabric glue on the scraped area and press the patch on the oilcloth under the hole.

Rips. Bring edges together. Glue a scrap of fabric underneath with fabric glue.

OIL TANK

Leaks. Have it inspected by the servicemen employed by your oil dealer. If they can plug leak, let them. If they say you need a new tank, you'd still better go along with them.

ONYX

Broken. Clean edges of break and coat with cellulose cement or epoxy glue. Press together until glue dries.

OUTDOOR FURNITURE, ALUMINUM

Unfinished aluminum pitted and corroded. It's too late to fix this. In the future, apply two coats of methacrylate lacquer after the metal has weathered a year, and renew coating every 2 years thereafter.

Unfinished aluminum stained. See ALUMINUM.

Painted aluminum scratched, chipped. Sand the bad spots and apply an oil-base exterior trim enamel.

Holes, dents. See ALUMINUM.

Hollow aluminum bent. If possible, carefully work piece straight again and drive in a tight-fitting dowel of hardwood.

Bolts, screws, and other fastenings rusted through. Some manufacturers have a bad habit of using steel fastenings in outdoor furniture made of aluminum. Remove the broken or weakened pieces. Clean surrounding aluminum with steel wool and refasten with aluminum bolts, etc.

OUTDOOR FURNITURE, IRON AND STEEL

See CAST IRON or STEEL.

Paint chipped. Remove weak surrounding paint and clean metal with sandpaper or a scraper until bright. Then apply red metal primer followed by one or two coats of alkyd exterior trim enamel.

If paint is chipped in many places, remove it entirely with a rasp or scraper. Take off rust with liquid rust-remover and coarse steel wool. Then prime and paint. Henceforth, paint furniture every 2 years whether it needs it or not.

OUTDOOR FURNITURE, RATTAN OR WICKER

Bindings loose. See FURNITURE, WICKER, RATTAN, REED, OR BAMBOO.

Strips broken, split. See FURNITURE, WICKER, RATTAN, REED, OR BAMBOO,

Varnish finish chipping, peeling. It must be removed if you want the furniture to be attractive, but the chore is miserable. Don't use paint remover, because it will gum up in the joints. Scrape and sand the dry varnish off down to the wood. Use commercial bleach to remove stains. Apply two coats of penetrating wood sealer for a clear finish, but a paint finish will wear much better. Apply an alkyd exterior primer followed by a coat of alkyd exterior trim enamel.

OUTDOOR FURNITURE— WEBBING

Dirty. See WEBBING.

Ends frayed. See WEBBING.

Woven webbing disintegrating. Tear it off and remove clips holding it. Remove rust stains made by clips. Out of Saran webbing—the only kind of woven webbing that is not quickly damaged by sun, moisture, etc.—cut new strips to the same length. Fold the ends into points, and fasten the ends to the framework with aluminum sheet-metal screws. Use screws with threads of slightly larger diameter than the holes.

OUTDOOR FURNITURE, WOOD

See FURNITURE, WOOD, for breaks, loose joints, and other major problems, but use resorcinol glue. To fill cracks, use plastic wood if furniture is unfinished or has a clear finish, exterior spackle or water putty if furniture is painted.

Holes, gouges, rotting wood, stains. See WOOD.

Finish damaged. If the damage is slight, touch up with paint or varnish, but if the entire surface is going to pot, remove the finish completely with paint remover, and sand wood smooth. For a new finish, apply an alkyd exterior primer followed by one or two coats of alkyd exterior trim enamel. Clear finishes do not stand up under exposure to sun and moisture. If you must use one, a penetrating wood sealer is as good as anything—and not very good at that. Do not use varnish.

PAINT BRUSH

Clogged with paint. See BASIC METHODS: HOW TO PAINT.

Loses bristles. All paint brushes lose a few bristles when new. If loss continues, however, brush should be discarded. The only alternative is to let some of the paint which accumulates just below the ferrule to harden around the bristles. This reduces the usability of the brush to some extent but not enough to worry about.

Bristles bent. If all the bristles are bent, put the brush in a can of thinner, bend bristles in other direction and wedge brush in position. Let it stand until bristles are straight again. Thereafter, never let the brush stand on its bristles when cleaning it; drill a hole through the handle and suspend it on a wire on the edges of the can holding paint thinner.

If stray bristles are bent around the edges of the brush, snip them off with scissors.

PAINT ROLLER

Clogged with dry paint. Soak in paintbrush cleaner until paint is soft; then work it out with your fingers, and continue soaking until clean. Wash in strong household detergent and rinse well.

Roller cover stuck to roller. You may be able to loosen it by soaking in paintbrush cleaner. If not, jab a knife through the roller and cut it off. In the future, after cleaning a roller, remove the cover.

Roller bulges in one spot; doesn't roll evenly. Remove cover and bend the frame holding it straight.

PAINTED SURFACE

For how to remove and apply paint, see BASIC METHODS: HOW TO PAINT.

Paint flaking, cracking, wrinkling, alligatoring. Remove paint down to the base. Make sure surface is dry. Apply primer and finish paint.

Paint chalking abnormally. Wash and scrub thoroughly to remove chalk. Let dry. Apply one or two additional coats of the paint previously applied.

Exterior paint blistered. Remove it down to the wood. Be sure surface is absolutely dry before applying primer and finish coat. Don't paint at all if blistering is a common occurrence, because you may have a condensation problem within walls, and until this is rectified, blistering will continue.

Exterior paint peeling. If paint peels down to the wood, treat it like blistered paint. If paint peels between coats, sand off peeling coat and roughen undercoat slightly; then apply new paint.

Paint deeply scratched. Sand to remove any loose paint. Fill scratch with spackle and sand smooth. Apply new paint.

Paint chipped. If surrounding paint is sound, fill in chipped area with spackle or gypsum-board joint compound. Wrap sandpaper around a block of wood to sand smooth and level. Repaint. If surface is chipped all over, remove all paint down to the wood before repainting.

Paint on iron and steel chipped. Remove rust from bare metal. Prime with red metal primer before repainting.

Paint on galvanized steel chipped. Scrape off loose paint. Prime metal with zinc-dust paint before applying finish coat.

Paint on plaster chipped, cracked. This happens to oil-base paint applied to new plaster that hasn't been allowed to cure for 6 months. It also sometimes happens to latex paint applied to old plaster, but in this case the cause is not clear. There is no simple cure. Remove all paint down to the plaster, wash and rinse plaster well, and repaint when dry.

Sanded paint flaking off. Scrape off all loose paint around holes, because once flaking starts it seems to spread. Brush on a prime coat.

For the final coat, mix a small quantity of paint with fine, clean, builder's sand or Perltex. Brush on. Try to achieve same texture and pattern as in surrounding paint.

Textured paint flaking, chipping off. This is very tough stuff to take off and also very tough stuff to match in texture. You may find it advisable to remove paint from the entire surface and start anew.

Remove as much as possible with a scraper. Then try paste-type paint remover. Then, if necessary, use a rotary sander. Then apply white textured paint with a brush and texture it while it is wet. Use a whisk broom, comb, sponge, or crumpled newspaper—whatever seems to have been used originally. (If paint was applied originally with a special texturing roller, you won't be able to match it.) If you don't get the right effect, wash off paint at once and start again. To match color of surrounding paint, overcoat the textured paint when dry with ordinary paint of the proper hue.

Brown spots show through paint. The stains are usually caused by the sap in knots or by old creosote stain. To stop them from bleeding through paint applied over them, brush an alcohol-base stain-killer on the stains. Then repaint.

Blotchy discoloration of paint applied to redwood or cedar siding. This is caused by soluble salts in the wood bleeding through the paint. Check and improve vapor barriers in the house so moisture cannot get into wood and release the salts.

Green copper stains. Sand thoroughly, wash with turpentine, then repaint surface. Clean and finish copper causing trouble.

Rust stains. Remove rust from metal and prime with red lead. Then sand discolored paint surface, wash with turpentine, and repaint.

If stains are caused by nails or screws that have been countersunk in siding, the only sure cure is to dig out putty covering nailheads and prime with red metal primer before reputtying and repainting. You may succeed in stopping further staining, however, simply by sanding the paint and applying a stain-killer over rust marks before repainting.

Mildew stains. Wash with a strong solution of chlorine bleach. To prevent recurrence of mildew, mix a prepared mildew retardant (available from paint stores) with your paint the next time you apply it.

Fingernail polish on painted surface. Nail polish remover will take it off, but may also mar the paint finish. Try scraping the polish off with the point of a sharp knife.

PAINTING, OIL

Dirty. Have oil paintings professionally cleaned every few years. About once a year between times, you can sponge them off very gently with a soft cloth well wrung out in clean water provided paint is not cracked. Don't scrub. Dry with a patting motion.

Canvas loose, bellying. Turn picture on its face and tap in wedges in back. Don't stretch canvas too tight.

Joints of frame open, loose. See PICTURE FRAME.

Other problems. Consult a reputable dealer or restorer.

PAINTING, WATERCOLOR

Mat discolored, torn. Buy mat board from an art supplies store. Remove painting and mat from frame and, using old mat as a template, outline new mat on mat board. Place mat board on clean plywood or other surface that won't be damaged by cutting. With a very sharp knife or single-edge razor blade (though the latter is not so easily controlled), cut mat board to size of frame. Then cut out opening for picture. Use a steel-edge ruler or straightedge. To hold it down tight, so you don't veer from the penciled outline, it is a good idea to fasten it to the cutting board with C-clamps. If possible, bevel the edges of the opening slightly.

Secure painting to back of mat with a single strip of masking tape stuck to the top edge. Carefully clean the face of the mat with art gum. Then reframe.

PAINT SPRAYER

Gun doesn't deliver paint, sputters, or leaks. Clean gun thoroughly according to manu-

facturer's directions. If paint has dried on fluid tip, soak tip in paint thinner. Clean air nozzle. Tighten packing nut.

Compressor makes hammering noise. Check and tighten loose pulley on motor or compressor shaft. Tighten setscrew holding eccentric to shaft.

Pressure is low. If air-intake filter on compressor is covered with paint, replace it. Tighten hose nuts and belt if it is slipping. Replace worn diaphragm.

Compressor pumps oil. Check whether oil level is too high. Examine for worn piston rings according to maker's directions.

PAPER

Torn. Patch with cellophane tape or a paper patch stuck on with rubber cement or white glue.

Separated from another material. Glue down with rubber cement or white glue.

PARTICLE BOARD

Cracked. Coat both edges with white or resorcinol glue; bring together carefully, without breaking flake-like layers; and let dry overnight. If board is subject to any strain, reinforce the break with a strip of wood glued to the back.

Scratched, gouged. Prime with paint or clear finish and let dry. Then fill hole with spackle or water putty. Sand smooth when dry. Note that if particle board is stained, matching stain should be mixed into the filling mixture before it is applied.

Pieces of particle board separated. Coat with white or resorcinol glue and clamp together overnight. Or fasten with nails or screws.

Particle board separated from another material. Use nails, screws, or glue to fasten together. Particle board has good nail and screw holding power if the nails and screws are driven into the face of the panels but not if they are driven into the panel edges. If glue is used, see HOUSEHOLD DECORATIVE ACCESSORIES and use glue specified for wood.

Finish marred. See LACQUERED SURFACE,

PAINTED SURFACE, SHELLACKED SURFACE, or VARNISHED SURFACE as case may be.

Stains. See PAINTED SURFACE or WOOD.

Burns. See FURNITURE, WOOD.

Edges rough. See PLYWOOD.

PATENT LEATHER

Cracked. You can't mend this. Just conceal the crack as best you can by dyeing the fabric underneath. In future, to prevent cracking, rub leather with petroleum jelly and don't expose to heat.

PEN

Fountain pen leaks. The barrel of the pen can be unscrewed or pulled from the finger-hold, and the rubber ink tube replaced. However, since the new ink tube must come from a pen dealer, it is just as well to have him make the repair.

Point broken. Same thing applies.

Plastic case broken at tip of ballpoint pen. Make sure ink tube is fully inserted in case. Then put a blob of cellulose cement or plastic mending adhesive on the broken tip.

Ballpoint pen skips or doesn't write when still full. Heat end of pen tip with match. Be careful not to melt plastic if nonrefillable pen.

PENCIL, MECHANICAL

Lead doesn't hold or doesn't draw back in. The tiny metal tube that holds the lead is clogged. To get at it, wrap the tip of the pencil case with adhesive tape and unscrew it with pliers. The lead-holding tube can then be brought into view by turning the top of the pencil to the right. Stick a pinpoint through the slit in the side of the tube and force out the obstruction.

PENCIL SHARPENER

Jammed with a broken pencil or crayon. Remove sawdust holder. Unscrew slotted bolt in

one of the grinding wheels and pull wheel to one side, but don't try to remove it entirely. You should then be able to reach and pry out the stoppage with a knife or small screwdriver. If you can't, loosen the other grinding wheel.

PEWTER

NOTE. If the pewter to be mended is a prized piece, let a professional fix it.

Small holes. Clean the metal inside the pewter object with steel wool, then cover hole with epoxy mender.

Joints between pewter surfaces cracked. Use epoxy mender as above if the repair cannot be seen. Otherwise, remove tarnish from the surfaces and clean metal carefully with fine emery cloth. With a warm soldering iron, melt shavings of tallow on the surface (this serves as a flux). Use a special tin-lead-bismuth solder. Hold the soldering iron against both the iron and the pewter, and melt solder into the joint. Do not hold soldering iron long in one spot because pewter has a low melting point.

Dents. First try to press it out with your fingers. If this doesn't work, hold a block of wood over concave side of dent and tap the reverse side sharply, but not too heavily, with another block of wood.

Pewter separated from other materials, such as felt. See HOUSEHOLD DECORATIVE ACCESSORIES (*metal*).

Tarnished. Clean with silver polish.

PHONOGRAPH RECORD

Dirty, greasy. Stand record on edge in a basin filled with tepid water to which a special record-cleaning detergent or light-duty laundry detergent has been added, and wash gently with a soft, clean sponge in a circular motion. Rinse at once in clean, cold water, shake off excess, blot almost dry with a lint-free towel, and stand upright in a rack to dry.

Clicks and skips during operation. If record has been scratched or cracked, there's nothing you can do about it. But if there's nothing visibly wrong with the record, the problem undoubtedly is caused by dust and hairs on the surface. To remove these, buy a Parastatik Disc Preener. Dampen the wick according to directions, and rub it lightly over the record as it revolves on the turntable.

Seams of jacket torn. Bind with adhesive-backed cloth tape.

PHOTOGRAPH

Torn. Coat both edges with a thin coat of rubber cement, and before this dries, press the edges together. Smooth carefully so as not to damage the emulsion. Then cover a sheet of paper or cardboard and the entire back of the picture with rubber cement. Let dry, and apply a second overall coat to the picture. Smooth it down on the paper.

Ink marks. Wipe lightly with a damp cloth if photo has a glossy finish. Same treatment minimizes but may not obliterate marks on dull-finish pictures.

Glue marks. Try wiping gently with damp cloth. Use a wad of dried rubber cement to remove old rubber cement.

PHOTO ALBUM

Page torn. See BOOK.

Punched page loose. Glue gummed reinforcing rings to page.

Photos loose. Try to remove glue from back of photos and pages by rubbing with your finger or an eraser. (Rubber cement will come off; any other adhesive will not—and you don't have to worry about it.) Dab white glue on back of photos at the four corners and stick down. This is the most reliable adhesive for the purpose.

Photos stained by rubber cement. There's no cure. Use white glue instead of rubber cement in the future.

PIANO

Keys stick. Raise heat and try to lower humidity in room for several days. Work the keys up and down and sideways. If stickiness doesn't disappear, call in a piano tuner.

Keys stained yellow. Age causes this and it cannot be corrected. Ordinary dirt stains can be removed with mild detergent and water.

Top off key. Carefully scrape off glue. Spread a thin layer of cellulose cement on back of key top and press down on the base for 5 minutes. Be sure to wipe off **any** glue that squeezes out at the sides.

Wood damaged. See WOOD.

PICTURE FRAME

Joints open, loose. Open joint wide enough to insert a thin knife or palette knife. Spread in white glue. Press joint together and tap in brad in edge of frame. To make sure corners are square, nail two strips of wood to a piece of plywood at right angles (use a carpenter's square). Set frame against these. Then nail two more strips of wood along the other sides and leave in place until the glue is hard.

Glass broken. See GLASS.

Easel warped on picture frame designed to stand on a table. Bend easel straight. Then glue a steel mending plate to the underside with epoxy glue.

Ribbon on easel frame broken. Cut it out and replace with a new piece of ribbon or cord cut to same length. Glue ribbon to back of frame and underside of easel with white glue.

Paper covering on back of frame torn or disintegrated. Remove picture wire and hooks. Scrape the paper off entirely down to the wood of the frame. Out of a smooth piece of heavy craft paper cut a piece slightly larger than frame. Spread white glue evenly on back of frame and smooth paper into this. When glue is dry, trim off excess paper with a razor blade.

Carving on gilt frame broken. Clean broken surface with a damp rag. Mix water putty with just enough water to make a thick dough and apply a large blob to break. Mold roughly to shape with your fingers while still damp. Then let dry and carve to correct shape with a sharp knife. Finish with sandpaper. Paint with gold paint.

PILLOW

Dirty. Have it dry cleaned. If you insist on laundering, wash feather pillows two at a time in washing machine filled with warm water and light-duty detergent. Agitate for 6 to 8 minutes. Rinse in warm water. Spin at normal speed. Dry in automatic dryer for 60 minutes at high heat.

Hand-wash polyester pillows in warm water with heavy-duty detergent. Don't twist them; force suds through them by pushing. Rinse thoroughly in warm water. Spin-dry in washer. Dry at low heat for 20 minutes or longer in dryer.

To wash foam pillows remove cover.

Holes. On bed pillows apply a patch with fabric glue. Holes in sofa pillows and the like are best mended by darning. See CLOTHING—FABRICS.

PING-PONG PADDLE

Rubber face loose. Scrape off glue and apply rubber cement to back of rubber and to wood. Let dry. Apply a second coat to one surface and smooth rubber down.

Cork face loose. Scrape off glue and reglue with white glue.

Sandpaper face loose, damaged. If face is simply loose, scrape off old glue and reglue with white glue. If paper is damaged, peel it off completely (wetting the surface will help). Stick down new sandpaper with rubber cement.

PING-PONG TABLE

Table wobbly. If filling loose screw holes with plastic wood and generally tightening screws and metal braces does not help, cut a 3-inch-thick board into 2-foot lengths. You will need one board for each table leg. Cut a 90-degree V-notch into end of each board. At the other end, hinge boards to short cross blocks of wood. Position the blocks on the bottom of the tabletop so that they are 18 inches from the legs and they bisect the corner angles of the table. Glue or screw the blocks to the bottom of the table top at this point. Press

notch of each brace against the leg it is designed to support. Drive a screw through one edge of brace into the table leg.

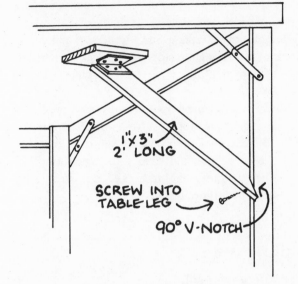

Veneer on tabletop split, delaminated. See VENEER.

Dents in top. Sand paint from dent. Fill with plastic wood. Sand smooth when dry and repaint.

Net torn. Sew torn edges together with strong cotton thread.

PIPE, HEATING

Insulation broken or missing. If broken or missing from a straight run of pipe, measure pipe size and buy a length of asbestos cellular insulation. Fold it around pipe and strap in place. If insulation is defective at a joint, cut and scrape it off. Smear on asbestos cement, which comes ready-mixed in can, and mold in place. The pipe should be cold.

Leaks in pipe run. See PIPE, WATER—COPPER.

Leaks at joints. See PIPE, WATER—COPPER or PIPE, WATER—STEEL.

PIPE VALVE

Shutoff valve doesn't shut off water. Turn off water and drain line. On stop valves (most commonly used type in homes), loosen cap nut. Then remove nut next below it. Screw out handle. Replace washer with one of proper size. On gate valves, unscrew large nut below cap nut. Pull out spindle, then pull out gate with pliers. Replace entire body of valve.

Shutoff valve leaks around handle. Tighten cap nut just enough to stop leak. If leaking persists, remove nut and wrap new graphite wicking around stem.

Shutoff valve frozen open by corrosion products. Don't try to force valve closed. Scrape off visible corrosion products. Saturate joint between cap nut and stem with penetrating oil. Then unscrew cap nut, take out stem, and clean both thoroughly.

PIPE, WATER

Also see entries following.

Leaks. See PIPE, WATER—COPPER; or PIPE, WATER—STEEL.

Clogged. Clogging may be caused by corrosion products or mineral deposits. There is no cure. Have pipe replaced with pipe of another material. Install a water softener if clogging is caused by hard water.

Sweats. Wrap with fiber glass tape.

Pipes thump or hammer. If this happens when a faucet is turned on, make sure cap nut on faucet is tight and faucet washer is in good condition (see FAUCET). If hammering is more or less continual, shut off main water valve, open all faucets in house, and drain system at lowest drain point. This will let in air which should cushion against hammer. However, if hammering persists or returns, call in plumber.

Frozen. Open all faucets on the line. Direct an electric heat lamp on the pipe, starting at the faucet end and working backward to the supply end. Or wrap rags soaked in boiling water around pipe. But do not use a torch of any kind.

PIPE, WATER—BRASS

Leaks in pipe. For temporary and permanent repairs, see PIPE, WATER—COPPER. If worm-drive screw-clamp is installed, buy same size as for steel pipes (see PIPE, WATER—STEEL).

Leaks at fittings. See PIPE, WATER—STEEL.

Leaks at unions. See PIPE, WATER—COPPER.

PIPE, WATER—COPPER

Leaks in pipe. Temporary repair: Apply a rubber patch with a worm-drive screw-clamp. To determine which size clamp is needed, tie a knot in a piece of string and loop string once around the pipe until it touches the knot. Remove string from pipe and measure from the "touching" point to the knot.

IF STRING MEASURES	COPPER PIPE SIZE IS
1 9/16 "	3/8 "
2 "	1/2 "
2 3/8 "	5/8 "
2 3/4 "	3/4 "
3 7/16 "	1 "
4 5/16 "	1 1/4 "

Cut a patch out of a rubber gasket material or old tire tube. It should be about 1 inch

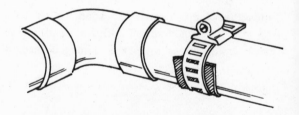

larger than hole in pipe. Turn off water. Center patch over hole. Open screw-clamp and slip it around pipe. Feed end of clamp strap into worm drive. Center clamp over hole and patch and tighten with a screwdriver. On a large hole, use two or even three screw-clamps side by side.

Permanent repair: Drain pipe. Clean hole and area around it with steel wool. Apply acid flux. Heat pipe with torch or soldering iron and apply solder.

NOTE. If copper tube springs many leaks, water should be treated to remove or reduce corrosive elements.

Leaks at soldered joints. Drain pipe. Clean joint with steel wool. Heat joint with torch until solder melts. Apply a little new solder.

Leaks at joints made with flared or compression fittings. Tighten the nut on the fitting with a wrench. If this doesn't stop leak, drain the pipe, loosen nut completely, pull joint apart, and make sure it is clean and properly aligned, then retighten nut. If leak continues, call plumber.

Leaks at unions. Leaks occasionally develop if the male and female sides of the union are not properly aligned or clean. Drain pipe. Loosen large central nut and pull joint apart. Check alignment and clean faces of joint. Retighten nut. If leak continues, call plumber.

Place the clamps over the ridged parts of the coupling and tighten with a screwdriver as much as possible.

For extra security, you can smear silicone caulking on the ridged parts of the coupling before making the joint. But this is really necessary only if the pipe is buried so deep that it's a nuisance to dig up if it should spring a leak or if the pipe carries water under very high pressure.

Leaks at joints. Tighten worm-drive screw-clamp. If this doesn't stop leak, remove pipe from fitting and smear silicone caulking on the ridged section of the fitting.

NOTE. Always use stainless steel screw-clamps with stainless steel screws on underground pipes and those exposed to moisture.

PIPE, WATER—FLEXIBLE PLASTIC

Leaks in pipe. For a temporary repair, cover leak with a rubber patch and a worm-drive screw-clamp. See PIPE, WATER—COPPER. For a permanent repair, cut the pipe in two with a fine-toothed saw. Pull the sections apart and slip a worm-drive screw-clamp over each end. Then insert a straight plastic coupling made for joining flexible plastic pipe in the cut ends.

PIPE, WATER—RIGID PLASTIC

Leaks in pipe. For a temporary repair, cover leak with a rubber patch and worm-drive screw-clamp. See PIPE, WATER—COPPER. A permanent repair may be difficult to make if there is not sufficient give in the pipe run. Start by cutting the pipe in two with a saw. Force the ends apart far enough to install a plastic

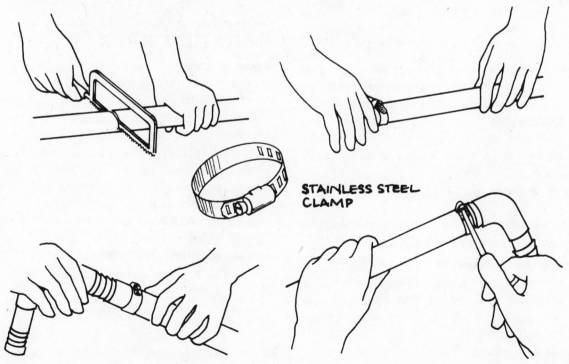

STAINLESS STEEL CLAMP

coupling made for rigid plastic pipe over the ends. If you can do this, clean the ends of the pipe with acetone. Brush special solvent-cement made for this type of pipe on the ends and inside the coupling. Then quickly slip the coupling onto the pipe ends. Force the pipe as far into the coupling as possible. Then give the coupling a half turn to spread the cement, and hold in place for a minute. Wipe off excess cement, leaving a small bead around the ends of the coupling. Don't turn on water for 6 hours, or the time specified on the can of cement.

Leaks at joints. Clean well. Clean again with a little acetone. Then brush a thin bead of cement into joint and let dry for 6 hours.

PIPE, WATER—STEEL

Leaks in pipe. There is not a satisfactory permanent repair. For a temporary repair, see PIPE, WATER—COPPER. To determine size of worm-drive screw-clamp needed, use string measuring technique.

IF STRING MEASURES	STEEL PIPE SIZE IS
2³⁄₁₆″	³⁄₈″
2⁵⁄₈″	½″
3¼″	¾″
4⅛″	1″
5¼″	1¼″
6″	1½″

Leaks at joints. Don't try to tighten fitting or pipe; you may only aggravate the problem. For a temporary repair, drain the pipe and dry fitting with a torch. Clean off rust, dirt, and pipe dope. Smear on epoxy mender and let set for several hours before turning on water again.

Leaks at unions. See PIPE, WATER—COPPER.

PLANE, CARPENTER'S

Bottom rough, rusted. Remove rust by rubbing with liquid rust-remover. Then, after removing or pulling back cutting blade, polish bottom with fine steel wool. To smooth out scratches, rub with emery cloth.

Blade dull, nicked. Here's a tricky job. You can use a grinding wheel, but it is safer to work on a large (about 2 inches wide) carborundum stone. The blade must be held firmly at an angle of about 25 degrees. You can buy a special blade holder or simply cut a block of wood to the proper angle. Hold blade against this and at right angles to the long side of the stone. Then move blade up and down the stone. Sharpen first on the rough side of the stone; finish on the smooth side. When job is done, turn blade over so that beveled edge is up; lay it flat on the smooth side of the stone, and move it sidewise several times.

PLANTER

Wood planter rotting at bottom. See PLANT TUB OR BOX. But a better remedy—possible with rectangular planters but difficult with round tubs—is to make a liner of aluminum flashing metal. Solder all seams. If planter has drainage holes, fit aluminum tube or a ring of aluminum flashing through holes and solder to bottom of liner.

Concrete planter broken. See CONCRETE (*thin sections of ornamental concrete broken*).

Hollow tile planter broken. See TILE, HOLLOW.

PLANT TUB OR BOX

Rotting at bottom. If rot has not progressed too far, unpot the plant. Clean and wash tub thoroughly and let dry. Dig out soft wood and fill holes with plastic wood. Apply two liberal coats of zinc or copper naphthanate wood preservative to the wood inside and out. Line bottom and well up the sides with freezer-grade aluminum foil or heavy polyethylene film and poke drainage holes through it to correspond with holes in tub bottom. Pour in 2 or 3 inches of coarse gravel before repotting plants. Keep tub raised off floor about 1 inch to provide air circulation underneath.

PLASTER

Plaster ornament broken. Coat broken surfaces with cellulose cement and let dry. Apply a second coat of cement to one surface and press together firmly.

Ornamental plaster surface chipped. Saturate with water. Mix plaster of Paris with water to form a stiff paste. Apply to chipped surface and mold roughly with your fingers. When dry, the plaster can be shaped accurately with a knife, file, and sandpaper.

Plaster ornament separated from another material such as felt. Apply cellulose or rubber cement to the separated surfaces and press together. See also HOUSEHOLD DECORATIVE ACCESSORIES. Hard plaster can be glued much like ceramics.

Plaster wall and ceiling problems. See INTERIOR WALL, PLASTER.

PLASTICS—FABRICS

NOTE. Plastic fabrics, such as rayon, nylon, Dacron, Orlon, Acrilan, etc., are mended like fabrics made out of cotton, silk, wool, etc. See CLOTHING—FABRICS.

Problems with vinyl fabrics. See VINYL.

PLASTICS—FLEXIBLE

See VINYL or POLYETHYLENE. Otherwise, if plastic is of unknown brand or type, see PLASTICS—GENERAL.

PLASTICS—GENERAL

NOTE. Plastics included under this heading are those used in kitchenware, appliances, radio cabinets, toys, decorative accessories, etc. If you cannot identify the type of plastics used in something that needs to be mended, follow directions below. If these repair methods do not work, chances are that you are dealing with polyethylene, and should check information in that entry.

Broken, cracked. Wash edges and dry thoroughly. Apply plastic-mending adhesive to one edge and press broken pieces together overnight. If the broken section is thin, it is then advisable to reinforce the joint by gluing a thin plastic patch over it. Use the same adhesive.

Scratched. Better leave well enough alone. However, if you want to take a chance, dip a rag in sewing machine oil or salad oil and then in powdered pumice. Rub on the scratch until it is obliterated. Then wipe surface clean and repeat the process with rottenstone. When the area dulled by the pumice begins to shine, wipe clean again. And then rub with powdered rouge (available at the hardware store) and water. This should restore the original shine pretty well.

NOTE. If you value the plastic article, test this scratch-removal method on the underside of the article or on a piece of similar plastic.

Deformed. Heat and very hot water soften and usually deform such thermoplastics as acrylics, nylon, polyethylene, styrene, and vinyl. All you can try to do—and it probably won't be successful—is to reheat the deformed object and try to mold it back into shape.

Stains. Wash in soap and water. Do not use abrasives. If stains remain, leave them alone.

Separated from another material such as wood. See HOUSEHOLD DECORATIVE ACCESSORIES. Plastics can also be drilled and screwed to wood or bolted or riveted to metal. The screw holes must be of slightly larger diameter than the fasteners.

PLASTICS—LAMINATED
(Formica and the like)

Plastic surface loose from wood base. Scrape out old adhesive as much as possible. Make sure surfaces are dry. With spatula, spread a thin layer of epoxy glue in crack. Then clamp or weight plastic in place. If plastic is under tension at a nearby point—for example, if a faucet escutcheon is bearing on it—release tension before clamping plastic.

Holes, deep burns. These are impossible to fill perfectly. The best you can do is to clean the hole well and fill with SeamFil, made by Kampel Enterprises, Inc., Dillsburg, Pennsylvania 17019. This is made in two dozen colors, and you can make additional colors by mixing the contents of the tubes together.

Simply fill the holes and smooth with a putty knife. If shrinkage occurs, repeat process an hour later. Sand smooth with very fine sandpaper.

Cracks between sheets of plastic. Scrape out dirt, clean thoroughly, and fill as above.

Stains. Wash with soap and water or mild household cleanser.

PLAYPEN, BABY'S

Plastic on top rails cracked. Don't try to fix it. Peel it off and either leave wood unfinished or apply nontoxic paint.

Slat broken. If broken with the grain, coat edges with epoxy glue and clamp together with C clamps for 12 hours. If break is across the grain, saw off slat flush with bottom rail and pull it out of mortise in top rail. Cut new slat the same length and shape top to fit in mortise. Apply epoxy glue in mortise and set in slat. To hold slat on bottom rail, daub epoxy glue on end and press in place on rail. When glue is dry, drive a long thin screw up through the rail into end of slat or join the slat to the rail with a steel corner brace.

Bottom weak. Check hinges, angle irons, or wood strips on which bottom rests. Reglue wood strips that reinforce the bottom.

PLIERS

Jaws do not meet squarely. Tighten nut that holds halves of pliers together. Then lock nut tight by holding a steel punch on the line where the nut goes through the bolt and rap with a hammer.

Teeth dull, rounded. Clamp pliers in vise and deepen grooves between teeth with a small triangular file.

PLYWOOD

Finish marred. See LACQUERED SURFACE, PAINTED SURFACE, SHELLACKED SURFACE, or VARNISHED SURFACE, as case may be.

Veneer loose, broken, bulging. See VENEER.

Burns, dents, scratches. See FURNITURE, WOOD.

Holes in painted plywood. Apply oil-base paint to all parts of hole. When dry, fill with spackle.

Holes in stained plywood. If hole is small, fill with plastic wood colored to match plywood finish, or with a shellac stick. If hole is large, cut out veneer around hole in a rectangle. Out of a scrap of matching veneer, cut a patch to fit, and glue into hole with white or resorcinol glue. Sand patch down to level of surrounding surface when glue dries.

Holes in plywood subfloor or underlayment under resilient flooring. Fill with latex cement.

Stains. See WOOD.

Warped. See FURNITURE—TABLE (*top or leaf warped*).

Pieces of plywood separated. Nail, screw, or bolt together, or coat with white or resorcinol glue and clamp pieces together overnight.

Plywood separated from another material. Refasten with screws or bolts. Or use appropriate glue (see HOUSEHOLD DECORATIVE ACCESSORIES and use same glues as specified for wood).

Edges rough, splintered. Wrap sandpaper around a block of wood and sand edges as smooth as possible. Fill deep holes with plastic wood or water putty. To conceal rough grain, brush on white glue or paste filler of the type used to fill pores in oak and other open-pore woods. Apply several coats as necessary. Sand smooth.

If plywood is stained, coat the edge after sanding with white glue. Press down a ribbon veneer trim. When glue dries, cut off edges of ribbon flush with plywood surface with a sharp knife. Stain trim to match plywood.

POLYETHYLENE

Holes, tears in thin material. Experiment first on some scrap material to get the hang of making this repair. Overlap the edges of the film or cut a patch out of polyethylene and lay it over the hole. Place a sheet of white paper on top. Heat an electric iron to about the middle temperature setting and hold it on the paper for several seconds. The polyethylene edges should heat-seal together. If they don't, increase iron temperature slightly. But beware of using too high a temperature, because it will disintegrate the plastic.

Breaks in thick polyethylene. A perfect repair is impossible. But broken parts can sometimes be joined by brushing the surfaces with the flame from a torch. Don't melt the plastic, just oxidize it. When cool, put a drop of water on the surfaces. If the water doesn't spread, heat the plastic further and test with water again. When the water drops do spread, dry the surfaces and apply plastic-mending adhesive. Let this set for five minutes, then press the pieces together.

PORCELAIN ENAMEL

Chipped. Clean chipped area and let dry. Then apply epoxy resin sold for porcelain repairs.

Rust or copper stains on surface. Wash with household ammonia and water, or a solution of 3 tablespoons Javelle water to 1 quart water. If this doesn't work, scrub with a nonabrasive cleanser such as Zud.

PORCH, MASONRY

Floor cracked, uneven. See BRICK, CONCRETE, or STONE, as the case may be.

Columns rotting. See COLUMN, WOOD.

Wood railings rotting. See FENCE, WOOD.

Iron railings wobbly. Chip out weak mortar around base of posts (or bolts holding posts). Blow out crumbs with vacuum cleaner. If opening is fairly small, force in epoxy mender. If opening is large, cram it full of a quick-setting cement available from hardware stores. In either case, brace the railing in vertical position until filler material hardens.

Collects water in low spot. Floor can be leveled by troweling on latex cement or by chipping out concrete in low spot to a depth of 1 inch and filling with mortar of 1 part portland cement and 2 parts sand. See BASIC METHODS: HOW TO MIX AND HANDLE CONCRETE. However, patch will not match surrounding surface unless you paint it; and paint does not hold up very well on concrete paving.

PORCH, WOOD

Floorboard weak, rotten. If entire board is gone, replace it. To remove, split it lengthwise in several places and pry it out from the center toward the edges. Be careful not to damage tongue and groove of adjacent boards. To set in a new board in a tongue-and-groove floor, chisel off the bottom part of the grooved edge. Tongue of new board can then be slipped into groove of adjoining board, and grooved edge will fit over tongue of the other adjoining board.

If only a small part of a floorboard is defective, locate position of nearest joists and draw pencil lines across the top of the floor to mark these. Then drill 1-inch holes in the corners between the pencil lines and the edges of the bad board. With a keyhole saw, cut across the two pencil lines from hole to hole. The saw cuts should be almost flush with the inner edges of the joists. Split defective board and pry it out. Nail 1-inch by 3-inch boards to the sides of the joists under the hole. Cut new board to fit the opening. Remove bottom part of the grooved edge. Then set in and nail.

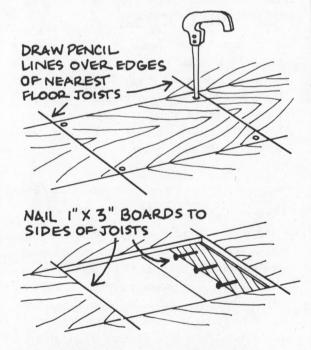

DRAW PENCIL LINES OVER EDGES OF NEAREST FLOOR JOISTS

NAIL 1" X 3" BOARDS TO SIDES OF JOISTS

Columns rotting. See COLUMN, WOOD.

Railings rotting. See FENCE, WOOD.

Railings wobbly. Secure to columns or floor with angle irons.

Porch sagging. Rent a steel jack post (or maybe two) and jack up sagging joists. Then place 4-inch by 4-inch timbers treated with wood preservative under joists and remove jacks.

POTTERY

See CHINA and EARTHENWARE. Use epoxy glue if pottery is used for cooking, cellulose cement if it is a purely ornamental piece.

POWER TOOLS (other than those common types listed under specific headings)

See BASIC METHODS: HOW TO CHECK OUT ELECTRICAL APPLIANCES.

Noisy. Lubricate according to manufacturer's directions.

Spark excessively. Carbon brushes probably need to be replaced. See ELECTRIC MOTOR.

PRESSURE COOKER

Gasket worn, cooker leaks. You can usually pull off the gasket (you may need pliers, because when it is old it sticks to metal) and replace with a new one available from the pressure-cooker dealer. But it's easier and costs no more to take the cooker to the dealer and let him do the whole job.

PROPANE TORCH

Out of gas. You need a new cylinder. Close valve. Unscrew old cylinder to left. Screw on new one to right until hand-tight and no more.

Doesn't light. You're probably giving it too much gas. Strike match and hold it directly against tip of burner tube. Open control valve just a hair until a small flame appears. Then, after a couple of seconds, gradually open valve all the way. Let the torch warm up a minute or two before using it in an inverted position.

Poor flame or none at all. Remove cylindrical burner head with a wrench. Lift or unscrew orifice from end of bent burner tube; reverse it and hold against the tube end. Then open and close the valve quickly, two or three times, to blow gas through the orifice. This should clean out the obstruction. Don't try to clean the orifice with a wire because you might damage it.

PUMP, PORTABLE WATER

Doesn't work. Has fuse blown? Is outlet into which pump is plugged defective? Is cord broken? Is extension cord (if there is one) broken? Does water rise high enough around pump?

Clean out small air-bleed hole near base of pump.

Open pump and check if impeller turns freely. If not, remove and clean it.

PUSH BROOM

Handle loose from broom head. Remove handle entirely and clean end and socket. Coat end of handle with epoxy glue and screw into head. Let glue dry for 6 hours. An alternative is to drill a small hole through the broom head into the end of the handle, and drive in a round-head screw.

PYROCERAM

Broken. Wash and dry well. Coat edges with epoxy glue and press together for 6 hours.

QUILT

Lining lumpy. Cut open surrounding stitches and readjust lining from the outside. Then resew.

Holes in cover. Snip out damaged area to within about ½ inch of surrounding stitches. Cut a patch to fit and tuck edges under surrounding fabric, and sew in place. To keep cut edges from raveling and improve their appearance, stick them down to patch with fabric glue.

Soiled. Quilts made with cotton covers and polyester lining can be machine-washed and dried at medium temperature. Have others dry-cleaned.

RADIATOR, HOT WATER

Radiator doesn't heat properly. Hold a pan under vent valve. Open valve with valve key to let out accumulated air; close valve when water begins to run out. If difficulty continues to arise, replace manually operated valve with an automatic one.

NOTE. If radiator is painted with metallic paint, heat output is reduced. Repaint with interior paint. (The metallic paint need not be removed first.)

Leaks at inlet valve stem. Tighten nut at top of valve. If leak doesn't stop, loosen nut completely and wrap graphite wicking around stem a couple of times. Bring nut down over this and tighten.

Paint chipped. Touching up is rarely satisfactory, because once paint chips in one place it usually chips in others. Disconnect radiator. Remove as much paint as possible with a coarse rasp or paint remover. Wash with detergent and dry with a towel (before rust can set in). Let dry thoroughly. Sand off remaining rust. If you can't get it all, apply red metal primer then an oil-base primer followed by a coat of oil-base semigloss paint.

RADIATOR, STEAM

Radiator doesn't heat properly. Unscrew valve from radiator, carefully clean venting port with a tiny wire. Blow hard through stem of valve. Shake out accumulated water. (Valves can also be cleaned by soaking in vinegar for 24 hours.) Then replace. If radiator continues not to heat, lay a carpenter's level on it to determine whether it is pitched properly. If it isn't, insert wood shims under legs. In a one-pipe heating system, radiator should pitch down to the supply line. In a two-pipe system, it should pitch toward the return line. If radiator still doesn't heat, replace valve with a new one.

NOTE. Heat output is reduced if radiators are painted with metallic paint. Overpaint with ordinary interior paint or special radiator paint.

Banging in radiator and pipes. Insert ½-inch blocks of wood under the legs of the radiator to correct the pitch of the pipe leading to it. If this doesn't work and it is possible to do so, insert thicker blocks of wood under legs. If this still doesn't work, call a plumber.

Water leaks from around stem of inlet valve. See RADIATOR, HOT WATER.

Paint chipped. See RADIATOR, HOT WATER.

RADIO

Doesn't work. If battery-operated, you probably need new batteries. Otherwise, take radio to repair shop and let them worry with it.

Tuning knobs loose. Remove knob. Coat hole in knob and end of spindle with plastic mending adhesive and press together. This, unfortunately, is not a very good repair because the knob will loosen up again. But if you use glue that will really hold, you may never be able to take the radio apart when it needs repairs again.

Plastic case broken. Clean edges and coat with plastic-mending adhesive. Fit pieces together and bind them with string or tape for 24 hours.

RAILING, WOOD

See STAIRS.

Porch railing weak. If railing is simply wobbly, you can strengthen it by screwing galvanized steel angle irons to the posts and floor. But if weakness is a result of rot, you must take the railing apart as necessary and replace the rotten members with new wood that has been saturated with wood preservative.

RAINCOAT

Tear in vinyl. Cut strip of vinyl to cover tear or use patch in plastic-mending adhesive kit. Apply plastic-mending adhesive to patch and smooth in place over tear.

Tear in polyethylene. See POLYETHYLENE.

Tear in rubber. Cut a patch out of rubber. Roughen undersurface of patch and area around hole with sandpaper. Apply thin coat of rubber cement to both surfaces and let dry. Then apply a second coat to the patch and smooth down.

Tear in cloth. Out of similar material, cut a small round patch and glue under tear with fabric glue.

Placket ripped in cloth coat. For a small rip, see CLOTHING—PLACKETS. If rip is large, rip out stitches in the entire back seam, pull edges together so that rip is concealed, and sew a new seam on a sewing machine. There is generally enough fullness to raincoats to make such a repair possible without materially changing the appearance of the coats.

RAKE, LEAF

Bamboo tines loose—too far apart or too close together. The tines are held with wire between two bamboo strips bolted to the bottom end of the handle and by laced wire and possibly a steel strip further down. Remove lower wire and position the tines properly. Remove old wire from bamboo cross brace and wrap new wire tightly around one end of it. Then lace it tightly between the tines and around the brace to the other end of the brace. Tighten at this point and lace back through the tines to the starting point.

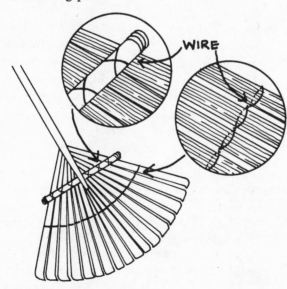

WIRE

Now take a long length of wire and bend it in half around the tine at one side of the rake 4 to 6 inches below the cross brace. Loop it around the tine and twist together three or four times. Then loop it around the next tine and twist together, and so on to the opposite side of the rake. The wire should form an arc more or less paralleling the arc formed by the ends of the tines.

Bamboo tine missing. If it is not broken, set it back in place in the rake and lace to the bamboo cross brace with wire. Also wire it to the other tines where they come together at the handle. If the missing tine is broken, either leave the rake alone or glue the broken tine together with epoxy adhesive and insert a small rivet through break when glue dries.

Head of bamboo rake wobbles on handle. Tighten the U-bolt or strap holding the tines to the handle. If the U-bolt or strap still wobbles, wrap the handle at this point with friction tape and tighten the bolt over this.

Bamboo handle split. See BAMBOO.

Tines in steel rake broken. There's nothing you can do to this kind of leaf rake except keep the head tightly bolted to the handle. Use the rake until a number of tines are broken and then throw it away.

RANGE, ELECTRIC

Nothing works. Have fuses blown at fuse box?

Single surface unit doesn't heat. Make sure switch is off. If unit is of removable type, plug it in tight. Replace it if it still doesn't work. If not removable unit, take out reflector and check if wires on units are loose or broken. Reconnect them. If unit still doesn't work, replace it.

Oven units don't work. If units are of plug-in type, remove and clean terminals and push units firmly into sockets. If they still don't work, replace item. If built-in unit doesn't work, have it replaced.

Oven temperature too low or too high. Something's wrong with the thermostat. Pull off temperature-control knob and change position on spindle. Move toward high heat to raise temperature, toward low to decrease temperature. (Note that this doesn't actually change the oven temperature—simply makes it agree with the indication on the dial. But the net result is the same.)

Convenience outlet doesn't work. Is 15-amp fuse in bottom compartment (or wherever it is located on your particular make and model) blown?

Oven light doesn't work. Bulb may be burned out. Replace with a new oven bulb. If this doesn't work, check whether 15-amp fuse on range has blown.

Oven food too light or too dark on top or bottom. The problem is probably with the utensil you are using and where you place it in the oven. Check the range instruction booklet.

Surface unit reflectors encrusted with spillages. Soak for several hours in a strong household ammonia solution. Then polish with fine steel wool and rinse clean.

Paint chipped. Touch up with porcelain enamel or epoxy touch-up enamel.

Stains on surface. Wash with detergent solution and/or rub with white appliance wax. Soak stains remaining in chlorine bleach.

Glass/ceramic cook top cracked. Don't use any part of cook top. Call a serviceman and have it replaced at once.

Aluminum or copper utensils leave marks on glass/ceramic cook top. Remove marks before you use cook top again, otherwise they may become permanent. Clean with Corning Cleaner Conditioner made for this purpose and available from appliance dealer. If spots remain, scour with a nonmetallic scouring cloth (such as Golden Fleece) and Bar Keeper's Friend, a nonabrasive scouring powder.

Other stains on glass/ceramic top. Clean as above. Make sure top is cool before you start work.

RANGE, GAS

Pilot light out. From the pilot follow the little gas inlet tube back to the manifold, where you will find an adjusting screw. Hold a lighted match at the pilot and turn the screw on the manifold counterclockwise until the gas ignites.

Then turn the screw clockwise till the flame is three-quarters of the height of the flashtube leading to the burner.

Top burners light but oven doesn't. This happens on only a few modern ranges. Check whether electric fuse on house circuit into which range is connected has blown. If it hasn't, call a serviceman.

Lights don't light. Check whether range is plugged into electric outlet. Check whether fuse on house circuit has blown.

Burners encrusted with spillages. Lift out burner and soak in solution of household ammonia. If necessary, boil in a weak solution of washing soda. Then dry thoroughly.

Oven food too light or too dark. See RANGE, ELECTRIC.

Oven temperature too low or too high. See RANGE, ELECTRIC.

Burner flame poor. If yellow, it's not getting enough air; if it jumps off burner, it's getting too much air. Rotate control on back of burner until flame is blue and quiet.

Pilot light goes out. Lift range top to expose pilot, and clean nozzle with a pin. This should correct problem, but flame may still be too small. Consult instruction booklet and adjust the screw near the end of the tube bringing gas to pilot.

RECORD PLAYER

Needle clicks, skips on record. Clean needle with camel's-hair brush. Always brush only from the base of the tone arm toward the tip.

Clicking is most likely attributable to hairs and dust on records. Buy a Parastatik Disc Preener and rub on record lightly as it turns. Preener wick must be damp.

Tone poor. Needle needs to be replaced (about once a year for average use). Follow directions in manufacturer's instruction booklet.

Needle comes down off the record or lands too far into record. Adjust needle set-down screw in base of tone arm.

Tone arm lifts too high or not high enough when record comes down. Adjust tone arm height screw in base of tone arm.

Tone arm skids all the way across record.

Adjust tracking force screw in base of tone arm until needle stays in grooves but does not bear down heavily into them.

Player hums. Try reversing position of plug in outlet. Connect a wire to metal chassis and ground it to a water pipe. (Be sure to unplug unit before making connection.)

Also see PHONOGRAPH RECORD.

REFRIGERATOR

NOTE. Call a serviceman if refrigerator doesn't work properly, but before doing so, check points below.

Doesn't work. Check: Has temperature-control dial been turned off? Is refrigerator plugged in? Is cord broken? Has fuse blown?

Feels warm on outside. Provide more air circulation at sides and especially at top if refrigerator exhausts heat from the back. If you have a modern front-exhaust box, call a serviceman.

Seems to labor. Clean out dust, lint, cobwebs from operating mechanism with a vacuum cleaner hose.

Interior not cold enough. Slip a dollar bill between gasket and door jamb; then close door and pull it out. If it comes out easily wash gasket with detergent solution and rinse. If door still doesn't close tight, have gasket replaced.

On old refrigerator with a latch rather than a magnetic gasket, loosen strike plate on jamb and move it into the box a fraction of an inch so that it pulls latch and door tight shut.

Water in refrigerator compartment. Trouble might be attributable to the door not closing tight. But chances are the drain line is clogged. If you can get at the line (it's usually clipped to back of cabinet), clean it out as well as you can with a small wire. Then pour a warm solution of household ammonia down through it until it runs out freely.

Odors in compartment. Wash compartment walls, shelves, and drawers with a heaping teaspoonful of baking soda in a quart of warm water. Keep an open box of baking soda in the compartment.

Door swings open or shut too fast. Pull off bottom front panel and raise or lower leveling screws under front corners. If refrigerator lacks leveling screws, slip pieces of wood shingle under the front feet.

Plastic parts broken. Clean with detergent and rinse. When dry, coat broken edges with plastic-mending adhesive and clamp together for 12 hours. If break needs to be reinforced, cover it with a strip of vinyl fabric glued to part with plastic-mending adhesive or vinyl cement.

Finish marred. Touch up with touch-up enamel after removing rust.

Stains on surface. Wash with detergent solution or rub with white appliance wax. To help protect surface against dirt and stains, wash the entire refrigerator and apply white appliance wax.

REGISTER, WARM AIR

Stains walls with soot. Remove grille and clean inside of duct with vacuum cleaner hose. Clean or replace furnace filters monthly.

RETAINING WALL

Cracked. This is caused by the pressure of the water and soil behind the wall. The crack may now permit adequate drainage, so if wall does not seem in danger of collapse, do not fill crack (you can grow vines over wall to conceal it). If you do fill crack, drainage tile must be installed behind wall so that water is carried away around the ends of the wall or through it.

The whole situation is complicated and possibly dangerous. Call in a mason who understands such things.

RIVET

Broken or loose. Cut or file off head. Poke out shank. Insert new rivet. If this is too long, cut off shank about 1/8 inch above surface. Place head on a vise or other heavy metal surface. Pinch pieces of metal being riveted together. Hammer down end of rivet shank until it overlaps hole.

ROOF—ALL TYPES

Moss growing on roof. Scrape or brush off completely. Brush pentachlorophenol wood preservative on wood roofs. On other roofs, brush on a solution of ½ ounce sodium arsenite in 10 gallons water.

Ice forms in gutters and backs up melt water which leaks through roof. See GUTTER, ALUMINUM.

Leaks at juncture with wall of house. This joint is flashed with metal, although the flashing may have been covered over when roof was reroofed. Easiest solution is to caulk joint with polysulfide rubber or silicone caulking.

ROOF, ASBESTOS-CEMENT SHINGLE

Broken shingles. If the shingles are lapped only at the bottom, shatter the cracked shingle with a hammer and remove the pieces. Slip a hacksaw blade up under overlapping shingles and cut off nails that held broken shingle. Insert a new shingle. To hold it in place, drill a hole through the joint between the overlying shingles and through the top of the new shingle. Drive one roofing nail through this until it is flush with the face of the new shingle. Then slip a 3-inch-wide strip of aluminum flashing between the shingles over the nail and bend it slightly so it will hold in place.

If shingles are lapped at the sides as well as at the bottom, have broken shingle replaced by a roofing contractor.

ROOF, ASPHALT ROLL

Small holes. Dab on asphalt roofing cement.

Large holes. Open the seam between pieces of asphalt roll below the hole and slip up through it a new piece of roll roofing large enough to extend 6 inches beyond all sides of the hole. When it is in place, spread asphalt roofing cement containing fibers under and around the edges of the hole. Press down torn roofing and close opening in seam below the hole.

Leaks in seams. If leaks are not stopped by

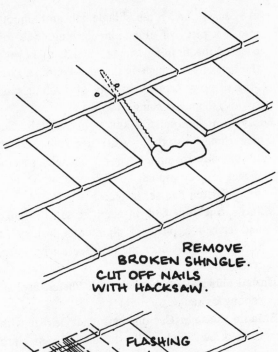

REMOVE BROKEN SHINGLE. CUT OFF NAILS WITH HACKSAW.

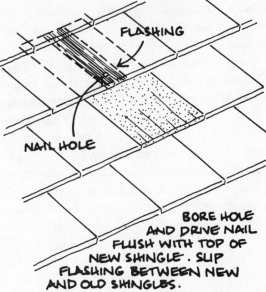

FLASHING

NAIL HOLE

BORE HOLE AND DRIVE NAIL FLUSH WITH TOP OF NEW SHINGLE. SLIP FLASHING BETWEEN NEW AND OLD SHINGLES.

applying asphalt roofing cement to them, coat the seam thoroughly with cement and then embed in it a 6-inch strip of 35-pound, smooth-surfaced, asphalt roll roofing. After the cement has set for 2 hours, paint the strip with unfibered asphalt roof cement.

ROOF, ASPHALT SHINGLE

Small holes, tears. Lift shingle carefully and put a dab of fibered asphalt roofing cement under hole.

Large holes, tears. Spread fibered asphalt roofing cement under the shingle tab and smooth into it a piece of aluminum flashing. The top edge of the flashing should extend up beyond the butt of the shingle in the next course above. Apply more cement to top of flashing and smooth damaged shingled into it.

Badly torn shingle. Cut out damaged tab. Cut new shingle to proper width and long enough to extend up under cut-off shingle several inches. Smear asphalt roofing cement on bottom of patch and set in place.

Shingle buckled. Cut through center of bulge and embed a piece of aluminum flashing in roofing cement under the tab. See *Large holes, tears,* above.

Curled shingle. Anchor tab with fibered asphalt roofing cement.

Shingle missing. Cut out nails that held it with a hacksaw blade. Slip a new shingle into place. You may have to cut off a bit along the top edge to position it properly. Smear asphalt roofing cement underneath and smooth shingle down into this. In a windy location, drive asphalt shingle nails through the tabs of the shingle overlapping the new one, and dab roofing cement on top of them.

Mineral surface wearing off. You can extend life of roof by applying an asphalt-base aluminum roofing paint. If roof is slightly cracked and pocked, use paint containing asbestos fibers; on a sound roof, use nonfibered paint.

Repair roof as necessary and brush clean. Apply paint with a brush and don't brush it out too much. A gallon should cover no more than 150 square feet and may cover less.

ROOF, BUILT-UP TAR AND GRAVEL

Leaks. Scrape back gravel and spread fibered asphalt roofing cement liberally over hole. Replace gravel. If roof seems badly worn, embed asphalt building paper in roofing cement, cover with additional cement, and replace gravel.

Blisters. Scrape back gravel and cut through blister with a knife. Spread roofing cement under blister and over it. Replace gravel.

ROOF, CLAY TILE

Leaks. Slip a piece of aluminum flashing metal under the tiles over the hole and hold in place with asphalt roofing cement applied to underside. The metal must be long enough so that its entire top edge is covered by the overlapping tiles.

Broken tiles. Call in a contractor.

ROOF, METAL

Small holes. Use steel wool thoroughly on the area and cover hole with exposy mender.

Large holes. Clean metal until it is bright. Cut a patch out of similar metal and solder in place. Use a soldering iron rather than a torch for safety's sake. For a less permanent repair, patch can be embedded in epoxy mender or fibered asphalt roofing cement.

Seams parted. Crimp together with pliers, and solder if possible; otherwise fill seam with epoxy mender or silicone caulking.

Steel roof rusted. Remove as much rust as possible. Prime with red metal primer and overcoat with two coats of oil-base house paint.

Factory-applied paint finish chipping, flaking. Scrape clean and sand off corrosion. Apply two coats of oil-base house paint.

ROOF, RIGID FIBER GLASS

Leaks at seams. Loosen nails. Clean out joint thoroughly with a knife or scraper and whisk broom. Run in a bead of mastic sealer supplied by fiber glass roofing manufacturer, or a bead of clear silicone caulking compound. Press sheets of fiber glass together well and nail them down again. Be careful not to drive nails down so hard that they crack the roofing.

Holes, cracks. See FIBER GLASS, RIGID.

ROOF, WOOD SHINGLE

Holes, cracks. Slip a piece of aluminum flashing metal up under the shingle over the hole and hold it in place with asphalt roofing cement.

The metal must be long enough to extend well up under the overlapping shingles.

Shingles rotten, badly damaged. Loosen overlapping shingles. Split defective shingle and pull out pieces. Slip a hacksaw blade up under overlapping shingles and cut nails that held defective shingle. Insert a new shingle. Put one or two dabs of asphalt roofing cement under this to hold it.

Shingles missing. Cut out nails which held them. Cut new shingles to fit gaps and slide into place. Fasten with two roofing nails driven just below butts of overlapping shingles.

Leaks in a closed valley. (A closed valley is one in which shingles come together instead of being separated by an open strip of flashing material.) Cut 12-inch- or 15-inch-wide aluminum or copper flashing metal into squares and bend into equal triangles. Push the metal up under shingles as far as possible. If a series of metal patches are required, work from the bottom of the roof up.

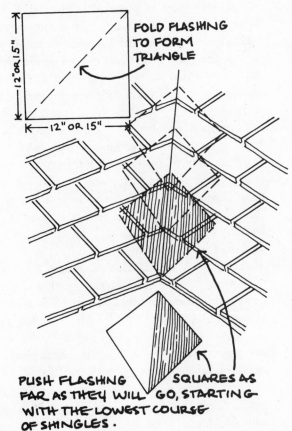

12" OR 15"

12" OR 15"

FOLD FLASHING TO FORM TRIANGLE

PUSH FLASHING FAR AS THEY WILL GO, STARTING WITH THE LOWEST COURSE OF SHINGLES.

SQUARES AS

ROPE

Broken. Cut the broken strands off cleanly, then separate the strands on each length of rope for several inches (the separation must be longer on thick ropes than on thin). "Crotch" the strands on the opposing pieces together just as you intertwine your fingers. Tie a string around the strands and the rope on your left. Then, starting with any strand on the right, tuck it over one strand and under one strand of the rope on the left. Do the same thing with the other two strands on the right. You may need a spike to open the strands in the rope in order to slip the loose strands through. Now remove the string and do the same thing with the strands on the left. When the splice is completed, do not cut the strands off next to the rope; let them protrude an inch or 2 to give extra strength.

Usually the strands need to be tucked only twice, as described. But for greater strength, you can make a third tuck.

End of rope raveling. Cut off cleanly and bind the end with friction tape. On a plastic rope, heat the end lightly with a torch until the strands are fused.

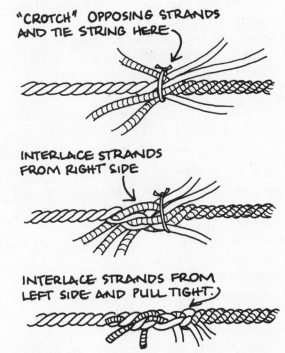

"CROTCH" OPPOSING STRANDS AND TIE STRING HERE

INTERLACE STRANDS FROM RIGHT SIDE

INTERLACE STRANDS FROM LEFT SIDE AND PULL TIGHT.

ROUTER

Doesn't work. Check whether fuse has blown, whether outlet into which router is plugged is defective, whether cord is broken.

Runs slowly or noisily. Lubricate according to manufacturer's directions.

Sparks excessively. Check if carbon brushes are worn down to about ¼ inch or less. If so, replace with new brushes of same size.

RUBBER

Small holes. Clean surface thoroughly with gasoline or benzine. Roughen with sandpaper. Spread on rubber cement.

Large holes, tears. Clean surface with gasoline or benzine and roughen with sandpaper. Cut patch out of an old tire tube or other rubber; clean and roughen surface. Coat both surfaces with rubber cement and let dry. Then apply a second coat to one surface and immediately smooth patch over hole.

A tire-tube patching kit will make a slightly stronger repair.

Rubber worn thin. Clean with gasoline or benzine and roughen with sandpaper. Apply plastic cement.

Rubber loose from another surface. Clean both surfaces, roughen with sandpaper and apply rubber cement. When this becomes tacky, press materials together and hold under pressure overnight.

RUG

Edges frayed. Whip the edge with carpet-binding thread or cover with gummed carpet-binding and press with a warm iron.

Worn in spots. Wear is caused by traffic and may be aggravated by condition of floor underneath. There is no way to mend worn spots satisfactorily, although you can conceal them to some extent by dyeing the rug backing to match the pile. If condition of floor contributes to the problem, take up rug and level the floor by sanding down high spots, filling wide cracks, and padding low spots with newspapers.

Holes. Stitch or glue burlap to wrong side of rug. Then, with a crochet hook, pull matching material through this to match the surrounding weave as closely as possible. To secure the yarn further, press gummed carpet-binding over the underside.

Rug indented by heavy furniture. Set steam iron in steaming position and hold over dents.

Rug limp. Have it sized by a rug cleaner. But if you don't care too much about it, mix 1 pound of wallpaper size with about 4 quarts of water. Stir smooth. Lay rug upside down on a flat surface. Brush size on back and let dry. If rug is loosely woven, make size mixture thicker than above formula.

Corners curled. Curl back by hand. Steam with a steam iron. If this method fails, fasten the corners down with double-faced adhesive tape.

Edges scalloped. Try steaming with a steam iron. Cut edge of rug cushion back 3 inches from edge of rug. In the final resort, fasten edges down with double-faced adhesive tape or tacks.

Fiber rug damaged. If fibers are only broken or frayed, glue them in place with white glue. If damage is extensive and rug is made up in small squares, cut out the bad squares and sew in new ones. But if rug is of overall weave, the only solution is to cut it into two or more smaller rugs. Finish the edges with gummed carpet-binding.

Burns in rugs. Carefully clip out the burned tufts, but don't cut too deep. Sponge with solution of 1 teaspoon mild detergent, 1 teaspoon white vinegar, and 1 quart warm water. Then weave fibers from a scrap of carpet into the hole through the backing. Glue bottom ends to rug backing with rubber cement. Trim off top ends flush with surface of rug.

Nongreasy food stains, alcohol stains. Sponge with water or detergent-vinegar solution.

Grease stains and materials. Scrape off as much greasy substance as possible. Apply trichloroethylene.

Thick grease, tar, crayon, lipstick, paint, chewing gum. Scrape off as much as possible. Clean with trichloroethylene. Let dry. Then apply detergent-vinegar solution if necessary. Repeat with trichloroethylene as necessary.

Blood stains. Apply detergent-vinegar solution. Dry. Then use trichloroethylene if necessary.

Ink stains. Sponge with detergent-vinegar solution. Only washable inks can be removed. Call a professional to remove others.

Urine stains. Blot up at once. Then sponge with detergent-vinegar solution, prepared puppy-stain remover, or carbonated water.

Vomit, excrement. Scrape up at once. Sponge with detergent-vinegar solution. Blot as dry as possible. Then sponge with 1 tablespoon household ammonia in ¾ cup water. Blot dry. Then sponge with 1 part white vinegar in 2 parts water.

RUG CUSHION

Edges frayed. If it's important to do anything at all about them, trim them off neatly, cover with gummed carpet-binding, and press with a warm iron.

RUG, GRASS

Soiled. Vacuum frequently to remove dirt and grit. When dirty, wash with heavy-duty detergent, rinse thoroughly and dry in sun.

Fibers broken. Glue in place with white glue.

Slides on floor. Brush neoprene rubber in an even coat on the underside. Or run a ribbon of plastic rubber around the edges and put dabs of rubber spaced about 6 inches apart on the area between. Let the neoprene or plastic rubber dry completely before putting down rug.

RULE, FOLDING

Broken between joints. Coat broken edges with epoxy glue and force together. When dry, cut a strip of aluminum or other metal flashing to width of rule and about 2 inches longer than the break, and glue it over the break with epoxy.

Broken at joints. Pry open the metal flanges wrapped around edges of blade. Coat broken blade edges with epoxy glue and coat the back of the broken-off section. Set into the joint and close the flanges.

SALTCELLAR

Top clogged. Clean out openings with a wire. Soak in warm water, and use wire again.

Top and base corroded together. Soak saltcellar in warm water until top can be removed. If this fails, soak in penetrating oil for several days. When pieces finally come apart, remove as much of the corrosion as possible with a rag; then use fine emery cloth or steel wool. To prevent recurrence of trouble, store saltcellars in a dry place only—preferably after emptying out the salt. Remove, clean, and thoroughly dry top frequently.

SANDER, RECIPROCATING, ORBITAL, OR DUAL

Doesn't work. Check whether fuse has blown, whether outlet into which sander is plugged is live, whether cord is broken. Check also if extension cord on which you may be using sander is broken.

Sluggish. Lubricate according to manufacturer's directions.

Sparks excessively. Replace carbon brushes with new ones of same size. Replace both even though only one is badly worn.

SAW, CHAIN

Won't start. Check whether it's turned on, whether choke is set properly, whether gas tank is full. If there's no spark, replace or clean the plug. Adjust carburetor according to instruction manual.

Doesn't run well. Clean air filter. Change fuel filter. Replace spark plug. Drain gas tank and carburetor, and clean. Adjust carburetor.

Go over entire saw thoroughly, outside and in, to remove dirt and caked-on sawdust. Check all nuts and screws for tightness.

Doesn't cut well. Sharpen chain. Make sure chain isn't reversed. Adjust tension on chain. Check whether bar holding chain is pinched, and pry it open.

Chain dull. You can touch up the teeth (called

cutters) with a small file. But for a first-class job, let an expert do the sharpening.

Chain edges forward as saw idles. Chain is probably too tight. Tension is about right if you can pull chain easily around the bar even though it fits snug to the bar. To adjust tension, loosen bar mounting bolt and turn tension-adjusting screw.

Chain broken. Lay broken link across a slightly open vise and knock out the rivets holding it with a steel punch. Insert new link and rivets, and set the rivets by tapping lightly. File link to width of adjacent links.

SAW, HAND

Blade bent. Reshape with hands. If the blade has a sharp kink, place it on a flat surface, lift handle slightly, then hammer out kink with a wood mallet.

Rusted. Smear on liquid rust-remover and rub with a rag. When blade is as clean as you can get it this way, go over it with fine steel wool.

Dull. Sharpening is a tedious job and trickier than it may appear. Let an expert do it.

SAW, PORTABLE CIRCULAR

Doesn't work. Is fuse blown? Is outlet into which saw is plugged defective? Is cord broken? If you're using an extension cord, is that broken?

Not running at top speed. Chances are you're running saw on an extension cord that is undersized. Up to 25 feet, use an extension cord with number 16 wires; from 25 to 50 feet, cord should have number 14 wires; from 50 to 75 feet, it should have number 12 wires.

Sparks excessively. Carbon brushes need replacement. (They should be replaced whenever either of the two brushes in a power tool or appliance is worn down to only ¼ inch long.) Unscrew caps; pull out old brushes and springs. Replace with new brushes and springs of the same size.

Doesn't saw straight. Check whether blade is warped and needs replacement. Make sure it is screwed on tight.

Cuts slowly. Replace blade with a new one.

Gum and pitch hardened on blade. Scrub with turpentine or kerosene.

SAW, SABER

Doesn't work. Check whether fuse has blown, whether outlet into which saw is plugged is defective, whether cord is broken.

Runs slowly. Lubricate according to manufacturer's directions with SAE number 20 oil.

Noisy. Lubricate.

Sparks excessively. Carbon brushes may need replacement. See ELECTRIC MOTOR.

SCISSORS

Don't cut—they simply fold material being cut. Tighten screw joining two halves of the scissors.

Dull. Cut a piece of medium sandpaper in two with the scissors. Turn sandpaper over and cut again. But for a real sharpening job, take the scissors apart and use a sharpening stone.

On a flat stone, lay the blades flat on their beveled edges (the entire beveled surface must be in contact with the stone) and draw the blades toward you. At the end of each cutting stroke, lift the blades and start over again (in other words, don't saw them back and forth). Take care not to let the blades rock.

On a grinding wheel, hold the blades at right angles to the edge of the wheel and with the inner sides of the blades on top. Then move the blades back and forth across the wheel as it turns. Take care not to change the bevels on the blades, and use very little pressure so you don't remove too much metal.

Point broken. File metal smooth. The scissors may not be perfect but they are still usable.

SCREEN, WINDOW

Holes in metal screening. If wires are simply pushed apart, as by a pencil point, straighten them with a small nail or ice pick. If wires are broken, buy screen patches at hardware store and hook into place over hole. You can make large screen patches out of a scrap of screening.

Holes in fiber glass screening. Push strands together if they are not broken. If strands are broken, you can fuse a fiber glass patch to the screening by applying heat. Practice on some scrap material until you get the hang of this. Have someone hold an iron frying pan or something similar to one side of the torn screening. Cut a patch to overlap hole and hold it against screening on other side. Then run the tip of a hot iron over it until it is stuck tight.

Holes in plastic screening. Cut a patch out of similar screening and sew it over the hole with nylon thread.

Metal screening corroded. Set on a flat surface and dust with a stiff bristle brush. Wash with soap and water; rinse and let dry. Paint both sides with two coats of spar varnish or prepared screen paint. To avoid clogging the mesh, apply finish with a piece of carpet.

Screening badly torn. Install new fiber glass screening (which is very durable, corrosion resistant, and easily stretched by hand). Pry off moldings on frame; remove tacks or splines holding old screening; rip off screening. Lay screen flat. Tack new screening securely across the top of the frame opening. Pull to the bottom and tack there. Then tack sides. Use ¼-inch copper tacks and space them about 2 inches apart. Or use a staple gun: it makes the work much easier. Cut off excess screening with a razor blade. Replace moldings.

If screening is held in place by splines instead of tacks, you can install new screening with these. Simply lay the screening over the grooves around the edges of frame and press it down into grooves with the splines.

Screen frame weak, wobbly. Brace four corners with iron angles. If you object to the appearance of these, drill ¼-inch holes deep into the corner edges. Holes must go through both of the joined pieces of wood. Coat ¼-inch wood dowels with resorcinol glue, drive them into holes, and cut off flush with frame edges.

SCREWDRIVER

Tip broken, rounded. Hold screwdriver in a vise and file across the tip. Hold file flat and file only on forward stroke. If repaired tip is too blunt, taper sides at the same gradual angle of original taper.

Shank loose in handle. Remove shank and squeeze a little epoxy glue into handle hole. Then insert shank as far as possible. Allow glue to set before using screwdriver.

SCREWS

Screw loose in screw hole. Remove from hole and cram hole with steel wool, solid wire solder, plastic wood, or a glued wood plug. Then reset screw.

Screw "frozen" in place. Heat screwhead with a soldering iron. Then unscrew it.

Head damaged so that screwdriver won't hold. If necessary to salvage screw, reslot head with a hacksaw.

Shank broken off in wood. If wood is thick enough and new screw must be reset in same place, drive screw deep into wood with a nail set. If this is impossible, punch a small hole in the top of the screw with a steel punch. Then drill out screw with an electric drill.

SEASHELL

Broken. Apply cellulose cement to both sides of break and press together until glue sets. If shell is used for cooking, apply epoxy glue.

SEPTIC TANK

Clogged. Despite claims to the contrary, chemical septic-tank cleaners and yeast are of very little value. Have tank pumped out. To prevent future clogging, have tank checked every 18 to 24 months.

Roots clogging pipes in disposal field. These must be cut out with a special auger. Call septic-tank service.

SEWING MACHINE

If you don't have an instruction booklet, get one by the manufacturer of your machine, and follow directions for maintaining and adjusting machine. Otherwise, take machine to a dealer.

SHAVER, ELECTRIC

Doesn't run. If power is on and the outlet into which shaver is plugged is operating, examine cord for a break, and replace it if you find one. If you still don't get action, take the shaver to a repair shop. Like a watch, this is one appliance that definitely needs professional attention. But you can avoid most problems if you keep the razor scrupulously clean according to the directions which came with it.

SHEET

Tears, holes. See CLOTHING—FABRICS (*holes*).

Hemstitching broken. This can be mended, but it's a painstaking job. Better separate hem edge from sheet entirely and rejoin with a strip of straight-edge lace. Or, if appearance is not important, simply sew the hem edge over the sheet edge on your sewing machine or by whipping.

Contour sheet split at corners. Apply press-on mending tape over the tears. Then, if you dry sheets in a dryer, stitch down the edges of the tape and the torn edges of the sheet.

SHELLACKED SURFACE

Shallow scratches. Rub with alcohol.

Deep scratches. Apply several coats of new shellac with a fine brush. Then rub lightly with alcohol to smooth out surface.

Shellac gummy. Remove with denatured alcohol. In future, don't use shellac that is more than 6 months old.

Alcohol spots on shellac. Alcohol dissolves shellac, so mop it up quickly. Then rub with rottenstone and a cloth dipped in salad oil or sewing machine oil. Remove residue with benzine.

Other stains. See VARNISHED SURFACE.

SHELVING

Sagging. If there is no support in the middle of the shelf, nail a strip of wood about 1 inch thick to the wall under the shelf. This should be 16 inches long or more so that you can nail through to two of the studs (which are spaced roughly 14 inches apart). An alternative is to screw an iron angle to the wall (the screws must enter a stud).

If the shelf is warped as well as sagging, install a metal shelf support under it. Or put a screw eye in the front edge of the shelf in the middle of the sag; install another screw eye in the ceiling overhead, and connect the two by a stout wire.

NOTE. Do not support a warped shelf from a stable shelf in this way, because it will only result in warping of the upper shelf.

Also see BOOKSHELF.

SHOES

Leather scuffed. Trim off flaps of leather with scissors or a razor blade. Rub rest of scuffed area with the palm of your hand. Brush on liquid stain-polish and buff. Then apply paste polish.

Leather water-stiffened. Rub a damp rag in saddle soap and rub vigorously on leather. Rinse with a rag dampened in clear water. Let dry (don't expose to heat). Then apply polish.

Patent leather cracked. You can't mend cracks, but you can prevent additional cracking by rubbing petroleum jelly vigorously into leather.

Moccasin seams split. Pick out broken threads. Resew with heavy cotton or linen thread coated with beeswax. Run thread through old holes.

Inner sole loose. Remove and scrape off old glue. Apply rubber cement to lining and to base. Let dry until tacky, then stick inner sole down.

Hole in leather lining. Trim out neatly with scissors. Cut a patch out of thin, soft leather like that used for inner soles. Feather the edges as much as possible with a razor blade. Then apply rubber cement to back of patch and around edges of hole. Let dry until tacky, then smooth patch in place.

Woman's shoe heel broken. Apply epoxy glue to both broken edges and press together for 12 hours.

Tap off heel. Reglue with epoxy glue.

Nail in heel. Hold heel on a solid metal surface. With a hammer and nail set, hammer down nail point on inside of shoe. If sole of shoe is so old and brittle that bent point of nail won't hold in it, however, grasp the point with pliers and pull nail out. Fill hole in inner sole with plastic rubber.

Hole in rubber sole. Clean rubber thoroughly with gasoline or benzine. Roughen surface if it is smooth. Fill hole with plastic rubber.

Hole in leather sole. If shoe does not warrant resoling by a shoemaker, apply a stick-on rubber sole. Clean old sole thoroughly and roughen with the rasp enclosed in the resoling kit (available at the five-and-ten). Apply thin coat of rubber cement to sole and let dry for 15 minutes. Apply a second coat and let it dry, too. Then remove paper backing from new rubber sole, apply cement to rubber, let dry for 20 minutes or more, and press on leather sole.

Leather sole delaminated. Clean out dirt. Wedge opposing surfaces apart and spread in flexible epoxy glue. Press surfaces together.

Sole squeaks. Try rubbing neat's foot oil deeply into the leather.

Polish on leather shoes blotched. Remove all polish with a cloth dampened with benzine. Then repolish.

SHOES, TENNIS

Holes in canvas. Cut a small round patch of canvas, coat with fabric glue, and stick on outside of shoe.

Rubber torn loose from canvas. Coat rubber and canvas with rubber cement and let dry. Then apply a second coat of cement to both surfaces and press together when cement is tacky.

Hole in sole or sole thin. Clean thoroughly with gasoline or benzine. Roughen surface with sandpaper. Fill with plastic rubber. Let dry 24 hours.

NOTE. Since plastic rubber is black, this repair looks good only on dark soles.

SHOWER CURTAIN

Tears in canvas. Glue a patch of matching canvas to the inside with fabric glue. See CANVAS.

Tears in rubber or rubberized material. Clean surface and let dry. Cut a patch from the bottom of the curtain. Coat curtain and patch with rubber cement. Let dry. Apply a second coat to patch and press in place.

Tears in oiled silk. Cover with cellophane tape.

Tears in plastic. Cut a patch out of matching plastic material and glue down with plastic-mending adhesive.

Mildew stains. Scrub stains with strong chlorine solution. Hang curtain out to dry.

SHOWER DOOR

Leaks. Examine "weather stripping" around the edges of the door and frame. Clean thoroughly and position properly. If torn or deteriorating, replace with new stripping from plumbing supplies outlet.

Works stiffly. This is primarily a problem with doors that slide in metal tracks. Clean tracks with a knife and old brush. Wash clean with strong household detergent solution or ammonia. Spray tracks with silicone lubricant.

White stains on door. Scrub with vinegar.

SHOWER HEAD

Clogged. If shower head is modern, take off head, clean out sediment with a wire, and rinse thoroughly. On old shower heads, poke a slim wire through the ports. Then soak head in vinegar.

SHOWER STALL

Leak at top of receptor (bottom of stall). Clean crack thoroughly and let dry. Fill with silicone caulking compound.

Leak in base of receptor. If leak is around edges of drain, clean out crack. Let dry for several days, then squeeze in silicone caulking. If cast-stone receptor is cracked, clean crack thoroughly. Let dry for several days, then fill with silicone caulking. If joints in a tile receptor are cracked, see TILE, CERAMIC. If these measures fail, call a plumber.

Water leaks into wall behind faucet escutcheons. Wrap escutcheon with adhesive tape and unscrew with a pipe wrench. Cut out weak plaster around faucet. Let dry. Then fill hole with silicone caulking and replace escutcheon.

Metal stall rusted out. If hole is small, clean surface with steel wool and apply epoxy mender. If hole is large, clean the surface and apply a thin layer of epoxy mender. Immediately embed in this a patch of wire screen cloth and cover it at once with more epoxy. When epoxy dries, spread on still more to form a smooth surface. Let dry. Then file and sand smooth.

Ceramic tile cracked, broken, missing. See TILE, CERAMIC.

Sliding doors stiff. Clean tracks with a toothbrush and detergent. Drop in a little light oil.

Drain clogged. See DRAINS, PLUMBING.

SHUTTER

Sagging. Remove loose screws from hinges and fill holes with plastic wood. Then reset screws and draw all screws up tight.

Rotting along top edge. Dig out soft wood and saturate the entire top of the shutter with pentachlorophenol wood preservative. When this has dried, fill holes with plastic wood. To protect against further rotting, tack a strip of aluminum flashing over top of shutter.

Adjustable louver broken. Try to glue pieces together with resorcinol glue and tack a strip of aluminum to the back of the louver for extra reinforcement.

If louver is beyond repair, remove it and make a new one. After you have shaped the wood pivots on the ends, cut a U-shaped slot about 1 inch long and the width of the pivot into the louver at the end of one of the pivots. With this pivot removed, you can now fit the

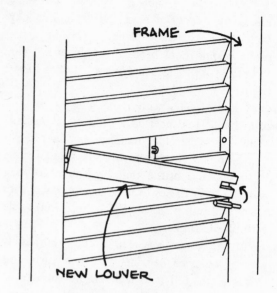

FRAME

NEW LOUVER

louver into the frame. Then coat the sawed-out end of the removed pivot with resorcinol glue. Insert the pivot end in the frame, slide the sawed-out end into the slot in the louver, and bind it in place with adhesive tape until glue dries. Final step is to secure the louver, at the middle, to the adjusting arm with small staples.

Panels in solid-paneled shutters rotten, delaminated, or warped. Smash out panel with a hammer and pull pieces out of the grooves in the rails and stiles. Then, with a sharp chisel, cut out wood forming back side of grooves to form a rabbet. Cut new panel from ⅛-inch tempered hardboard to fit in opening. Set it in opening and nail ¼-inch quarter rounds around the four sides to hold it in place. Use 1-inch galvanized finishing nails. Paint front and back of hardboard.

SILL, HOUSE

Rotting. If rot has not progressed too far, chisel out the soft wood. Brush pentachlorophenol wood preservative into the holes and over the surrounding wood. Apply at least two coats. Then fill holes with plastic wood.

If rot has progressed so far that sill must be replaced, the entire rotten section should be sawed and chiseled out. Let a carpenter do this job if the cut-out piece is over 4 feet long, but you can replace a shorter piece yourself. Don't worry about the wall collapsing. Just cut a new timber to size, saturate it with wood preservative, and shove it into place under the studs.

After repairing a sill, be sure to correct whatever condition caused it to rot.

Riddled by termites. Replace sill as above. To control further infestations of termites, dig a trench 8 inches wide and 1 foot deep next to the foundation walls. With a crowbar, make a series of holes 1 foot apart in the bottom of the trench. Make the holes as deep as possible. Pour in chlordane at the rate of 1 gallon per 2½ lineal feet of trench for each foot of depth from the bottom of the trench to the footing. (In other words, if the distance from the bottom of the trench to the footing is 7 feet, pour in 7 gallons per 2½ lineal feet.) Then fill trench halfway and pour in ½ gallon per 2½ lineal feet. Finally, fill trench to the top and pour in another ½ gallon per 2½ lineal feet.

This treatment assumes that you have a basement or concrete-floored crawl space. If your house is built on a slab or over a crawl space without a concrete floor, have the soil treated by a professional.

In all cases, make sure that the ground outside the house is at least 6 inches lower than the bottom of the sill or siding.

SILVER

NOTE. Whether you want to repair silver or let an expert do it depends on how much you value the piece. You can do the job, but without a professional's tools and experience, you may not produce a good-looking result.

Small holes. Clean metal. Apply acid flux. Solder with solid-core solder.

Joints broken between metal pieces. Clean metal and flux with acid. Clamp joints together. Heat metal with tip of soldering iron and melt solid-core solder on surface.

Dents. Try to bend out with your fingers. Otherwise, let a jeweler work on them.

Silver separated from other materials, such as plastics, felt, etc. See HOUSEHOLD DECORATIVE ACCESSORIES.

Silverplate off, base metal exposed. Have it replated by a jeweler. In the future, don't wash plated silver in a dishwasher. Never clean it with a dip cleaner.

Tarnished. Rub on silver polish (paste or liquid) with a soft cloth. Use a toothbrush to get into crevices. Rinse in hot soapsuds and dry.

SINK, BATHROOM

Surface stained, damaged. See BATHROOM FIXTURES.

Faucet leaks. See FAUCET.

Drain clogged. See DRAINS, PLUMBING.

Pop-up stopper leaks. Some stoppers can be lifted right out. To remove others, you must loosen and pull out control arm at the back of the drainpipe under the lavatory.

First step is to remove stopper and clean off edges and edges of drain opening. Squirt a little light household oil into sleeve around stopper handle and work handle up and down. This should correct problem in most old stoppers.

New stoppers are made of plastic and have a rubber flange at top which keeps water from running out. In time, however, the rubber becomes deformed. When this happens, take stopper to plumbing supplies house and replace the flange.

SINK, KITCHEN

Porcelain chipped. See BATHROOM FIXTURES.

Stains. See BATHROOM FIXTURES.

Drain clogged. See DRAINS, PLUMBING.

Faucet problems. See FAUCET.

Basket-type strainer-stopper leaks. These are very unreliable gadgets, and when they no longer can be made to seat properly in the drain opening, it is best to buy new ones.

SKATES, ICE

Blade dull, rough. Buy a skate sharpener if you do a lot of skating. Otherwise have a sports shop do the sharpening.

Problems with shoes. See SHOES.

SKATES, ROLLER

Action sluggish. Take off wheels and soak in kerosene to remove dust, dirt, gummy grease, in bearings. Fill bearing sleeves with petroleum jelly and replace wheels.

SKI

Wood split. Apply epoxy glue to one of the split edges and clamp pieces together for 12 hours. For reinforcement, screw small brass mending plates or a sheet of aluminum flashing across the break.

Wood splintered. Splintering usually occurs along the edges of a ski. Trim out the broken wood as cleanly as possible with a knife or small chisel. Form a piece of hardwood to fit roughly into the gap. Glue in place with epoxy glue; clamp, and let dry for 12 hours. Then trim down with a plane and sandpaper.

Holes in wood. Fill with plastic wood and sand smooth when dry.

Steel edges loose. Fill screw hole in wood with plastic wood, let dry, and then set in a screw. If this doesn't hold, fill hole again with plastic wood. Then drill a new hole through the metal and slightly into the wood about 1 inch from original screw. Drive in screw.

NOTE. While some simple repairs such as the above are possible with wooden skis, other types of skis must be fixed by an expert.

SKIN-DIVING EQUIPMENT

Rubber suit torn. Patch like a tire. (See TIRE.) Or cut a small patch out of matching rubber. Coat the back and torn surface with rubber cement. After this has set for about 5 minutes, press pieces together.

Neoprene foam suit torn. Coat torn edges with rubber cement, let set, then press together. Then apply a narrow strip of plastic rubber over back of tear.

Flippers cracked. Keep out of the sun as much as possible to prevent cracking. If crack doesn't go all the way through, fill it with rubber cement and press the edges together. A through crack is repaired in the same way, but in that case it is advisable to apply a patch of thin rubber to one or both sides with rubber cement.

Face mask leaks. Caulk joint between glass and mask with automobile windshield sealer or with silicone rubber caulking.

Rubber articles stick together in storage. Sprinkle with talcum powder.

SKI POLE

Basket worn out, broken. Baskets are held on poles by friction. If basket is difficult to remove, coat end of pole with soap. Basket will then come off fairly easily and can be replaced by new basket.

Pole broken. A bamboo or metal pole can be fixed by inserting a dowel of wood or steel in the pole, across the break. Fasten in place with epoxy glue. Note, however, that a ski pole is supposed to bend—not break—and if it should snap again—propably in the same place—the dowel might spear you.

SKYLIGHT

Leaks. Go up on roof and clean the seams around the edges of the plastic dome. Fill with silicone or polysulfide rubber caulking. Also clean and caulk joints between skylight and roof. Use fibered asphalt roofing cement or silicone or polysulfide rubber caulking.

If a hinged dome is leaking around the edges, check the weather stripping. It may be out of place or it may need to be replaced.

Condensation on skylight. Consult dealer about replacing the single-thick plastic dome with a double-thick insulating dome.

SLATE

Broken. Clean edges well and apply epoxy glue. Press together for 12 hours.

Loose in floor. See STONE.

Stains. See STONE.

SLED

Stiff. Sometimes the runners are actually stiffer than they should be for easy steering. But, as a rule, the stiffness is traceable to the binding of the various moving metal parts. First examine the way the sled is put together, and as you move the handle back and forth, notice the points at which there is some give, or slippage, between wood and metal. Clean rust from metal at these points. Slip sandpaper between metal and wood, and sand wood lightly. Rub paraffin on wood surfaces that you can reach, and squirt powdered graphite on inaccessible surfaces. Oil rivets holding metal to metal.

Seat broken. The planks are screwed or nailed to the wood cross braces but may be riveted to the rear strap of the metal steering yoke. File off the rivet on the broken plank, then unscrew the rest of the plank from the frame. Replace with a new hardwood plank. If large-headed rivet like the original one is difficult to obtain, replace it with a nut and bolt. Be sure to use lock washer under nut.

Center plank attached to steering handle cracked at end. Replace plank if you wish, but it can be reinforced adequately by screwing one or two short steel mending plates across the break.

SLEEPING BAG

Holes, tears. Cut a patch out of matching fabric, coat lightly with fabric glue, and smooth over hole.

SLIDE PROJECTOR

Pictures soiled. Blow dust off slides or clean with a camel's-hair artist's brush. If slides are covered with glass, clean glass with a damp cloth.

Clean projector lens with camel's-hair brush or lens paper from a photographic supplies store. If lens is smeary, use lens fluid cleaner, too.

Clean slide holder well.

Slides stick in projector. Clean the slide holder and check if it is damaged in any way. But the chances are that the slides are poorly mounted and should be remounted.

Slides don't feed into projector. This is a fairly common problem in simple projectors in which one slide pushes the other through. The problem is usually caused by slides which are mounted in such thin cardboard that they slide past the preceding slide rather than pushing against its edge. To correct, remount the slides.

Bulb burns out rapidly. Don't close up projector as soon as you're finished using it. Leave it open for 15 minutes or more so bulb's heat can be dissipated. If projector has a fan, turn it on.

SLIPCOVER

Cording worn. Rip seam, remove cording, and rip off covering. Cut matching or contrasting material on the bias into 1½-inch strips. Fold these around cord and stitch. Then sew covered cord into slipcover seam.

Other problems. See CLOTHING—FABRICS.

SLIPPERS

Inner sole loose. Coat with fabric glue and smooth down.

Bow off. Staple in place with an office stapler. If it is impossible to get the stapler into the slipper, coat back of bow and top of slipper with rubber cement. When this is tacky, press bow in place for 15 minutes or more.

Pompon off. Apply fabric glue to the back and press down.

Patch of fur torn from furry slippers. Glue down with fabric glue.

Problems with leather slippers. See SHOES.

SNAP FASTENER

Won't hold. With pliers, slightly flatten the prong on the male side of the fastener.

Won't close. Squeeze sides of the prong on the male side.

NOTE. In the long run you'll be better off to replace defective fasteners. Inexpensive kits of fasteners and the tools used to install the non-sew-on types are available.

SNOWMOBILE

Doesn't start. Are you out of gas? Are spark plugs clean and sound? Are they dry? Is choke properly adjusted?

Starts hard, performs poorly. Remove exhaust pipe and muffler, and clean carbon from ports with a small wooden dowel and vacuum cleaner.

Smokes too much. Adjust carburetor according to your operator's manual.

Track too loose, too tight, or not equally tight on both sides. Jack up rear end of snowmobile and adjust tension nuts on back or sides of machine. Then have someone start engine and accelerate slightly so you can inspect track as it turns. If it doesn't ride evenly, adjust further until it is centered.

Track damaged. Jack up snowmobile and cut across track with a sharp knife. Use a carpenter's square so ends of track are parallel and at right angles to edge of track. Then splice track with metal lacing available from snowmobile dealer.

Cleats damaged or missing from track. Replace with new cleats using a repair kit from snowmobile dealer.

Skis out of line. The skis should toe in about ¼ inch. Place rules across the skis at toe and heel. Then adjust tie rod.

Belt worn. Remove belt by holding stationary half of driven pulley and turning movable half until belt is loose and can be slipped off. Install new belt by reverse procedure.

Clutch malfunctioning. Remove spark plug and insert a length of nylon rope through hole. Jam it down against piston to hold clutch sheave in place. Then remove nut and pull off outer sheave. Remove any rust on exposed shaft with emery cloth and apply a little petroleum jelly. Remove corrosion and burnt-on rubber from inner surfaces of pulley, and put outer sheave back on shaft.

Then remove driven pulley by taking out holding pin and twisting pulley to release spring pressure. Clean and lubricate shaft and clean inner surfaces of pulley. Then replace and reinstall belt. Jack up machine, start engine and watch belt. If it creeps or runs, you have to do further cleaning or, if this doesn't work, have compression spring replaced.

Drive chain too loose or too tight. Generally, you should be able to depress the chain only ¼ inch, but this varies somewhat among makes of snowmobile. Reset adjusting screws as necessary.

Windshield scratched. See ACRYLIC, RIGID.

SNOW SHOVEL

Edge of blade bent, knicked. If made of steel, file with a metal file. If made of aluminum, saw off the edge with a hacksaw and file.

Handle broken. If made of wood, see GARDEN TOOLS. If made of metal, replace it with a hardwood rake or hoe handle and rivet into place.

Handle strap loose. File heads off rivets and remove strap. Bend into shape. Then install with new rivets or nuts and bolts.

Snow sticks. Rub vegetable oil on surface as needed or spray with vegetable or silicone lubricant.

SNOW THROWER

See LAWN MOWER, POWER. The machines are essentially the same. But remember that snow throwers get wet when you use them and must therefore be dried off well to prevent corrosion and resultant malfunction or breakdown. Spraying frequently with silicone lubricant is advisable.

Snow sticks in chute. Dry off chute and spray with silicone lubricant.

SOLDERING IRON

Tip pitted. Smooth tip with a fine-metal file, then apply flux to surface and melt solder on it.

Tip worn out. Most tips can be unscrewed. Then all you do is screw in a replacement tip. However, if tip refuses to turn, do not try to force it. Let serviceman make repair.

Electric iron won't heat. Heater has burned out. If you have manufacturer's instruction sheet, disassemble iron according to directions and put in a replacement heater.

SPARK PLUG

Inoperative or not sparking properly. Replace the plug with a new one if the insulator in the center is cracked or chipped, the curved electrode is partially eaten away, or the straight electrode is eaten away. But you may be able to clean and continue to use the plug otherwise, even though it is pretty badly coated with carbon or whitish deposits. Note, however, that the only sure way to fix a fouled or slightly bent plug is to find a gasoline station that has a sandblaster and a tool for gapping plugs. If you can't find such a station, you'll just have to take your chances.

Carefully clean the electrodes, the top of the plug body, and the insulator with a tiny knife or other scraper and emery cloth. With a fingernail file, touch up the top of the straight electrode and the bottom of the curved electrode. Take pains not to bend the curved electrode and change the gap.

SPRING, COILED (as in door springs)

End broken off. With pliers firmly grasp the top coil at a distance from the end equal to a full turn of the coil. Hold spring below this point with another pair of pliers. Bend top coil sharply upward. Form new loop that will hook into the screw eye or whatever the spring was attached to.

Coils misshapen. All you can do is pinch them together with pliers.

Not springy enough. Lengthen slightly by stretching.

SQUEEGEE

Rubber blade nicked. Remove blade by taking out screws in the head of the metal holder.

Reverse blade and replace in holder. If blade is badly damaged, buy a replacement. Or cut a new blade out of a tire tube or, better, rubber gasket material. Be sure to cut the edge straight and smooth.

STAINLESS STEEL

Dents. If you can get at the back of the metal, hammer out dent—preferably with a hard-rubber mallet. Work from edges of dent toward the center.

Seams cracked, open. Clean well. Close seam and resolder. Use special flux and solder recommended for stainless steel. For how to solder, see BASIC METHODS: HOW TO SOLDER METAL.

Steel bent. Hammering is difficult because stainless steel is very strong and resilient. Try to squeeze out bend in a vise. Or place one end of the steel piece in a vise and bend the other end by hand.

Blotchy looking. Clean with special stainless steel cleaner.

Scratched. Better leave well enough alone. Rubbing with superfine emery cloth may remove scratches but will simply dull a larger area.

Separated from another material. See HOUSEHOLD DECORATIVE ACCESSORIES. If you use screws or bolts, be sure they are of stainless steel.

STAIRS

Risers deeply scarred. This happens if treads are unusually shallow. For a temporary repair, fill scars with plastic wood. For a more permanent repair, cover the risers with some material that will not scar so badly as wood: tempered hardboard, vinyl flooring, linoleum, laminated plastic. Glue to risers with appropriate glue.

Treads badly worn. Call in a carpenter.

Balusters loose. If balusters are set into treads, as they usually are, the only thing you can do is to try to squeeze white glue into the joints and hope. If balusters are nailed to top of treads, drill some holes diagonally through them into the treads and then anchor with finishing nails. Fasten loose balusters to the handrail with glue.

Newel post wobbly. Additional nails and glue should strengthen it. Or screw to bottom tread with iron angles.

Stairs creak. If you can get under them, drive thin wedges into grooves of stringer, and nail risers to treads. Otherwise, try to pinpoint source of creak. Then drive 3-inch galvanized finishing nails into stringer. Or drive nails diagonally through ends of risers into stringers. (In both cases, drill small holes for nails first.)

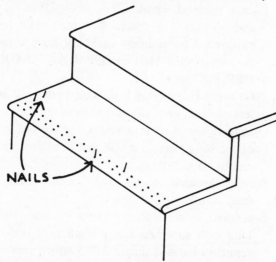

NAILS

If squeak is between a riser and tread, drive long slender flathead screws down through top of stringer into riser. Countersink the screwheads and cover with plastic wood stained to match treads.

STEEL

Dented. If you can get at the back of the metal, hammer out the dent. If this is impossible, clean surface with steel wool and fill dent with epoxy mender. Sand smooth when dry.

Rusted, pitted. Clean with steel wool and apply paste or liquid rust-remover. Fill pits with epoxy mender. Prime with rust-inhibiting paint and apply finish paint.

Small holes. Use steel wool on area around hole and edges of hole. Fill with epoxy mender.

Large holes. Cut a patch that overlaps hole about ½ inch on all sides. Hold in place over hole and drill a series of holes through both

pieces of metal. Insert steel rivets, cut off all but about ⅛ inch of ends, and hammer the ends down. If hole is to be made leakproof, spread epoxy mender between metal surfaces before riveting. The epoxy alone will hold the patch in place only if the steel is not subjected to any strain.

Another way to patch holes, large or small, is by soldering. See BASIC METHODS: HOW TO SOLDER METAL.

Steel broken. If no strain is put on broken piece, you can solder pieces together or glue with epoxy glue. But if break is under strain, have the steel welded.

Seams open. Rivet together. Or clean thoroughly and solder.

Steel bent. Depending on the thickness of the metal, you may be able to hammer out the bend. Hit sharply, but do not pound. An easier method is to bend the metal in a vise.

Steel separated from other materials. Screw, bolt, or rivet them together. Or use glue (see HOUSEHOLD DECORATIVE ACCESSORIES).

Joints broken in a steel wire grille (as in charcoal grills, bicycle baskets, etc.). Clean wires with steel wool. Bring them together and, if necessary, clamp with a C-clamp or with a loop of light wire. Heat with a soldering iron or torch and apply solder.

STEPLADDER

NOTE. Don't break your neck because of a patched-up job. Make repairs properly.

Ladder wobbly. The rivets holding the side rails to the iron angles under the top step are undoubtedly loose. Remove them by filing off the heads and replace with bolts. Brace the iron angles, if necessary, by screwing wood blocks to the bottom of the step and tight against the iron angles.

Also replace rivets or screws holding the spreader to the rails with bolts. Tighten cross braces, if any, on the back of the ladder.

Step of wood ladder broken. Loosen nut which holds the steel tie rod under the step. Cut step in two and carefully pull pieces out of mortises in side rails. If they resist, split the pieces into narrow strips. Remove nails holding the step. Cut new step out of clear white pine. Coat mortises. Set the step into the rails and secure with a couple of small finishing nails. Tighten tie rod.

Rail of wood ladder broken. Out of yellow pine, cut a splint that overlaps both ends of the break at least 24 inches. Spread epoxy glue on broken edges of rail and press them together. Then screw splint to outside of rail.

Aluminum ladder comes apart. Put it back together again with aluminum—not steel—nuts and bolts. That's all there is to it.

STEPS, BRICK

Bricks broken, loose. See BRICK.
Iron railings loose. See PORCH, MASONRY.

STEPS, CONCRETE

For cracks, holes, roughness, see CONCRETE.

Edges chipped, broken. Clean thoroughly. Coat edge with latex liquid that comes with latex cement. Mix latex cement to thick consistency and trowel on step. Shape properly and hold in place with boards if necessary.

Iron railings loose. See PORCH, MASONRY.

STEPS, STONE

Stones loose. See STONE.
Iron railings loose. See PORCH, MASONRY.

STEPS, WOOD

Treads split, broken, weak. Replace with new boards which have been saturated with pentachlorophenol wood preservative.

Steps sagging. If they have simply pulled loose from a porch, renail them with spikes and then screw iron angles to the stringers and the porch. If the posts under the stringers have rotted out, replace with new posts saturated with pentachlorophenol wood preservative.

If the stringers are cracked or rotting, take the steps apart carefully and use the pieces as patterns for new steps. Or buy precut stringers from a lumberyard. The new steps should be built, if possible, out of wood that has been pressure-treated at the mill with preservative. Otherwise, brush two coats of preservative on all boards and timbers after they have been cut to shape. Don't let bottoms of stringers touch the ground or rest directly on flat paving; raise them about 2 inches on bricks or concrete so they will be above standing water and moisture and not so easily attacked by termites.

STONE

Mortar joints between stones cracked or eroding. Chip out bad mortar. Blow out crumbs with vacuum cleaner. Fill with mortar made of 1 part portland cement and 3 parts sand. Trowel to match other joints.

Stone broken, chipped. Where it is impossible or inadvisable to use concrete mortar (as in the case of a statue), dry broken surfaces thoroughly. Spread silicone adhesive on one and press surfaces together firmly for at least 24 hours.

Stone ornament separated from some other material. See HOUSEHOLD DECORATIVE ACCESSORIES.

Stains, efflorescence on stone. See BRICK.

Smoke stains. See FIREPLACE, MASONRY.

STONE WALL, DRY

Collapsed. Lift off stones that have been dislodged, and rebuild. Set largest stones at the base of the wall. Arrange all stones so that joints are staggered. Support teetering stones with stone chips.

Heaved by frost. Take down broken section of wall. Dig a trench about 18 inches deep under wall and fill it halfway with rubble. Tamp well. This should provide the drainage necessary to prevent heaving.

STONE WALL, MASONRY

Cracked. Open crack as much as possible with a cold chisel; blow out crumbs and fill with a wet mixture of 1 part portland cement and 3 parts sand.

Stone out. Chip out mortar from hole and remove dust and particles. Trowel 1:3 mortar into the back of the hole and onto the base, and set in stone. Then cram mortar into the joints around the sides and top.

Joints open. See STONE.

STORM WINDOW

Pane broken. See WINDOWPANE.

Adjusting arms stiff. They're undoubtedly rusted. Clean with emery cloth and apply oil.

Loose in frame, leaks cold air. Apply rubber weather stripping that has a flat nailing flange and a fat, round edge. Tack flange to edge of sash so that, when sash is closed, the round edge of the strip presses tight against the crack between the sash and the frame.

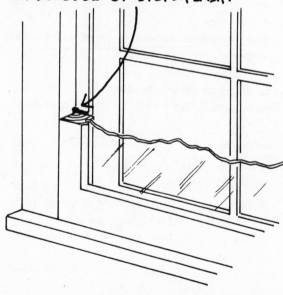

TACK WEATHERSTRIPPING TO INSIDE EDGE OF STORM SASH.

STRAW, WOVEN

Weave broken. Coat broken ends of straw and body of weave with a little white glue. Cover glued surface with wax paper. Then clamp the break between boards. If necessary, break can be reinforced on the wrong side of the straw with cloth coated with white glue.

Holes. Leave ends of broken straws jagged: they will be less obvious than if you cut them off cleanly. Cut a patch out of matching straw, coat edges with white glue, and paste under the hole. Cover both sides of straw with wax paper and clamp patch between boards.

A better-looking mend is made by weaving in new straw, but this is possible only on simple, coarse weaves like those used in old farm hats.

STUFFED ANIMAL

Seams split. Resew edges with tiny overcasting stitches.

Losing its stuffing. Coarse wool or shreddings from an old fiber rug cushion makes the best stuffing. Cram in tightly and then restitch the torn seam.

Glass eye loose or off. First try looping a small hairpin through the eyelet in the back of the eye. Pinch the bend in the hairpin closed. Put a dab of cellulose cement on the back of the eye and on the hairpin wires. Stick hairpin all the way into the head. Give the cement an hour or 2 to dry before testing whether eye is secure. If it comes loose, remove the hairpin. Thread a needle with heavy cotton thread and poke it through from the back of the head to the eye socket. Run thread through the eyelet in the back of the eye. Then poke needle back through the head to the point you started from. Pull eye up close to the head, squeeze the head slightly, and tie a square knot in the ends of the thread so that when you release pressure on the head, the thread will be tight.

Also see DOLL and TOYS.

STYROFOAM

Broken. Glue pieces together with white glue. This is not a very sturdy repair but will hold if you don't put strain on the joint.

Holes. Break off a piece from a scrap of Styrofoam. Fill hole with white glue. Press scrap into it. When glue is dry, shape the scrap with a knife.

SUEDE

Holes, tears. If a hole, trim it out neatly. If a tear, bring edges together. Sew a patch of matching suede under opening. If garment is old and will not be dry cleaned, patch can be glued on with rubber cement or fabric glue.

Shiny spots. Rub with medium-fine sandpaper.

Soiled. Rub very lightly with medium-fine sandpaper.

Ballpoint-pen ink. Place paper towel under stain. Apply Inknix, available from stationary store, and rub with a hard-bristled brush. If stain is old, let Inknix soak in for a while before scrubbing. Repeat application if necessary. Then rinse with warm water.

Other stains. Take garment to dry cleaner. If he can't remove stains, he may be able to conceal them by spray-dyeing.

SUITCASE

Vinyl torn. Glue down with vinyl cement or patch with matching vinyl and vinyl cement.

Fabric slashed. Spread fabric glue underneath and smooth down.

Fabric of lightweight, unreinforced bag cut. Cover cut on the inside with adhesive-backed mending tape, or cut a patch out of lightweight canvas with pinking shears, coat with fabric glue, and smooth over back of tear.

Leather torn. Lift edges, spread rubber cement underneath, and smooth down.

Leather on handle worn, torn. Sew down loose flaps of leather if possible. Otherwise, glue in place with rubber cement. If wire hooks in ends of handle are loose, bind lightweight wire tightly around them and glue leather over them.

Leather edge bindings worn, torn. Cut out worn spot. Apply a little rubber cement under ends of remaining bindings. Out of matching leather, cut a new binding to fit. Apply rubber cement to back of patch and to edge of suitcase. Let dry until tacky, then press binding in place.

Leather scuffed. Trim off little flaps of leather with scissors. Rub scuffed area vigorously with palm of hand. Then apply appropriate polish.

Metal side dented. Tap it out carefully with a block of wood.

Lining loose. Paste back in place with fabric glue.

Travel labels loose. Place a sponge or piece of felt dampened in warm water on top and weight down. Peel label off when loose. Decals can be removed in the same way after being soaked overnight. Or brush nail polish remover over them and peel off.

SUMP PUMP

Doesn't go on. Check: Has fuse on house circuit blown? If basement is flooded and fuse box is down there, don't go near it until you shut off the house current at the meter. Is there trouble in the motor? See ELECTRIC MOTOR. Did float fail to rise with the water level in the sump? Clean the rod on which it is mounted with steel wool and coat lightly with grease. If this doesn't correct the problem, float may have a hole in it and be waterlogged. Remove, empty, and solder hole, or cover with plastic steel. Or buy a new float.

Motor working but pump not pumping. Check whether sump is filled with muck and pump intake is clogged. If these are OK, call a serviceman.

NOTE. Don't fool around in a sump without first turning off the electricity to the motor.

SWIMMING POOL, CONCRETE

Leaks in pool. Draw water down below leak. If pool is cracked, chip crack open to a width of about ½ inch and a depth of ¾ inch. Blow out crumbs. Cram tight with hydraulic cement and let dry at least 12 hours before painting and/or filling pool.

If leak is through a joint in pool, dig out the old sealant as much as possible. Dry surfaces thoroughly. Fill joint with polysulfide rubber or silicone caulking compound.

Tiles in ceramic tile trim loose or broken. Remove them. Scrape old adhesive from the back and from the wall of the pool. Apply silicone caulking compound to backs of tiles, press in place, and let dry for 24 hours. Then fill joints with ceramic tile grout.

Rubber-base paint peeling, blistered. Have it removed completely by sandblasting. Take it off yourself with a rented sandblaster (although, unfortunately, such machines often lack the power for the job). Or scrape it off inch by inch with paste-type paint remover and a scraper. Repair concrete as necessary. Wash it with muriatic acid to etch it and rinse well. Then apply epoxy primer followed by one or two coats of epoxy pool paint.

Epoxy paint worn thin. Scrape as necessary and sand. Wash with trisodium phosphate to kill algae and get off dirt. Rinse, wash again with muriatic acid, and rinse. When dry, apply epoxy primer and one coat of epoxy finish paint.

Cement paint loose, powdery. Scrape, sand, and wash with trisodium phosphate to remove dirt and algae. Rinse. Scrub on one coat of cement paint while surface is damp.

Paint on wooden diving board flaking, worn. Wash and rinse. Fill cracks with plastic wood. Sand entire board smooth. Apply two coats of epoxy diving board paint with abrasive added to make it skidproof.

Stains. Scrub stains above water line with chlorine bleach as it comes from bottle. Below water line, use chlorine powder. Just sprinkle it on stain and scrub, or wrap it in a soft cloth and scrub.

Trisodium phosphate is also effective on stains.

Use a stiff nylon scrub brush for most work, but if stains prove very stubborn, use a stainless steel brush or a block of pumice.

Scale deposits. Scrub with dilute muriatic acid.

SWIMMING POOL, FIBER GLASS LINER

Leaks in liner. See FIBER GLASS, RIGID. Pool water must, of course, be drawn down below the hole before repair is made.

Stains, scale deposits. See SWIMMING POOL, CONCRETE, but don't use a stainless steel brush or pumice block on fiber glass.

SWIMMING POOL PIPING

Leaks. These are extremely difficult to find unless you can actually see them. Look for spongy areas in ground. If you can persuade your local water utility to cooperate, have them check for the leak with the stethoscopelike device they use for water-main leaks.

Once leak is found and pipe is exposed, it is advisable to replace that section of pipe or even the entire run. But you can make good temporary repairs that should see you through the swimming season. See PIPE, WATER.

SWIMMING POOL—PLASTER FINISH

Cracks. Scrape open and fill with polysulfide rubber or silicone rubber caulking.

Large holes. Have these repaired by a plastering contractor who specializes in pool work. But if you decide to paint the plaster instead of keeping it its basic color, you can make repairs by chipping out all loose plaster. Clean base well and let dry. Then fill holes and cracks with latex cement.

Stains, scale deposits. See SWIMMING POOL, CONCRETE.

SWIMMING POOL PUMP AND FILTER

Doesn't start. Has fuse blown? Is extension cord (if any) on pump broken? Is cable connected securely to pump?

Pump works but doesn't pump water. Make sure pump is primed and all valves are open. Is water level in pool at proper height? Check piping to make sure all joints are tight.

Pump running too slow or too hot. Turn it off for half an hour just in case there has been a voltage drop. Then turn it on. If it still runs slow, call your pool dealer.

Pump not pumping enough water. Clean out strainer in pump and/or skimmer. Clean filter (see below). Make sure valves in suction and return lines are not partly closed. If problem continues, there is probably some stoppage in the suction line. Try pushing a stiff wire from the strainer before the pump into the suction line to see if you strike anything. Hold one end of vacuum cleaner hose over inlet on return line and push the other end of hose down into the skimmer. The force of water from the return may loosen the stoppage and push it into pump strainer. If trouble persists, open the suction line at a joint and drive a plumber's snake through it.

Pump noisy. It might be that something is wrong with the pump, but before leaping to that conclusion and calling a serviceman, try shutting down the valve in the return pipeline until the noise stops. If it does stop, leave valve at this setting.

Filtering action poor even after filter has been cleaned. If you have a sand filter, introduce a prepared filter-cleaning compound according to directions on package. If you have a diatomaceous earth filter, clean filter with special cleaner; or remove filter elements and soak and carefully scrub them in warm detergent solution or dilute muriatic acid. If you have a cartridge filter, replace the cartridges.

SWIMMING POOL—VINYL LINER

Holes in liner. Cut a patch from matching material sold for the purpose and stick down with cement sold with the material. Repair can be made just as well below water as above. (Some patching materials come with pressure-sensitive adhesive applied to the back side.)

Stains, scale deposits. See SWIMMING POOL, CONCRETE. Be sure not to use a stainless steel brush or pumice block on vinyl liner —only a fairly soft brush.

SWING, PORCH

Creaks, squeaks. There is little you can do to stop creaking permanently. Remove rust on chains or springs with emery cloth, steel wool, and liquid rust-remover. Apply a light coating of automobile grease if clothing will not touch it. Otherwise, keep lightly coated with oil.

Holes, tears in cushions. See CUSHION, BENCH.

Enameled steel rusting. Remove all rust with steel wool or emery cloth. Apply red metal primer. Then apply oil-base trim enamel.

SYRINGE, RUBBER

Collapses when pinched, slow to suck up water. Coat joint between nozzle and bulb with rubber cement. If bulb is thin, and cracked in one spot, spread thin layer of rubber cement over it. If there is an actual hole, cut a patch out of rubber, roughen back and the area around the hole with sandpaper, brush rubber cement on both surfaces. When dry, apply another coat of cement to patch and press down.

TACK

Reins, checkstraps, etc., broken. Overlap ends and rivet or sew together. For extra strength, coat both pieces with rubber cement, let set for 5 minutes, and press together before riveting or sewing.

Leather dry. Soak everything except saddle and other large items in neat's-foot oil until it will not soak up any more oil. Then wipe dry. Work oil into saddle.

Soiled. Scrub hard with saddle soap, brush, and/ or sponge.

Bits, stirrups, curb chains discolored. Brighten with steel wool and scouring powder.

TAPE, AUDIO

Squeals, wows. Buy special silicone-impregnated jockey cloth. Hold lightly around tape and put recorder in rewind. This is not a permanent cure.

Echoes. This is caused by "print through," when the tape layers are wound too tightly to one another. It cannot be corrected, but can be prevented by rewinding tapes slowly or by leaving them in "tail-out" position when finished playing and rewinding just before the next playing. The tapes should also be played periodically and stored in a cool place.

TAPE RECORDER

Doesn't work. Check: Is fuse blown? Is outlet defective? Is cord broken? Is power off at the recorder? Is pause button depressed? Is tape twisted or sticky?

Tape breaks. Belt tension may be wrong. Adjust according to manufacturer's directions.

Performance poor. Clean recording and playback heads well with a cotton swab soaked in rubbing alcohol. Clean capstan and pinch wheel the same way. Demagnetize heads.

Music sounds dull, lifeless. The heads are probably out of alignment. Buy a special alignment tape and play it while turning adjusting screw on playback head.

TEFLON

Scratches. Leave them alone. In future, use plastic, rubber, Teflon-coated, or wooden spatulas, spoons, etc., or be very careful with steel utensils. Never cut with a sharp knife in a Teflon-coated utensil.

Stains. Minor staining is normal. To remove dark or widespread stains, clean with Stain-Aid or Dip-It. Or mix 2 tablespoons baking soda, ½ cup liquid chlorine bleach, and 1 cup water. Simmer for 5 minutes in stained pan. Remove from heat and check Teflon surface. If stain remains, repeat treatment. But note that this may cause dark-colored Teflon to turn a little lighter.

Heavy soil. Wash with hot, sudsy water. If necessary, scrub with a plastic mesh scouring pad. Do not use metal scouring pads or brushes, steel wool, or coarse scouring powder.

TELEPHONE

Wire pulled loose from outlet. Unscrew outlet cover and reattach wire to the terminal. You can't electrocute yourself.

Cord cut. Call for the phone repairman.

Phone too loud or not loud enough. Adjust volume control on bottom of receiver.

TELESCOPING TUBES (as in an indoor TV antenna, camera tripod)

Jammed. If the metal has been dented, try to straighten the dent by inserting a metal rod, heavy wire, or wood dowel up inside the tube. Or you can try to squeeze out the dent with pliers wrapped with adhesive tape to prevent scarring of the metal. But either job is very difficult and success is highly uncertain.

If the tubes are jammed by corrosion, saturate the joints with penetrating oil.

Bent. If you want the tubes to telescope, your only hope is to work out the bend by inserting a metal rod, etc., as above.

TELEVISION ANTENNA

Antenna leaning, loose at mounting. If antenna is mounted on chimney, tighten metal straps holding it. If one of these is broken, replace it with a new strap or with baling wire.

If antenna is clamped to wood siding, a window, or the fascia board at the eaves, remove U-shaped pipe hangers and screw them to firm wood (don't count on the ability of screws to hold in plastic wood crammed into old screw holes). Install additional pipe hangers if needed.

If antenna is bolted to masonry siding, lead anchors in the wall have probably pulled out. Replace with new anchors. If these are also loose, replace anchors with machine-screw anchors.

If antenna is mounted on roof, it should be held upright by guy wires. If you have these, check whether they have broken or come loose. If you don't have these, attach three or four to antenna pole and to large screw eyes at edges of roof.

Antenna twisted, not aimed at station. Loosen antenna pole from brackets holding it and reorient. If antenna is badly rusted, you'll probably need to saturate brackets with penetrating oil before you can turn pole. Have someone check the picture on the TV set while you are adjusting the aim.

Antenna pole bent. You'll have to take the whole thing down and bend it on the ground. Better get a serviceman, and probably a new antenna.

Antenna rods out of position. Reset the rods and tighten bolts.

Inside antenna damaged. See TELESCOPING TUBES.

Lead-in wire connections at antenna broken. Strip about ½ inch of insulation from the ends of the wires, scrape with a knife, and twist strands together. Clean terminals with emery cloth. Wind the wires to the right around the terminals and tighten. Then wrap cellophane electrical tape around them. If wire has been hanging loose from the antenna, strap it to pole with several strips of electrical tape.

Lead-in wire supports loose. Reset the supports in a sound surface if very loose and fill the old holes. If only slightly loose, straighten them and pack mastic into the holes around them. Use asphalt roofing compound for supports nailed or screwed into roof, caulking compound for those in siding.

Lead-in wire broken. It is best to have this replaced, but it can be spliced. Cut out broken wires, strip back insulation for a distance of about ½ inch on opposing wires. Twist these together, solder, and wrap with cellophane electrical tape. See ELECTRIC CORD.

Antenna rusted. Remove rust with liquid rust-remover and sandpaper. Prime with a red metal primer and overcoat with an alkyd gloss trim enamel.

Rust streaks on roof below antenna. Clean and paint antenna as above.

TELEVISION SET

NOTE. Don't under any circumstances try to repair a TV set. True, you shouldn't have any trouble replacing blown tubes, but you're likely to have plenty of trouble locating them and having them tested. Furthermore, if you have a new solid-state set, you don't have any tubes to fiddle with. In other words, call in a serviceman for most problems. There are, however, several minor ailments you can take care of yourself.

Not working. Has fuse blown? Is outlet dead? Is cord broken?

Suddenly quits. Press overload reset button on back.

Picture bad. Check electric cord for break. Check whether antenna lead-in is connected properly at back of receiver. Look for breaks in the lead-in wire, especially where it might have been mashed under a door or window. Broken wires can be cut out and ends of sound wires twisted together and soldered.

Ghosts. Antenna may have been knocked around in a windstorm and may need to be reaimed or even replaced.

Snow. Check lead-in wire and antenna.

Picture too short. Adjust the "vertical" and "height" screws on the back of the set. First, mark their present positions with pencil lines, then turn right or left, keeping track of number of turns. You can do this safely while set is on.

Picture too narrow. Adjust "horizontal" screw on back of set.

Picture fuzzy. Adjust focus control on back of set.

Picture won't hold. Adjust "horizontal" screw on back of set.

TENT

Beckets (peg loops) frayed or torn loose. You can replace them with new loops made out of canvas, but they'll probably come apart quickly, too. Buy heavy belt-webbing and cut to proper length. Punch a small hole near each end. Make corresponding holes in bottom seam of tent. Insert a metal rivet through a small washer and then through the webbing and the tent seam. Place another washer over the shank. Then hammer down end to shank. The loop should be formed so that the two rivets are about 3 inches apart.

Holes, tears. Dry tent. Cut patch out of matching material and glue down with fabric glue.

Tent leaks, though no holes are to be seen. Erect tent in a warm place and let it dry. Brush or spray on prepared waterproofing compound available from camping supplies store.

Window netting torn. Sew torn edges together with overcasting stitch.

Holes in window netting. Cut edges cleanly. Out of matching netting, cut a patch at least 2 inches larger in all directions than the hole. Coat patch heavily with fabric glue and place over hole. Press between wax paper and two boards.

Seams split. Stitch seam together on one side with running stitches. Use heavy cotton thread coated with beeswax. Then spread a thin layer of fabric glue in seam and, before this dries, stitch along other side.

Holes in floor. Make sure floor is dry, then cut a patch out of matching material, coat with fabric glue, and paste over hole. If tent pole is the cause of the hole, paste down two or three layers of canvas under the pole. Or, after patching the hole with fabric, paste a piece of tire tube over it with rubber cement.

Umbrella tent spreader arms slide down pole. If pole is too slick or thumbscrew too small to hold arms, drill a hole through the pole at the right height and stick a blunted nail through it every time the tent is raised.

TERMITE SHIELD

Joints open. Crimp metal together. Solder if possible. If not, seal with fibered asphalt roofing cement.

Holes. Clean metal with steel wool and cover holes with epoxy mender.

TERRACE, BRICK

If bricks are set in mortar, see BRICK. If bricks are set in sand, see WALK, BRICK.

TERRACE, EXPOSED-AGGREGATE CONCRETE

Cracked. Since there is no way of concealing cracks, you'd better leave well enough alone. If you insist on filling them, clean them out with a knife and hose but don't widen them any more than you have to. Then fill with latex cement.

Badly broken. Break out area with a sledge hammer. Wet edges with water. Fill with 1 part portland cement, 2¼ parts sand and 3 parts pebbles. Compact thoroughly to eliminate voids. Draw a board across the patch to level it. Then scatter pebbles or stone chips matching surrounding surface on patch. Cover surface evenly. Then with a 2-by-4 pat the aggregate into the concrete until it is completely embedded. When concrete starts to set, brush mortar away from upper part of aggregate with a fairly stiff stream of water from a hose. Cover patch with damp burlap for at least 48 hours.

Wood strips between sections of concrete rotten. Dig them out with a chisel. Replace with strips of redwood, cypress or any other wood soaked in wood preservative. Simply hammer the strips into the joints. They don't need to be fastened.

TERRA-COTTA

Broken. Clean edges thoroughly and make sure they are dry. Apply epoxy glue and press together for 6 hours.

Terra-cotta ornament rough on bottom, scratches surface on which it stands. Out of felt or cork, cut a covering for the bottom. Apply rubber cement to one side of covering, and let dry. Then apply cement to covering and to bottom of object. Let set until tacky, and smooth covering down.

TERRAZZO

Cracks. Unfortunately, the cracks are less obvious when open than when patched. Better leave them alone.

Soiled. Scrub with a mild household detergent solution and rinse thoroughly. When dry—and if you are sure the terrazzo is spotlessly clean —brush on a penetrating masonry sealer.

Stains. See BRICK.

THERMOMETER

Mercury separated. Shake thermometer hard. If this doesn't work, immerse the bulb (tip) in water, and heat water on the range until the mercury column rises and reunites.

THERMOS BOTTLE

Liner broken. Buy replacement liner and follow manufacturer's directions for installing.

Plastic cup broken Wash in water and dry thoroughly. Coat broken edges with plastic-mending adhesive and press together for 24 hours.

TILE, CERAMIC

Broken. If tile is loose (used as a hot mat, for instance), coat broken edges with cellulose cement. Let dry. Apply a second coat to one edge and press pieces together until cement sets. If tile is fixed (as in a wall), you may be able to conceal break with porcelain glaze. Otherwise, chip out tile and replace as below.

Loose or missing from wall, floor, table, etc. Remove tile. Chip out mortar joints. Clean mortar base if concrete, or remove it entirely if adhesive. Coat back of tile with silicone adhesive and press it into center of hole. (To hold in in place, insert toothpicks around the edges). Let adhesive set for 24 hours or more. Then soak joints with water, remove excess from the bottoms of joints, and fill joints with a commercial grout. Remove excess cement with a sponge. Tool joints with the end of a toothbrush handle when they begin to set.

Ornamental tile separated from some other material. See HOUSEHOLD DECORATIVE ACCESSORIES.

Rust stains on tile. Rub with a cleanser containing oxalic acid, such as Zud.

Grease stains. Wash with washing soda and let the solution stand on the stain for an hour. Then rinse well.

Coffee, mustard, ink, blood stains. Wash with a strong chlorine bleach solution.

Nail polish on tile. Wipe off with nail polish remover.

Tile joints stained. Scrub with a strong solution of chlorine bleach and let it stand for a few minutes before rinsing. If stains persist, make a slurry of a bleach-containing cleanser such as

Ajax or Comet and water. Brush on the joints and let stand for 10 to 15 minutes. Then scrub with a stiff brush and rinse.

TILE, HOLLOW

Broken. Clean edges and dry. Apply epoxy glue to one edge and press the pieces together firmly for 12 hours.

Tiles separated. Scrape off old concrete. Spread concrete (1 part cement to 3 parts sand) on edges of bottom tile. Press next tile into this. When concrete has set but is still workable, trim off excess. If the arrangement of the tiles permits, an easier method is to spread silicone adhesive on edges of bottom tile and press next tile into this.

TIRE

Tube punctured. If hole is not visible, inflate tube and place it in a tub of deep water. Bubbles will show location of leak. Use a tire-tube patching kit. With the top of a can, roughen the rubber around the puncture. Apply rubber cement evenly to tube and let dry to tackiness. Apply a second coat of cement in same way. Remove fabric backing from patch and press on to cement. Roll flat.

Tubeless tire punctured. Use a tubeless-tire patching kit. Tire does not have to be dismounted. With pliers, pull out object that punctured tire. Clean the hole with rubber plug needle (in kit) dipped in cement. Work more cement into hole with needle. Roll small end of a rubber plug that is about twice as large as the hole into needle eye. Dip plug and needle into cement and push plug into hole. Unhook needle by pulling straight out. Trim plug off ⅛ inch above tread.

TOASTER, ELECTRIC

Doesn't toast. Check whether fuse has blown, whether outlet in which toaster is plugged is operating. Disconnect toaster and examine cord for break. Replace if necessary. If these measures fail, take toaster to service shop.

Toast doesn't pop up. Remove crumb tray and clean. With a vacuum cleaner, blow crumbs out of inner workings. If pop-up mechanism still doesn't work, you'd better take toaster to service shop. However, you can remove outer shell by removing handles (some screws may be hidden under metal nameplates embedded in handles—these can be pried out) and unscrewing from base. Examine mechanism to see if anything is out of place. But don't force parts.

TOBOGGAN

Bottom board broken. Unscrew the board from the cross braces and break the glue bonds. Cut the board in two immediately under one of the braces in front of the break. Angle the cut so that the front edge of the board is slanted upward toward the front of the toboggan. Cut a hickory board to the proper length and angle the back end to overlap what remains of the broken board. Glue the angled edges together with epoxy glue. Then glue and screw the old and new lengths of board to the cross braces.

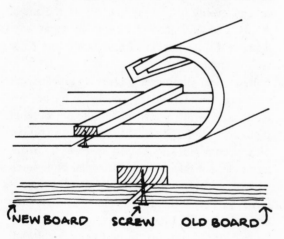

NEW BOARD   SCREW   OLD BOARD

TOILET

Water runs steadily into toilet. Is stopper ball dropping squarely into the outlet seat? If not, see if rod is bent and make sure the guides attached to overflow pipe are in line. If this

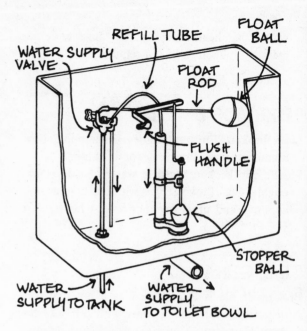

WATER SUPPLY VALVE   REFILL TUBE   FLOAT BALL   FLOAT ROD   FLUSH HANDLE   STOPPER BALL   WATER SUPPLY TO TANK   WATER SUPPLY TO TOILET BOWL

is not the problem, replace stopper ball with a new one of the same size. Clean the edges of the outlet at the same time.

If toilet is a modern type with a cylindrical plastic stopper that slides up and down on a small pipe, empty toilet and turn off water. Swing refill tube to one side. Unscrew cap above stopper. Lift out stopper and clean edges of outlet. If rubber ring at bottom of cylinder is worn, replace it.

Water runs into overflow pipe. Lift the copper or plastic float ball as high as possible. If this stops the overflow, bend the float rod downward slightly to lower the float. If overflow continues, unscrew float ball. If it is full of water, replace with a new one. If overflow still continues, release the screws that hold the float arm in place and lift out valve plunger in top of inlet pipe. Unscrew metal collar at bottom of plunger, remove the flat washer, and install new one of the same size.

Tank does not fill enough. Bend float rod upward. Tank should fill to within ¾ inch of top of overflow pipe.

Water leaks from valve at top of water supply pipe. Turn off water and empty tank. Remove screws from mechanism at end of float rod and lift out valve plunger in top of inlet pipe. Replace flat split washer on plunger.

Refill tube broken. The break usually occurs at point where tube is connected to supply pipe, and the broken piece in the pipe is hard to remove. Insert a narrow screwdriver in the piece and try to turn it out. If this is impossible, coat the end of a new plastic refill tube with silicone adhesive and push it down into the broken piece. When adhesive is dry, bend tube down into overflow pipe. Let adhesive dry 3 hours or more before turning on water.

Entire toilet tank mechanism broken or leaking. Replace it with a new mechanism.

Leak in joint of large supply pipe between tank and bowl. Carefully loosen nut: it's easily bent or damaged. Remove old string inside. Wrap new cotton string several times around pipe at the joint. Slide nut over it and tighten.

Supply pipe between tank and bowl cracked. For appearance's sake, replace the pipe. You can, however, stop the leak by cleaning corrosion out of the crack and smearing on epoxy mender. Let dry for 24 hours before flushing toilet.

Drain clogged. See DRAINS, PLUMBING.

Tank top broken. Make sure edges are clean and dry. Coat with epoxy glue and press together.

Tank or bowl cracked. Turn off water and empty out all water. Dry surface completely. Scrape crack open slightly with an ice pick. Be sure to remove all dirt. Spread epoxy or silicone adhesive over crack and force it in as much as possible. Let dry 24 hours before using toilet.

Ceramic caps covering bolts that hold toilet to floor loose or off. Clean top of bolt and scrape old plaster out of cap. Fill cap with patching plaster or silicone adhesive and reset it firmly over bolt.

Tank sweats. Install a toilet tank cover. It will help to keep warm air from the tank while the water temperature rises to room temperature and will also soak up the drip. But it's not a perfect answer. There isn't one.

TOILET SEAT

Stained. Wash with detergent solution first, then with a fairly strong chlorine solution. Then call it quits.

Chipped. No matter what you do it's always going to look chipped. Remove loose paint. Sand surrounding paint. Prime bare spot with alkyd primer. Then paint spot with alkyd gloss enamel. Finally, you may decide to paint the entire seat—in which case, wash and sand it well beforehand.

Plastic film peeling from wood seat. Glue down with plastic-mending adhesive or vinyl cement.

Rubber bumpers disintegrated. Pull them off and take out nails, if possible; otherwise, cut them off and file smooth. Screw on new bumpers.

Seat needs replacement. If the seat fits the bowl attractively (meaning that it should be about the same shape as the bowl and should overhang the rim about ½ inch), loosen the nuts that hold it in place at the back of the bowl and take it to a plumbing supplies outlet to make sure you get a seat of the same shape and size. If the seat doesn't fit the bowl, draw a careful outline of the entire bowl top on newspaper and use this to help you pick out the right seat.

TOOLS, HAND

See AX; BRACE AND BIT; CHISEL; ELECTRIC DRILL; FILE, CARPENTER'S; HAMMER; KNIFE, POCKET; PLANE, CARPENTER'S; PLIERS; POWER TOOLS; various entries for SAW; SOLDERING IRON; WRENCH, PIPE.

NOTE. The greatest enemy of all tools is rust. If it forms, rub it off with fine steel wool and then with liquid rust-remover. Wipe an oily rag over tools that are stored in a damp place.

Other common problems are broken or loose handles, dull and nicked cutting edges, clogged teeth, and stiff movement of such jointed tools as braces and wrenches. The methods for correcting these problems are obvious and generally similar to those used for the tools for which specific entries appear.

TOWEL

Edges of terry-cloth towels frayed. Trim off edges. Run two lines of machine stitches along edges.

Holes, tears in terry cloth Discard the towel or cut it into smaller towels or washcloths. Machine stitch the edges as above.

Other problems. See CLOTHING—FABRICS.

TOYS

See also BALL, INFLATED LEATHER; BALL, INFLATED PLASTIC; BALL, INFLATED RUBBER; DOLL; and STUFFED ANIMAL.

NOTE. There are so many different toys on the market that it is impossible to cover them all individually. But all are relatively easy to repair if you (1) examine the problem and the way the toy is put together; (2) have patience, and (3) follow the proper methods for fixing the different materials used. Above all, remember that the greatest problem with toys is that they are often flimsily constructed and need to be reinforced.

Plastic toys cracked, broken. Clean edges of break, apply plastic-mending adhesive, and clamp together overnight. Reinforce the break with a strip of rigid plastic or wood, and glue in place with plastic-mending adhesive. Or if contours of toy prohibit use of rigid strip, try bolting aluminum flashing to back of plastic or, if worse comes to worst, glue down heavy sheet vinyl with plastic-mending adhesive.

Plastic loose from wood or metal. Drill holes through the plastic and other material and secure with small bolts. For a neater repair, use rivets. Insert these from the plastic side and do not pound too hard on shank or you may crack the plastic.

Plastic or metal caterpillar treads come apart. Drill tiny holes through the edges of the treads that have separated. Loop fine steel wire or nylon fishing line through them and twist or tie ends together.

Dents in steel toys. If metal is thin, bend out dents with your fingers. Otherwise, hold a block of wood against the concave side of dent, and tap the other side with a hammer or wood block.

Flanged joints in steel toys broken. Toy joints are often formed by inserting a metal tab through a slot and then bending down the tab.

If the tab breaks off, try cleaning the metal inside the separated pieces with steel wool, tie the pieces together with string or C-clamps, heat with a soldering iron, and run in a little solder (see BASIC METHODS: HOW TO SOLDER METAL).

If the steel pieces in the joint overlap ¼ inch or more, you can, instead of soldering, drill matching holes through them and bolt together. Or drive in self-tapping screws from the outside and blunt the points with a file.

Heavy steel broken. Coat broken edges with epoxy glue and press together overnight.

Steel loose from wood. Secure with screws or, better, bolts.

Wood toys broken, split. Coat broken edges with glue and clamp together. Use white glue on toys used indoors, resorcinol glue on those used outdoors. Reinforce breaks with wiggle nails, steel mending plates (see BASIC METHODS: HOW TO FASTEN WOOD), or by gluing on wood splints.

Joints in wood open. Pry far enough apart to scrape out old glue and spread in new glue, as above. Clamp for 24 hours. Reinforce with nails or screws.

Wood models broken. Reglue with white glue. If gluing surfaces are very small, reinforce joint by cutting a sewing pin in two and tapping into the joint.

Tears in flexible rubber toys. Cut a patch out of a scrap piece of rubber and roughen back surface with sandpaper. Roughen area around tear. Coat both surfaces with rubber cement and let dry. Then apply a second coat of cement to patch and smooth over tear.

Hard rubber gouged, broken. Clean with paint thinner and roughen with sandpaper. Spread on plastic rubber.

Fabric in toys torn. Cut a patch out of appropriate material, coat lightly with fabric glue, and paste over tear.

Wheels off toys. On such large toys as doll buggies and wagons, wheels today are held on with cap nuts which are simply hammered on. Replace missing nut with one of these or, better, drill a small hole through the axle, slip a steel washer or two on the axle, then insert a cotter pin in the hole.

On cheap small toys, the axles are flattened

at the ends. To make repair, push wheel back on axle, being careful not to widen the hole in the hub. Then melt a blob of solder on the end of the axle.

Wheels wobble. Pry off cap nut and slip one or more steel washers on the axle; replace wheels, and add more washers. Then replace nut or drill a hole through the axle and insert a cotter pin. The washers should fit tightly around the axle. The greater the diameter of the washers next to the wheel the better.

Steel wheels bent. You can remove these and try straightening, but it's a tough job. Try to find replacement wheels.

Wood wheels broken. Apply epoxy glue to broken edges and press together for 24 hours.

Solid or semipneumatic tire loose or off wheel rim. Clean tire with gasoline and roughen with sandpaper. Remove rust and dirt from wheel rim with steel wool and spread in plastic rubber. Then work tire back on rim. If rim lips are bent, hammer straight after tire is on.

TRAILER, CAMPER

Body problems. See AUTOMOBILE BODY.

Gas leaking. Sniff around close to the floor to see if you can pinpoint the likely point of the leak. Then open doors and windows. Brush sudsy water on all suspicious joints. If this forms a sizable bubble, gas is escaping at that point and you must tighten the joint, remake it, or replace the fitting and/or tubing.

TRAILER, SMALL (for boats, etc.)

Frame loose. Tighten all bolts. If this is impossible, saturate them with penetrating oil to loosen nuts. Clean out threads and oil. Then tighten.

Frame rusted. Make a habit of going over it frequently. Chip or file off rust and sand metal bare. Prime with red metal primer. A couple of coats may be advisable to assure complete coverage. Then paint.

Springs stiff. Clean thoroughly with whatever tool can do the job. Lubricate.

Lights out. Check connection with car and make

sure it's tight. Remove bulb, clean off corrosion on base, and test it. If it doesn't work, replace. If you still don't get light, examine the wiring system from stem to stern. Tape worn spots in insulation. Pull on splices and remake them if loose. Solder the joints if possible, then overwrap with electrical tape. Tape wires to trailer so they don't flop around.

Wheel bearings overheated, jammed. Jack up trailer. Pry off dust cover, pull out cotter pin, and remove nut. Take out bearings and clean them. Then clean hub and shaft thoroughly, removing almost all the grease. Put wheel-bearing grease into hub, then place the bearings in a kitchen plastic bag with plenty of grease and work the grease all over the bearings. Replace bearings in hub and add more grease until cup is about half full. Then screw on nut hand-tight or just a shade more. Replace cotter pin (you may need a new one if you have packed the bearings often). Finally replace dust cover.

Coupler loose. Adjust and tighten it. Also tighten hitch on car. Lubricate with SAE number 30 oil.

TRASH COMPACTOR

NOTE. If compactor doesn't work properly, you should call a serviceman. But check the following points first.

Doesn't work. Has fuse blown? Is compactor plugged in? Is the outlet live?

Doesn't compress trash. Lubricate rams according to manufacturer's instruction book. Clean out the guideposts. Adjust tension on belt.

TRAY

Rim of gallery tray loose. If possible, clean metal and solder rim in place (see BASIC METHODS: HOW TO SOLDER METAL). Otherwise, run a small bead of epoxy mender around bottom of rim where it joins the base.

Decorative insets loose from heavy plastic tray. Clean loose piece and hole in which it fits thoroughly and let dry. Try fitting piece into hole; you will probably discover that it is a bit too big and must be trimmed down very slightly with a knife and sandpaper. Then coat with plastic-mending adhesive and glue in place. Let dry 6 hours before using tray.

Glass in tray broken. Pry off wood or hardboard back. Replace glass with a new pane. Reglue back with white glue.

Scratches, stains. See entry for material of which tray is made.

TROUSER HANGER

Trousers fall out. Stick strips of felt to inside surfaces of the wood cuff-holders with white glue. If hanger still doesn't close tightly enough, bend the heavy wires inward.

Wires pull out of cuff-holders. Coat wires with epoxy glue and set into the holes in the wood.

TRUNK

Lock bent. This is very difficult to straighten, but try to do so with pliers. If this doesn't work, pull away trunk lining, and file heads off rivets holding lock. Remove lock and straighten it in a vise and by hammering. Then rivet back on the trunk.

Leather handles broken. Remove trunk lining and file heads off rivets holding the end caps. Remove caps and handle. Cut heavy webbing belt to proper length and whip ends with thread. Then make a hole in both ends and rivet or bolt the webbing to the trunk. Re-rivet end caps or try sticking them down with epoxy glue.

Metal corners pulled off. Glue down with epoxy glue.

Lining torn. Stick back in place with fabric glue.

TYPEWRITER

Keys work stiffly. With a toothbrush, loosen eraser crumbs in the key slots. Then blow out crumbs and dust with a vacuum cleaner hose. Run a very little sewing machine oil into key slots and work keys.

Carriage moves sluggishly. Put a drop of light oil on either end of the rod or bar on which carriage glides. Work carriage back and forth.

Letter head on key loose. You can fix this temporarily by raising key half way and supporting it there. With a small pair of pliers, carefully position head. Be careful not to mar the letters. Hold with pliers and heat one side of head with soldering iron briefly. Remove heat but not pliers and let solder harden.

Key sticks at ribbon slot. Check on which side of slot key is binding; then bend key head slightly to other side. Often if you just wiggle key back and forth several times it will straighten out.

Keys punch holes through paper. Platen is probably worn and hard. Have it recovered. If electric typewriter, check pressure control.

UMBRELLA

Tears. Cut a small matching patch and paste to underside of umbrella with fabric glue. Use as little of the glue as possible.

Fabric torn from the end of a steel bow. Resew the seam if it has ripped. Then sew the fabric to the tip of the bow. It may be advisable also to glue it to the tip. Use rubber cement and apply to the fabric and the tip; let dry until tacky, and then stick fabric down.

Fabric needs to be replaced. Send umbrella to an umbrella repair shop.

Bows bent. Umbrella bows are small U-shaped strips. When bent, the sides bend inward or outward. To prevent breaking the bow as you bend it straight by hand you must also bend the sides back to their proper positions with pliers. The whole job must be done very gradually: straighten the bow a bit, then bend the sides a bit until finally the job is done.

Bows broken. Better let an expert take over. However, it is sometimes possible to join the broken pieces with a metal splint. Use a 1-inch to 1½-inch length of baling wire or a finishing nail and glue this into the channel in the bow with epoxy glue.

Handle loose. If this is a perennial problem, remove handle and coat hole in it with epoxy glue. Replace on shaft and let glue dry at least 24 hours.

Upper catch won't hold. Take umbrella to a repair shop.

URETHANE FOAM

Torn. Apply plastic-mending adhesive to one edge and press torn pieces together.

VACUUM CLEANER

Doesn't work. Disconnect and examine cord for a break. Check whether plug is broken. Make necessary repairs (see ELECTRIC CORD). If this doesn't work, take vacuum to service shop.

Suddenly stops after making rattling noise. Whatever caused the rattle (a nail or safety pin, for example) is jammed in the fan. Disconnect vacuum, disassemble enough to get at fan, and loosen it by turning. Object should fall out.

Doesn't pick up dirt. Remove threads wound around brush. Replace brush if worn. Replace drive belt. Check whether outlet from machine into bag is clogged and poke out lint and dirt with a stiff wire. Check whether hose is similarly clogged and clean with a long wire.

Hole in bag. If bag is plastic, use a plastic-mending adhesive kit. Cut plastic patch so it overlaps hole about ½ inch. Cover one side with plastic adhesive. Stick over hole on inside of bag. If bag is cloth, cover hole on inside with adhesive-backed mending tape or press-on mending tape.

Hole in hose. If hose is plastic, seal small holes with plastic-mending adhesive. If hole is large, use plastic patch and plastic adhesive as above. If hose is covered with fabric, cut a patch out of matching material. Coat one side of patch and area around hole with fabric glue. Stick on patch and let dry before using vacuum.

Hose loose from metal tube. This is a fairly common problem with new vacuum cleaners that have hoses made out of plastic over a flexible metal coil. If plastic sleeve on end of hose is separated from the hose, coat end of hose with plastic-mending adhesive and screw into the sleeve. Let glue dry overnight. If plastic sleeve is loose from metal tube, wrap ½-inch adhesive tape around end of tube to form a ridge; then force sleeve over this.

Tubes battered at ends, won't hold together or hold on cleaning tools. Straighten ends with pliers. Check whether the metal clips that are sometimes used to secure the joints are catching properly. If these measures don't work, about the only thing you can do is bind the tubes permanently together with cellophane electrical tape or adhesive tape.

Retractable cord doesn't retract. Open vacuum and clean dirt out of cord reel. If this doesn't work, replace reel.

VARNISHED SURFACE

Minor scratches. Rub with the meat of a walnut or similarly oily nut, or with floor paste wax.

Larger scratches. These can be filled by rubbing with a wax stick made for use on furniture. Or you can touch up the scratches with matching oil stain applied with a small artist's brush.

The alternative is to sprinkle rottenstone, available from a paint store, on the scratch and rub with a cloth dipped in salad oil or sewing machine oil. Work with the grain. This will take off quite a lot of the finish, and it may be necessary to refinish with oil stain. But if you haven't cut through the varnish to the wood, several applications of paste wax should pretty well hide the blemish.

Varnish rough, gummy. This may happen if the varnish is very old or has not been applied under the proper conditions. The best answer is to strip the surface with paint remover. Use steel wool on the undersurface. Then apply new varnish (see BASIC METHODS: HOW TO PAINT).

Water spots. First try rubbing spot with cigarette ashes and a cloth dipped in salad oil or sewing machine oil. If this doesn't work, put spirits of camphor on a cloth and daub on spot. Let dry for about 30 minutes. Then rub on rottenstone with cloth dipped in oil. Remove residue with benzine.

Heat marks. Wipe spot with camphorated oil and then dry quickly. If surface is rough, rub with very fine steel wool. If this doesn't work, rub with rottenstone and a cloth dipped in salad oil.

Alcohol spots. Rub with rottenstone and a cloth dipped in salad oil.

Paint spots. Paint remover will play havoc with the finish. About the only thing you can do is scrape off the paint with the point of a sharp knife. Then, if surface is damaged, rub it with rottenstone and oil as above.

Nail polish on varnish. Don't apply nail-polish remover or other lacquer thinner. Scrape off with a knife like a paint spot (see above).

Candle wax on varnish. Remove as much as possible with your fingers, then scrape off the rest with a dull table knife. Wipe residue off quickly with benzine or paint thinner.

Crayon or lipstick marks. Rub with white appliance-cleaning wax.

Paper stuck to varnish. You may not be able to get it off, but at least you can try. Saturate the paper with paint thinner or turpentine and try to peel off. If unsuccessful, you'll have to rub it off. Don't rub too hard. If the varnish left underneath seems to be fairly thick, let it dry for a couple of days, then go over it with fine steel wool to smooth it out. If the film is thin, sponge it lightly with paint thinner until smooth.

Surface streaky, foggy, slightly grayish. There's too much wax or polish on the surface. Try removing it with a soft cloth dipped and wrung out in white vinegar. If this doesn't work, use an automobile body cleaner such as Simoniz. Then refinish—preferably with an oily polish, or with a paste wax if surface gets hard wear. Use very little, and don't reapply often.

VASE

Leaks through cracks or seams. If vase is metal, clean surface well with steel wool and cover crack on inside with epoxy mender. If vase is pottery or translucent glass, spread a ribbon of silicone caulking on crack. If vase is clear glass, coat crack with clear epoxy glue.

Broken. See entry for material of which vase is made.

Glass vase broken in many pieces. If it's worth saving, glue the pieces together with cyanoacrylate glue or cellulose cement. Then coat the entire vase on the inside with Liquitex Gel Medium, a transparent acrylic emulsion sold in art supplies stores. Squeeze on surface from tube and brush it out evenly over the glass. When dry, apply a second coat. The film not only waterproofs the vase but also helps to reinforce it.

Glass vase covered inside with whitish film. Wash or soak in vinegar to remove the calcium deposit.

VENEER

Loose. Carefully bend veneer away from its base and scrape out old glue. Apply white or resorcinol glue and press veneer back in place. Cover with wax paper, then a piece of wood. Clamp or weight. Wipe off glue that oozes out from under veneer.

Broken or missing. Buy new veneer of matching wood. With very sharp knife, cut out broken veneer in a rectangle or diamond. Be sure cuts are clean and straight. Scrape out old glue. Cut new veneer to fit hole exactly. Apply white or resorcinol glue and set patch in place. Cover with wax paper and weight down for 24 hours. Then sand patch level with surrounding veneer and apply matching stain.

Blistered. If wood is stiff and brittle, cover with damp rags until it becomes more flexible. Slash blister with a sharp knife, cutting with the grain. Lift edges carefully and squirt or spread white or resorcinol glue underneath. Press down. If edges overlap, trim one to match the other. Wipe off excess glue, cover with wax paper, and weight down.

Scratched, dented, etc. See FURNITURE, WOOD.

VENETIAN BLIND

Tapes broken. Take down blind. Remove the raising cords, then slide out slats and remove the tapes (which are tacked to the top and bottom boards in wood blinds; clamped in place in metal blinds). Buy new tapes at department or variety store. Cut to right length and attach to top of blind. Then rehang blind and slide slats into tapes and attach tapes to bottom board. Knot cords at one end and slip other end up through the bottom board, the slats, and top board. Then run cords over pulleys and down through the hole in which cord catch is located. Adjust tension on cords so that blind does not tilt when raised.

Wood slat broken. If break runs with grain, coat the edges with epoxy glue and press together. Then, with epoxy glue, stick a patch cut from thin aluminum or a tin can to the back of the slat over the joint. Clamp with C-clamps until dry.

If break is across the grain or if you don't like the patched-up repair above, loosen tapes and cords from the bottom of the blind and take out the broken slat. Replace with a new one or, if blind is too long anyway, simply shorten it by one slat.

Metal slat bent. Straighten it by hand and with pliers (cover the jaws of the pliers with adhesive tape so you don't mar the finish on the slat). If slat cannot be straightened decently, remove and replace it as above.

Cord catch doesn't hold, blind sags. Take down blind, scrape rust from catch and oil. While blind is down, clean and oil other moving parts, too.

VINYL

Tears in vinyl fabric. Bring torn edges together and overlap if possible. Coat with vinyl adhesive and let dry overnight.

Holes in vinyl fabric. Use plastic-mending adhesive kit, which contains a vinyl patch, or cut a patch out of matching vinyl. Clean surface around hole. Apply vinyl adhesive to edges of patch and press over hole.

Breaks in rigid (or reasonably rigid) vinyl. Clean edges and apply vinyl adhesive to one. Press pieces together overnight. If glued edges are thin, reinforce the joint by gluing a scrap of vinyl or other rigid plastic over it.

Problems with vinyl floors. See FLOOR, VINYL.

VINYL WALL COVERING

Loose. Lift edges carefully and scrape off some of the old adhesive. Then apply new adhesive made specifically for hanging vinyl wall covering or, in a pinch, white glue. Smooth down edges, taking care to remove all bubbles.

Holes. It is best to tear out a patch to cover the hole since it will show less than a cut patch. But tearing vinyl covering is hard because it tends to delaminate, leaving a wide edge on one side of the tear. Keep trying until you produce a patch that doesn't have white edges. Then paste it over hole with vinyl adhesive.

Pigment film missing in spots. If the spot is large, either apply a patch or hang an entirely new strip of vinyl. But you can touch up small spots very nicely with colored pencils.

Dirt, stains. Wash with detergent solution.

VULCANIZED FIBERBOARD
(like that on trunks, laundry mailing boxes)

Broken. Cut a patch out of vulcanized fiberboard or aluminum flashing. Roughen area around tear. Apply epoxy glue to patch and press together.

Alternative is to cut a patch out of aluminum flashing, hold it back of tear, and drill small holes through the two materials. Then insert aluminum rivets.

WADERS

Holes, tears. See TIRE (*tube punctured*). Clean surface and rub with sandpaper. Cut a patch out of matching material. Apply a thin coat of rubber cement to both surfaces; let dry for 5 minutes, and smooth the patch over the hole.

WADING POOL, FIBER GLASS

Scratches, breaks. See FIBER GLASS, RIGID.
Stains, scale deposits. See SWIMMING POOL, CONCRETE.

WADING POOL, PLASTIC

Holes, tears. Repair with mending kit sold by pool maker, or cut a patch out of sheet vinyl

and glue over hole with plastic-mending adhesive or vinyl cement. The pool surface must, of course, be absolutely clean and dry.
Stains, scale deposits. See SWIMMING POOL, CONCRETE.

WAFFLE IRON

Doesn't heat. Check whether fuse has blown, whether outlet into which iron is plugged is operating. Inspect cord for a break and replace it if necessary. If grids are easily removed from appliance, look for a broken heating element. You can make a temporary repair by twisting the ends of the wires together several times. Make sure they don't touch the shell of the waffle iron. As soon as possible thereafter, remove the heating element and replace it with a new one available from a wiring supplies store or appliance service shop.

If none of these repairs works, take waffle iron to serviceman.

Grids dirty, stuck up. Wash nonstick grids in detergent solution. Don't wash others, however, because that will destroy the grease film that keeps waffles from sticking.

Batter and grease encrusted on body of waffle iron. See CHROMIUM PLATE.

WALK, BRICK

Cracks in mortar joints. See BRICK.

Bricks set in sand heaved, sunken, or broken. Lift out brick and make new base of sand. Tamp smooth. Set in brick and fill around it with more sand. If bricks heave or sink frequently, sand base is of insufficient depth. Remove all bricks in the area, dig out soil, and provide a cushion of sand or hard cinders 3 or 4 inches deep.

Border bricks of walk set in sand sunken or slanting. To prevent this, all border, or edging, bricks should be installed perpendicularly. Remove them, dig a straight-sided trench, and set in bricks. Pack soil around them firmly.

Bricks spalled or badly pitted. If set in sand, lift them out and replace with new bricks. Replacement is also the best solution if bricks

are set in mortar, but this is a time-consuming job. It's easier to fill holes with latex cement mixed with red pigment from masonry supplies outlet.

WALK, CONCRETE

Water stands in low spots. If walk is laid in sections, try raising the troublesome section with a crowbar and filling underneath with gravel. If water collects in middle of walk, clean surface thoroughly and trowel on latex cement. Note that patch will not match surrounding surface.

Crack between walk and house foundations. Scrape out crack and let dry (use a torch if necessary). Fill with asphalt roofing cement. If crack is very wide and roofing cement would be unsightly, fill crack to within 1 inch of top with roofing cement and strands of manila rope. When cement has hardened, fill crack the rest of the way with latex cement or mortar made of 1 part portland cement and 3 parts sand.

Other problems. See FLOOR, CONCRETE.

WALK, STONE

Cracks in mortar joints between stones. Chip out broken and weak mortar with a cold chisel. Blow out crumbs. Pack in mortar made of 1 part portland cement and 3 parts sand.

Stone loose. Lift it out. Chip away mortar joints around edges of hole and chip out top of mortar bed to a depth of 1 inch below old level. Clean out crumbs and dirt. Saturate mortar bed overnight with water, then let dry until no standing water remains. Brush on a soupy mixture of cement and water. Then immediately spread on mortar bed a new layer of mortar made of 1 part portland cement and 3 parts sand. Set in stone and level it with surrounding surface. Fill in around edges with more mortar. Wipe off mortar on stones with a wet rag. Keep covered for about 48 hours with damp burlap.

Stones set in sand heaved or sunken. See WALK, BRICK.

WALLET

Seams ripped. You can resew them. Or if wallet is leather, apply a thin coat of rubber cement to both edges. Let dry until tacky and press edges together. On plastic wallets, use plastic-mending adhesive.

Leather or plastic worn through at fold. Out of thin matching or complementary material, cut a strip that will overlap the sides of the holes and will wrap over the top and bottom edges of the wallet about ¼ inch. Glue up and down the fold and at top and bottom on the inside with appropriate glue (see above).

Ornamental metal corners off. Coat the groove in the metal corner with cellulose cement, place on corner of wallet, and crimp lightly.

WALLPAPER

Loose. Lift carefully (wet with water if very stiff). Spread thin wallpaper paste underneath. Smooth down with clean, damp rag.

Blistered, bulged. Soak with water until paper is soft. Cut across blister with a razor blade. Lift edges carefully and spread thin wallpaper paste underneath. Smooth down with a clean, damp rag. If edges overlap, let them overlap, or slice through the center of the lap, from end to end, with a razor blade. Remove cut strips and press down.

Tears, holes. Tear a patch out of a leftover scrap (torn edges are less noticeable than cut edges). Smear thin wallpaper paste on the back. Position patch to match pattern and smooth down over tear.

Dirt and stains on washable paper. Wipe off with mild detergent solution.

Crayon marks on washable paper. Remove with white appliance wax.

Dirt on nonwashable paper. If the dirty spots are isolated, you can remove the worst of them with an art-gum eraser or with a wad of dried rubber cement. Test on an inconspicuous spot first and don't rub too hard. If the eraser doesn't work, try cleaning with Goddard's wallpaper spot remover: it may not work, but if it doesn't, it won't do any harm.

Generally, however, if nonwashable wallpaper is dirty all over, it's best to leave it alone, because while you can clean some areas, you won't achieve a uniform result—and the resulting unevenness will look worse than the dirt.

Grease stains on nonwashable wallpaper. Spray with Goddard's wallpaper spot remover. Or make a stiff paste of dry starch and trichloroethylene. Spread a ½-inch layer on stain and let dry. Then brush off.

WASHING MACHINE

Doesn't work. Is washer plugged in? Has fuse blown? Is cord broken?

Doesn't fill with water. Are water valves open? Make sure supply hoses are not kinked. Unscrew hoses from faucets and look in them for small filter screens. If there are any, remove and clean them.

Doesn't empty. Check whether drain hose is kinked.

Oversudses. Check: Did you use too much detergent or a new kind of detergent? Let suds settle and then pump out. Follow instructions in your use-and-care manual.

Water comes in cold. Probably because you've overdrawn supply elsewhere in house. But check whether inlet valves are turned on. Maybe you should raise water-heater thermostat setting. Maybe you need a larger water heater.

Clothes not clean. Are you using proper amount of detergent? Is water hot enough?

Washer "walks" across floor. It isn't level. Set it in its proper place in the laundry. Then raise or lower the leveling feet underneath. Check with a carpenter's level to make sure top of washer is level from front to back and side to side.

Paint nicked. Clean metal at once with sandpaper and apply touch-up enamel. If you delay repair, make sure scratch is free of rust before touching up.

Rust spots on underside of top, especially around lid hinges. Scrape with a knife and clean with emery cloth till metal shines. Paint with porcelain glaze or epoxy touch-up enamel.

WASTEBASKET

Paper or fabric covering torn or loose. Glue with glue.

Leather covering torn or loose. Coat back of leather and base with rubber cement. Let dry until tacky, and smooth the leather down.

Top binding badly torn. Replace with binding cut from adhesive-backed mending tape.

Plastic basket cracked. Coat cracked edges with plastic-mending adhesive and clamp together for 24 hours.

Fancy perforated metal strip broken from solid metal below. This will never look the same, but you can mend the basket pretty well by sanding off paint on inside of strip and metal below it. Out of metal window screen cloth, cut a strip 1 inch to 1½ inches wide and long enough to cover the break. Spread a thin coat of epoxy mender on basket and embed mesh in it. Do not add additional epoxy unless mend seems weak when patch dries.

WATER HEATER

Leaks. See WATER TANK.

Doesn't work. Call a serviceman. But if you have a gas water heater and the pilot light is out, you can proceed as follows: First shut off the A valve, which is the main gas valve to the burner, and the B pilot valve. Wait 5 minutes. Then turn on B valve and ignite with a match. Then turn on the A valve.

NOTE. Instructions for lighting pilot lights are printed on a tag attached to heater. Don't lose these.

Water too hot or too cold. Adjust aquastat.

Not delivering enough hot water. Chances are heater is clogged with scale. Call a serviceman. It may also be advisable to install a water softener.

Sediment in hot water. Open valve in side of heater, and drain until water runs clear.

Rust in hot water. Either the tank is corroding or something is wrong with your main water supply. Call a serviceman.

Gas heater smells. Shut off main gas control valve at once and call a serviceman. Don't look for leaks with a lighted match.

Gas or oil heater's flue pipe corroded, out of line. See FURNACE FLUE.

WATERING CAN

Holes in galvanized can. Remove rust from around hole with steel wool and spread on epoxy mender.

Seams in copper can open. Clean thoroughly inside and out with steel wool. Bring edges together. Then apply solder (see BASIC METHODS: HOW TO SOLDER METAL).

End of spout collapsed. Depending on the size of the spout, open it as much as possible with a screwdriver or nail. Then, to shape the opening properly, tap in a round of hardwood (such as a broomstick or dowel) which has been sharpened slightly at the end.

Sprinkler head clogged. Remove from can and and scrape the inside of the head with a screwdriver. Then open the holes by inserting a stiff wire from the outside. Soak in vinegar.

WATER PUMP

Doesn't operate. Is switch on? Has fuse blown? Is wiring loose?

If you haven't been operating pump for some time, drive shaft may be frozen, so grasp it with a pair of pliers and turn it until it's free. Examine pressure switch and clean contacts by sliding a piece of paper between them. If you still can't get pump going, call a serviceman.

Motor slow, overheating, sparking. See ELECTRIC MOTOR.

Pump operates but produces no water. Check whether water level in well has dropped too low. Clean or, if necessary, replace strainer and foot valve at bottom of well. Open priming plug and reprime pump. Look for leaks in suction line and fix them. Check whether jet is plugged and clean it according to manufacturer's instructions.

It is also possible that the pipes from the pressure tank to the house are frozen, in which case they should be thawed out carefully (see entries for PIPE, WATER). As soon as possible, they should be installed below the frost line. In the meanwhile, you can keep them open by wrapping with electric heating cable.

Pump doesn't deliver water at full capacity. Water level in well may be too low, piping may be clogged. Look for a leak in the seal around the drive shaft and replace seal according to manufacturer's directions.

Pump pumps but doesn't shut off. Adjust or replace pressure switch. A faucet may be left open somewhere or there may be a leak in the supply pipes. Jet may be clogged.

Pump goes on and off too frequently. Check for an open faucet or leak in supply pipes. Adjust pressure switch. Tank is waterlogged (see following).

Tank waterlogged. This happens when the air cushion in the tank is too small. The result is to make the pump turn on and off frequently. If you have an automatic air control, the situation can be corrected by removing the valve core in the air valve and replacing with a new one of the same type. If this doesn't do the trick, pump air through the valve into the tank with a tire pump. If trouble keeps on, call a serviceman.

If your system does not have an automatic air control, there is what looks like an ordinary tire valve on the pump. Remove the cap. If the valve core is OK, it will now suck in air as the pump operates. When proper air cushion is restored (it takes a day or so), replace cap. If the valve core doesn't suck in air, replace it with a new core. If this still doesn't work, drain the system entirely by turning off the pump, opening a valve or pipe on the outlet side of the tank to let in air, and opening the valve at the bottom of the tank to let out water. When tank is empty, close valves and refill.

Air spurts from faucets. Look for and fix leaks in suction line to pump. But trouble usually occurs when tank has too large an air cushion, causing water to flow from faucets in violent bursts. To remedy situation, drain system entirely as above and refill.

Also see PUMP, PORTABLE WATER.

WATER TANK

Leaks. These are easy to stop—at least temporarily—with water tank repair plugs available at plumbing and hardware stores. The size required depends on the size of the hole, but since you can't be sure how strong the metal is around the hole, buy several sizes.

The simplest plug is a self-tapping screw with a rubber washer under the large head. To use this, just twist it into the leak with a wrench (there's no need to drill a hole) until the gasket begins to mushroom out and the leak stops.

Other plugs are a little more reliable in a tank with a good head of air pressure. With these you must first drill a hole, which means that the tank should be drawn down before you start making the repair. One type of bolt is held in place with a spring toggle. Another type is something like a hollow-wall screw anchor.

Air-bound or waterlogged. See WATER PUMP.

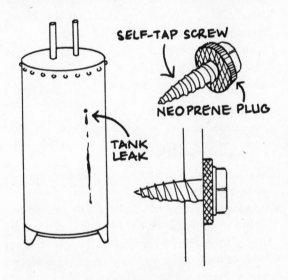

WEATHER STRIPPING

Felt or rubber weather stripping hardened by paint. Tear it off and replace it with new stripping.

Metal-weather-stripped door or window closes and opens hard. Rub weather strips with paraffin or spray with silicone lubricant.

Interlocking metal weather stripping prevents door or window closing. Clean out under and over the weather strips with a knife, screwdriver, etc. Vacuum out all the dirt. This may be all that's wrong. If not, straighten edges of strip so they mesh when closed.

Make sure that door or window hinges are tight.

Metal stripping vibrates noisily when wind blows. With a putty knife or screwdriver, bend the unattached edge of the strip outward so that it presses more tightly against the door or window.

WEBBING

Dirty. Clean plastic webbing with detergent solution. If this doesn't work on vinyl, use a special vinyl cleaner. Canvas webbing is usually hopeless, but if it can be removed, wash in hot water and heavy-duty detergent in washing machine. Use chlorine bleach on white webbing.

Ends frayed. Put several rows of stitches through canvas webbing. Use a sewing machine if possible. On plastic webbing, trim off the frayed ends and coat the first inch of material below with plastic-mending adhesive. You can also fuse the strands in polypropylene webbing by heating slightly with a torch.

WHEELBARROW

Holes in metal. Sand thoroughly and spread on epoxy mender.

Wood bottom rotted out. Build a new one preferably out of maple or oak. But you can get by for a long time by covering the old bottom with ¼-inch tempered hardboard. Use screws rather than nails to hold it down.

Wheel stiff, noisy. Saturate it with SAE number 30 oil.

WICKER

Broken. Coat break with white or resorcinol glue. Apply glue to area around break. Cover wicker on both sides with wax paper and then clamp the broken piece between boards for 24 hours.

Break can be further reinforced with wire woven through surrounding wicker.

See also FURNITURE—WICKER, RATTAN, REED, or BAMBOO.

WINDOW, AWNING

Window stiff or stuck. Lubricate operator and adjusting arms with powdered graphite and remove any paint on them. If window still works badly, you may need a new operator. Call in carpenter.

Leaks at top of window frame. See WINDOW, DOUBLE-HUNG.

Other problems. See entries for DOOR. Solutions are similar.

WINDOW BOX

Holes in metal box. With steel wool, clean metal until it is bright. Then cover hole with epoxy mender. To prevent recurrence of rusting, coat inside of box with liquid asphalt roofing cement. To make sure drainage is adequate, drill additional holes in bottom.

Wood rotting. See PLANT TUB or BOX.

WINDOW, CASEMENT

Window stiff. Lubricate adjusting arm and make sure it is free of paint. If window has a rotary operator, squirt powdered graphite into joint at base of handle. Then open window and squirt more graphite into back of operator and on to sliding track.

Air leaks around edges of window. If windows are metal, install rubber stripping that is slotted to fit over the edges of the frame. A flange laps over the window edges and prevents air from entering. Flexible metal weather stripping is better but should be installed by an expert. If windows are wood, tack one edge of metal stripping to the frame and bend up the other edge so that it presses against the edges of the sash. The tacked edge should face outward for outswinging casements so that it won't interfere with the closing of the window.

Water leaks at top or sides of window frame.
See WINDOW, DOUBLE-HUNG.

Window sags. Remove sash and square it up.
Install flat steel angle irons at corners.

Other problems. See DOOR, HINGED.

WINDOW, DOUBLE-HUNG

Window sticks. If painted shut, run point of a
sharp knife repeatedly around edge of sash.
Don't exert too much pressure lest the knife
slip and gouge the surrounding wood. If necessary, drive a thin putty knife between the sash
and stop.

If sticking results from swelling of wood,
rub paraffin on the pulley stiles. Or spray stiles
with silicone lubricant.

If this still doesn't work, pry off the stops.
Work from the back edges so you don't damage
the exposed faces of the stops. Hold the bottom sash against the parting strips. Reposition
the stops a fraction of an inch away from the
sash, and renail them. If the top sash is stuck,
take out the bottom sash and pull out the
parting strips with pliers. Then scrape or sand
down the back edges of the parting strips
slightly until the sash works freely.

Lower sash rattles in wind. Remove the stops.
Hold the sash against the parting strips. Renail
the stops closer to the sash.

Upper sash rattles in wind. Remove stops, bottom sash, and parting strips. Cut strips of
fabric to the length of the parting strips and
just wide enough to cover the portion that is
exposed when the strips are inserted in the
jambs. The thickness of the fabric depends on
the space between the rattling sash and the
parting strips: use anything from thin canvas
to felt. Glue the fabric to the back of the parting strips with white glue. When glue is dry,
replace parting strips in jambs. Test how easily
the sash slides, then replace lower sash and
stops.

Sash cord broken or stretched. Pry off inside
stop bead on one side of sash and remove
lower sash. Unscrew top of pocket cover in
the stile and take out sash weight. Cut off cord.
Push new cord over pulley at top of window
frame and run it down through slot in frame.

Tie it securely to sash weight, replace weight
in frame, and pull it up to the pulley. Set sash
on windowsill and pull cord down 3 inches
below hole in edge of sash. Knot cord at this
point and wedge knot in hole. Replace window
in frame and work it up and down. Adjust
length of cord. Then replace pocket cover and
stop bead.

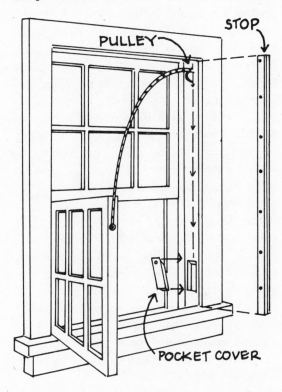

If sash cord on upper sash is broken, repair
is made in same way. To remove sash it is
necessary first to remove bottom sash as above
and then pull out the parting strip between
the two sashes with pliers.

NOTE. Sash chain can be used instead of cord.
It won't stretch.

Unique balance broken or kinked. This is a
patented window balance in which a spiral strip
of steel moves up and down inside a tube
fastened in the stiles at the top of a window.
If one of the balances breaks or kinks, remove
the stops. Pry the foot of the defective balance
from the bottom of the sash. Swing the sash
partway out of the frame, and pry the balance
from the stile. Replace with a new Unique
balance. But note that the groove in the side
of the sash may have to be widened and deep-

ened if the new balance tube is larger than the original.

If more than one of the Unique balances in the window are broken or kinked, it is better to replace all of them with a pair of modern aluminum jamb liners. To use these, remove the stops, bottom sash, parting strips, upper sash, and four Unique balances. Enlarge the grooves in the edges of the sashes if necessary. Nail the clips that hold the jamb liners to the stiles. Then set the sashes between the jamb liners and lift the entire bundle into the window frame. Squeeze the liners into the clips. Replace the stops.

NOTE. Aluminum jamb liners can also be substituted for sash cords. In this case, after taking out the stops, parting strips, and sashes, remove the pulleys from the stiles. Cut grooves in the edges of the sashes to fit the liners. Then install liners and sashes as above.

Window doesn't latch. Catch on lower sash is either out of alignment with hook on upper sash or hook is too low. If out of alignment, take off hook; fill screw holes, and set hook in new position. If hook is too low, remove it, slip a piece of hardboard or plywood underneath, and screw hook down.

Horizontal mullions on upper sash splintered, gouged. Remove paint and rust from catch on lower sash, and oil it.

Air leaks around edges of window. Install weather stripping. Metal stripping is best and also permanent, but installation is difficult. Installation of rubber or felt stripping, on the other hand, is simple. Just nail to the frame so that the edge presses firmly against the sash. Use aluminum nails spaced every 2 inches. The strips go on the inside of the bottom sash, outside of the top sash.

Water leaks at sides of window frame. Squeeze caulking compound into the cracks and smooth down flush with the siding.

Water leaks at top of window frame. Clean out old caulking compound between window frame and siding. Force in new compound. If siding is of any material other than masonry and if window is not flashed, cut a strip of aluminum or copper flashing 4 inches longer than width of window. Center over window frame and force it up under siding as far as possible. Bend

metal at base of siding and then bend down over top of window frame. Nail to the front of the frame.

FORCE FLASHING UP UNDER SIDING, BEND OUT OVER DRIP CAP, AND NAIL

WINDOW, JALOUSIE

Air, water, enter through louvers. Despite manufacturers' claims, this is inevitable. There is nothing you can do that will not spoil appearance of window. But check whether hinges are working properly and allow louvers to close all the way.

Stiff. Clean crank and closing mechanism on sides. Apply light oil and work louvers up and down.

WINDOWPANE

Broken. Crack out glass and pull out glazier's points. Carefully cut out old putty. All of it should be removed so wood is bare. If you are setting new pane with glazing compound, brush an oil-base exterior primer on the wood and let dry. If you use old-fashioned putty, coat the wood with linseed oil and set new pane immediately.

Have new pane cut $\frac{1}{16}$ inch to $\frac{1}{8}$ inch narrower and shorter than opening. Spread a thin bed of putty (or glazing compound) evenly on the rabbets. Press pane firmly into place and tap in glazier's points around the edges. Space points about 6 inches apart. Spread a thick layer of putty on rabbets with a putty knife. Then, holding putty knife at an angle against the glass and the outside edge of the rabbet, press putty into place with a smooth, even stroke that starts at one corner of the opening and runs to the next. The angle of the putty should be such that it is invisible when you stand indoors and look out the window. Let the putty dry until it doesn't show finger marks when you touch it. Then repaint.

Broken panes in metal windows are handled the same way. After cleaning out the old putty, sand the metal clean but don't prime it. The glass is held in place with special metal clips rather than glazier's points. Use special metal-sash glazing compound.

Putty broken, crumbling, missing around edges of pane. Scrape it all off down to the wood. Take care not to gouge wood. Then prime wood with oil-base exterior primer and apply glazing compound as above, or prime with linseed oil and apply oil-base putty.

If some of the old putty is very hard to remove, simply square off the ends and apply new putty in the opening between.

Insulation glass cracked. Have it replaced: it has lost some of its insulating value.

Moisture inside insulating glass. There is a leak or break somewhere, and glass should be replaced.

WINDOW SHADE, ROLLER

Shade too tight, snaps up. Raise it to the top, remove from brackets, and unroll it about 18 inches. Replace and test. If still too tight, repeat until it works well.

Shade too loose, rolls up slowly. Pull down about 18 inches from top, remove from bracket, and roll up by hand. Replace in brackets and test. Repeat as necessary until tension is right.

Falls out of brackets. If shade is mounted on front of window casings, simply move one of the brackets a little further in. If shade is hung inside window opening, pull the round pin in the roller out about ¼ inch (you'll probably

need pliers). If this doesn't correct problem, remove one or both of the brackets and install a shim of cardboard, hardboard, or wood underneath.

New shade too long for brackets mounted inside window opening. You should take it back to the store that made it and have it remade. But if you prefer, you can file a little off the ends of the roller pins. Or recess one of the brackets slightly in the woodwork.

Won't catch when rolled down. Remove roller from brackets. Clean and oil ratchets on the flat rotating pin.

Shade torn. Apply a patch of cotton or vinyl fabric with fabric glue or plastic-mending adhesive.

Bindings broken on bamboo or split wood shades. Unroll shade on floor and remove broken bindings. Cut a new cotton cord about three times the length of the shade and fold it in two equal lengths. Loop it around bottom wood strip and tie with a square knot; then loop it around the next strip and tie, and so on to the top of the shade.

WINDOWSILL

Cracked. If cracks are large and/or go all the way through the sill, drive long galvanized finishing nails through the edge of the sill to close the cracks as much as possible. Scrape the cracks open a little and fill with plastic wood or water putty. Apply a couple of coats of alkyd trim enamel.

Rotten. Dig out rotten areas and saturate wood with pentachlorophenol wood preservative. Let dry for 24 hours. Then fill holes with plastic wood or water putty, and paint.

Disintegrating. Clean off old paint. Cut a piece of fiber glass to cover entire surface. Work polyester resin into it, brush additional resin on sill, and smooth down fiber glass. See FIBER GLASS, RIGID (*breaks in opaque fiber glass*).

WINDOW, SLIDING

Window sticks. Check whether it is painted shut. Run point of sharp knife around edge of sash to break paint film. Rub tracks with paraffin or beeswax or spray them with dry lubricant. Clean tracks every few months.

Leaks at top or sides of window frame. See WINDOW, DOUBLE-HUNG.

WOOD

Finish marred. See LACQUERED SURFACE, PAINTED SURFACE, SHELLACKED SURFACE, VARNISHED SURFACE, as case may be.

Burns, dents. See FURNITURE, WOOD.

Holes in painted wood. If there is backing behind the wood (as in house siding, for example), brush paint into hole and let dry. Then fill with spackle. If there is not backing behind the wood (as in a box), tack a scrap of thin aluminum behind hole and fill with spackle. For a neater repair, cut the hole to a geometrical shape with a coping saw. Be sure sides of hole are straight. Then cut a plug of wood to fit, and glue it into the hole with white or resorcinol glue.

Holes in stained wood. Treat as above, but use plastic wood instead of spackle. Mix the wood with stain before applying it: it will not take stain when dry.

Gouges in painted wood. If the gouge has paint in it, fill with spackle, sand smooth when dry, and apply paint. If gouge does not have paint in it, brush paint on the bare wood and let dry before filling.

Gouges in stained wood. Mix matching stain into plastic wood, smooth into gouge, and sand when dry. Stick shellac can be used as an alternate filler (see FURNITURE, WOOD). For a neater repair, whittle a strip of matching wood to fit in the hole. Soak it in stain matching the damaged wood and let dry for 24 hours. Then glue it into gouge with white glue. Let excess glue fill cracks around the patch. When glue dries, sand the patch smooth.

Wood split. Coat edges of split with white or resorcinol glue and clamp together. If necessary, reinforce with nails, screws, or wiggle nails.

If wood siding is split and edges cannot

be brought together, coat the edges with linseed oil and then fill split with putty.

Wood rotting. If rot is widespread, wood should be replaced. But if rot is just setting in, dig out the soft wood with a knife and gouge. Saturate surfaces with pentachlorophenol wood preservative (zinc or copper naphthanate can also be used). Let dry for about 48 hours. Then fill holes with plastic wood or water putty.

Rotten wood can also be treated with Git-Rot, available in marine supplies outlets, but the material is expensive.

Knots loose. Either remove knot and fill hole with spackle or push knot out, coat edges with glue, and reset in the hole.

Wood warped. See FURNITURE—TABLE (*top or leaf warped*).

Joints in wood loose, broken. Rejoin with white or resorcinol glue and/or metal fasteners.

Wood separated from another material. Refasten with screws or bolts. Or use appropriate glue (see HOUSEHOLD DECORATIVE ACCESSORIES).

Sawed edges rough, soak up paint. Wrap sandpaper around a block of wood and sand edges as smooth as possible. Roughness that remains can be eliminated by brushing with several coats of paste filler or white glue.

Stains. These are very difficult to remove because of the absorbency of wood. First try wiping off the stain with paint thinner, turpentine, or benzine. Then sand. If this doesn't work, bleach the spot with a commercial bleach according to manufacturer's directions; or use a solution of ½ cup oxalic acid crystals in 1 quart water. Keep swabbing this on the stains until the proper color returns. Then neutralize the bleached area with 1 cup borax dissolved in 1 quart hot water. When wood is thoroughly dry, sand smooth to eliminate the raised grain.

WOOD BOWL

Worn, marred. Scrub thoroughly with detergent solution and let dry completely. Fill gouges with plastic wood after sanding them. Then sand entire bowl to obliterate scratches and general roughness.

Cracked. If bowl is not used for salad, force epoxy glue into crack from both sides. If bowl is used for salad (in which case wood may be too oil-soaked for glue to adhere), cut out crack in a V on the inside of the bowl and pack in plastic wood. Smooth down firmly and sand well when dry. Then force epoxy glue into crack from the outside.

NOTE. Salad bowls are rarely painted on the inside, but plastic wood mars the appearance to such an extent that you may want to paint a bowl that has been patched. If so, the wood must be scrubbed and soaked in warm detergent solution to remove as much of the oil as possible. For the toughest possible paint finish, brush on epoxy primer followed by one or two coats of epoxy enamel.

WORLD GLOBE

Split at seam. If globe is made of cardboard, coat edges with white glue and press together. Reinforce with cellophane tape if necessary. If globe is metal, bring halves together and put tiny dabs of epoxy glue across the joint at three or four points.

WRENCH, PIPE

Teeth dull, rounded. Clamp wrench in a vise and deepen grooves and sharpen teeth with a small triangular metal file.

WROUGHT IRON

Joint separated. Try soldering (see BASIC METHODS: HOW TO SOLDER METAL) but it is better to have the joint welded.

Pitted. Clean pits with steel wool and smooth in epoxy mender.

Rusted. Clean with a wire brush, steel wool, and liquid rust-remover. Apply a red lead primer and finish paint.

ZIPPER

Slider on metal zipper sticks. Rub zipper with a candle or paraffin.

Slider on metal zipper separated from one toothed edge. Open stitches at base of zipper, slide slider down below toothed edge, and then pull it back up.

Metal zipper jammed. Repair with a zipper repair kit from a variety store. The type made by Penn Products Company is especially easy to use. Remove old slider and install new one in kit. Follow directions on package.

Teeth missing from metal zipper. A few isolated missing teeth usually don't make much difference. But if several in a row are gone, replace entire zipper.

Slider comes off nylon zipper. Open stitches at base of zipper. Pry off the small metal stop at lower end of toothed edges. Slip slider up over ribbed edges of zipper binding. Make sure teeth are aligned. Then pull slider up to top of zipper. Replace metal stop, if possible; otherwise stitch across end of toothed edges several times.

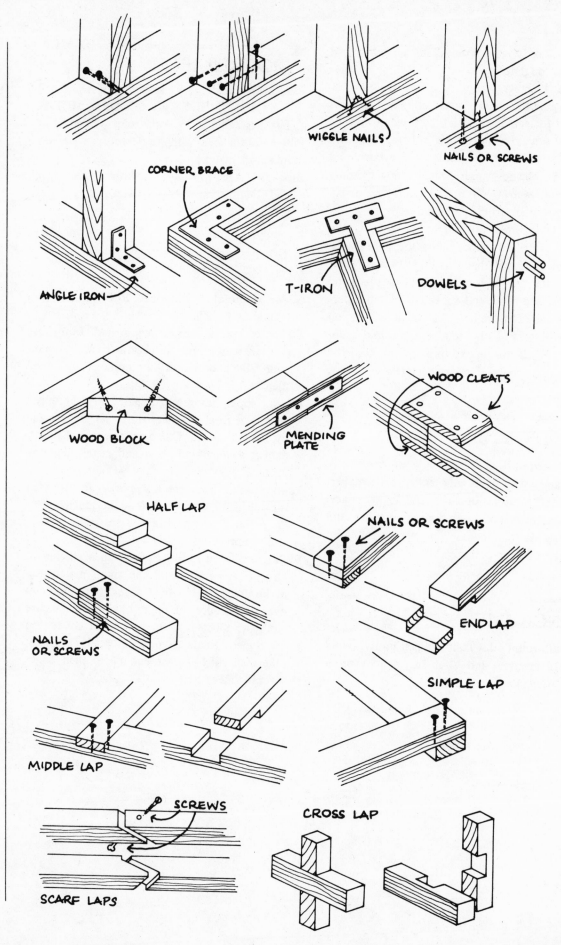

WIGGLE NAILS

NAILS OR SCREWS

CORNER BRACE

ANGLE IRON

T-IRON

DOWELS

WOOD BLOCK

MENDING PLATE

WOOD CLEATS

HALF LAP

NAILS OR SCREWS

NAILS OR SCREWS

END LAP

MIDDLE LAP

SIMPLE LAP

SCREWS

SCARF LAPS

CROSS LAP

Section 2/Basic Methods

HOW TO FASTEN WOOD WITH NAILS, SCREWS, AND OTHER METAL FASTENERS

Nails are the easiest fasteners to use. Common nails with large flat heads are for rough work. Box nails also have large heads but are thinner and help to prevent splitting of wood. Finishing nails have small heads that are easily countersunk below the surface of the wood.

In addition to these basic nails, there are a number of others with greater holding power. Some are coated with rosin or cement; some have spiral shanks; some have annular-ring (ring-grooved) shanks. These are used as noted in the mending section.

The worst drawback of nails is that they tend to split the wood into which they are driven. This can be prevented to some extent by blunting the points with a hammer. A much more reliable method—especially when nailing in oak or yellow pine—is to drill holes slightly smaller than the nails almost through the wood.

Screws. A screwed joint is stronger than a nailed joint and can be easily taken apart. To facilitate driving a screw, drill a hole for it first. Use flathead screws if you want the head to be flush with the surrounding surface. (In hard wood it is usually necessary to drill a shallow hole into which the screw head can be countersunk, but in soft wood the head usually countersinks itself as you turn the screwdriver.) Oval-head screws project slightly above the surface, while round-head screws are entirely exposed.

Bolts are used mainly for joining metal but may be used in wood in cases where nails or screws won't hold or if the joined wood is frequently disassembled and reassembled. To use bolts, drill a hole the size of the shank all the way through the wood. Before screwing on the nut, insert a flat metal washer to protect the wood and then a lock washer to prevent loosening of the nut.

Wiggle nails, also known as corrugated fasteners, are used for joints that are subject to little strain. Hammer them into wood slowly, with light taps; and to avoid splitting the wood, do not run them parallel with the grain.

Skotch fasteners are a substitute for wiggle nails. They are not as strong but are easier to use and less likely to split the wood.

Flat metal mending plates are known by a number of names depending on the design. Screwed to the wood, they make a strong joint but add nothing to its attractiveness.

Joints. Many of the joints used by professionals are difficult to make. But there are plenty of others that you can handle. Their strength varies as noted below. But the use of glue in addition to metal fasteners will make even the weakest sturdy.

Butt joints are among the easiest to make but are not very strong. The end of the piece to be butted must be cut off perfectly square. Joining is done in the ways shown.

Lapped joints are another easy-to-make type. The simple laps, however, are not likely to hold too well because they depend for strength entirely on the screws or nails driven through the two pieces. Laps in which part of the wood is cut away are much stronger.

Miter joints can be made accurately only if you have a miter box that controls the angle of the cuts. Such joints are usually held together with glue and a single nail but can be strengthened in the ways shown.

The dado joint is made with saw and chisel. Even without special fasteners it is considerably stronger than most butt joints.

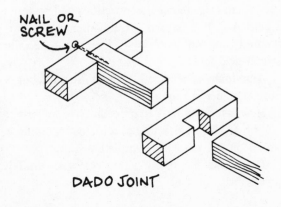

NAIL OR SCREW

DADO JOINT

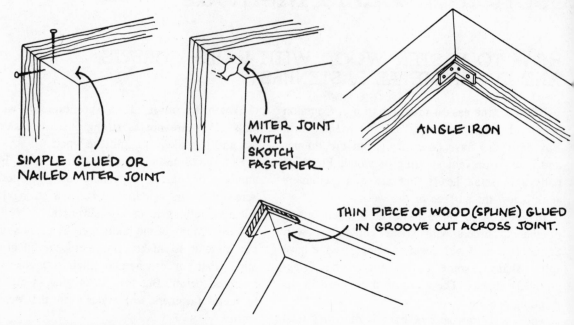

SIMPLE GLUED OR NAILED MITER JOINT

MITER JOINT WITH SKOTCH FASTENER

ANGLE IRON

THIN PIECE OF WOOD (SPLINE) GLUED IN GROOVE CUT ACROSS JOINT.

HOW TO SOLDER METAL

Soldering is an easy way to mend metals permanently. Small soldering jobs are best done with an electric soldering iron of the conventional type or of the faster gun type. Large jobs are done with a propane torch. The tips of soldering irons must be kept smooth, clean, and tinned (coated with a thin layer of solder). Torch tips must also be kept clean and undamaged if they are to give a steady blue flame of the proper size and shape.

Solder is a mixture of tin and lead. It is available in the form of wire, bars, or paste. Wire solder may be solid solder or contain a core of acid or rosin flux. Bar solder is solid. Paste solder comes mixed with acid flux.

Whenever solid solder is used, a flux which cleans the metal must first be applied to the metal. This is available as a liquid or paste. Rosin flux is used in making electrical connections and on terne metal. Acid flux is used for all other work. Galvanized iron and stainless steel require especially strong acid fluxes.

Aluminum is soldered without fluxing, but a special solder is required.

Here is the step-by-step procedure for soldering:

(1) If the object to be soldered contains a liquid or gas, empty it completely.

(2) Clean the metal with steel wool until it shines brightly.

(3) Apply flux to the cleaned surface if the solder does not contain flux.

(4) Heat the metal until it is hot enough to melt the solder applied to it. Except in the case of lead and pewter, the solder should always be melted by the metal being soldered—not by the soldering iron or torch. If the metal is not heated sufficiently, the melted solder looks dull, granular, and rough. It should flow and form a smooth, bright film.

(5) To join two pieces of metal (except in plumbing work), it is advisable to tin (flow a film of solder on) each piece separately. Then place tinned surface to tinned surface and apply heat until the solder melts. Remove heat and hold the metal pieces together with a screwdriver, pliers, etc., until the solder hardens.

(6) To solder copper pipe into a plumbing fitting, clean both pipe and fitting and brush on an acid flux. Insert pipe into fitting and apply heat to the joint. Then touch solid solder to the joint. It will be drawn by capillarity into the joint and seal it.

(7) When acid flux is used, wash off the residue thoroughly with water after the metal has cooled.

HOW TO FASTEN METAL WITH BOLTS, RIVETS, ETC.

In addition to joining pieces of metal by soldering and, to a very limited extent, by gluing, you can often do the job with the following metal fasteners:

Bolts. The most commonly used types are machine bolts, which have square or hexagonal heads that are gripped with a wrench, and stove bolts, which have rounded, slotted heads for a screwdriver. To use bolts, drill holes just slightly larger than the threaded shank. Slip on lock washers before screwing on the nuts.

Self-tapping screws are threaded right up to the head. They are used primarily to join thin sheets of metal which are exposed only on one side (for example, the back of an automatic washing machine is attached to the side flanges with self-tapping screws). To use the screws, first drill holes slightly smaller than the widest diameter of the screw threads. Then just screw into place.

Rivets. Steel, copper, and aluminum rivets are available at hardware stores in various sizes. They are used to make neat, unobtrusive, permanent joints. To use, drill through the pieces of metal to be joined a hole the size of the rivet shank. Insert the rivet and place it head down on a hard metal surface. Clip off all but about ⅛ inch of the exposed shank. Then hammer down the shank with light blows so that it overlaps the hole. Do not hammer so hard that the rivet is completely flattened. It should have a rounded contour.

Cotter pins are used to hold together metal pieces which may be frequently disassembled or which move. The hole for the pin should be just slightly larger than the shank. Insert the pin and bend the two halves of the shank in opposite directions.

HOW TO GLUE THINGS TOGETHER

The glues described here are just a few of the many on the market, but with one exception, all are easy to use and have superior holding power. Most are available in hardware stores as well as large building supplies outlets.

Cyanoacrylate glue. This is a new adhesive which has been highly touted as a superglue for use on nonporous materials such as metal, glass, ceramics, plastics, vinyl, and rubber. But I have found it produces a very poor bond and include it for only two reasons:

(1) It sets in an incredibly short time and is therefore useful for making repairs when time is of the essence.

(2) Because it is as thin and clear as water, it makes an almost invisible joint and is therefore valuable for mending china, earthenware, glass, etc., that is used for decorative or display purposes only.

Apply to only one of the surfaces being bonded. Use sparingly—about 1 drop per square inch. Bring surfaces together and hold for about 30 seconds. The article can then be handled, although the glue does not achieve full strength for about 12 hours. Take care not to get the glue on your skin, because you can stick yourself together as easily as you can glue china.

Cellulose cement. This is an excellent glue for china, glass, phenolic plastics, and other nonporous materials, and can also be used on wood, leather, and paper. It makes a slightly neater joint than epoxy glue but cannot withstand much contact with water and breaks down under heat. To use on nonporous materials, spread a thin coat on both surfaces and clamp together for about 24 hours. On porous materials, apply a thin coat to both surfaces and let dry. Then apply a second coat and press pieces together.

Epoxy glue. Epoxy is the strongest adhesive in general use. It is outstanding for bonding all nonporous articles and is also excellent for wood (but is usually used on wood only to make very difficult mends—for example, fixing a chair rung that is broken almost straight across). It is so impervious to moisture and heat that, even after boiling a piece of mended china for 15 minutes, I could not break the bond.

Epoxy is packaged in several formulations—for general use on rigid materials, as well as for special uses on flexible materials, boats, etc.

Epoxy is also the base of a number of thick, filler-type adhesives such as epoxy mender and plastic steel.

The best epoxy glue is a so-called two-part adhesive that is packaged in two tubes or sometimes two cans. To use, squeeze out equal parts of part 1 and part 2 on a piece of wax paper, aluminum sheet, etc., and mix thoroughly to a uniform color. Apply a thin coat to one surface, and press the pieces together for about 6 hours. Clamping is not essential but makes for a neater joint.

NOTE: Do not mix part 1 of one brand with part 2 of another brand, or vice versa.

Fabric glue. Sold in variety and notion stores, this is a white glue which is used on fabrics, leather, and leatherette. It is water- and heat-resistant but is dissolved by dry cleaning and cleaning fluids. Squeeze a small amount into a saucer and spread a thin layer on one surface. Then smooth the pieces together and let dry. Excess glue can be rubbed off when dry. Stubborn spots are removed with trichloroethylene.

Plastic-mending adhesive. This is a clear, waterproof glue which can be used to bond most plastics and also to stick plastics to wood. Spread a thin coat on both surfaces and clamp them together for 24 hours. If bonding plastic to wood, apply two coats to the wood. Let the first dry before applying the second.

To use plastic-mending adhesive on polyethylene, lightly brush the surfaces to be joined with a flame, as from a propane torch. Don't melt the surface, just oxidize it. After flaming, apply a drop of water to the surfaces. If this spreads, the polyethylene is ready to be glued. If it doesn't spread, heat the surfaces further.

Resorcinol glue. This is the best adhesive for gluing wood that is exposed to moisture. It consists of a red liquid and a powder which are mixed together just before application. Allow to dry for 24 hours. The red stain that remains can be removed by sanding or can be concealed with paint.

Rubber cement. The rubber cement used in offices is generally suitable only for gluing paper but can be used in a pinch on other materials. Rubber cement for general repairs is considerably stronger. Use it for bonding flexible materials to

both flexible and rigid materials. You can also use it for filling small holes.

Apply to both surfaces to be joined and let it set for about 5 minutes. Then smooth the pieces together firmly and allow the adhesive to dry for about an hour.

Silicone-rubber adhesive. Silicone is a thick, rubbery mastic smelling like vinegar. It is used on nonporous materials as well as on leather and paper. Although its bond strength is not exceptional, it is completely resistant to water. Unlike other adhesives, it can glue together materials with nonconforming surfaces; in fact, it can bridge gaps of up to about ¾ inch. It comes in clear, white, gray, and black. Paint does not adhere to most types.

Smear the glue on one surface and press the pieces together for 24 hours. The excess should be removed immediately with a paper towel, since it is difficult to get up after it has set.

Silicone-rubber adhesive is the same as silicone caulking.

Vinyl cement. This is a clear adhesive for bonding vinyl and leather to themselves or to other materials. It produces a strong, water-resistant bond. When used on vinyl, roughen the surfaces slightly with sandpaper. Apply to one surface and press the pieces together for 12 hours.

White glue. More properly called polyvinyl-acetate or PVA glue, white glue is a fairly thin, white liquid which dries colorless. Although only moderately strong, it is the most widely used adhesive for sticking wood to wood, and can also be used on paper, fabrics, and other porous materials. But it should not be used on articles that are exposed to dampness. To use, simply apply to one surface and clamp the pieces together for 24 hours.

The rules for using glue are generally similar, no matter which one you are working with:

(1) Scrape off old glue from the article to be mended.

(2) Remove dirt, dust, oil, etc., from the surfaces.

(3) Sand or plane wood surfaces smooth.

(4) Apply glue in thin coats and spread it over the entire area.

(5) If a patch is to be applied, round the corners of the patch slightly. They are not so likely to come loose as square corners.

(6) Align surfaces to be glued and press together. In most cases, clamping is then required. Several types of small clamps are illustrated, and other larger or specialized clamps are available. Generally C-clamps are used because they are easy to handle and apply strong pressure. To protect the surfaces of the thing you are gluing, place strips of wood under the jaws of the clamp. The strips also help to spread the pressure.

In cases where clamps are unusable, use tourniquets or weights. Broken edges of fragile objects can be held together with strips of masking or adhesive tape.

(7) To prevent glue that squeezes out from a joint from sticking to an adjacent surface, wipe off as much as possible; then lay wax paper between the glued surface and the one you have to protect.

(8) If you try to glue a tight-fitting dowel or chair rung into a hole, the glue collects at the bottom of the hole and prevents the dowel from being inserted all the way. To solve this problem, flatten the dowel slightly on one side with a knife, file, or plane. This permits the excess glue to be squeezed out of the hole as the dowel is driven in.

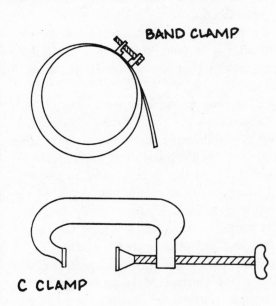

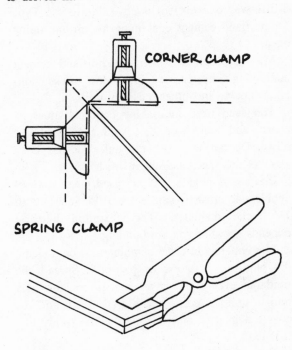

HOW TO MIX AND HANDLE CONCRETE

If you are trying to save work (but not money), the best concrete to buy is that delivered ready-to-pour in a cement truck. Next best are the ready-mixes to which you simply add water or, in some cases, liquid latex or epoxy.

Unlike ready-to-pour concrete, which is sold only by the full or (sometimes) partial truckload, the ready-mixes come in relatively small packages and are consequently best suited to small jobs. Conventional ready-mixes made with portland cement are formulated for various purposes such as pouring a sidewalk or building a brick wall.

Other ready-mixes are put up in even smaller packages. These include latex, epoxy, vinyl and acrylic cements, which are used for patching and for leveling uneven surfaces (unlike convenient cements, they can be troweled to an edge only $\frac{1}{16}$ inch thick). Another specialized ready-mix is hydraulic cement, which is used to stop active leaks in basement walls and floors.

If you mix your own concrete, it is important to measure accurately to the proportions given in the mending section. All measurements, unless otherwise stated, are made by volume, not by weight. For this reason, people who do a lot of concrete work usually build a measuring box holding exactly 1 cubic foot. One sack of portland cement also holds exactly 1 cubic foot.

The cement, sand, coarse aggregate, and water used in mixing concrete must be clean and free of vegetable matter and dust. Cement is usable as long as it can be crumbled in the hand easily. If lumpy, screen it.

Ordinary gray or white Type I portland cement can be used for all pouring and forming projects. But in cases where the concrete will be exposed to freezing and thawing or to salt action (as on a driveway or walk), it is advisable to use Type IA portland cement containing an air-entraining agent.

Masonry cement, which is a portland cement containing lime, is used for laying bricks, concrete blocks, and other masonry units.

The sand used in making concrete must be coarse and sharp—not fine stuff that is almost dusty. Do not use sea sand unless it has been washed and washed again in fresh water.

Coarse aggregate, when used, consists of pebbles or crushed stones from ¼ inch up to 1½ inches diameter. (The maximum diameter depends on what you are building.)

Mix concrete in clean containers or on a clean, flat platform of wood or plywood. Spread the sand out evenly and cover it with cement. Mix until a uniform color is achieved. Then add the coarse aggregate and mix until it is evenly distributed.

Form a hollow in the center of the mix and add water slowly, mixing all the time with a hoe or spade. The batch should be uniformly damp—smooth, plastic, and sticky when you work it with a trowel. It should not be runny or crumbly.

The mortar should be used within 45 minutes. Do not add water if it begins to stiffen. (On the other hand, mortar made with masonry cement is usable for about 2 hours, and can be re-tempered with a little water.)

If placing concrete in forms, make sure the forms are built of strong wood or plywood and are firmly braced so they will not bulge or collapse under the weight of the concrete. Coat the forms thoroughly with automobile oil or grease.

Pack the concrete thoroughly into the form to eliminate air pockets. Slice into it with a spade, trowel, or mason's trowel and then press down and smooth off.

If a rough surface is desired, finish the concrete after it is quite stiff with a wood float. For a smooth (but less wearable) finish, use a steel trowel.

Just as soon as the concrete is hard enough so you can press it without leaving a thumbprint, sprinkle it with water and cover it with damp burlap or straw. Keep this damp and in place for at least 7 days so the concrete can cure properly.

If concrete is to be colored, use dry powdered pigments made for the purpose. Mix these with white portland cement before adding the cement to the sand and other ingredients. The amount of pigment should not exceed 10 percent of the weight of the concrete. Make up sample batches of concrete to determine exactly how much pigment to use.

Although concrete can be used in freezing weather, the work requires so much attention that it is best delayed until the temperature is higher. Pouring concrete in very hot weather also requires special attention.

HOW TO MAKE BASIC SEWING STITCHES

Back stitch. This is the strongest hand stitch. Make a short, straight stitch through the fabric, double back, and start the second stitch in the middle of the first. The stitches underneath are ⅛-inch to ¼-inch long; those on top, made by doubling back, are half that length.

Basting stitch. This is a temporary stitch used to hold fabric in position until permanent stitches are put in. The stitches are ¼-inch to ½-inch long; they do not have to be even.

Blanket stitch. This is a decorative stitch used for making thread loops and edging heavy materials. Hold the thread at the left. Take a stitch upward through the fabric, then bring the thread down through the thread you are holding; take another stitch upward and down through the thread, etc.

Chain stitch. This is a decorative stitch. Insert needle from the reverse side of fabric, form a loop and hold it, stick needle back through fabric at the starting point; bring needle out through fabric and through the bottom end of the loop; form another loop, etc.

Diagonal basting. This is slightly stronger than the ordinary basting stitch and is sometimes left in permanently. It is particularly useful when you are working with slippery material. The diagonal stitches are made on top of the material and may be up to 4 inches long. The short stitches are underneath and are up to ¾ inch long.

Herringbone stitch. This is primarily a decorative stitch but has strength and is used for mending sails. Starting at your left, make a slanting stitch upward; then on the reverse side of the fabric

make a short stitch backward; then make a slanting stitch downward across the first stitch; then make a short stitch backward and make another slanting stitch upward.

Overcasting. This stitch is used to prevent raveling of fabric edges. The stitches loop diagonally around the edge and extend about ¼ inch into the fabric. Do not pull the thread up tight or you may pucker the material.

Running stitch. Most common of all permanent stitches, this is best made by running the needle through the fabric several times, pulling the needle through, then repeating. The shorter the stitches the better.

Whipping. This is similar to overcasting but the stitches are not so deep. The purpose is to hold down a fabric edge that has been turned under.

Zigzag stitch. This is a strong, decorative stitch used for applying lace, appliqué work, etc. Each stitch goes at an angle to the one before it. Zigzagging is best done on the sewing machine with a zigzagger.

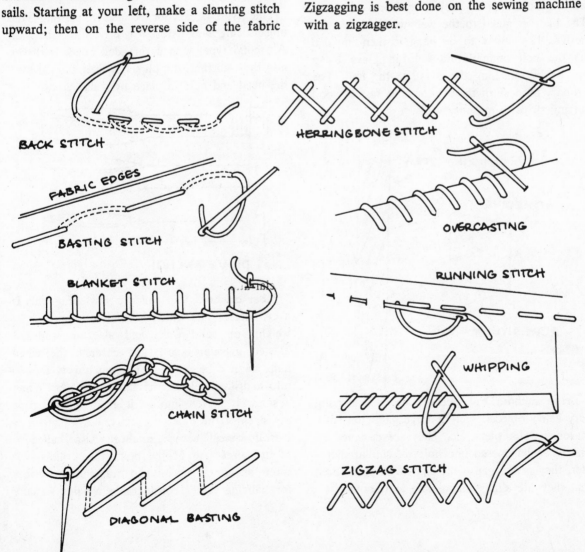

BACK STITCH

FABRIC EDGES

BASTING STITCH

BLANKET STITCH

CHAIN STITCH

DIAGONAL BASTING

HERRINGBONE STITCH

OVERCASTING

RUNNING STITCH

WHIPPING

ZIGZAG STITCH

HOW TO SUPPORT THINGS ON WALLS THAT WILL NOT RECEIVE OR HOLD NAILS AND SCREWS

Hanging things on difficult walls usually presents no problems if you know which fasteners to use. The following are sold in almost all hardware and building supplies stores. Most are available in a range of sizes.

A anchor. This new anchor gets its name from the fact that the short plastic sleeve into which a screw is driven expands to an A shape. It is mainly useful for supporting moderate weights on hollow-core flush doors and similar thin-surfaced walls with very shallow hollows. To use the anchor, drill a hole of similar diameter, tap the anchor in flush with the wall surface, then drive in the screw that comes with the anchor. This pushes the anchor through the wall and flattens it against the inside wall surface.

Adhesive anchor. This old but rarely used device consists of a large, perforated metal plate with a bolt or nail projecting from one side. The plate is glued to the wall with silicone adhesive. The object to be hung is then impaled on the bolt or nail and held in place by a nut or by clinching the point of the nail. The primary purpose of the anchor is to fasten wood furring strips to masonry walls.

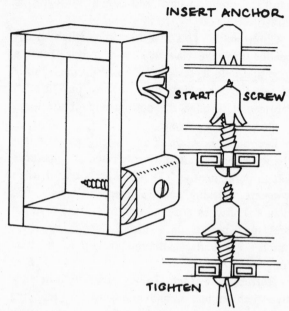

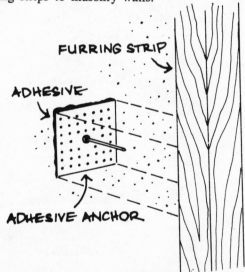

Drive anchor. Drive anchors are used to hang very heavy objects, such as large gates, on solid masonry walls, piers, etc. They are designed so that when hammered into holes of similar diameter, they press against the sides with such force that they are almost impossible to remove.

One type of anchor is inserted through the object being hung before it is driven into the wall. A second type, with a threaded head, is driven into the wall first; the object is then slipped over the head and held in place by a nut.

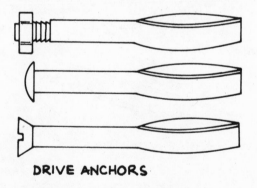

DRIVE ANCHORS

Fiber anchor. Also called a rawl plug, this is a cylinder of jute which is used to support light weights on solid walls and also on walls of plaster, gypsum board, and ceramic tile when nails cannot be trusted. The anchor is tapped into a drilled hole of the same diameter. When a screw is driven into it, it expands and grips the sides of the hole.

Hollow-wall screw anchor. Also called a Molly screw or Molly bolt, the hollow-wall screw anchor is one of two outstanding devices for hanging rather considerable weights on any thick hollow wall. It consists of a long slender bolt and metal sleeve.

Drill a hole through the wall the same size as the sleeve. Insert the bolt through the object you are hanging and then through the sleeve. Push the sleeve through the wall and tighten the bolt. As you do so, the sleeve collapses and grips the inside surface of the wall.

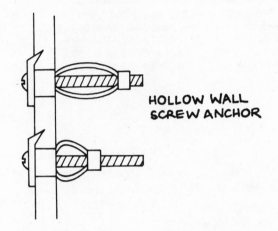

HOLLOW WALL SCREW ANCHOR

A less common type of screw anchor has a sharp point, so it can be hammered through a soft wall surface without drilling.

Lead anchor. Also called a lead shield, this cylinder of lead is usually the first choice for supporting heavy weights on solid masonry walls because, although not as reliable as a drive bolt or machine-screw anchor, it costs a little less and is easier to use. The anchor is installed like a fiber anchor. Simply drill a hole of the same diameter in the wall, tap in the anchor, and then drive in a screw until the sides of the anchor grip the sides of the hole. Be sure to use a screw of the size specified for the anchor.

LEAD ANCHOR

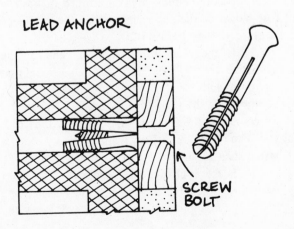

SCREW BOLT

Machine-screw anchor. Machine-screw anchors are used to support very heavy weights on solid masonry walls. They are made in several ways, but the operation is the same in all cases. A boltlike machine screw is inserted in a metal sleeve and, as it is tightened, it jams the sleeve against the sides of the hole in which it is inserted. Unlike a drive anchor, it can easily be removed.

MACHINE-SCREW ANCHOR

In using a machine-screw anchor, you must take care:

(1) to buy a machine screw that is exactly sized for the anchor and

(2) to drill a hole the exact diameter and length of the anchor.

Masonry nail. The quickest way to fasten things to a masonry wall is to hammer in a masonry nail, but the strength of the nail cannot always be trusted. The best masonry nails have thick, spiral-grooved shanks which can be driven into poured concrete. Cut nails with flat, tapered shanks should be used only in softer masonry and mortar joints.

Nylon anchor. This is the closest thing to an all-purpose fastener but is not widely available. It is a cylindrical device which is inserted in a drilled hole. A screw or screwlike nail is then driven into it.

Although nylon anchors will support only moderate weights, they can be used in both solid and hollow walls. They even hold in very thin surfaces such as ¼-inch hardboard.

Plastic anchor. Plastic anchors are similar to fiber anchors and are used interchangeably with them.

Stud. This is a naillike fastener made of heat-treated steel which is driven into solid masonry either with a special hammer-actuated stud driver or with gunpowder in a pistol. The principal advantage of the device is that no hole must be drilled for it; consequently, it can be installed very rapidly. It is used primarily for attaching wood furring strips to basement and other masonry walls.

Toggle bolt. This is the other outstanding device for hanging heavy things on thick, hollow

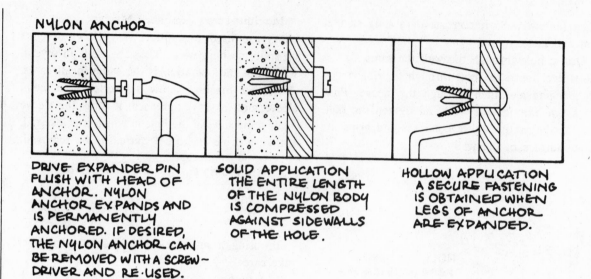

NYLON ANCHOR

DRIVE EXPANDER PIN FLUSH WITH HEAD OF ANCHOR. NYLON ANCHOR EXPANDS AND IS PERMANENTLY ANCHORED. IF DESIRED, THE NYLON ANCHOR CAN BE REMOVED WITH A SCREW-DRIVER AND RE·USED.

SOLID APPLICATION THE ENTIRE LENGTH OF THE NYLON BODY IS COMPRESSED AGAINST SIDEWALLS OF THE HOLE.

HOLLOW APPLICATION A SECURE FASTENING IS OBTAINED WHEN LEGS OF ANCHOR ARE EXPANDED.

walls. The most common type, known as a spring-wing toggle bolt, consists of a long, slender bolt and a nut with two wire wings that automatically spring open when inside a wall.

To use, drill a hole the same size as the winged nut when closed. Insert a bolt through the object being hung; screw the nut on partway, push the nut through the wall, and pull it back so the open wings bear against the inner surface of the wall. Then screw the bolt tight.

Toggle bolts and hollow-wall screw anchors are pretty much interchangeable. The bolts come in more and longer lengths. On the other hand, they require a larger drilled hole which is sometimes hard to conceal. And if you ever unscrew the bolt, the nut falls down inside the wall and is lost forever.

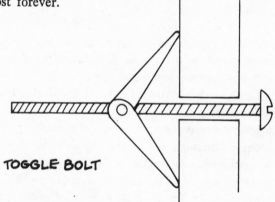

TOGGLE BOLT

HOW TO CHECK OUT ELECTRICAL APPLIANCES

Electrical appliances are pretty complicated gadgets and difficult to repair. They are also hazardous to repair because you may either get a shock in the process or cause a fire later.

Nevertheless, before you rush out for a serviceman, there are several obvious checks to make:

(1) Is the appliance plugged in and turned on? It's surprising how often people call a serviceman without determining this.

(2) Are the prongs on the end of the cord plug loose in the outlet? Bend them outward slightly and try plugging in again.

(3) Is the outlet into which the appliance is plugged operative? To check this, simply plug a light into it. If the light doesn't go on, the outlet may need to be replaced (see ELECTRIC OUTLET).

(4) Has the circuit breaker tripped or has the fuse blown on the circuit into which the appliance is plugged? See FUSE BOX.

(5) Is the plug loose from the end of the appliance cord? Disconnect and make sure that the bare ends of the wires are screwed down tightly inside the plug (see ELECTRIC CORD). Of course, if the plug is molded on to the cord, you can't do this. But trouble rarely occurs inside such a plug.

(6) Is the appliance cord broken? If the cord is of the detachable type, substitute another one for it. If the appliance then works, you know the

original cord is defective. If the cord is not detachable, unplug it from the wall outlet and examine it carefully. If you find a break, either make the necessary repairs or replace the cord entirely (see ELECTRIC CORD).

(7) Is a built-in type of cord disconnected from the terminals in the appliance? Sometimes it is easy to open up the appliance and check this; more often it is not.

If the appliance still doesn't work after you have taken these steps, it is now advisable to call in a serviceman or take the appliance to him. But if you feel like exploring further, be sure to disconnect the appliance before you proceed.

There are several other things you should know about electrical appliances:

Many minor troubles can be prevented or corrected if you have the instruction books that come with all appliances. Never throw these away. Keep them together in some convenient place.

Keep appliances clean and free of dust. They will work a lot better.

Don't oil appliance motors unless the manufacturers recommend it. Follow their directions exactly.

If an appliance doesn't run at what you think should be the right speed or if it doesn't heat properly, your house wiring may not be adequate. But sometimes the slowdown occurs because there is a voltage drop in the utility's power lines and you are not getting the normal amount of power. (In this case it usually doesn't continue for long.) Both conditions should be checked out by an electrical contractor.

HOW TO PAINT

Removing old finish. Of course it is not always necessary to do this. On the other hand, it is necessary if you want to replace a paint finish with a natural finish, if the old finish is badly scarred or eroding, if the old finish is too thick, or if the old finish is of a type which cannot be covered.

First, scrape off as much of the finish as you can with a putty knife, paint scraper, and pocketknife. Don't work too hard at this; just take off the loose film.

Don't burn off the remaining finish with a torch. It's too dangerous. Electric removers are safer, although even they can cause the paint film to flame up. They are especially useful in removing paint on siding and exterior trim. Just move the tool slowly over the surface and strip off the paint with a putty knife after it.

Liquid removers are best in most jobs. The water wash-away type is preferred by many people because, after it softens the finish, you just remove the sludge with a wet cloth. But I have found this type less effective than the others. I prefer the nonflammable benzol type. In any case, the paste removers are easiest to use on vertical surfaces and work as well as the thin liquids on horizontal surfaces.

When using paint remover, always work in a well-ventilated place. Wear gloves. It's advisable also to wear goggles.

Follow manufacturer's directions. Flow on the remover with an old paintbrush and don't brush back over it. Let stand for 15 minutes or so until finish is soft. Make a test scraping. If finish comes up easily, strip down the entire surface. On stubborn areas, apply more paint remover. Do the scraping with a putty knife, paint scraper, or pocketknife. If the old finish is thin and the surfaces are contoured, use coarse rags, steel wool, and a toothbrush. Complete the job by washing the surface with paint thinner or water.

While paint removers are useful for most jobs, there are better methods for others:

Whitewash and calcimine come off with warm water. Casein paint comes off with warm water to which household ammonia is added.

Floor finishes should be removed by sanding with electric floor sanders.

On ornamental metal use simply a scraper, knife, stiff wire brush, rasp, or cold chisel. These won't remove all the paint, but liquid removers are too time-consuming.

Penetrating stains can be removed only by sanding, planing, or bleaching with a commercial bleach.

Preparing surfaces. When the old finish is

removed, fill imperfections in the wood. Then smooth the entire surface with sandpaper.

If old finish does not have to be removed (as on a wall), wash the surface with a mild solution of washing soda or household detergent, then rinse with clear water. Fill holes and cracks with spackle, plastic wood, etc. (for the appropriate filler for a given material, see individual entries in front section). When this is dry, sand smooth. Then, if spackle or patching plaster were used, prime the patches with paint. Prime knots in wood with shellac or stain-killer.

If the painted surface is very shiny (a hard gloss enamel, for example), roughen with sandpaper.

Painting tools to use and how to use them. Whether you use a brush, roller, or spray gun (or spray can) depends on the contours of the surface, the area and accessibility, and the finish desired.

A brush is the best all-around painting tool. It can be used to apply any type of paint on any type of surface and to achieve any type of finish. A roller is much faster, but its use is pretty well limited to large surfaces and it leaves a slightly stippled finish; furthermore it is very difficult to clean if used with anything other than water-based paint. A spray gun, when properly used, is extremely fast and leaves an almost perfectly smooth paint surface, but the fine mist it produces is a nuisance. A spray can has similar advantages and disadvantages. I recommend that you use sprayers only for painting intricate surfaces (wicker chairs and shutters, for example), for applying lacquer, and for refinishing kitchen cabinets where an extremely flat finish is desired.

Buy the most expensive brush you can afford. It flows the paint on better, doesn't lose its bristles, lasts longer. If you're starting with a new brush, shake out the loose bristles, then suspend the brush in linseed oil for 12 hours so the paint will not cling so tightly in the bristles. Squeeze out the oil with a stick, and spin the handle between your palms to remove the last drops.

Dip the brush only halfway into the paint and slap off the excess on the inside of the can (don't scrape it across the rim). Apply paint with light, short strokes using only the ends of the bristles. Brush back and forth; then smooth the paint with cross strokes. Then, to eliminate brush marks almost entirely, smooth out again in the direction you started.

Paint should be brushed on. Enamel, varnish, and lacquer are applied with a somewhat fuller brush and flowed on.

Use short-nap rollers for most jobs; long-nap rollers when painting rough surfaces (stucco or concrete, for instance). Do not overload the roller when filling with paint. Start rolling on paint a slight distance from the previously painted area and work toward that. Roll lightly back and forth—in any direction—but finish by rolling all strokes in one direction.

Instead of buying a spray gun, rent one. Tell the dealer what you are going to paint and have him give you the correct nozzle. Mix the paint thoroughly and strain through cheesecloth or wire screening. Thin it according to manufacturer's directions.

Before starting to spray, cover everything that is not to be painted with canvas, newspaper, masking tape. Wear a mask—preferably a respirator—when painting.

Spraying is done with a full arm motion. Hold the gun nozzle 6 inches from the surface and keep it pointed toward it at right angles. Start your stroke before pulling the trigger and release trigger before reaching the end of the stroke. Always keep the gun moving to avoid building up paint in one spot. Generally, it is advisable to spray from side to side, then top to bottom. Overlap spray patterns about one-quarter to one-half.

Painting sequence. If you paint things in logical sequence you will save time, do a better job.

Always start by removing hardware—door knobs, catches, light switch plates, curtain rods, etc. Cover areas you don't want to paint.

• In a room, paint the ceiling first, then the walls, then the woodwork.

• On a ceiling, start in a corner and work across the width of the room (not the length) to the other corner. Then come back to the wall at which you started and paint another strip across the room. Make each strip only as wide as your arm can reach. Work fast so that edges of first strip are still wet when you paint the second strip (otherwise the overlap cannot be smoothed out).

• On a wall, start at the ceiling and paint down to the baseboard. Paint in narrow strips. Don't stop work until entire wall has been painted from corner to corner.

• On a paneled door, paint the edges first, then the panels, then the horizontal rails, and finally the vertical stiles.

• On a window, paint the mullions first, then the frame.

• On the exterior of the house, paint the siding first and then the trim (except when you are painting the peak of a tall house, when it is easier to paint siding and trim at the same time). Follow the sun around the house; don't paint in its hot rays.

• On chairs and tables, paint the bottoms first, then the tops.

• On chests and cabinets, paint from top to bottom—the interior first, then the sides, then the front.

What paint to use where. Many modern paints have excellent coverage and are sold for "one-coat" application. But two coats do a better job. For the first coat, use a primer or undercoater of the type recommended for use with the final finish.

Most paints and clear finishes are easy to apply if you use the right tools and prepare the surface properly. But two present problems.

Lacquer is tricky because it dries so rapidly. It must be flowed on with a full brush in one quick stroke that leaves an even film. Strokes should overlap very little and you shouldn't brush over a covered surface unless the lacquer has sagged. Spraying is easier.

Another problem with lacquer is that it wrecks most other finishes on which it is applied. Therefore, do not use lacquer if you cannot positively identify the original finish as lacquer.

Varnish is somewhat annoying in another way. Because it dries slowly, it picks up dust from the air. In refinishing furniture, therefore, work in a clean, draftless room and, as an extra precaution, it is advisable to hang a tent of newspapers over the piece before you go to work.

SURFACE	PAINT TO USE
Aluminum	Zinc chromate primer followed by any oil-base exterior paint.
Automobiles	Red metal primer followed by auto enamel.
Basement walls	
Masonry	2 coats cementitious coating or exterior latex paint.
Gypsum board	2 coats interior latex paint.
Wood, plywood	For a paint finish, apply alkyd primer followed by alkyd paint. For a clear finish, apply oil stain followed by 2 coats varnish or wax.
Boats	
Bottoms	2 or 3 coats antifouling marine paint.
Topsides, wood decks	Marine undercoater followed by 2 coats marine paint. For a clear finish, 2 or 3 coats spar varnish (if you start with bare wood, apply a marine wood-sealer first).
Canvas decks	2 or 3 coats nonskid deck paint.
Canvas	On awnings, beach umbrellas, and the like, canvas paint.
Ceilings	2 coats latex paint. But use semigloss alkyd paint in kitchen and bathrooms.
Decks, wood	2 coats clear exterior oil stain.
Exterior trim, doors, windows	Alkyd undercoater followed by alkyd trim enamel.

Exterior walls

Wood, plywood — Oil-base primer followed by oil-base house paint. Or 2 coats opaque exterior oil stain. For a clear finish, 2 coats clear exterior oil stain; or 2 coats water repellent.

Masonry — 2 coats exterior latex paint.

Hardboard — Oil-base primer followed by oil-base house paint.

Asbestos-cement — 2 coats exterior latex paint.

Fences

Wood — Oil-base primer followed by oil-base house paint. For a clear finish, 2 coats clear exterior oil stain.

Steel — See Iron.

Floors

Wood — For a clear finish, 2 coats penetrating sealer. For a paint finish, oil-base undercoater followed by 2 coats oil-base deck enamel.

Concrete — Epoxy undercoater followed by 1 or 2 coats epoxy floor enamel.

Furniture — For a clear finish, 1 or 2 coats stain followed by 1 coat white shellac (3-pound cut) followed by 1 coat interior varnish. For a paint finish, alkyd undercoater followed by gloss alkyd enamel.

Furniture, children's — See Toys.

Furniture, outdoor — Alkyd undercoater followed by 1 or 2 coats alkyd trim enamel. For a clear finish (but it won't last very well), 2 coats penetrating wood sealer.

Galvanized iron — Zinc dust primer followed by any oil-base paint.

Interior trim, doors, windows — Alkyd undercoater followed by alkyd interior enamel. For a clear finish, 1 or 2 coats oil stain followed by 1 coat white shellac (3-pound cut) followed by 1 coat interior varnish.

Interior walls

Gypsum board — In kitchens and bathrooms, latex primer followed by 1 or 2 coats alkyd semigloss wall paint. Elsewhere, latex primer followed by 1 or 2 coats interior latex paint.

Plaster — In kitchens and bathrooms, alkyd primer followed by 1 or 2 coats alkyd semigloss wall paint. Elsewhere, 2 coats interior latex paint.

Wood, plywood, hardboard — Alkyd primer followed by 1 or 2 coats alkyd semigloss wall paint. For a clear finish, interior oil stain followed by 1 coat white shellac (3-pound cut) followed by 1 coat interior varnish.

Iron — Red metal primer follower by 1 or 2 coats alkyd gloss enamel (exterior or interior, depending on location of iron).

Machinery — Red metal primer followed by a machine-and-implement enamel.

Pools — Epoxy primer followed by 1 or 2 coats epoxy pool paint.

Radiators — Red metal primer (if radiator is rusted) followed by 2 coats alkyd interior enamel (semigloss or gloss).

Screens — 2 coats spar varnish or 2 coats screen paint.

Steel — See Iron.

Toys — Never use paints containing lead. For a paint finish, alkyd undercoater followed by 1 or 2 coats alkyd interior gloss enamel. For a clear finish, 1 coat oil stain followed by 2 coats interior varnish.

Cleaning up after the job. Remove spatters of water-base paint with water, or other types of paint with paint thinner or turpentine.

Wash brushes and rollers used with water-base paint under a stream of running water. Clean out pan used for roller painting at same time.

Rinse brushes used with other paints in paint thinner, then slosh up and down in paintbrush cleaner. Then wash in a strong solution of heavy-duty household detergent such as Mr. Clean. Rinse, shake dry, and hang up to dry completely.

To revitalize an old brush, soak it in brush cleaner for a couple of days. Work it up and down occasionally and scrape out paint as it loosens with a splinter of wood. As cleaner becomes fouled with the paint, strain it through cheesecloth into another container. Keep soaking brush until bristles are clean. Then wash in strong household detergent.

Clean rims of paint cans with a rag before putting on lids. Don't hammer lids down. Step on them firmly and squarely.

HOW TO CUT GLASS

It costs so little extra to have glass cut for you that I recommend you do it that way. However, if you want to do the job yourself, you can very easily (but only on single-thick glass like that used in small windowpanes).

Wash the sheet of glass with soapy water. Place it on a clean, firm surface. Use a wood yardstick as your straight edge. Hold glass cutter, slots down, between your first and second fingers with your thumb under the handle. Hold cutter straight up and down and, starting ⅛ inch from edge of glass farthest from you, press it firmly to glass. Then draw it in a straight, continuous stroke with even pressure along the straight edge toward you.

To break glass, clasp it at end of cut between the fingers of your two hands. Hold firmly on either side of line. Snap quickly downward (away from cut). Another way to break glass is to hold one of the cut ends off the table several inches and tap directly underneath the cut with the end of the glass-cutter handle. To break off a narrow strip of glass, hold it in one hand, slip cutter slot over the edge, and snap downward. If uneven edges are left after breaking the glass, you can break them off with the glass-cutter slots or with pliers.

To cut glass in a perfect circle requires a special cutter which turns around a spindle. Cut the circle first. Then cut straight lines from the circle to the edges of the sheet. Break out the waste glass in sections.

HOW TO STOP CONDENSATION

You can't see condensation—water vapor—except when it collects on your windows. But it is likely to be the cause of rotting timbers in the attic, rotting joints in the floor over a crawl space, rotting sills in a crawl space, blistered and peeling paint on the outside walls, falling plaster, stained and loose wallpaper, eroding paint, and even rotting wood on windows and windowsills.

There are four ways to reduce this invisible menace.

(1) Reduce humidity in the house. You can do this by improving housekeeping and living habits (for instance, cover pots on the range, use as little water as possible when mopping floors, take shorter and cooler showers). But you should also equip kitchen and bathroom sinks, tubs, and showers with mixing faucets so that you will not saturate the air with steam. Cover the ground in unexcavated areas with the largest possible sheets of heavy polyethlyene film or with 55-pound roofing felt laid with 2-inch lapped joints.

(2) Improve ventilation. You probably have a ventilating fan in the kitchen, but it may not be as large as it should be. You can hardly have a

kitchen fan that is too large. For efficiency, make sure it is ducted to the outdoors by the shortest and straightest possible route.

Ventilate your clothes dryer to the outdoors by a 4-inch plastic or metal duct. Install small ventilating fans in the bathroom—especially in the most frequently used bathrooms or in those with shower baths.

Increase the size of screened ventilated openings under the house in all unexcavated areas, or install additional openings. This is a job for an expert who understands the rules for sizing ventilators.

(3) Install vapor barriers in all outside walls, top-floor ceilings, or roof and floors over unheated spaces. The purpose of these is to prevent condensation from seeping out of the rooms into the wall, roof, and underfloor cavities. In an existing house, the easiest way to install the barriers is to paint the walls and ceilings on the inside with two coats of oil, alkyd, or latex paint and to coat wood floors with penetrating sealer or varnish. Vinyl wall coverings, resilient flooring, and ceramic tile are also excellent vapor barriers.

(4) Insulate the house. This will raise the surface temperature of walls, ceilings, and floors and prevent water vapor from condensing on them. Note, however, that if you don't have vapor barriers, insulation should not be installed, because it may increase the danger of condensation forming in the wall, ceiling and floor cavities.

HOW TO CONTROL INSECT PESTS

Ants. Sprinkle chlordane dust on anthills outdoors. Indoors, spray ants with pyrethrin spray. Also spray behind sink, refrigerator, along baseboards—wherever the pests travel or congregate. Ant traps are effective, but keep them out of reach of children and pets.

Bedbugs. These flat, smelly, brown insects infest mattresses, bed frames, and upholstered furniture. If they suddenly turn up in your house, spray mattresses and beds with pyrethrin. Also spray cracks along baseboards.

Bees, hornets, wasps. Keep them out of the house by screening roof and eaves ventilators and by plugging all cracks and holes under the eaves and in the siding with caulking compound. To destroy the insects that get into the house despite all precautions, spray with pyrethrin. There are aerosols that will wipe out nests at a distance of 15 feet or even a bit more.

Carpet beetles. The larvae of these small, more or less oval beetles feed on wool, mohair, carpets, upholstery, and clothing. Vacuum backs and bottoms of upholstered furniture, under rugs, in closets and dark corners to remove lint and dust in which insects settle. Clean all articles to be stored and wrap with paradichlorobenzene crystals. Mothproof carpets. Spraying with pyrethrin kills carpet beetles on contact.

Centipedes. Spray with pyrethrin. Note, however, that centipedes are valuable since they kill many other insects.

Cockroaches. If you hit cockroaches with a pyrethrin spray, you will kill them. But to rid a house that's infested with them, you must also apply poison under sinks, kitchen appliances, and radiators, inside cabinets, and around pipes. Use a combination boric acid and pyrethrin spray. Or simply sprinkle boric acid through a flour sifter and spray over it with pyrethrin.

Fleas. If dogs and cats are not allergic to them, put flea collars on them, and change every 2 or 3 months. Stray fleas that are not killed by the collars can be destroyed by spraying the animals with a pyrethrin spray or washing them with flea soap. Spray pyrethrin on floors and baseboards in rooms where your pets sleep.

Flies. Hang up sticky flypapers, get out the swatter, and dispose of food wastes more frequently. If this doesn't solve the problem, spray pyrethrin around a closed-up room for about 6 seconds; then get out and leave it closed for 15 to 30 minutes.

Mosquitoes. Check all door and window screens and make sure they are sound and fit tightly in frames. Improve springs on doors. To get rid of a swarm in the house, spray pyrethrin around each room for about 6 seconds; then close up room for 15 minutes or more.

You can use sprays and foggers outside the house, but you won't have too much success now that DDT has been banned. Pour a little oil into standing puddles.

Moths. Clean closets, trunks, boxes, etc., used for storing fabrics. Have wool rugs mothproofed or treat with a moth spray. Dry clean or wash woolens, furs, and other materials of animal origin before storing; then place in tight containers or plastic wrappings with paradichlorobenzene crystals.

Silverfish. Spray basements, bookcases, shelves —all warm, damp places—with pyrethrin. When storing cottons and rayons, clean well but don't starch.

Spiders. Spray with pyrethrin or simply squash the bugs and their eggs. Look for black widow spiders in rubbish heaps, under stones, around basement windows, and in dark sections of the garage and spray with pyrethrin.

Termites. There are four ways to tell if you have termites:

(1) The insects look like ants but have thick waists and four wings of equal size. Ants have pinched-in waists and wings of different size.

(2) When termites swarm out of the ground— usually in the spring—they lose their wings. You may find these in little piles on the ground.

(3) Termites build small tunnels of earth on foundation walls.

(4) Termite damage to wood is not always visible; but if you find that a piece of wood is soft enough for you to stick an ice pick in deeply, tear off the outer layer. If termites have been at work, you will find tunnels running with the grain and littered with small gray specks.

The following steps are essential to get rid of termites.

• Scrape the tubes off the foundation walls. Fill holes and cracks in the walls with concrete or fibered asphalt roofing cement.

• Remove wood, paper, and other cellulose material from around and under the house. It even pays to dig up the soil and remove the debris from this.

• Don't let any wooden part of the house touch the ground. Raise it at least 6 inches on concrete blocks or piers.

• If your basement or crawl space is damp, do everything possible to get rid of the dampness: Pipe roof water away from the house. Slope the ground away from the house. Waterproof the foundation walls. Install larger ventilators in crawl spaces.

• Treat the soil under and around the house with chlordane. See SILL, HOUSE.

Whenever you have to replace a sill or other wood structural member of the house, use lumber that has been pressure-treated at a mill with wood preservative or saturate the wood yourself with pentachlorophenol, zinc, or copper naphthanate.

Ticks. The best way to control ticks is to put flea collars on your dogs and cats, and to inspect your pets every day and pick off and burn every bug you find. Once ticks get established in the house, there's almost nothing you can do to stop them from spreading short of calling in a qualified exterminator.

GLOSSARY OF TERMS AS
USED IN THIS BOOK

Aerator. A device on the end of a faucet that introduces air into the water and thus breaks up the hard flow. This is done by a system of tiny screens inside a screw-on cap.

Angle iron. An L-shaped piece of rigid steel or brass used for joining and bracing the corners of doors, windows, etc.

Allen screw. A small screw with a hexagonal slot or hole in the head.

Allen wrench. A small tool made of a hexagonal rod of steel bent like an L.

Auger. A plumber's boring tool resembling a long coiled spring with a claw at the tip and a handle to crank it.

Bail. The wire handle on a bucket.

Batten. A strip, usually of wood, fastened over a crack between adjacent materials.

Becket. One of the loops by which the edges of a tent are held to the ground.

Bevel. To cut the square edges of, say, a board at an angle. A bevel is an angled surface.

Bulkhead. The outside basement door which is installed above the steps leading down from the yard into the basement.

Butt. To bring together. In a wood floor, for example, the wood strips are butted together.

Caulk. To fill and seal a crack with some plastic material such as putty or caulking compound.

C-clamp. A clamp shaped like the letter C. Probably the most frequently used clamp in carpentry.

Cementitious coating. A paintlike cement coating which is applied to basement and other damp masonry walls to make them waterproof. It comes as a powder which is mixed with water before use.

Chuck. On a drill, the sleeve which tightens around a bit and holds it on the brace.

Coarse aggregate. The clean stones or pebbles of varying size used in concrete mixes.

Cold chisel. A heavy steel chisel for cutting stone, brick, metal, etc.

Commutator. The round, segmented copper collar on the shaft of some electric motors.

Compression faucet. The most common type of faucet, though now being displaced. It can be identified by the rubber or composition washer screwed to the end of the faucet spindle.

Cotter pin. A device used to join two things that are usually made of metal. The pin has a ring-like head and two parallel prongs which are bent to the side after the pin is installed.

Countersink. To drive beneath the surface. Nails are countersunk with a steel punch called a nail set. Screws are countersunk by drilling a hole large enough to receive the screwhead.

Disk sander. An electric drill converted to use as a sander by inserting in the chuck a round, flat, sandpaper-covered disk in place of the drill bit. There are also electric tools which are equipped only for disk-sanding.

Dowel. A straight, round pin, usually of wood but sometimes of metal, which is inserted in opposite holes in two materials that are to be joined together.

Eccentric. A device that revolves in an unusual pattern.

Efflorescence. The crusty, whitish stains that appear on masonry surfaces.

Emery cloth. A sandpaperlike material made of cloth which is covered on one side with an abrasive substance called emery.

Epoxy mender. A very thick epoxy adhesive used primarily for filling holes in metal. There are several types: some are packaged in two containers, others come ready for use in one. They are often sold under such names as Plastic Steel or Plastic Aluminum.

Escutcheon. A more or less ornamental covering plate, such as the plate behind a doorknob.

Fascia. The outward-facing board under eaves and cornices.

Ferrule. A ring of metal used to strengthen and hold together a tool head and handle.

Finial. The ornamental top on lamps, bedposts, etc.

Finishing nail. A slender nail with a small head that is easily countersunk.

Flange. A projecting edge or rim which holds a thing in place. At the bottom of an official

U.S. mailbox, for instance, there are four flanges which fit around the board on which the mailbox sits.

Flashing. The sheet material—usually metal—used to prevent leaks at joints in the roof and exterior walls.

Float. A wooden tool used to smooth concrete. In essence, it is a short, thick board with a handle centered on one side. After concrete is floated, it has a slightly rough, nonskid texture.

Flux. Liquid or paste material used to clean metal that is to be soldered. It assures that the solder will adhere to the metal.

Friction tape. Black, sticky fabric tape, sometimes called tire tape.

Furring strip. A strip, usually of wood, which separates and permits the easy joining of one flat surface to another. For example, when gypsum board is to be applied over a basement wall, wood furring strips are first attached to the wall and the gypsum board is nailed to these.

Gasket. A device made of more or less flexible material which seals a joint. On a water pump, for example, gaskets are used to seal the joints between sections of the suction chamber.

Gate valve. A plumbing valve that controls the water flow by means of a metal tongue which screws in and out of the valve body.

Gland nut. The metal nut which holds stuffing material, called a gland, in place. The gland prevents water leakage through a propeller shaft or a piston rod in a water pump.

Glazier's point. A small triangular or diamond-shaped piece of metal used to hold a windowpane in a frame. It is covered by the putty on the outside of the pane.

Grout. A soupy mixture usually of portland cement and water used either to fill small joints (as in a ceramic-tile floor) or to ensure the adherence of a stiffer mortar.

Gypsum. A mineral used for making plaster or the rigid, paper-covered boards used in place of plaster.

Gypsum-board joint compound. A smooth, light-grayish-brown filler material used to conceal joints between gypsum boards and to cover the nails holding the boards. It is also an excellent material for filling and leveling other wall-surfacing materials.

Jamb. One of the three sides of a doorway or window opening.

Joist. A large horizontal timber supporting a floor or almost-flat roof.

Lath. The base to which plaster is applied. In modern construction, lath is commonly a flexible roll of perforated steel sheet or a rigid panel of gypsum. Wood laths are thin strips of unfinished wood which, in walls, are nailed parallel to one another across the studs.

Louver. One of the slanted strips of wood, metal, or glass set in a frame that is designed to admit air but not water. The word is also used to describe the entire ventilating device: an attic louver, for example.

Miter. To cut at an angle of other than 90 degrees. As a noun, the word means the acutely angled joint formed by mitering.

Miter joint. The joint formed by two pieces of material that are mitered—for example, the joint at the corner of a picture frame.

Mortar joint. The cement-filled joint between bricks, stones, concrete blocks, etc.

Mortise. A hole or recess into which something fits. For example, a hinge is set into a mortise in a door jamb.

Mullion. A wood or metal strip that divides one windowpane from another.

Muriatic acid. Hydrochloric acid. A dangerous chemical used to clean and etch masonry and metal surfaces and to remove efflorescence from masonry.

Packing nut. The large nut which holds flexible stuffing material in place around the stem of a faucet.

Paint thinner. Any liquid used to thin a paint. The term, however, is most often applied to the petroleum distillate used for thinning oil-base paints.

Paste filler. A thick, pigmented, oil-base material used to fill the pores in such open-pore woods as oak and chestnut. It can also be used to fill other minor roughness in wood.

Penetrating oil. A thin oil which is squirted into metal joints that are rusted together. It softens or releases the rust so the joints can be opened with wrenches.

Placket. An opening or slit in a garment. For instance, a skirt has a placket at the waistline to permit putting it on and it may have plackets at the hemline to provide ease of movement.

Plastic rubber. A soft, thick, gooey rubber packaged in a tube and used to fill holes in rubber. It can also be used as a caulking material.

Plastic wood. Also called wood dough, this is a mixture of tiny wood fibers and chemicals that is used to fill holes in wood. The most common plastic wood dries to a dirty yellow and is impenetrable to stain, so it must be mixed with stain before application. However, the material is also made in various colors to match many woods.

Plumber's friend. A bell-shaped rubber device with a wood handle. It is used to dislodge stoppages in plumbing drains.

Polysulfide rubber caulking. One of the best caulking compounds presently in use.

Pumice. A fine abrasive powder used for rubbing down materials to obtain a smooth finish.

Quarter round. A strip of wood which, viewed end on, forms one-quarter of a circle.

Rabbet. A groove in the edge or face of a piece of wood, metal, etc. For example, mullions are rabbeted to receive windowpanes.

Rail. One of the horizontal members of a paneled door. Compare *Stile*.

Ratchet. The device that engages a toothed or cogged wheel and either makes it turn or prevents it from turning.

Red metal primer. A brownish-red paint that is used to prime steel and iron to prevent rusting. It was originally made of red lead, which has been legally banned from the market.

Riser. The vertical part of a step.

Rottenstone. A fine abrasive powder used for rubbing down materials to obtain a very smooth finish. It is slightly finer than pumice.

Rouge. A very, very fine red abrasive powder.

Scale. The rough whitish deposit left by hard water in plumbing pipes, water heaters, dishwashers, sinks, etc.

Self-tapping screw. A screw used in metal work, primarily to join thin sheets.

Shank. The leg or part of a device by which it is connected to another device—for example, the threaded portion of a screw.

Sheathing. The boards or panels nailed to the outside of studs or rafters to form a base for the finish siding or roofing.

Shim. A thin piece of wood, metal, stone, cardboard, etc., which is inserted under or between something in order to make it level or to move it outward or upward.

Siding. The outside covering of the walls of a building.

Silicone caulking. A caulking made of silicone rubber. It is the same as silicone rubber adhesive.

Spackle. A type of plaster for filling holes, cracks, and dents in plaster, gypsum board, wood, etc. One type of spackle is a powder which is mixed with water. A superior type comes ready-mixed in a can. Some formulations can be used indoors only, others can be used indoors and outdoors.

Spline. A thin strip of wood or metal. In a screen, a spline is laid over the screen cloth and the two are pushed into a slot in the frame to hold the cloth tightly in place.

Spreader. A metal gadget used to brace wobbly chairs and tables. It consists of a turnbuckle to which four wires are attached. The wires, in turn, are attached to the chair or table legs.

Sprocket. A toothed wheel that engages with a chain used to drive a machine.

Stain-killer. A white-pigmented, shellac-base paint used to cover knots in wood and prevent them from bleeding through the finish coat of paint.

Stile. One of the vertical members of a paneled door or window. Compare *Rail*.

Stop. One of the strips against which a door rests when it is closed tight, or which holds a window sash in its frame.

Stop valve. A plumbing valve which controls the water flow by means of a flat washer which can be turned tight against a valve seat. It is the type of valve most often found in homes on the supply lines leading to lavatories, tubs, sinks, etc.

Strike plate. The metal plate that is screwed to a door jamb and engages the latch when the door is closed. Also called simply a strike.

Stringer. One of the saw-toothed timbers to which stair treads and risers are attached.

Stud. One of the vertical timbers in a wall. These are usually 2 inches by 4 inches and are spaced 16 inches from center to center.

Stuffing box. The small chamber around a propeller shaft or water pump piston rod. It is stuffed with flexible material, sometimes called a gland, which prevents water leakage around the shaft or rod.

Tang. The slender, pointed end of a knife, fork, file, etc., which fits into the handle of the implement.

Tenon. The thing which fits into a mortise.

Terne. Steel coated with lead and tin. Thin terne sheets are used on roofs.

Trichloroethylene. A nonflammable cleaning fluid. It has generally taken the place of carbon tetrachloride and should always be used instead because it is much less toxic.

Turnbuckle. A device used to join and tighten two threaded rods or sometimes wires. The rods are threaded in opposite directions so that when you turn the turnbuckle to the right it simultaneously draws the rods toward each other and when you turn to the left it pushes the rods apart.

Valve seat. The surface inside the body of a faucet on which the washer is seated when the faucet is turned off.

Water putty. A plasterlike material that is mixed with water and used to fill holes in wood.

White appliance wax. A liquid wax used for cleaning and polishing kitchen appliances. It is equally useful for cleaning and polishing other materials.

Wiggle nail. Colloquial name for a corrugated metal fastener—a small strip of corrugated steel with sharp points along one side.

Wire nut. Also called a solderless connector, a screw device for joining wires in an electrical circuit.

Worm-drive screw clamp. A steel ribbon that is specifically designed to clamp flexible plastic pipes to fittings but which is also used to stop leaks in pipes. It is slipped around a pipe and then tightened with a screwdriver.

INDEX